Human Security

Benny Teh Cheng Guan
Editor

Human Security

Securing East Asia's Future

Editor
Benny Teh Cheng Guan
School of Social Sciences
Universiti Sains Malaysia
Penang, Malaysia
ben@usm.my

ISBN 978-94-007-1798-5　　　　e-ISBN 978-94-007-1799-2
DOI 10.1007/978-94-007-1799-2
Springer Dordrecht Heidelberg London New York

Library of Congress Control Number: 2011937553

© Springer Science+Business Media B.V. 2012
No part of this work may be reproduced, stored in a retrieval system, or transmitted in any form or by any means, electronic, mechanical, photocopying, microfilming, recording or otherwise, without written permission from the Publisher, with the exception of any material supplied specifically for the purpose of being entered and executed on a computer system, for exclusive use by the purchaser of the work.

Printed on acid-free paper

Springer is part of Springer Science+Business Media (www.springer.com)

To my parents

Contents

Introduction: Human Security Development and the Future of East Asia 1
Benny Teh Cheng Guan

Part I The State, the People and Responses to Human Security Concerns

1 **Human Insecurities or Liabilities? The Changing Security Paradigms and the Case of the North Korean Refugees** 17
Jaime Koh

2 **Human Insecurity in the People's Republic of China: The Vulnerability of Chinese Women to HIV/AIDS** 39
Anna Marie Hayes

3 **From National Security to Human Security: Population Policy Shifts in Vietnam** 59
Kathleen A. Tobin

4 **Irregular Migration in Thailand: New Possibilities for Anti-Trafficking and Development Programs** 75
Jennryn Wetzler

5 **Security in Labor Migration in the Philippines: National Honor, Family Solidarity, and Migrants' Protection** 95
Asuncion Fresnoza-Flot

Part II Regional Approaches to Human Security and Policy Implications

6 **Insecurity Within and Outside the State: The Regional and Local Dynamics of Environmental Insecurity in the Mekong** 115
Duncan McDuie-Ra

7 **The Association of Southeast Asian Nations (ASEAN) and Climate Change: A Threat to National, Regime, and Human Security** 135
Alfred Gerstl and Belinda Helmke

8 **Depoliticizing Natural Disasters to Enhance Human Security in a Sovereignty-Based Context: Lessons from Aceh (2004) to Yangon (2008)** 157
Delphine Alles

9 **Human Health Threats and Implications for Regional Security in Southeast Asia** 173
James R. Campbell

10 **The Proliferation of Trading Agreements and Implications on Human Livelihood** 193
Benny Teh Cheng Guan

11 **Human Security, Capital Punishment, and East Asian Democracies** 217
Sangmin Bae

12 **An Emerging Human Security Threat on Pacific Island States: Analyzing Legal and Political Implications of Territorial Inundation** 231
Chih-Chieh Chou

Index 249

Contributors

Alfred Gerstl is an Editor-in-chief of the Austrian Journal of South-East Asian Studies (ASEAS). He has been a lecturer for politics and International Relations at the Universities of Vienna (Austria), Passau (Germany) and Macquarie (Australia). His research interests include International Relations theories and regional cooperation, mainly in East Asia.

Anna Marie Hayes is a Lecturer in International Relations at University of Southern Queensland located at Toowoomba, Australia and is a member of the Public Memory Research Centre. Her research interests include Chinese history, gender issues in China, gendered perspectives of human security and pandemic illnesses, such as HIV/AIDS, as a source of global human insecurity.

Asuncion Fresnoza-Flot is a Sociologist associated with the Unité de Recherches Migrations et Société (URMIS) at the Université Paris Diderot – Paris 7. Her research interests include international migration, the question of gender and the place of the family and religion in migration phenomena, immigrant entrepreneurship, and majority-minority relations.

Belinda Helmke is a Political Risk Analyst in the corporate sector. She is also a Visiting Scholar at the Centre for Peace and Conflict Studies in University of Sydney and a member of the ASEAS Editing Board. Her research focuses primarily on international law and international relations, particularly the use of force by states and armed conflict. She is the author of *Under Attack: Challenges to the Rules Governing the International Use of Force* (Ashgate 2010).

Benny Teh Cheng Guan is a Senior Lecturer at the School of Social Sciences, Universiti Sains Malaysia, Penang, Malaysia. Apart from human security, his research interests include the political economy of regionalism and the building of security communities in East Asia. He is the co-editor of *The Shape of the East Asian Economy to Come: Lonely Rhetoric or Global Reality* (Cambridge Scholars Publishing 2007).

Chih-Chieh Chou is an Associate Professor in the Department of Political Science and Graduate Institute of Political Economy at National Cheng Kung University and an Adjunct Associate Professor in International Law Program at Soochow University, Taiwan. He is also a member of the Board of Directors of the Chinese Association of Human Rights in Taiwan. His research interests include international organization, human rights, human security, regional security and political change. He is the author of *Triggering or Halting? Impacts of International Efforts and Geopolitical Order on Transition to Democracy* (VDM Verlag 2009).

Delphine Alles is a Doctoral Candidate and Lecturer at Sciences Po and CERI (Centre for International Studies and Research), Paris, France. Her research focuses on the role of religion in the foreign relations of Indonesia and Malaysia, as well as human security and regionalism.

Duncan McDuie-Ra is a Senior Lecturer in development studies in the School of Social Sciences and International Studies at the University of New South Wales, Australia. His current research focuses on identity and environmental insecurity in the Himalayas and the Pacific. He is the author of *Civil Society, Democratization and the Search for Human Security: The Politics of the Environment, Gender, and Identity in Northeast India* (Nova Science 2009).

Jaime Koh is a Doctoral Candidate in the Cultural Studies in Asia program at the National University of Singapore. She is a former journalist with special interest in the history and politics of East Asia and the co-author of *Cultures and Customs of Singapore and Malaysia* (Greenwood 2009).

James R. Campbell is a Professor at the College of Security Studies, Asia-Pacific Center for Security Studies, Honolulu, Hawaii. Prior to that, he served as manager for biosecurity and biodefense at the Pacific Northwest National Laboratory in Richland, Washington. Campbell completed 27 years as a biomedical research scientist in the U.S. Navy Medical Service Corps, retiring from active duty in 2005.

Jennryn Wetzler works for the Bureau of International Information Programs at the U.S. Department of State. She was a Boren Fellow in Thailand, a critical languages Scholar in Egypt, and a Peace Corps Volunteer in Niger. Her interests lie in transnational migration, human trafficking and human security. She is the co-author of "Education and Post-Conflict Recovery" in *Peacebuilding in Traumatized Societies* (University Press of America 2008).

Kathleen A. Tobin is an Associate Professor of history at Purdue University Calumet in Hammond, Indiana. She has written on various aspects of birth control and population policy. She is the author of *Politics and Population Control: A Documentary History* (Greenwood 2004) and *The American Religious Debate over Birth Control, 1907–1937* (McFarland 2001).

Sangmin Bae is an Associate Professor of political science at Northeastern Illinois University, Chicago. Her research interests include international norms, human rights, and international relations theory. She has written widely on capital punishment and human rights issues and is the author of *When the State No Longer Kills: International Human Rights Norms and Abolition of Capital Punishment* (State University of New York Press 2007).

Abbreviations

ACWF	All China Women's Federation
AFTA	ASEAN Free Trade Area
AOSIS	Alliance of Small Island States
CBCP	Catholic Bishop Conference of the Philippines
CHS	Commission on Human Security
COP15	Copenhagen Climate Change Conference
ECMI	Episcopal Commission for the Pastoral Care of Migrants and Itinerant People
FDI	foreign direct investment
FTA	free trade agreement
GAM	Gerakan Aceh Merdeka (Free Aceh Movement)
GMS	Greater Mekong Subregion
IDU	intravenous drug use
ILO	International Labor Organization
IPCC	Intergovernmental Panel on Climate Change
LSCW	Legal Support for Children and Women
MRC	Mekong River Commission
MTCT	mother-to-child-transmission
NAFTA	North American Free Trade Agreement
OFWs	Overseas Filipino Workers
PDA	Population and Community Development Association
PHR	Physicians for Human Rights
PLWHA	people living with HIV/AIDS
R2P	responsibility to protect
RTA	regional trade agreement
RTI	reproductive tract infection
SAARC	South Asian Association for Regional Cooperation
SIS	small island state
STDs	sexually transmitted diseases
STI	sexually transmitted infection
TAGP	Trans-ASEAN Gas Pipeline Infrastructure Project

TIP	Trafficking in Persons
TNCs	transnational corporations
TNI	Tentara Nasional Indonesia (Indonesian Armed Forces)
TVPA	Trafficking Victims Protection Act
UNAIDS	United Nations Joint Program on HIV/AIDS
UNDP	United Nations Development Program
UNEP	United Nations Environmental Program
UNESCO	United Nations Educational, Scientific & Cultural Organization
UNFCCC	United Nations Framework Convention on Climate Change
UNHCR	United Nations High Commissioner for Refugees
UNICEF	United Nations Children's Fund
WHO	World Health Organization
WTO	World Trade Organization

List of Tables

Table 10.1	Free trade agreement status by country (as of January 2010)	194
Table 10.2	Projected GDP and export changes based on FTA between Japan and Asian Countries	197
Table 10.3	Projected GDP changes among various FTA partnerships in East Asia	198

Introduction: Human Security Development and the Future of East Asia

Benny Teh Cheng Guan

> *The security of states is essential, but not sufficient, to fully ensure the safety and well-being of the world's peoples.*
>
> *(Lloyd Axworthy 2001)*

The international relations of East Asia have, for too long, been dominated by inter-state politics. Regional security has been, and unfortunately continues to be, understood within the traditional framework of preserving territorial sovereignty and regime survival. In line with the Western notion of states as the prevailing actor, discussions on security issues in East Asia have focused largely on states' interactions and behaviors.

While this has led to a wealth of knowledge on East Asian politics, such understandings are obviously biased and fail to capture the broader fundamentals of issues and challenges facing the peoples of East Asia. Part of the reason for this failure is the idea that humans are less important than states. This reason derives from the conventional understanding that the welfare of the people is subsumed under the concept of state security and that the existence of the former is contingent upon the success of the latter.

Though traditional security plays a significant role in nation building, it does not necessarily correlate positively with human security. There have been numerous cases ranging from cross-border human trafficking activities and organized crimes to environmental and health disasters that greatly threaten the security of individuals and communities rather than the survival of states. Cases of women trafficking for the sex industry from the Philippines to Malaysia, for example, have been well reported (Ciralsky and Hansen 2007a, b). In Japan, 95% of victims identified in trafficking for sexual exploitation originated from East Asia.[1] Regarding communicable

---

[1] The UNODC (2009a) reported that out of the 175 victims identified from 2005 to 2006, 70 were from the Philippines, 58 from Indonesia, 24 from Thailand and 14 from China (including Taiwan).

B.C.G. Teh (✉)
Universiti Sains Malaysia, Penang, Malaysia
e-mail: ben@usm.my

diseases, the World Health Organization (WHO) declared in mid June 2010 that Southeast Asia had reached Phase 6 pandemic (widespread human infection) due to the continuous reporting of new cases of the Influenza A (H1N1) virus in all six WHO reporting regions (WHO 2010). The United Nations Office on Drugs and Crime recently published a report on the globalization of crime highlighting East Asia as a source for the trafficking of wildlife, timber and drugs to places as far as Europe (UNODC 2010). Recent news reports on seizures of drugs fashionable with club-goers such as ketamine and methamphetamine from South Asia and the Middle East suggest that demand for these substances is increasing in popular destinations such as Thailand, Indonesia and Malaysia.[2] Since such cases are clearly transnational in nature and directly affect individuals, it would be improper to categorize them as secondary to state security or to simply view them as domestic concerns.

This however does not imply that comparable cases did not exist previously. Although these are not new to human history, they are becoming more profound and noteworthy and deserve not only the attention but also the cooperation of state and non-state actors. The United Nations Secretary-General Ban Ki-moon expressed at a Security Council debate that, "With transnational threats, States have no choice but to work together. We are all affected – whether as countries of supply, trafficking or demand. Therefore we have a shared responsibility to act" (Department of Public Information 2010). The same would apply to non-governmental organizations (NGOs), multinational corporations and civic groups.

Indeed, the advent of globalization has shrunk the regional and global spaces and time that used to separate human beings and limit their ability to interact. This has further contributed to the process of economic regionalization leading to higher interdependence of the East Asian region as evidence by the 1997 Asian financial crisis, which in turn led to the development of civil societies that are much more aware of universal human rights and critical of their governments' policies. The change of governments in Indonesia and more recently in Japan, the prolonged political crisis in Thailand and the strengthening of the opposition parties in Malaysia reflect to various degrees the maturation of societies and their concerns in the region.

The integration of East Asian economies into the global economic system through the implementation of progressive trade liberalization policies in the last three decades has led to a rise in the insecurity of people. On one hand, globalization has contributed to the economic growth and prosperity of nations but on the other hand, it has provided opportunities for shadow economies to thrive. In Malaysia, underground economy has been growing and is reported to be worth approximately USD3.1 billion (The Star Online 2010c). Cases of victims losing their hard earned

---

[2] See *The Star Online*, 2009a,b,c, 2010a,b; The Straits Times, 2010. UNODC's 2009 report on Patterns and Trends of Amphetamine-Type Stimulants and Other Drugs in East and South-East Asia have also indicated the increasing role played by Thailand, Malaysia, Indonesia, Vietnam and the Greater Mekong Subregion as either markets or locations for production of such illicit drugs.

savings and retirement funds through unscrupulous ideas such as the Ponzi scheme, pyramid selling schemes or remittance scams have too often been heard.[3]

Situations are made worse when there is an economic crisis. Nothing could be more palpable than the extent of anxiety caused by the 2008 global economic crisis. Not only did it intensify income insecurity due to pay cuts and layoffs but it also presented long term effects owing to the erosion of savings, the disruption of social safety nets and the rise in food prices.[4] Food insecurity is further exacerbated by environmental disasters brought about by climate change. This will have a direct impact on the poor and the vulnerable. It is without doubt that economic crises can transmit between economically integrated countries and "wipe out years of poverty reduction" efforts (FAO 2009). The Asia Pacific still remains the highest undernourished region compared to Latin America and Africa, with a steady rise in number of people from over 500 million in 1995 to 642 million in 2009 (FAO 2009: 9–11). This can only suggest that the integration of Asian countries into the world economy does not assure the sustainability of human livelihoods.

Thus, the demand for greater consideration and solution of non-traditional problems illustrates the complexities and challenges of societal progress that inescapably require a more constructive approach, one that is different from the common, cooperative and comprehensive security approaches associated with traditional state security.

The Concept of Human Security

The development of human security can best be understood as a progression of international efforts to refine and broaden the definition of traditional security. However, it also represents a contradiction from and challenge to the more conventional forms.

One of the earliest forms was the common security idea that called for international cooperation to prevent the escalation of arms that has characterized most parts of the Cold War period. The successful formation of the Conference on Security and Cooperation in Europe (CSCE) in the early 1970s and the subsequent 1975 Helsinki Accords revealed the strong determination of the European states to prevent Europe from becoming a theatre of nuclear war and replace nuclear deterrence – increasingly seen as unsustainable – with a common process of cooperation. In 1982, The Independent Commission on Disarmament and Security Issues, in support of the CSCE, called for the development of a common security to overcome

---

[3] The Ponzi scheme refers to the infamous investment fraud by Bernard Madoff that robbed investors of their lifetime savings. In Japan, a ringleader was sentenced to 20 years for masterminding the well known "Ore, ore" (Hey, it's me!) remittance scam, raking in 146 million yen (approx. USD1.6 million) from victims. (The Japan Times 2010).

[4] For an interesting account of the impacts of the economic crisis in East Asia, see Turk and Mason (2009).

the unrealistic build up of armaments in international politics based on the balance of power principle. Partly seen as a critique of realism it warned that stability anchored in an arms race is too fragile and "a more effective way to ensure security is to create positive processes that can lead to peace and disarmament" (1982: 7). The report of the Commission provided the impetus to expand the narrow understanding of traditional military threats by highlighting developmental issues pertaining to the Third World.

In 1986, Mikhail Gorbachev proposed that the Asia Pacific region too should have its own security conference and once again broached the same idea in September 1988, reflecting the relevance of the report and the CSCE concept.[5] In December, Gorbachev (1988) delivered an important speech (below) at the United Nations that not only led to the end of the Cold War but bolstered the common security model.

> We are talking first and foremost about consistent progress toward concluding a treaty on a 50 percent reduction in strategic offensive weapons, …about elaborating a convention on the elimination of chemical weapons …and about talks on reducing conventional weapons and armed forces in Europe. We are also talking about economic, ecological and humanitarian problems in the widest possible sense.
> …One would like to believe that our joint efforts to put an end to the era of wars, confrontation and regional conflicts, aggression against nature, the terror of hunger and poverty, as well as political terrorism, will be comparable with our hopes. This is our common goal, and it is only by acting together that we may attain it.

The speech provided a clear indication for a number of things: First, the reduction of offensive weapons resonated with the call for disarmament under the common security framework. Second, it acknowledged that a superpower arms race leads to destruction. Finally, it explained the need to move beyond militarism by embracing economic and social development strategies through cooperative measures.

'Cooperative' became the keyword for security cooperation as the world moved into the post-Cold War era. Seen as an adaptation of common security, it emphasizes more the importance of multilateralism rather than unilateral action and stresses more the use of diplomatic tools such as political dialogues, confidence building measures and conflict resolution as means to establish a stable world order (Acharya 2001). Cooperative security, thus, connotes an incremental approach centered on joint efforts among states (Butfoy 1995).

However, a security concept with a slightly different emphasis was being developed in East Asia during the Cold War. Traced back to the early 1980s, the formulation of a comprehensive security framework was undertaken by Japan. Apart from preserving the military dimension, the framework also emphasized economic security. The importance placed on the latter can be explained by the 'hostility' that Japan was experiencing in its rise to become an economic power and the changing security environment compelling Japan to play a more proactive role than

---

[5]For more details, see Fukushima (1999). Interestingly, she wrote that Japan and others saw the Soviet Union's proposals as "mere propaganda".

to remain fully dependent on the United States.[6] Leveraging on its economic strength, Japan sought a framework that would allow it to justify its role in contributing to international peace through the use of its official development assistance (ODA) program and in safeguarding stable supplies of food and energy resources (Akaha 1991).

By incorporating non-military rudiments in the understanding of post-Cold War security, Japan has been seen by some scholars, primarily Amitav Acharya (2001) and Christopher Hughes (2005), as playing an important role in the articulation and subsequent acceptance of the human security concept by Asian countries. Japan's penchant for human security became more profound at the turn of the twentyfirst century. Lam Peng Er's article on *Japan's Human Security Role in Southeast Asia* (2006) clearly identified elements of human security in Japan's foreign policy. Working in tandem with Japanese NGOs and business groups, the Japanese government has played an active role in providing financial, medical and armed forces assistances to several Southeast Asian countries stricken by humanitarian disasters such as the SARS outbreak, the Aceh tsunami and the cyclone Nargis. Throughout 2009, Japan provided a series of its Grassroots Grant Assistance (GGA) to assist Myanmar in its post-Nargis reconstruction projects.

At this point, it is best to provide a brief historical background on the idea of human security that originated from the United Nations and a number of interpretations and approaches that resulted from it.

Defining Human Security

The genesis of human security can be traced back to the Human Development Report titled "New Dimensions of Human Security" under the United Nations Development Program (UNDP 1994). Led by the late Mahbub ul Haq, the report introduces human security as a new concept that equates security with people rather than with territorial states. It is a move to inject distinctiveness and separation into how the notion of security should be perceived. By collectively pushing for a wide arrangement of people-centered projects, it is meant to be an 'integrative' concept as opposed to a 'defensive' one.

The idea behind human security stemmed from the over attention placed on securing states' interests at times at the expense of human lives. Historical wars were mainly about the survival of states and regimes rather than the protection of the people from threats. Thus, lives were sacrificed in the name of country and

---

[6] According to Akaha (1991: 325), the need to look at economic security was due to "a series of unsettling international developments in the 1970s and early 1980s: the superpower strategic parity and short-lived detente, the Sino-American rapprochement, the collapse of the Bretton Woods system, the deepening Sino-Soviet rift, the two oil crises, and the U.S. defeat in the Vietnam War. Of the major developments during that period, none exposed Japan's vulnerability as acutely as the 1973–1974 oil crisis".

nation. Even then, it has not resolved the many conflicts that continue to occur within states and among societies such as the South Thailand conflict, the Rohingyas issue and the Xinjiang unrest. The problem lies in the delineation of territories either fought through wars or colonialism that failed to properly capture the composition of various ethnic groups. In short, the arrangement of the international system was based primarily on states rather than on societies. In many instances, societies were required to organize themselves within the boundaries that had been predetermined and pledge allegiance to their respective states even if they found it difficult to accept. Cases that have led to unfortunate bloodshed such as in the Balkans clearly showed what happens when there is a grave mismatch between nation building and societal make-up. Irredentist hegemony and migration across borders further complicate matters and generate international concern in a globalized world.

Thus, the conventional argument that human security can only be advanced if there is state security[7] no longer upholds since it clearly implies prioritizing the latter over the former. For decades, North Korea's paranoia with national security has brought about widespread suffering and refugee outflow of its people (see Chap. 1). As the world emerged from the ashes of the Cold War and as globalization becomes manifested in every layer and spectrum of the global society, the meaning of security has to be broadened beyond the typical narrative. This means putting in the *human* dimension that has been lost in oblivion. To do so, the 1994 report explicitly defined the term as having two important components: the freedom from want and the freedom from fear. The former focuses on the "…safety from such chronic threats as hunger, disease and repression" that reflects a slow and silent process and the latter on the "…protection from sudden and hurtful disruptions in the patterns of daily life" that reflect "an abrupt, loud emergency" (UNDP 1994: 23–24). Furthermore, the report identified seven key areas of the human security concept deemed important: economic security, food security, health security, environmental security, personal security, community security and political security.[8] Many of these areas are in fact touched upon by the contributors of this book.

In the following years, Canada, under the leadership of Foreign Minister Lloyd Axworthy (1996–2000), began to consider human security as part of its foreign policy, seeing the concept as a new measure of global security. It defined the term along the lines of the UNDP report but put a greater stress on threats such as human rights abuse and terrorism that directly affect individual's rights and safety (Bajpai 2000: 36). Together with Norway, a Human Security Partnership was established in May 1998 to address landmine and child soldier issues, among others. A year later, Canada led a group of like-minded countries, who gathered in Lysøen, Norway, to push for the concept as a policy agenda, defining it as "freedom from pervasive threats to people's rights, the safety or even their lives".[9] Furthermore, that year saw

---

[7] Abad (2000) argues that state security is "an essential prerequisite" of human security.
[8] For more details, see UNDP (1994: 24–33).
[9] "A Perspective on Human Security: Chairman's Summary" (1999).

the launching of human security under the United Nations Centre for Regional Development (UNCRD) that sought to integrate the concept into sustainable development strategies at the regional and local levels.

In 2000, UN Secretary General Kofi Annan strongly called for the building of a world "free of want" and "free of fear" at the Millennium Summit. In response, the Government of Japan initiated the establishment of the Commission on Human Security (CHS) in 2001, which lasted for 2 years.[10] Co-chaired by former UN High Commissioner for Refugees Sadako Ogata and Nobel Laureate Amartya Sen, the CHS took on the task of defining and developing the concept as an operational tool for policy implementation. Its 2003 report, *Human Security Now*, incorporates two approaches – bottom-up and top-down. The former "concentrates on empowering people" through development programs that "can best attained in a community context" while the latter puts the onus on the state to protect the people's well-being through sound "rule of law and judicial institutions" (Ogata 2006: 2–3). Despite some shortcomings, the combination of the two approaches is thought to provide the framework for human security.[11]

The 2003 report demonstrated Japan's stance on human security, which differs from those pursued by Canada and Norway. For the latter two, human security ought to be defined in a narrower form based particularly on the 'freedom from fear' and should thus focus on the two areas of political and personal securities – protection from political oppression and physical violence. The remaining five areas (economic, food, health, environmental, and community securities) are considered more suited to human development, which the two countries felt were already being pursued under various UN programs, and therefore a clear distinction should be made between human security and human development (Alkire 2003). Instead of prioritizing one over the other, Japan, on the other hand, followed the 1994 UNDP report that saw a need to pursue human security in its broadest sense, arguing that access to food and clean water as well as freedom from diseases and natural disasters affects the survival of individuals and are therefore of equal importance.[12]

Since 2003, there have been further efforts taken by the UN to move away from the fixation on state security towards human security by drawing up a new security consensus that would legitimize international interventions in places that undermine human security (Alkire 2003: 4). Therein lies the difficult challenge of addressing the issue of humanitarian intervention due to the overarching principles of sovereignty and non-interference in domestic affairs. One of the earliest efforts to address this concern was the International Commission on Intervention and State Sovereignty,

---

[10] To be certain, Japan had been advocating human security as a new strategy as early as 1995 through Prime Minister Murayama's speech to the UN (Acharya 2001).

[11] Muthien and Bunch argue that there are limitations in the CHS report for what they see as a failure to address women insecurities due to what they alleged to be a male-centered reporting (Schwartz 2004).

[12] Fukushima (2009) notes that there is now less focus on debating the concept of human security and more focus on operationalizing it.

set up in 2000 and largely sponsored by Canada. In their 2001 report, the Commission sought to emphasize that sovereignty is not about "control" but about "responsibility". Sovereignty does not only mean respect for the territorial integrity of other states but the responsibility to respect and protect the dignity and safety of citizens. This dual meaning showed resoluteness to hold national authorities accountable for their actions within their geographical borders and signified that the international community through the UN has a responsibility to act collectively should states fail to uphold their basic duties. The meaning of sovereignty and intervention is thus broadened to cover individuals – the core focus of human security. It also strengthened the notion of human rights as being universal.

Building on the report and in line with the development of human security, a High Level Panel on Threats, Challenges and Change that was created by Kofi Annan to review the new security landscape endorsed in their 2004 report the idea of 'responsibility to protect' (R2P) and the importance of development in building security. This endorsement was again reiterated under the three freedoms – freedom from want, freedom from fear and freedom to live in dignity – that formed the UN Secretary-General's proposed agenda for the High-level Plenary Meeting of the General Assembly (World Summit) in September 2005. At the Summit, the world leaders came to consensus that "[e]ach individual State has the responsibility to protect its populations from genocide, war crimes, ethnic cleansing and crimes against humanity" (UN 2005b: 31).[13] This was a momentous breakthrough particularly for the enhancement of freedom from extreme fear and reflected the changing tide of politico-security values.

In early 2009, the R2P was further refined with the introduction of the three pillars by Secretary-General Ban namely "the protection responsibilities of the State; the international assistance and capacity-building; and the timely and decisive response" to arrest crimes against the human race as a strategy to operationalize and transform the concept into a policy. The first pillar reinforces the 2005 endorsement that places the responsibility to protect civilians from harm squarely on the state. The message was clear – the UN opposes atrocities, unlawful killings and systematic attacks by states on their vulnerable populations. In 2010, the Secretary-General took the R2P a step further by addressing early warning and assessment capabilities. While efforts appeared to have been made, the practice of the R2P remains limited and its capacity to prevent crimes debatable.

Human Security for East Asia

The UN has played a major role in refocusing the debate on security by recognizing individual human beings as worthy of protection from threats, including those originating from states' actions. However, the UN has yet to provide an exact and legal

---

[13] Following the Summit, two bodies were created – the Human Rights Council and the Peacebuilding Commission – in March and June 2006 respectively.

definition of human security and as such the term remains contested. The difficulty of providing a precise definition stems from the different approach that human security takes in comparison to state-focused security such as the common, cooperative and comprehensive securities previously discussed. In critically asking "[i]f the values of the person conflict with the values of the state, which prevail?", Acharya argued that human security "is certainly not new wine in an old bottle. Comprehensive security answered the question: which threats to state security? Human security answers 'whose security'?" (2001: 453–454).

Human security in its strictest sense is about the security of the people and therefore prioritizes individuals over states. Therein lies the distinction. The UN is a representation of its members and any conceptual and operational development of the term would hence entail states' input and commitment. For human security to take a stronger hold there is a need for greater recognition of the values of individuals and communities vis-à-vis the states. This does not necessarily imply that human and state securities are stacked on opposite ends but more needs to be done to bring human security issues to the forefront of international attention. This is where efforts should be made to enable the UN to function as an inter-societal organization representing the world citizens apart from its traditional role as an intergovernmental institution.

For the purpose of this study, human security is defined along the lines of the 1994 UNDP and the 2003 CHS reports and so without doubt puts people at the heart of the security lexicon. The study does not only see the protection from pervasive threats as instrumental, but it also sees sustainable development as essential to the enhancement of human freedom and fulfillment. This provides a single framework to address and highlight the various issues pertaining to the safety and wellbeing of individuals living in East Asia. Home to nations with high economy and population growth rates, the region has observed various human insecurities including income disparities made worse by globalization and the lack of safety measures to cushion and rescue those who fall. Human security is indispensable if ever globalization is to have a human and ethical face.

The interdependence of states and societies in East Asia further illustrates the increasingly multifaceted and transnational nature of people-related problems that require regional cooperation and swift solution. Just like traditional security, human security necessitates coordinated responses and collective efforts. It is within these understandings that the study aims to provide valuable insights into the complex relationships between the different levels of people, state and region, and to examine the extent of human security being mainstreamed into state and regional activities.

The future of East Asia and its people lies not in military buildup for the protection of sovereignty but in human development for the protection of human lives and the realization of human potential. After all, shouldn't that be the focus of East Asian regionalism? Is the effort to build an ASEAN community and subsequently an East Asian community through the ASEAN+3 and the East Asia Summit frameworks for states or for the people? For too long, ASEAN has been criticized for being an organization catering solely to the interest of its member states. This is perhaps best reflected in former Thai Foreign Minister Surin Pitsuwan's speech in 2002 when he said,

> In 1998, at the time the idea of flexible engagement was proposed at the Association of Southeast Asian Nations (ASEAN) ministerial meeting, I proposed the creation of a "caucus for social safety nets." None of my ASEAN colleagues supported me. Most of the support came from outside ASEAN, particularly the West—Australia, the United States, Russia, and even India. I proposed a caucus of social safety nets because all of a sudden *millions of our people* had slid back into poverty and they needed help to sustain them through the crisis. My colleagues thought the idea was another Western idea and another way of coming through the back door in order to interfere with the internal affairs of member states. So we should not underestimate the problems, the resistance, the doubt that could occur as we work to shift from the supremacy of the state to a focus on individuals (2002: 56; emphasis added).

Hence it is not too difficult to see that while ASEAN identified Socio-Cultural Community as one of the three important pillars of its community it is by far the weakest primarily because bottom-up processes played by civic groups and NGOs have yet to be given ample attention and support. According to the ASEAN Charter, the purposes of ASEAN, among many, are "to alleviate poverty…; to enhance the well-being and livelihood of the peoples of ASEAN…; to strengthen cooperation in building a safe, secure and drug-free environment for the peoples of ASEAN; to promote a people-oriented ASEAN…" (2008: 4–5). If these aims are what ASEAN sets out to achieve, then the significance of human security to the future of Southeast Asia is obvious. Coupled with the role that Japan has been playing in promoting human security[14], such similar purposes as outlined by ASEAN should aptly apply to the wider regional agenda in securing the future of East Asia as well. In fact, the East Asia Vision Group report that was produced in 2001 for the ASEAN+3 cooperation identified "people focus" as one of the guiding principles, explaining that "their security, welfare and happiness are our ultimate goal" (2001: 8). Therefore, regional security frameworks such as the ASEAN Regional Forum, which has been disparaged for its inability to move beyond the first phase of confidence building, should be reconfigured into a body for the championing of human security concerns (Teh 2009).

The lack of thrust of Asian regional organizations in championing the causes of human security lies less in their intergovernmental structures and more in the deficiency of spaces for civic groups to voice their concerns and lobby for greater attention on human related issues, particularly on the freedoms from fear and want. A more dynamic relationship between states and societies with substantial amount of bottom-up pressures are necessary to reorient the elitist image of regional institutions considering the fact that many of the issues such as food scarcity, illicit drugs and organized crimes increasingly demand a multilevel approach.

Chapters in This Volume

This book is divided into two parts and consists of a total of twelve chapters. Part I has five chapters that discuss the problems of human security within the conundrum of state-society relations. Chapter 1 provides an in-depth analysis into the problems

---

[14] For a detailed analysis of Japan's human security policy, see Edström (2008).

of North Korean refugees as a critical case study. The author argues that the refugee issue highlights the ineffectiveness of the human security paradigm in transcending the deep-rooted traditional security agenda and views ethics and morality as indispensable in creating a sustainable security culture of reconciliation. Chapter 2 takes up the issue of health security, focusing on the vulnerability of women to HIV transmission in mainland China. Chinese women, due to the patriarchal nature of the society, will continue to suffer from the lack of empowerment and remain highly insecure unless a gendered response to HIV based on international best practices is appropriately enforced. Empowerment is undeniably the key to forestalling the spread of communicable diseases. Chapter 3 looks at the historical trend of population policy in Vietnam and its relations to human security. In discussing Vietnam's demographic changes, the author shows that the level of transition from state to human security approaches in the four important areas of migration, reproductive rights, food supply and the environment, and minority rights has remained unclear due to various internal and external developments.

Thailand's migration situation and anti-trafficking initiatives are carefully explored in Chap. 4. Though the Thai government has infused certain international practices to stem human trafficking, the author finds that such development is still ineffective in addressing the wider range of exploitations especially on unforced migrants and street children unless collaboration between anti-trafficking and development efforts are properly established. In contrast to the previous chapter that looks at migrants in the country, Chap. 5 discusses the dynamics of interaction between the state and society in the Philippines concerning Filipino labor migrants abroad. Employing both top-down and bottom-up approaches, the author examines the concept of human security as viewed by the government and by the people and reveals that while the state concerns itself with the protection of its citizens working abroad, it fails to provide protection for the migrants' families at home from insecurities that are seen as the reason for migrants to emigrate in the first place.

Part II covers the remaining seven chapters. This part deals with the broader regional issues in the key areas of health, environmental, economic and political securities and implications for policy consideration. Chapter 6 anchors its discussion on the environmental problems affecting the lower Mekong region that covers parts of the territory of Cambodia, Laos and Vietnam. Looking at intra- and extra-regional factors the author points out that addressing insecurity is a complex process that depends on dynamic interactions of actors at various levels and can only be fully tackled if ample space is created for the voices of those directly affected to be heard. Chapter 7 takes issue with the environment as well but fixes squarely on the inability of ASEAN to mitigate the ill effects of climate change due to its outdated diplomatic culture. Seeing a need to unlock the traditional mindset, the authors believe that continuous pressure from Indonesia and civil societies inside and outside of the region is needed to help develop a common policy with effective measures in line with international practices.

One of the hurdles for ASEAN is the removal of its overzealousness on the principle of non-interference. Chapter 8 attempts to provide a solution by discussing the issue of natural disasters. It elaborates that collaborative measures including more sophisticated mechanisms can be taken on issues that are considered politically neutral citing the example of what the author sees as an encouraging regional response carried out by ASEAN in the 2008 Nargis cyclone aftermath.

However, environmental security is not independent from the other areas of security as outlined in the UNDP report. In fact, they are clearly interrelated and interconnected. In Chap. 9, the interrelatedness and the dangers of other human security threats primarily on the food supply and safety to health security are examined and highlighted. Providing a number of case studies as support and seeing multi-sectoral cooperation as compulsory to sustainable solution, the author argues that health security is crucial. The failure of governments to protect their citizens risks exposing them to extremism and threatens the security of states. It clearly illustrates and strengthens the point that human security is not inferior to traditional security as conventionally thought.

Chapter 10 assesses the extent of economic security being considered in the process of proliferating free trade agreements (FTAs). Engaged in competition to outdo each other in the number of FTAs signed, governments have largely centered attention on national economic interests rather than giving sufficient consideration to long-term effects and structural transformations that could negatively impact peoples' economic wellbeing. Turning to political security, Chap. 11 discusses one of the major issues on the international human rights agenda – the death penalty. Despite democratic progress, the death penalty continues to exist in most parts of East Asia. Contrasting the experiences of South Korea and Japan, the author shows that the former has achieved great progress in abolishing capital punishment because of reform-minded leaders' ability to generate change regardless of public opinion while the latter has been incapacitated by its own enjoyment of political stability to take bold and unfavorable initiatives to enact reforms. Lastly, Chap. 12 sets the course for an examination into the principle of sovereignty and the legal-political and ecological impacts of sea level change affecting small island states (SISs). Sovereignty as traditionally defined, argues the author, is a hindrance to resolving environmental threats to SISs. Legal and political consensus among the international community is a necessity to address and prevent human misery due to the perils of inundation.

While there have been some efforts in implementing human security in East Asia, there is still a considerable lack of awareness, recognition and political will particularly among state actors to deal with the vast array of human-related transnational issues and to seek collective actions across traditional boundaries especially in cooperation with non-state actors, which are pertinent in securing a peaceful sustainable future for the region and its inhabitants.

References

(1999, 20 May). *A perspective on human security: Chairman's summary*. Lysoen, Norway. http://www.nisat.org/export_laws-regs%20linked/norway/lys%C3%B8en_20_may_1999.htm. Accessed 19 February 2007.

Abad, M. C., Jr. (2000). *The Challenge of balancing state security with human security*. ASEAN Secretariat. http://www.aseansec.org/14259.htm. Accessed 6 July 2010.

Acharya, A. (2001). Human security: East versus West. *International Journal, 56*(3), 442–460.

Akaha, T. (1991). Japan's comprehensive security policy: A new East Asian environment. *Asian Survey*, *31*(4), 324–340.

Alkire, S. (2003). *A conceptual framework for human security*. Working Paper 2, Centre for Research on Inequality, Human Security and Ethnicity (CRISE), University of Oxford.

ASEAN. (2008). *The ASEAN charter*. Jakarta: The ASEAN Secretariat.

Axworthy, L. (2001). Human security and global governance: Putting people first. *Global Governance*, *7*, 19–23.

Bajpai, K. (2000). *Human security: Concept and measurement* (Kroc Institute Occasional Paper #19:OP:1). http://www.hegoa.ehu.es/dossierra/seguridad/Human_security_concept_and_measurement.pdf. Accessed 6 July 2010.

Ciralsky, A., & Chris, H. (2007a, 8 August). *Sex trafficked: Anna's story* (Transcript). Dateline NBC. http://www.msnbc.msn.com/id/20182993/. Accessed 27 June 2010.

Ciralsky, A., & Chris, H. (2007b, 10 August). *Women rescued from human traffickers* (Transcript). Dateline NBC. http://www.msnbc.msn.com/id/20185681/. Accessed 27 June 2010.

Commission on Human Security. (2003). *Human security now*. New York: Commission on Human Security. http://www.humansecurity-chs.org/finalreport/English/FinalReport.pdf. Accessed 6 July 2010.

Department of Public Information. (2010, 24 February). *States have shared duty to fight transnational threats to international peace, security, Secretary-General says in Security Council Debate*. New York: Department of Public Information. http://www.un.org/News/Press/docs/2010/sgsm12763.doc.htm. Accessed 28 June 2010.

East Asia Vision Group (EAVG). (2001). *Towards an East Asian Community: Region of peace, prosperity and progress*, EAVG Report. Jakarta: The ASEAN Secretariat.

Edström, B. (2008). *Japan and the challenge of human security: The founding of a new policy 1995–2003*. Stockholm-Nacka: Institute for Security and Development Policy.

FAO (Food and Agriculture Organization of the United Nations). (2009). *The state of food insecurity in the world: Economic rises – impacts and lessons learned*. Rome: FAO.

Fukushima, A. (1999). Japan's emerging view of security multilateralism in Asia. In *Security multilateralism in Asia; views from the United States and Japan*, Institute on Global Conflict and Cooperation (IGCC) Policy Paper (pp. 23–37). University of California.

Fukushima, A. (2009). East versus West?: Debate and convergence on human security. In P. Sorpong (Ed.), *Human security in East Asia: Challenges for collaborative Action* (pp. 46–60). Oxon: Routledge.

Gorbachev, M. (1988, 7 December). *Address to 43rd General Assembly*. New York: United Nations.

Hughes, C. W. (2005). Japanese military modernization: In search of a 'normal' security role. In A. J. Tellis, & M. Wills (Eds.), *Strategic Asia 2005–06: Military modernization in an era of ncertainty* (pp. 105–136). Seattle: The National Bureau of Asian Research.

International Commission on Intervention and State Sovereignty. (2001). *The responsibility to protect: Report of the International Commission on Intervention and State Sovereignty*. Ottawa: International Development Research Centre.

Lam, P. E. (2006). Japan's human security role in Southeast Asia. *Contemporary Southeast Asia*, *28*(1), 141–159.

Ogata, S. (2006). Speech presented at the UNU Junior Fellows Symposium on Development, Peace and Environment. Tokyo: United Nations University.

Pitsuwan, S. (2002). *Human security as a policy framework for new cooperation in Asia*. Presentation for session II, health and human security: Moving from concept to action-fourth intellectual dialogue on building Asia's tomorrow. Tokyo: Japan Center for International Exchange.

Schwartz, A. (2004). *Is human security a useful concept for achieving gender justice human rights and development? An interview, Association for Women's Rights in Development*. http://www.awid.org/eng/Issues-and-Analysis/Library/Is-human-security-a-useful-concept-for-achievinggender-justice-human-rights-and-development.

Teh, B. C. G. (2009). Managing threats in the Asia-Pacific region: A new role for the Asean Regional Forum (ARF). In B. Edström (Ed.), *Security and development in Asia: New threats and challenges in the post-postwar era* (pp. 82–109). Stockholm: Institute for Security and Development Policy.

The Independent Commission on Disarmament and Security Issues. (1982). *Common security: A blueprint for survival.* New York: Simon & Schuster.

The Japan Times. (2010, 25 March). *'Ore, ore' ringleader gets 20 years.* The Star Online. (2009a, 7 July). *Drugs entering via KLIA.* http://thestar.com.my/news/story.asp?file=/2009/7/7/nation/4266520&sec=nation. Accessed 28 June 2010.

The Star Online. (2009b, 30 October). *RM38m worth of drugs seized in Batu Ferringhi.* http://thestar.com.my/news/story.asp?file=/2009/10/30/nation/5005151&sec=nation. Accessed 28 June 2010.

The Star Online. (2009c, 10 December). *Ketamine worth RM1.2mil seized at KLIA.* http://thestar.com.my/news/story.asp?file=/2009/12/10/nation/20091210152640&sec=nation. Accessed 28 June 2010.

The Star Online. (2010a, 22 January). *Customs on alert at KLIA.* http://thestar.com.my/news/story.asp?file=/2010/1/22/nation/5521180&sec=nation. Accessed 28 June 2010.

The Star Online. (2010b, 28 June). *Indian authorities foil attempt to smuggle ketamine to Malaysia.* http://thestar.com.my/news/story.asp?file=/2010/6/28/nation/20100628122612&sec=nation. Accessed 28 June 2010.

The Star Online. (2010c, 23 June). *Underground economy growing with many illegal activities.* http://thestar.com.my/news/story.asp?file=/2010/6/23/nation/6527973&sec=nation. Accessed 30 June 2010.

The Straits Times. (2010, 16 June). *Thai customs seize ketamine.* http://www.straitstimes.com/BreakingNews/SEAsia/Story/STIStory_541186.html. Accessed 28 June 2010.

Turk, C., & Andrew, M. (2010). Impacts of the economic crisis in East Asia: Findings from qualitative monitoring in five vountries. In A. Bauer, & M. Thant (Eds.), *Poverty and sustainable development in Asia: Impacts and responses to the global economic crisis* (pp. 51–76). Philippines: Asian Development Bank.

UNDP (United Nations Development Program). (1994). *New dimensions of human security.* United Nations: Human Development Report

United Nations. (2004). *A more secure world: Our shared responsibility.* Report of the high-level Panel on threats, challenges and change. New York: United Nations.

United Nations. (2005a). *In larger freedom: Towards development, security and human rights for all.* Report of the Secretary-General, March, Fifty-ninth session, Agenda items 45 and 55, United Nations General Assembly.

United Nations. (2005b). *Draft resolution referred to the high-level plenary meeting of the General Assembly by the General Assembly at its Fifty-ninth Session.* World Summit Outcome, Sept, Sixtieth session, United Nations General Assembly.

United Nations. (2009). *Implementing the responsibility to protect.* Report of the Secretary-General, January, Sixty-third session, United Nations General Assembly.

UNODC (United Nations Office on Drugs and Crime). (2009a). *Global report on trafficking in persons.* http://www.unodc.org/documents/Global_Report_on_TIP.pdf. Accessed 28 June 2010.

UNODC (United Nations Office on Drugs and Crime). (2009b). *Patterns and trends of amphetamine-type stimulants and other drugs in East and South-East Asia (and Neighbouring Regions).* A Report from the Global SMART Programme.

UNODC (United Nations Office on Drugs and Crime). (2010). *The globalization of crime: A transnational organized crime threat assessment.* Vienna: United Nations Publication.

WHO (World Health Organization). (2010). *Respiratory disease activity in SEA region during 13 June – 19 June 2010, Communicable diseases.* http://www.searo.who.int/EN/Section10/Section2562.htm. Accessed 26 June 2010.

Part I
The State, the People and Responses to Human Security Concerns

Chapter 1
Human Insecurities or Liabilities? The Changing Security Paradigms and the Case of the North Korean Refugees

Jaime Koh

1.1 An Escalating Crisis?

> There must be a new conception of how to get along in the world, a recognition that only the individual person is of ultimate value – not governments, not abstractions, not collectivities – and that if we do not cherish the life embodied in such persons, there is no point to our other pursuits, much less to contention over ideologies, economic systems, and political policies (Holmes, 1989:263).

Between 50,000 and 300,000[1] of North Korean refugees are said to be in northeast China, where they mix with a significant population of ethnic Koreans of Chinese citizenship. A smaller number – between 300 and 12,000 – are in Russia's maritime province bordering North Korea (Yoon, 1999; Lee, 2003).[2] These refugees are the subjects of this chapter.[3] The phenomenon of refugees from North Korea is a paradox. On one hand, refugees are not unknown in Korean history: Since the nineteenth century, many have sought refuge overseas in times of economic deprivation and social upheavals to escape political oppression or simply as part of the regular migratory movement. Yet contradictory to the assumption that more people are as

---

[1] There are no official records of the exact number of refugees, only estimates. See Foster-Carter (2001).

[2] Amnesty International puts the figure as between 2,500 and 6,000. The US State Department also puts the number at 6,000 while the South Korean Intelligence Agency puts it at 12,000 (in 1999). See Amnesty International (1996).

[3] North Korean refugees referred to in this chapter do not include North Koreans who had made their way to South Korea from North Korea directly, or those who are already in the South. Theoretically, Seoul regards North Koreans as overseas South Koreans, extending legislative protection and economic assistance such as education and residence allowances to all arriving North Koreans.

J. Koh (✉)
National University of Singapore, Singapore
e-mail: jaimekoh@gmail.com

likely to flee an oppressive regime as during times of conflict and upheavals, available documents point to little migration from North Korea since the end of the Korean War (1950–1953).[4] The establishment of the authoritarian regime under Kim Il-Sung would be a logical push factor for an exodus of North Koreans. Yet the number of refugees from North Korea since 1953 is relatively low. South Korea said it received 4,662 North Korean defectors between 1954 and February 2004, the majority of them arriving in 2003 and 2004 (Ministry of Unification, n.d.). In comparison, the United States admitted more than 233,000 refugees from communist states between 1956 and 1968 (Loescher, 1993:59). Prior to 1988, most defectors from North Korea were soldiers stationed at or near the demilitarized zone (DMZ) who crossed the DMZ into South Korea.[5] There were also a small number of non-military defectors, mostly students and party officials, who defected while studying or while on overseas missions, motivated by a general discontent with the communist regime.[6] Since the late 1980s, most of the North Korean defectors were civilians who cited economic reasons and survival as their reasons for escape.

Refugee flow from North Korea intensified in the 1990s as a result of the widespread famine and its ripple effects (Lohman, 1996; Foster-Carter, 1999; Amnesty International, 2004; Human Rights Watch, 2002; Refugee International, 2005; *Voice of America,* 2005; Charny, 2003). The situation had not deteriorated into one of mass exodus, but the lack of official recognition of these North Korean's refugee status as defined by the United Nations High Commission for Refugees (UNHCR); the presence of these North Koreans has raised issues concerning their legal status and treatment by the various authorities. Despite extensive documentation of their plight, the international community has hitherto paid little attention to this humanitarian crisis. The world's attention on North Korea remains centered on its military and nuclear ambitions, political intransigence, and on human rights violations within its borders.

According to the 1951 Refugee Convention, a refugee is one who,

> owing to well-founded fear of being persecuted for reasons of race, religion, nationality, membership of a particular social group or political opinion, is outside the country of his nationality and is unable or, owing to such fear, is unwilling to avail himself of the protection of that country; or who, not having a nationality and being outside the country of his former habitual residence as a result of such events, is unable or, owing to such fear, is unwilling to return to it.[7]

---

[4] The number of refugees from North Korea, which peaked during the Korean War, was significantly reduced by war's end. See Kim (1998:30).

[5] This information is drawn from articles and reports in various issues of the *Korea Newsreview* magazine. See for example, Korea Newsreview (1979a, b) (1981a, b) (1983a, b) (1986), (1988a, b) (1989a, b, c).

[6] This is based on an informal and random sample of articles published in *Korea Newsreview*, a South Korean English newsletter. It is *not* a comprehensive survey of all possible sources on North Korean defectors.

[7] *1951 Convention Relating to the Status of Refugees,* Article 1(2). Hereafter referred to as the Refugee Convention. The *1967 Protocol Relating to the Status of Refugees* removed the time and geographical limitations of the 1951 Convention which originally applied only to refugees from Europe before 1951.

Instead, the North Korean refugees have been variously referred to as "defectors," "escapees," and "illegal immigrants." These labels accord them little legal protection. Advocacy groups have argued for these North Koreans to be officially recognized as refugees on two fundamental premises. First, they have a well-grounded fear of persecution – a key determinant of refugee status – as a result of the oppressive social and political control in North Korea (Choi, 1999:235; Refugee International, 2005:13). Second, the North Koreans are considered refugee sur place, that is, refugees who did not leave their country of origin for fear of persecution but who fear persecution upon return. Claims of severe punishment, including death, incarceration in labor camps, and further discrimination, have been documented to support the North Koreans' bid for asylum.

1.2 Human Security and the North Korean Refugees

The growth of human rights mechanisms and norms has brought people – one of the most basic but neglected units of analysis in international relations – into the spotlight. It was in this context and in response to the growing limitation of traditional security that the concept of human security emerged, as articulated by the *1994 Human Development Report* (hereafter, HDR). In contrast to protecting the state from external attacks by rival states as premised by the traditional paradigm, human security is about "security for people" and "a concern with human life and dignity". It is a human-centered vision that advocates for the human individual to be protected from the freedom from want – "safety from such chronic threats as hunger, disease and repression," and from fear – "protection from sudden and hurtful disruptions in the patterns of daily life" (ibid:23). The threats to well-being are mapped out in seven categories: economic, food, health, environmental, personal, community, and political (ibid:25–33). Human security is achieved when these needs and rights are adequately provided for. Even before the concept took its present form,[8] the idea of human security formed the foundation of international refugee work which was to protect the well-being and security of a vulnerable group of people. The former United Nations High Commissioner for Refugees, Sadako Ogata, clearly articulated human security as a fundamental premise of refugee work.

This statement sums up, in a nutshell, the case of the North Korean refugees:

> As a rule, people do not abandon their homes and flee from their own country or community unless they are confronted with serious threats to their life or liberty. Flight is the ultimate survival strategy, the one employed when all other coping mechanisms have been exhausted.

---

[8] Enhanced by the International Commission on Intervention and State Sovereignty's 2001 *The Responsibility to Protect* report and the Commission on Human Security's *Human Security Now* report, published in 2003.

Measured against the seven categories of threats to human security identified by the *HDR*, the insecurities of the North Korean refugees are clear, as the following points illustrate:

1. Environmental insecurities – The natural disasters that had plagued the country since 1994 have destroyed approximately 90% of North Korea's limited arable land (Amnesty International, 2004; World Food Program 2005a), leading to widespread famine. The severity of the situation had led Pyongyang to appeal publicly, for the first time, to the international community for help in September 1995 (Natsios, 2001:1). By 1996, North Korea sustained US$15 billion in damages, having lost 1.9 million tons of grain, equivalent to 17% of the previous year's production, and 330,000 ha of farmland. More than 5.4 million people were displaced (Ahn, 2005:3). Food shortage is still critical, and areas of North Korea are still experiencing famine.
2. Economic insecurities – The famine was "an extreme manifestation" (Forster-Carter, 1999:8) of North Korea's economic crisis which began in the late 1980s (Ahn, 2005:11; Amnesty International, 2004:6). It was also the inevitable result of Pyongyang's flawed economic and agricultural policies, coupled with external developments such as the collapse of the communist bloc and deterioration in relationship between Pyongyang and its patrons, China and the Soviet Union. The situation was compounded by North Korea's unsuccessful reforms to salvage its faltering economy, including the failures of the special economic zones (SEZ)[9] and inappropriate macro-economic reforms. The July 2002 macro-economic reforms aimed at introducing a market economy only served to worsen the impact of the famine with adverse effects, including runaway inflation, unpaid wages, cuts in government rations, and high unemployment rates (Cho, 2002; Cooper, 2005; World Food Program:2005b).
3. Food insecurities – The threat to food security for the North Koreans started with the onset of North Korea's economic crisis in the late 1980s (Ahn, 2005:1). By 1987, it was importing some 438,000 metric tons of grain, almost three times the amount imported the year before (ibid:9). It was a sign of serious trouble for a country that has claimed one of the world's highest rice yields and had sent about 7,000 tons of food to South Korea in 1984 when floods drastically reduced the latter's harvests (ibid:1). The food shortages and the subsequent famine of the 1990s led to the breakdown of the Public Distribution System (PDS), the main

---

[9] They include the Rajin-Sonbong SEZ established in 1991 in the northeast of the country; Shinuiju, established in 2002 which was also to double up as a special administrative region; and Kaesong. The city of Shinuiju in the northwest of the country, bordering the booming Chinese city of Dandong, was declared a Special Administrative Zone in September 2002. It was the most promising of the lot, touted to have independent legislative, judicial, and administrative powers, and is "totally capitalist." But it was mired in political difficulties when the North Korean-appointed Chinese governor of the region, Yang Bin, was arrested by Chinese authorities for alleged commercial misconduct just days after the SAZ was declared. It raised speculation that the arrest was a show of Chinese displeasure at Pyongyang's appointment of Yang which was apparently made without Beijing's blessing. See Koh (2004) and Chosun (2002a, b).

means of food and services in North Korea. Between 1992 and 1993, the PDS rations, which had been consistent since 1973, were reduced by 20% (ibid:9). By 1997, the peak of the famine, the PDS could only reportedly supply 6% of the population with food as compared with the system's pre-famine reach of 60% of the population (Amnesty International, 2004:8–9). In 1998, rations dropped from more than 300 g per person per day to just 100 g (ibid:8–9), less than half of the amount needed for survival (World Food Program, 2005b).

4. Health insecurities – The social costs of the famine and related health and sanitation services were high, with expectant mothers, children, and the elderly being the most vulnerable (Amnesty International, 2004:25–29). Chronic malnutrition, anemia and other diseases, and high infant mortality were common problems (ibid:25–29; European Union, UNICEF, WFP, 1998). North Korea acknowledged in 2002 that more than 60% of its children under 5 years old suffer from acute respiratory infections, that more than 20% suffer from diarrhea, and that the death rate for these diseases was as high as 80% (Amnesty International, 2004:25).

5. Community and personal insecurities – An estimated 2–3.5 million[10] of North Korea's population (10–17%) have died from hunger and related diseases since 1994. The family unit has been broken up with the death of members and/or the dispersal of members in search of survival. Many orphans became street children and have been reduced to foraging or begging for food on the streets of North Korea or China (Chung, 2003:191–211), with no access to food aid or physical protection. Women have reportedly been trafficked, voluntarily or otherwise, to China as rural brides or prostitutes (Muico, 2005; Charny, 2004:75–97; Hughes, 2005). North Korean police patrols have reportedly been given shoot-to-kill orders against potential defectors crossing into China (Human Rights Watch, 2002:10; Choi, 1999:252) by way of the Tumen River. For those who have made it to China, they still often have to dodge the Chinese police or North Korean agents patrolling the area (Human Rights Watch, 2002:11–16) and are at the mercy of those who shelter them. Those caught are then deported back to North Korea where they would be sent to labor camps, subjected to torture and cruel treatment, or executed in extreme cases (Amnesty International, 2004:32–37; Life Funds for North Korean Refugees 2004; UN Commission on Human Rights 2004).

6. Political insecurities – The North Koreans' exposure to such threats to their physical well-being reflects their lack of political and freedom both domestically and when outside their country. The crossing of the Tumen River is more than just an illegal trespassing of a national boundary; it is "a decisive moment of separation when (the refugees) cross…the border between being a citizen

---

[10]The latter figure is estimated by Hwang Jong Yop, the former ideologue and philosopher of the North Korean self-sufficiency ideology – *Juche* – who defected to South Korea in 1997. He was said to be the highest-ranking North Korean Communist party member to have defected (Natsios 2001:6).

and a criminal or ... traitor" (Human Rights Watch, 2002:10). It is considered an act of "ultimate resistance" to the Pyongyang regime (Refugees International 2004:6). According to the North Korean penal code, leaving the country without permission is a criminal act punishable by imprisonment in a labor re-education camp or execution. The severity of such punishments is not unthinkable for such a tightly regulated society in which even the mobility of its citizens within the country is highly controlled (Choi, 1999:251). International protection for those who made it out of North Korea is lacking. China and Russia do not recognize these North Koreans as refugees as defined by the 1951 Refugee Convention. Instead, they are regarded as "illegal immigrants," "economic migrants," "escapees," or "defectors." More often than not, these refugees are not given access to UNHCR. Aid is also not forthcoming from the local population.

If the aim of the human security paradigm is to "identify the missing gaps of what must be restored, rebuilt or replaced to achieve peace and stability" (Henk, 2005:100), it has failed in this case. The following section will discuss why the issue of human security remains at the periphery of the traditional state- and military-centric understanding of security.

1.3 Human Security – Subject Non Grata?

Despite its Asian pedigree (Acharya, 2001:444), the concept of human security has made a virtually negligible impact in Northeast Asia (NEA). This mirrors the region's lukewarm reception to the notions of human rights and democracy. With the exception of Japan, most NEA states have neither adopted nor included human security in their security policy and discourse. The region's obsession with security continues to be dominated by the realist school with its emphasis on the absolute sovereignty of the state, unity and stability of the state, and military strength. But the less-than-welcome reception of human security is not just specific to NEA, it is also in tandem with the lack of significant global impact of the human security paradigm. Except in a few countries such as Canada,[11] Norway,[12] and

---

[11] Canada has taken on human security as part of its foreign policy paradigm. See the Department of Foreign Affairs and International Trade (1999, 2005) and McRae and Hubert (2001).

[12] Norway has entered a bilateral initiative with Canada reaffirming human security as a leitmotif of their foreign policies. See *Norway-Canada Partnership for Action, The Lysoen Declaration*, accessed at The Norwegian Initiative on Small Arms Transfer website, http://www.nisat.org/export_laws-regs%20linked/norway/lysoern.htm, 21 June 2006. Norway, Canada, and nine other countries formed the Human Security Network in 1999. It was the first attempt at institutionalizing the human security agenda. See Human Security Network (2005). For Norway's foreign policy approach, see Lunde (1999) and Ministry of Foreign Affairs, Norway (2005).

Japan,[13] the concept of human security operates in the peripheries of mainstream policies.[14]

Human security implies not just a shift of focus from state to individual, but of a fundamental reordering of state–society relations, putting individual needs and rights above that of the state. If democracy and democratization are key components of human security as argued (Anwar, 2003:545), then it is no surprise that the concept of human security as articulated by the various international organizations and academia is not a welcome guest in Asia. Although military strength underpins the region's definition of security, the latter has expanded in the past 30 years to include economic and social security. Yet, this expanded security paradigm – in the form of comprehensive security, a term first coined by Japan in the 1970s – is still "conventional security" given that it has been established as the security norm in the region. One of the main tenets of comprehensive security is to build up a state's economy. Despite the rapid pace of economic development in the region in the past few decades, these efforts remain a means to protect and promote the security of the state (ibid:536) rather than for the ultimate well-being of the people as the end goal. Most of the national interests do not always include the interests of the collective, such as access to food, water, shelter, education, and health, and possession of political and civil rights.[15] Threats to these interests rarely feature in the national agenda. At best, the task of addressing any human insecurity is the means to the end of maintaining power and stability. At worst, it is relegated to the periphery as an idealistic vision. Respect for state sovereignty, rather than respect for human rights and dignity, inevitably dictates the affairs of the states.

These issues open up a whole new set of questions regarding the human security-realpolitik nexus: To what extent has geopolitics played a part in the neglect of humanitarian concerns for the North Korean refugees? Does security for one group (for example, states) necessarily have to be at the expense of the security of another (individual citizens)? What does security mean? How can we reconcile the seemingly divergent interests of state security and security of individuals and groups? How do we juggle the ethical and moral imperatives that inform the humanitarianism of human security and the pragmatism of realpolitik?

The human security paradigm, said to include the excluded (Commission on Human Security, 2003:5), has failed the North Korean refugees due to several

---

[13] In addition to incorporating human security principles into its diplomacy, Japan also initiated the establishment of the Human Security Trust Fund (HSTF) in the United Nations Secretariat in 1998, advocated for the Commission on Human Security (CHS) in 2000, and established the Advisory Board on Human Security to follow up on the final report of the CHS and to advise the HSTF. Numerous grassroots projects around the world have benefited from funds disbursed through the trust fund. See Japan's Ministry of Foreign Affairs (2005) and Japan (2005).

[14] For example, as an indication of the spread of "human security" in security discourse, two surveys in 2002 found that the term "human security" is referred to or used in less than 0.3% and 5% in English newspapers and journal articles, respectively (Evans, 2004: 37).

[15] Take for example the case of the reluctance of the Myanmar military junta in allowing aid into the country following the devastating Cyclone Nargis in May 2008. Its fear of foreign intervention and the desire to maintain its power override the concern for its people.

limitations of the paradigm: The disparity in practice between state sovereignty and individual rights, the humanistic nature of the paradigm, and finally the paradigm's disregard for realpolitik. The role of geopolitics in humanitarian affairs cannot be discounted. The refugee issue is not an issue independent of the surrounding political and security environments. Instead, it is inextricably entwined with the region's prevailing political and security concerns. Human security and traditional security intersect and cannot be separated into distinct concerns. Human security is not just a concern of the state, the individual, or the humanitarian groups exclusively, it involves an array of players.

Here, I draw inspiration from the school of critical security studies in arguing for a need to re-conceptualize the meaning of security. This task involves more than simply expanding or narrowing the security agenda; it requires a fundamental re-evaluation of the dynamics of international relations that includes asking the question: Is there a place for ethos in international politics? I believe that ethics is not irrelevant to international relations; the international order has its foundations in ethics in ideas such as the notion of human security, albeit intertwined with conventional security both pragmatically and ethically in an increasingly interdependent world. More importantly, it has to be one that is founded on cooperation among the players involved.

The state-centered security paradigm that has served Northeast Asia well is no longer adequate in dealing with emerging issues that extend beyond the scope of the conventional understanding of security. Non-traditional threats to security such as the Asian financial crisis, health pandemics (avian flu and SARS), and natural disasters (the December 2004 tsunami, the May 2008 earthquake that caused extensive damage in China, and the destructive impact of Cyclone Nargis on Myanmar) demonstrate the breadth of issues with security implications for both the governments and people.[16] Even in an expanded "comprehensive security" agenda, the resulting conventional security paradigm remains deficient in dealing with human security issues. First, the continued centrality of the state ensures that the "national interest" issues of territoriality, sovereignty, and national survival remain paramount. As such, only issues that the state considers critical to its security and welfare are included on the "national interest" agenda. This ineffectuality is due to the second limitation of the conventional security paradigm: The notions dealt with are too abstract for a consistent policy that takes into account humanitarian concerns. While "nation," "state," "sovereignty," and "territoriality" have important philosophical and political significance, they are nevertheless highly abstract and contested concepts. As with the concept of security, these concepts are a result of their historical context within which they developed. The contested nature of such concepts allows for a fluid definition of security and, hence, of national interests. Furthermore, since security in this case is built on these normative contexts which are constantly shifting, this leads to "a certain complacency in the international community that has come to accept many things…as immune to change",

---

[16] The impact of "non-traditional" security threats on East Asia is dealt within Dupont (2001).

unlike human security which is built on common values. Finally, the conventional security paradigm discounts the humanistic[17] aspect of security and treats every security issue as static, embodied in numbers and definitions. To take a more humane view is regarded by the political elites as being too "soft" and inappropriate for state matters as "there is no rule for civic virtue and comity" (Falk, 1995:38).

Yet are the increasingly vocal claims of human security the proverbial final straw that breaks the back of the conventional security camel? The case of the North Korean refugees has demonstrated otherwise. The human security paradigm has failed the North Korean refugees just as the conventional security paradigm has. The "ostensible harmony" between upholding both state and individual sovereignty and security as international law purports does not exist. Although the rights of individuals to seek asylum is embodied by Article 14 of the Universal Declaration of Human Rights,[18] they are neither accompanied by a corresponding duty of states to accept them nor are entry rights enshrined in the Refugee Convention. Although the Convention establishes the norm of *non-refoulement*, "it fails to address the crucial question of access to an asylum state in an effective and unequivocal manner" (ibid:278). This leaves the door open for the state to define not just what its own interests and security are, but also that of the refugee who already has little voice in the conventional security discourse. In the case of the North Koreans, their rights to asylum have been denied not only by their country but also by China and Russia. Worse, China contravenes the norm of *non-refoulement* by knowingly and systematically deporting those who are caught back to North Korea in the purported adherence to its treaty obligations with North Korea (Human Rights Watch, 2002:5).

Secondly, and perhaps ironically, because of human security's relative humanistic nature, it is difficult to quantify human security, unlike conventional security, which can be concretized by the size of armies, weapon arsenals, and economies. Although the Human Development Index produced by the UN is to some extent a quantification of human security, it risks falling into the same danger of reducing the very basic premise of human safety and dignity to statistics and definitions. And it is into this crevice that the North Korean refugee issue has fallen. The human security paradigm has failed the North Korean refugees at the very stage of definition. While refugees are theoretically accorded protection by the Refugee Convention, such protection is only given to those who fall within the scope of the definition that the Convention has spelt out. Except for a lucky few, most of the North Korean refugees are considered as illegal economic migrants, a status that does not have the appended protection as that of a refugee or asylum seeker. The political reluctance of China and Russia to grant the North Korean refugee status has sought to justify itself on an international legal basis as is the prerogative of the receiving countries, not the UNHCR, to accord refugee status.

---

[17] I am using this word in the broadest sense.

[18] Article 14 of the UDHR reads: "1. Everyone has the right to seek and enjoy in other countries asylum from persecution."

The third failure of human security in addressing the North Korean refugee issue is the apparent lack of consideration for the political agenda of the parties involved. This is perhaps the most important factor. Despite the advent of humanism in various forms – as human rights, human security, and humanitarianism – the impact and influence of politics in humanitarian affairs remain as critical factors that cannot be dismissed. As Gil Loescher has eloquently argued, politics plays an important role in the case of the refugees because refugees are essentially a political issue that requires a political solution (Loescher, 1992, 1993; Loescher & Monahan, 1989). The formulation of a refugee policy, on a national or international basis, "illustrates the conflict between international humanitarian norms and the sometimes narrow self-interest calculations of sovereign nation states" (Loescher & Monahan, 1989:8). Furthermore, it is also argued that refugees can be used as foreign policy instruments "by governments in pursuit of larger geopolitical and ideological objectives" (ibid:11–12), such as destabilizing the government of the receiving state. Conversely, as the case of the North Korean refugees shows, the neglect of the refugees is in itself undoubtedly a political act as much as North Korea's prohibition of unregulated population movement within and outside the country. The role of politics is even more critical in the case of non-Convention refugees, such as the North Koreans, for it raises several questions: What might be the motivation for going beyond the Convention and according the North Koreans recognition and protection? Would it be based on the belief of basic universal human rights or on the political decision to grant any North Korean defector refugee status as a means of discrediting the communist dictatorial Pyongyang regime?

What then should be the role of politics in human security vis-à-vis refugees? Is there no place for politics in humanitarianism? Human security, which embodies human needs and human rights, cannot be divorced from political and conventional security concerns. Former UNHCR High Commissioner Jean-Pierre Hocké argued that the humanitarian objectives "on behalf of refugees are no longer sufficient if made without reference to the political situations which have given rise to the refugees' flight" (Hocké, 1989:42). Indeed, in refugee work, "political considerations are hardly ever absent" (Hambro, 1955:3) as refugee crises throughout history have shown. From the decision to protect Russians and Jews fleeing communism in the 1920s, the exodus of Chinese refugees to Hong Kong post 1949, the flood of Indochinese refugees in the 1980s to the long-running deadlock over the state of the Palestinian refugees, the humanitarian notion of helping the vulnerable has been mired in political wrangling among and between the state parties and humanitarian organizations. The case of the North Koreans is no exception.

1.4 Competition or Cooperation?

Although proponents of the human security paradigm have often reiterated that the paradigm does not exclude the state and its concerns, and that they are complimentary, the two paradigms have, instead of working together, operated in mutual exclusivity. It is paradoxically the failure of human security in protecting the North Korean refugees that paved the way for the continued realpolitik approach. Geopolitical concerns of regional political and military security have taken precedence. The state remains the referent of security while the needs and security of the refugees have been relegated to the periphery. The conventional security paradigm has, in this case, ignored the moral and ethical imperatives of humanitarian action. Conversely, the human security paradigm does not take into consideration the practical aspects of the interstate relations – geopolitics. Humanitarian and human rights advocacy groups seem to have discounted the complex historical and political contexts of the region in which the refugee issue is situated. Instead, they have regarded the refugee issue as existing almost in a contextual vacuum, with their insistence that China in particular recognizes the North Koreans as refugees and that Pyongyang must reform its political and social systems.

The handling of such controversial issues as the North Korean refugees is ultimately "a balance test" (Yonhap 2006) between humanitarianism, security, and political considerations. Balance is not just about finding the equilibrium between the two contending and static sets of issues. Instead, it is about responding to the dynamics of the interactions between the two, constantly re-evaluating and reshaping responses accordingly. Such a balance, however, cannot take place if both sets of paradigms are seen as static, fixed, and unchanging. It must be recognized that, on the issue of refugees, the conventional and human security paradigms are not mutually exclusive but intersect with each other on several fronts. There needs to be cooperation between the state parties, the UNHCR, and other humanitarian groups for the issue to be constructively resolved. None should be excluded.

But while the UNHCR and other humanitarian groups play an important role in engaging the issue, the states remain the primary players as refugees challenge three fundamental concerns of conventional security: state sovereignty, territoriality, and the maintenance of balance of power. The North Koreans have, in physically crossing borders illegally, challenged not just their own government's ability to control and manage its population, to maintain security of their border areas and the occupation of their territories, but also that of the neighboring countries. In addition, the North Korean refugees have also brought the various parties' implementation of international laws, conventions, and treaties under scrutiny. In so doing, the North Koreans are testing, again incidentally, the diplomatic skills of the states and international agencies in maintaining the regional status quo or in generating a new equilibrium.

The refugees also underscore security implications for the states in that they are no longer simply passive by-products of conflicts, but are themselves potential causes of conflicts. The history of refugee crises has demonstrated that their consequences do not stay within national borders but that the impact of the human insecurities leading to refugee flows can affect the security, and hence policies, of neighboring countries (Loescher, 2003:39–40; Goodwin-Gill, 1999:3). The issue of the North Korean refugees could potentially pose not just socio-economic threats to the host countries but also increase the political tensions between the states involved given the already tense regional geopolitical context. Could the refugee issue pose an obstacle to the achievement of peace and security in the region? Would it be used as a justification for international intervention that could trigger a region-wide conflict? Would the continued impasse of the situation develop into the volatility and endemic instability that Africa's Great Lakes region has experienced (UNHCR 2005:68)? Will the interplay of the presence of the North Korean refugees, regional politics, and international legal inaction create a scenario of further political and socio-economic tensions? What additional insecurities will the refugees face with an extended period of deadlock? It is no longer adequate to treat the refugee problem as a purely humanitarian one in which the resolution ultimately depends on the wider political and diplomatic actions, given the security implications. Even for North Korea, labeled the world's most isolated country, the consequences of human insecurities within the country have spilled over into China, Russia, and elsewhere. The North Korean refugees have indeed, in this unspoken manner, affected the already delicate balance of security in the region.

Unlike the relatively precise nature of refugee migration in the past, the nature of contemporary refugee movement has become more ambiguous. In such "mixed migration" (UNHCR 2006:1,9), it is often difficult to differentiate between the various groups of refugees and their reasons for flight. The situation is further complicated by the use of people traffickers and smugglers in addition to the use of "traditional" avenues, adding to the dimensions of criminality and illegality of such movements. The use of such illegal channels not only lends credence to state security and asylum policies, more critically, it undermines the legitimacy of the asylum seekers and refugees (ibid:2). The overarching concern for the security and safety of the state remains paramount even within the rhetoric of human rights. Can such heightened security fears and the non-traditional nature of contemporary refugee movements justify the overshadowing of the protection needs of these individuals? Do the inadequacy of the current international refugee regime in addressing such non-typical situations – such as that of the North Koreans' – and the increasing securitization of movement of humans justify the inaction that results in such a prolonged state of impasse?

Protracted refugee situations have just as many security implications for states as emergency situations such as that in Darfur. The UNHCR defines protracted refugee situation as one in which refugees find themselves in a "long lasting and intractable state of limbo" where "their lives may not be at risk, but their basic rights and essential economic, social and psychological needs remain unfulfilled after years in exile" (ibid:106). A more formulaic definition of a protracted refugee situation is one in which more than 25,000 persons have been in exile for more than 5 years in a developing country (ibid:106). While such situations may be relatively more stable than that in an emergency, the security risks are no less in such forgotten situations, which now account for the majority of the refugee situations in the world. In fact, such instances could be more insidious as they are largely the result of the lack of political will to address not just the human insecurities that resulted in the refugee flows in the first place, but also the refugee situation itself (ibid:109–110). The significant security implications of such situations include strained diplomatic relations between host states and the states of origins, which could directly result in the prolonging of conflict, and creating obstacles to peace and development (ibid:117). In addition, the prolonged period of irresolution puts the very security and rights of the refugees at risk. The potential of instability and further conflict could prompt intervention (ibid:117–118), the very situation that many states do not want to see happen.

While the numbers and definitions of the status of the North Koreans in China and Russia remain debatable, there is no doubt that the situation is a protracted one in need of a long-term resolution. A case-by-case approach with the objective of avoiding major political embarrassment is not the answer. To delay addressing the situation until it develops into a security emergency could prove to be even more problematic. Thus far, the theoretical approach that informs the pragmatic attitude toward the North Korean refugees appears to be one of competition: conventional security concerns versus human security interests. But this competition has created a situation in which neither the security concerns of the North Korean refugees are addressed nor is the political stalemate over North Korea anywhere near resolution.

1.5 Sustainable Security

The implications of the international failure in addressing the situation of the North Korean refugees demonstrate the need to reassess the notion of security. The question "what does security mean?" needs to, yet again, be reexamined. In reiterating the call for a new understanding of security, which in this case includes a more conscious and ethical approach to international relations, it is not my contention that the actors have to choose between morality and strategic political concerns. It is not a binary issue of either or. There is no denying that governments have to be pragmatic in managing their domestic and international policies. Yet, these political concerns do not have to be diametrically opposed to ethical concerns. The establishment of humanitarian agencies and their participation in the workings of the international community, for example, has demonstrated the possibility of having an ethical dimension to the framework of international relations without being detached from reality. The need for a re-conceptualization of the notion of security is not just about readjusting or overhauling the definition of the concept. Ever more so, it is about being able to step outside any given framework and view it from various perspectives that are not confined to any theoretical orthodoxy. While critics might argue that this is an invitation to chaos, I maintain that this can create the space so needed for a serious and open-minded engagement of intellectual knowledge and practical realities. A paradigm shift requires more than a re-packaging of the frameworks of analysis; it requires a rethinking about the relationship between knowledge and power (Burke, 2001:223) – the knowledge of the situation and the power to act on a resolution.

Just as the world is constantly changing – the actors, problems, and their scope and nature – so must the analytical frameworks through which the world is studied develop and evolve in tandem. The understanding of threats to peace and security has come to include non-traditional security issues such as the economy, HIV/AIDS, and human rights violations. Linkages have been made between the traditional understanding of state security and the need to include the various non-traditional issues such as economic development and environmental degradation into the security paradigm. More importantly, the articulation of the human security paradigm indicates that the security referent has to shift to the individual in its own right, not just because it is the base level of analysis. Yet the current understanding of the paradigm shows that the rights and realpolitik are still not successfully integrated conceptually or practically into a broader security paradigm that includes conventional security considerations without compromising on human security principles.

In rethinking the meaning of "security," we have to reconsider the meaning of "threat" and "vulnerability." Security is commonly linked to threats – the deliberate intention to cause harm. Security is "about the pursuit of the freedom from threats" which are visible, often external, danger that is "identifiable, often immediate, and requires an understandable response" (Liotta, 2005:50). Threat assessments, in which the probabilities of threats happening are weighed against the consequences, are at the heart of national security policies. The conceptual discourse on human security is also framed in terms of threats albeit with different referents. Yet there is another underlying notion for human security: vulnerability. Vulnerability is related to the weaknesses of the subject of threat vis-à-vis the capabilities of the other players in the system (Buzan, 1991:113). While issues such as hunger, disease, unemployment, poverty, and social upheavals threaten the security of the people, it is also an indication of the susceptibility of the people because of their lack of capabilities. Unlike a threat, vulnerability is often just an indicator that is not as clearly identifiable (Liotta, 2005:51), is "often linked to a complex interdependence among related issues, and does not always suggest a correct or even adequate response" (ibid:51).

In the context of human security the primary consideration for responding to vulnerability lies at the identification of it being an "extreme vulnerability": a situation often of imminent danger and can be the result of living under severe conditions of deprivation (ibid:51). Vulnerabilities are categorized to allow for the prioritization of aid and intervention. The three broad categories of extreme vulnerabilities include (1) victims of war and internal conflicts, (2) persons who live below the subsistence line and thus face socio-economic disasters, and (3) victims of natural disasters (ibid:182). Extreme vulnerability can be understood by the imagery of "a man standing permanently up to the neck in the water, so that even a ripple is sufficient to drown him" (Liotta, 2005:51).

But unlike threats, not all vulnerabilities require immediate intervention nor are their impacts on security immediate. Within the category of vulnerabilities is a more "problematic conditionalit(y)" of "creeping vulnerabilities" (ibid:52): long-term vulnerabilities that are neither visible nor in need of urgent responses, unlike extreme vulnerabilities or threats. In other words, they are structural violence and inequalities that are present, yet invisible. These non-emergencies are often characterized by uncertainty, complexity, and are non-linear (ibid:52), proving difficult for causal analysis. More often than not, these creeping vulnerabilities require long-term strategic planning and development rather than crisis management or responses. Yet because of the ambiguous nature of such conditions, they are frequently ignored by decision makers in the classic but erroneous response to "situations of clear ambiguity" as Liotta argues (ibid:52). If left unattended, the impact of creeping vulnerabilities – such as uncontrolled urbanization and population growth, outbreak of diseases, scarcity of natural resources, and climate change – could "boomerang" back to haunt those who made the decisions as the 9/11 terrorist attacks demonstrated (Liotta, 2002:473–488).

From the realpolitik perspective, the case of the North Korean refugees is a threat. It is a political embarrassment that spans several countries, with the potential to destabilize the regional security status quo. Humanitarian groups, on the other hand, see these refugees as vulnerabilities; they are the consequences and victims of political, social, and economic deprivation who deserved to be helped. More accurately, the North Korean refugees fit the profile of "creeping vulnerabilities" on three accounts. Although potentially destabilizing, they do not yet threaten the political and social stability of North Korea, China, Russia, and South Korea. It is perhaps the non-urgency of the refugee issue that has allowed it to remain relatively latent for more than a decade. Furthermore, the refugees themselves are manifestations of the numerous kinds of structural violence within the North Korean society that include poor governance and the resultant poverty, as well as the appended social discrimination. Thirdly, the international community's response is that of doing nothing or, at best, as little as possible. Paradoxically, the creeping vulnerabilities, which are incidentally human security issues, do not go away simply because they are ignored. While they "will not mitigate or replace more traditional hard security dilemmas" (Liotta, 2005:53), they have to compete with the various other "threats-based" conditions for the attention of policy makers (ibid:53).

Vulnerabilities and threats cannot be distinctly separated into the opposite ends of the security spectrum. Although not all vulnerabilities are threats, untreated weaknesses left to fester over time can potentially develop into a threat to security. Similarly, while not all threats are vulnerabilities, some apparent threats are revealed to be vulnerabilities when the layers of perspectives are peeled away. Is it possible to reconcile the seemingly divergent security paradigms – the conventional as represented by threats and human as represented by vulnerabilities? Some have argued that this can be achieved through the convergence of the two, as this will allow for all the issues that impact security to be addressed. This means that attention is not overly focused on one set of concerns at the expense of the other, for an unbalanced focus could lead to detrimental boomerang impact. Scholars have argued that human security and national security are one and the same. The difference between the two lies in the securitization of particular sets of issues that reflect the contemporary contexts of the society. Implicit in this argument is that both human and national securities are different routes to the same end, the only difference being that of the security referent. This, however, assumes that human security and national security are not in conflict with each other.

Yet the contrary is true: The security of the people can be threatened and conflicts with that of the state. This happens not only in dictatorial regimes such as

Khmer Rouge Cambodia, the military-run Myanmar, or dynastic communist states such as North Korea. In the wake of 9/11, the human security of citizens of democracies such as the USA, United Kingdom, and Australia has been increasingly threatened by the state's emphasis on "homeland security" against external terrorist threats. Discursive arguments aside, the convergence of the two security paradigms may not be the practical way forward. While the expansion of the security agenda to include issues of concerns to both state and human beings highlights the range of issues at hand, it could potentially become a policy nightmare. Not only does it risk what critics fear would de-value the importance of each issue, it could also bring about what Kyle Grayson labels a "security policy 'Frankenstein's Monster'" (Grayson, 2003:337), one that is open to the politicization of securitization. This then paves the way for the state to justify "previously unjustifiable security actions" (ibid: 339) and to augment national security instead of the security of the individual citizens (ibid:339–340).

The second approach takes a longer-term perspective. It calls for an ongoing dialogue in which the concerns of each are aired and heard, instead of being ignored as in the case of the North Korean refugees. Through this process of open dialogue, a "sustainable security" can be established. The idea of sustainable security is adapted from Khagram, Clark, and Raad's article on the connection between human security and the natural environment (Khagram, Clark & Raad, 2003:289–313). What this concept offers is "a more open space for deliberation, analysis, and action could help connect analysts and practitioners" (ibid:301) of the various aspects of security for an ongoing dialogue that would eventually and hopefully lead to a common purpose of bettering lives for all. The idea of a sustainable security is not based only on threats and vulnerabilities, but with a focus on creeping vulnerabilities. Instead of having various adjectives prefixed to security, all of which deal with the same issues from different perspectives and different levels of analysis, sustainable security is an inclusive concept which allows all aspects and perspectives to come together in dialogue. This draws on the foundation of the school of critical security studies, which argues that security is essentially a derivative concept (Booth, 2005:13). So sustainable security is an attempt to analyze, explore, and appraise the security framework by stepping outside of it (ibid:11). The approach, following the critical school, is one of being self-reflective, and hence rendering it more responsive to the changing realities (ibid:11). It is in this intellectual spirit of challenging normative orthodoxies through dialogue that the concept of security can become sustainable.

The "sustainable security" framework is not so much a framework as an ongoing approach that is responsive to the changing environment. The need for such an approach is even more urgent now if lasting solutions are to be found for the numerous insecurities that many are facing around the world. The inability or the unwillingness to address these insecurities satisfactorily is the underlying cause for the continual outbreaks of violence and conflicts. The reluctance to move beyond the theoretical rigidity has blinkered the policy approach of many governments. The ability to break through the paradigmatic inflexibility is imperative if the international community is to fulfill its promise of "never again" will it allow the inhumanity of unbridled genocide, ethnic cleansing, famines, and other human tragedies.

The concept of security then has to be sustainable if it is to be able to respond to the changing milieu without overhauling the underlying theoretical frameworks every time. Sustainable security thus calls for a more conscientious and ethical approach to international relations. Instead of branding human security as a theoretical framework or a policy strategy, the concept of sustainable security puts forward the alternative of human security as an ethos, as Grayson suggested. This approach thus enables the moral and ethical dimensions underlying human security to be considered when implementing the vision. Despite the persistence of the realist paradigm in international relations, the moral foundations of the international world order cannot be discounted. If in adopting human security as an intellectual framework and as a policy strategy has failed the North Korean refugees, perhaps human security as ethos could contribute to the resolution of their insecurities.

1.6 Conclusion: Human Security as an Ethos?

Human security has been offered as a policy agenda for human development and international relations. It has been put forward as a useful concept to justify humanitarian intervention, and for identifying, prioritizing, and resolving emerging transnational security threats. But it has also been argued that human security would function better as a "radical discourse of critique" (Bellamy and McDonald, 2002:376) that "interrogate(s), evaluate(s) and criticize(s) the practice that makes people insecure in the first place" (ibid:376). Yet positioning human security either as a policy agenda or as a conceptual framework does not take into account the moral and ethical dimensions that are implicit in human security. The ethical grounding of the human security paradigm lies in its concern with

> transcending the dominant paradigmatic orthodoxy that views critical concerns of migration – recognition (i.e. citizenship), basic needs (i.e. sustenance), protection (i.e. refugee status) or human rights (i.e. legal standing) – as problems of interstate politics and consequently beyond the realm of the ethical and moral (ibid:17).

It has been argued that morality has little impact and, indeed, little position in international relations. Moral norms, it has been said, are qualifiers, not initiators or ends of behavior. The arguments against ethics and morality in international relations are traditionally rooted in the nature of interstate relations.[19] One argument holds that the essential and perennial relation between states is one of competition and self-interest; hence, moral imperatives are irrelevant and even dangerous for they could lead to a "crusading fervor" and "lack of reasonable perspective" (Maxwell, 1990:13). A second argument is that there can be no morality in politics as there is no international law, since law precedes morality (ibid:16). Other realists

---

[19] Realist tenets and arguments against morality in international relations are treated in the following which are considered realist "classics." The list is not exhaustive. Morgenthau (1951, 1958, 1984), Machiavelli (1961), Kennan (1986), Hobbes (1991), and Hinsley (1986).

argue that morality is irrelevant in international relations because of the sacrosanct notion of state sovereignty and because of certain characteristics in group behavior that lower the moral standards of its action. This is especially true for states that are governed by the ideas of self-interests, self-protection, nationalism, and sovereignty (ibid:23. See also Niebhur, 1936; Hare and Joynt, 1982). A survey of the contemporary world order seems to attest to the validity of realism.

Yet, despite the skepticism of the idealistic vision, there are moral foundations to the international world order, even if in practice these are not necessarily recognized. Ideas such as just war theory underscore the belief that there is still a universal standard of right and wrong.[20] The theory has developed from its Christian ethics origins into the current debates about the conduct of war, such as the rights and wrongs of targeting civilians,[21] the proportionality of force, and humanitarian intervention, among others, issues that are still very real in today's world.[22] Immanuel Kant's belief that the man's rationality is guided by the categorical imperative derived from the concept of duty (Kant, 2002) is reflected in the establishment of the various international conventions and covenants, and the advent of the human rights movements. The Stoic philosophy of cosmopolitanism has taken the form of the United Nations and its agencies, regardless of their imperfections.

Ethics is already present in the international community. The rationale for the relevance of ethics in international relations lies in the reality that decisions have an impact on everyone (Grayson, 2003:340). It is for this reason that policymakers "need to be steeped in ethical considerations" (ibid:340). This, of course, raises numerous problems, both philosophical and empirical. These problems, some of them long-running in the philosophical debates relating to international relations, include how to prioritize the issues and choose between conflicting ones, who is the agent of action and change, and which principles (for example, sovereignty and non-interference in domestic affairs of others) take precedence over ethical concerns? Conversely, should or to what extent do ethical concerns override issues of national interests and security? Are ethics universal or are they culturally bound? In trying to understand why the North Koreans who fled their famine-ravaged country are not officially recognized as refugees, this chapter has addressed the failure of the human-centered vision of human security. But the failure of the human-centered vision is not due to the flaws of the paradigm per se; rather, it points to the failure in the implementation of the paradigm in a world dominated by conventional security concerns. The failure is of the two seemingly divergent security frameworks working in mutually exclusive zones rather than together, despite the claims of human security to complement the conventional security agenda.

---

[20] This idea is borne out in the arguments of Aristotle, St Augustine, and St Thomas Aquinas among others.

[21] The most illustrative example of this would be the My Lai massacre in Vietnam by the Americans during the Vietnam War.

[22] For the debates on morality and war in the contemporary world, see Walzer (2004). In the book, Walzer raises the issues of ethics of war with contemporary examples including Kosovo, the Israel/Palestinian conflict, the two Gulf Wars, and the war on terrorism.

In conclusion, more questions have been raised: What does security mean? What is the role of politics in humanitarianism? Is there no place for ethics and morality in politics? Is an ethical policy framework feasible? The challenge is to consider beyond one's vested interest and that of the other parties'. How to do that without sounding idealistic? Is that possible? These questions are applicable not just to the North Korean refugees, but to almost any issues that involve a conflict of interests and agendas related to security. Perhaps, the ultimate question is: How can we bring conflicting parties to dialogue? How can we create a culture of reconciliation? That, I believe, has to begin in questioning the basis of our actions and the questioning of how the world operates. The lack of clear-cut answers should not be the obstacle to raising the questions in the first place.

References

Acharya, Amitav. (2001). Human security: East versus west. *International Journal, 56*(3), 442–460. Summer.
Ahn, Christine. (2005). *Famine and the future of food security in North Korea*. California: Institute for Food and Development Policy. Policy Brief No. 11.
Amnesty International. (1996). *Pursuit, Intimidation and Abuse of North Korean Refugees and Workers*, ASA24/06/96, http://www.amnestyusa.org/refugee/document.do?id=BBFB03F8365BDCD98025690000692E19. Accessed 5 July 2005.
Amnesty International. (2004). *Starved of rights: Human rights and the food crisis in the democratic people's republic of Korea (North Korea)*.
Anwar, D. F. (2003). Human security: An intractable problem in Asia. In Alagappa Muthia (Ed.), *Asian security order: Instrumental and normative features* (pp. 536–567). California: Stanford University Press.
Bellamy, A., & McDonald, M. (2002). The utility of human security: Which humans? What security? A reply to Thomas and Tow. *Security Dialogue, 33*(2), 373–377.
Booth, K. (Ed.). (2005). *Critical security studies and world politics*. London: Lynne Rienner.
Burke, A. (2001). Caught between national and human security: Knowledge and power in post-crisis Asia. *Pacifica Review, 13*(3), 215–239.
Buzan, B. (1991). *People, state and fear: An agenda for international security studies in the post-cold war Era* (2nd ed.). Brighton: Wheatsheaf Books.
Charny, J. R. (2004). North Koreans in China: A human rights analysis. *International Journal of Korean Unification Studies, 13*(2), 75–97.
Charny, J. R. (2003). *North Korean refugees in China: The current situation and strategies for protection*. Testimony by J. R. Charny, Vice President for Policy, Refugees International to the Senate Committee on Foreign Relations. http://www.refugeesinternational.org/content/article/detail/1143/. Accessed 5 Apr 2005.
Cho, M-Y. (2002, August 30). N. Korea farm reform seen insufficient to end hunger. *Reuters*.
Choi, Sung-Chul Choi. (1999). *Human rights and North Korea*. Seoul: The Institute of Unification Policy, Hanyang University.
Chosun, I. (2002a, September 24). Shinuiju special administrative region.
Chosun. I. (2002b, October 6). Yang Bin under house arrest.
Chung, Byung-Ho. (2003). Living dangerously in 2 worlds: The risks and tactics of North Korean refugee children in China. *Korea Journal, 43*(3), 191–211.
Commission on Human Security. (2003). *Human security now: Final report of the commission on human security*. New York.

Department of Foreign Affairs and International Trade, Government of Canada. (1999). *A perspective on human security: Chairman's summary*. Ottawa: Department of Foreign Affairs and International Trade. http://www.dfaitmaeci.gc.ca/foreignp.HumanSecurity/lysoen-e.htm. Accessed 20 Oct 2005.

Department of Foreign Affairs and International Trade, Government of Canada. (2005). http://www.humansecurity.gc.ca/menu-en.asp. Accessed 20 Oct 2005.

Dupont, A. (2001). *East Asia imperilled: Transnational challenges to security*. Cambridge: Cambridge University Press.

European Union, UNICEF, WFP. (1998). *Nutrition survey of the democratic people's republic of Korea*. New York: UNICEF.

Evans, P. (2004). Asian perspectives on human security: A responsibility to protect?. In Proceedings, international conference on human security in East Asia, 16–17 June 2003, Seoul, Republic of Korea. Seoul: UNESCO, Korean National Committee for UNESCO, Ilmin International Relations Institute of Korea University.

Falk, R. (1995). *On humane governance: Toward a new global politics*. Cambridge: Polity Press.

Foster-Carter, A. (1999). *North Korea: Prospects, scenarios and implications*. WRITENET report for UNHCR.

Foster-Carter, A. (2001). *North Korean refugees: An escalating crisis?* WRITENET report for UNHCR.

Goodwin-Gill, G. (1999). Refugees and security. *International Journal of Refugee Law, 11*(1), 1–5.

Grayson, K. (2003). Securitization and the boomerang debate: A rejoinder to Liotta and Smith-Windsor. *Security Dialogue, 34*(3), 337–343.

Hambro, E. (1955). *The problem of Chinese refugees in Hong Kong*. Report submitted to the United Nations High Commissioner for Refugees. Leyden: A.W. Sijthoff.

Hare, J. E., & Joynt, C. (1982). *Ethics and international affairs*. New York: St Martins.

Henk, D. (2005). Human security: Relevance and implications. *Parameters, 35*(2 Summer), 91–106.

Hinsley, F. H. (1986). *Sovereignty* (2nd ed.). Cambridge: Cambridge University Press.

Hobbes, Thomas. (1991). In Tuck Richard (Ed.), *Leviathan*. Cambridge: Cambridge University Press.

Hocké, Jean-Pierre. (1989). Beyond humanitarianism: The need for political will to resolve today's refugee problem. In Loescher Gil & Monahan Laila (Eds.), *Refugees and international relations*. Oxford: Oxford University Press.

Holmes, R. L. (1989). *On war and morality*. Princeton, New Jersey: Princeton University Press.

Hughes, D. M. (2005). How can I be sold like this? The trafficking of North Korean women refugees. National Review Online, http://www.nationalreview.com/script/printpage.p?ref=/hughes/hughes200507190734.asp. Accessed 14 Dec 2005.

Human Rights Watch. (2002). *The invisible exodus: North Koreans in the people's republic of China*. New York: Human Rights Watch.

Human Security Network website. (2005). http://www.humansecuritynetwork.org/menu-e.php. Accessed 31 Oct 2005.

International Commission on Intervention and State Sovereignty. (2001). *The responsibility to protect: Report of the international commission on intervention and state sovereignty*. Ottawa: International Development Research Centre, http://www.iciss.ca/menu-en.asp. Accessed 31 Oct 2005.

Japan. (2004). *Diplomatic blue book 2004: Efforts to tackle various global issues to promote human security*, p 184, http://www.mofa.go.jp/policy/human_secu/. Accessed 31 Oct 2005.

Japan's Ministry of Foreign Affairs webpage (2005) http://www.mofa.go.jp/policy/human_secu/assistance.html, Accessed 31 Oct 2005.

Kant, I. (2002). *Groundwork for the metaphysics of morals*. (A. W. Wood, Trans., Ed.). New Haven: Yale University Press.

Kennan, G. (1986). Morality and foreign policy. *Foreign Affairs, 64*, 205–219.

Khagram, S., Clark, W. C., & Raad, D. F. (2003). From the environment and human security to sustainable security and development. *Journal of Human Development, 4*(2), 289–313.

1 Human Insecurities or Liabilities? The Changing Security Paradigms...

Kim, C. S. (1998). *Faithful endurance: An ethnography of Korean family dispersal*. Tucson: University of Arizona Press.
Koh, D. W. (2004). Dynamics of Inter-Korean conflict and North Korea's recent policy changes. *Asian Survey, 44*(3), 422–441.
Korea Newsreview. (1979a, July 14). Northern officer defects to south.
Korea Newsreview. (1979b, August 4). N.K soldier defects for liberty.
Korea Newsreview. (1981a, April 11). N.K scientist defectors.
Korea Newsreview. (1981b, April 25). N.K soldier crosses DMZ into freedom.
Korea Newsreview. (1983a, March 5). North Korean pilot defects to ROK.
Korea Newsreview. (1983b, May 14). North Korean captain defects to ROK.
Korea Newsreview. (1986, January 11). N.K soldier defects to south.
Korea Newsreview. (1988a, April 21). Two N.K stowaways defect to south.
Korea Newsreview. (1988b, June 11). Overseas mission failure prompted defection.
Korea Newsreview. (1989a, March 4). 2 N. Korean college students defect to Seoul.
Korea Newsreview. (1989b, March 25). Seoul Olympics motive for defection.
Korea Newsreview. (1989c, May 13). 2 More N.K students defect to Seoul while studying in Poland.
Lee, J. (2003). The Korean Chinese (Chosonjok) in the Russian Far east: A research note, In *Human flows across national borders in Northeast Asia*, T. Akaha (Ed.). http://www.miis.edu/rcenters-ceas-pub.html. Accessed 3 Sept 2005.
Life Funds for North Korean Refugees. (2004). *Are they telling us the truth? Brutality beyond belief*. Seoul: Life Funds for North Korean Refugees.
Liotta, P. H. (2002). Boomerang effect: The convergence of national and human security. *Security Dialogue, 33*(4), 473–488.
Liotta, P. H. (2005). Through the looking glass: Creeping vulnerabilities and the reordering of security. *Security Dialogue, 36*(1), 49–70.
Loescher, G. (1992). *Refugee movements and international security*. London: Brassey's for The International Institute for Strategic Studies.
Loescher, G. (1993). *Beyond charity: International cooperation and the global refugee crisis*. New York: Oxford University Press.
Loescher, G. (2003). Refugees as grounds for international action. In N. Edward & J. van Selm (Eds.), *Refugees and forced displacement: International security, human vulnerability and the state*. Tokyo: United Nations University.
Loescher, G., & Monahan, L. (Eds.). (1989). *Refugees and international relations*. Oxford: Oxford University Press.
Leiv Lunde. (1999, May 15–16). *Humanitarian assistance, conflict resolution and development, speech at CARE International board of directors CARE Norge meeting in Oslo*, http://odin.dep.no/odinarkiv/norsk/dep/ud/1999/taler/032005-090036/dok-bn.html. Accessed 3 Nov 2005.
Lohman, D. (1996). North Korea: A potential refugee crisis? WRITENET report for UNHCR.
Machiavelli, N. (1961). *The prince*. Translated with an introduction by George Bull. Harmondsworth: Penguin
Maxwell, M. (1990). *Morality among nations: An evolutionary view*. New York: State of New York Press.
McRae, R., & Hubert, D. (Eds.). (2001). *Human security and the new diplomacy: Protecting people, promoting peace*. Montreal: McGill-Queen's University Press.
Ministry of Foreign Affairs, Norway. (2005). *Strategic framework: Angola 2003-2005*. http://odin.dep.no/ud/english/topics/bilateral/032131-220007/dok-bn.html. Assessed 3 Nov 2005.
Ministry of Unification. (n.d.). http://www.unikorea.go.kr/en/EUF/EUF0101R.jsp. Accessed 21 May 2006.
Morgenthau, H. J. (1951). *In defense of national interests*. New York: Knopf.
Morgenthau, H. J. (1958). *Dilemma of politics*. Chicago: Chicago Press.
Morgenthau, H. J. (1984). *Politics among nations*. New York: Knopf.
Muico, N. K. (2005). *An absence of choice: The sexual exploitation of North Korean women in China*, London: Anti-Slavery International.

Natsios, A. (2001). *The great North Korean famine*. Washington, DC: United States Institute of Peace.
Niebhur, R. (1936). *Moral man and immoral society*. New York: Scribners.
UN Commission on Human Rights (2004, April 8). Situation of human rights in the democratic people's republic of Korea, E/CN.4/2004/L.21.
UN Human Rights Commission (2005). Situation of human rights in the democratic people's republic of Korea, January, E/CN.4/2005/34.
UNHCR. (2006). *State of the world's refugees: Human displacement in the new millennium*. Oxford: Oxford University Press, 2005.
Voice of America. (2005). *N. Korean defectors testify about human rights abuses back home and in China*.
Walzer, M. (2004). *Arguing about war*. Connecticut: Yale University Press.
World Food Program. (2005a). *Country brief: DPRK*. http://www.wfp.org/country_brief/indexcountry.asp?country=408. Accessed 30 June 2005.
World Food Program. (2005b). *Emergency food assistance to vulnerable groups in DPR Korea*. Project number EMOP 10141.3
Yonhap. (2006, March 17). Presidential adviser urges US to do more for North Korean refugees.
Yoon, Y-S. (1999). *Situation and protection in Russia*. In Proceedings of the 1st international conference on North Korean human rights & refugees in Seoul. http://www.nkhumanrights.or.kr/bbs/board2/files/57_yeo-sangyoon.doc. Accessed 22 Sept 2005.

Chapter 2
Human Insecurity in the People's Republic of China: The Vulnerability of Chinese Women to HIV/AIDS

Anna Marie Hayes

2.1 Women and HIV/AIDS in the People's Republic of China

In China, HIV/AIDS has spread to new groups of the population and it has been estimated that around 740,000 people were living with HIV/AIDS (PLWHA) at the end of 2009 (Ministry of Health of the People's Republic of China 2010: 5). There are serious localized HIV/AIDS epidemics in several provinces; Yunnan, Guangxi, Henan, Sichuan, Xinjiang and Guangdong. These provinces alone account for 70–80% of China's overall HIV/AIDS rates (Ministry of Health of the People's Republic of China 2010: 5). Xinjiang Autonomous Region and Yunnan Province have both experienced HIV/AIDS epidemics resulting from high rates of needle sharing among injecting drug users and up until 2005 the sharing of intravenous drug equipment was the main mode of HIV transmission in the PRC. In addition, blood and plasma selling to centres practising unsafe blood-donation procedures has led to approximately 69,000 former blood and plasma donors and recipients to contract HIV mainly in Henan, Hubei, Anhui, Hebei and Shanxi (National Centre for AIDS/STD Prevention and Control 2006: 1).[1]

For the purposes of this chapter, the definition of human security is aligned closely with that of the United Nations which states that human security is both 'freedom from fear' and 'freedom from want', incorporating components such as economic, food, health, environmental, personal, community and political security. This definition challenges the more restricted notions of human security and is centred on the principles that human security is a universal concern, its components are interdependent, that it is best achieved through prevention rather than intervention and that it is people-centred (UNDP 1995: 232–34).

[1] The transmission of HIV through blood selling is relatively unique to China and has caused many of China's rural poor to become HIV positive. It has also been a very sensitive issue for the Chinese government due to the role of the Henan Provincial Health Department in both Henan's blood trade and the initial cover-up of the emerging HIV/AIDS epidemic there. For further reading, see Hayes (2005).

A.M. Hayes (✉)
University of Southern Queensland, Toowoomba, Australia
e-mail: anna.hayes@usq.edu.au

Figures from the Ministry of Health (MOH) show sexual transmission is now the main mode of HIV transmission in the PRC, signalling that China has moved into the 'growth period' of its HIV/AIDS epidemic. At the close of 2009, it was reported that 59% of the total number of HIV/AIDS cases in China were caused by sexual transmission, with heterosexual transmission accounting for 44.3% of those infections and homosexual transmission accounting for 14.7% (Ministry of Health of the People's Republic of China 2010: 22). Of the total reported number of HIV/AIDS cases, 30.8% of PLWHA in the PRC are women demonstrating the vulnerability of women to HIV transmission and increasing the concerns that the country is in a growth period (SCAWCO and UNAIDS 2007: 4). Also concerning is that since 2005, sexual transmission has been the fastest growing mode of HIV transmission in China (Hong et al. 2009).

Further evidence of China's HIV epidemic moving into its growth period are the country's figures on mother-to-child-transmission (MTCT). Since 2005, it has estimated that MTCT of HIV accounted for approximately 1.3–1.5% of the total number of new HIV cases (National Center for AIDS/STD Prevention and Control 2006: 2; Ministry of Health of the People's Republic of China 2010: 23). According to the United Nations Joint Program on HIV/AIDS (UNAIDS) MTCT rates in excess of 1% demonstrate that a HIV/AIDS epidemic meets the criteria for the categorization of a 'generalized epidemic' as MTCT highlights rates of HIV among women in the general population who do not belong to any particular high-risk group (Gill et al. 2007).

Therefore, the above results are further evidence that China's overall HIV/AIDS epidemic has moved into its growth period. If effective prevention and control measures are not introduced prior to or during the growth period, and the country's HIV/AIDS epidemic moves into the 'rampant prevalence period', large scale HIV transmission is inevitable. Although rates of HIV among the general population remain low in the PRC, with rates believed to be between 0.042% and 0.071% (Ministry of Health of the People's Republic of China 2010: 5), the spread of HIV through heterosexual intercourse among the general population is very much a warning that the numbers of PLWHA may soon explode across the country. If this occurs, it would make the epidemic very difficult to prevent and control and Chinese women's vulnerability to HIV transmission will increase substantially, particularly because the prevalence rate of HIV among the general population would increase rapidly.

Physiologically, women are two to four times more vulnerable to HIV transmission than their male counterparts when engaging in unprotected vaginal intercourse (UNAIDS 2002: 57).[2] In addition to physiological risks, women worldwide face a number of vulnerabilities to HIV/AIDS, deriving from a variety of social, cultural,

---

[2]This is largely because the surface of vaginal mucosa is much bigger than penile mucosa. Furthermore, semen from an HIV infected male is usually higher in HIV concentrations than are the vaginal secretions from a HIV positive female. Also, if a woman has a reproductive tract infection (RTI) or a sexually transmitted infection (STI), her vaginal mucosa is changed and can become irritated, ulcerated or more prone to scratches, all of which result in the vagina becoming more vulnerable to HIV infection (UNAIDS 2002: 57).

economic and political factors. A society's gender roles have considerable influence on three main areas of HIV/AIDS vulnerability; accurate sexual and reproductive health knowledge, sexual passivity and aggression, and promiscuity. In addition, 'enabling environments' such as social, cultural, political and economic environments, can all fuel HIV vulnerability among women and these vulnerabilities are largely the result of gender inequality (Feinstein and Prentice 2000).

Thus, in order for a state's HIV/AIDS response to be effective it must include gender-specific factors. Therefore, women must be recognized as a vulnerable group. However, when asked whether she believed Chinese women were particularly vulnerable to HIV transmission, Interviewee D (2003, pers. comm., 27 August),[3] who was the Director of a government organization that played a key role in HIV/AIDS prevention and treatment, responded that she believed 'women are less vulnerable [than men] to HIV/AIDS' and that women's vulnerability to HIV/AIDS largely depended on whether a woman was a sex worker, an intravenous drug user (IDU), if she had donated her blood, had a blood transfusion or had used other blood products (Interviewee D 2003, pers. comm., 27 August).

This point of view was supported by another interviewee, who was the National Programme Officer for an international non-governmental organization (INGO) responsible for HIV/AIDS prevention and treatment. In response to the same question, this interviewee stated that 'gender does not play any role [in its HIV/AIDS policies], and it is not part of mainstream discussions' (Interviewee C 2003, pers. comm., 22 August). These responses are alarming because they ignore the patterns of HIV transmission to women in much of the rest of the world, whereby women in the general population have been found to be extremely vulnerable to HIV transmission in areas with high rates of HIV/AIDS.[4]

However, while Interviewee C's organization did not incorporate a gendered response into its overall HIV prevention and treatment programs, her responses indicated that the intersection of gender and HIV vulnerability was being considered (2003, pers. comm., 22 August). Interviewee C believed that gender and economics were important issues in HIV/AIDS prevention and treatment, even though

---

[3] All interviewees spoken to during fieldwork were employed in government or non-governmental organizations that were responsible for HIV/AIDS prevention and treatment. Furthermore, none of the interviewees wanted to be identified, nor did they want the identity of the organization in which they worked to identified. This was largely due to the continued sensitivity of HIV/AIDS in China, particularly when discussing the issue with international researchers or reporters. Thus, the interviews were conducted upon the agreement that the interviewees' details would be kept confidential. It is for this reason that neither the interviewees, nor the organizations they worked for, have been identified in this chapter.

[4] Women now make up approximately 50% of those infected with HIV/AIDS globally. HIV infection rates in many countries also reflect that more women than men have contracted HIV. For example, HIV infection rates in Sub-Saharan Africa reveal that 60% of PLWHA are women. In the Caribbean the figure has reached approximately 50%, and if it follows the patterns of Sub-Saharan Africa it can be expected that women infected with HIV/AIDS will soon outnumber men there also. In Asia, approximately 35% of PLWHA are women, a figure that has increased since 2000 when the percentage was 19% (UNAIDS and WHO 2009).

they were not yet widely recognized or were a part of China's official HIV/AIDS response and policies. On the issue of what factors increased female vulnerability to HIV transmission, she said:

> Women are vulnerable... for a number of reasons. These include the status of women - political, economic and social status of women. Also, the educational level of women is lower than their male counterparts, and unemployment rates are a great deal higher. This has a lot to do with remaining views on the role of women, which follow closely with the traditional stereotypes of women as wives, devoted to house and raising children. They are still seen in this caregiver role. Women are also restricted in their access to information, so this also makes them vulnerable because they don't know what HIV/AIDS is or how to prevent it (Interviewee C 2003, pers. comm., 22 August).

Responses from other interviewees also demonstrated that organizations were aware of the links between gender and HIV vulnerability. When asked what factors he believed increased Chinese women's vulnerability to HIV/AIDS, Interviewee E (2003, pers. comm., 27 August), a health specialist for an INGO that included HIV/AIDS in its health framework, responded that he felt unemployment and low education levels were key factors because they led to economic insecurity that could lead women to prostitution. He stated that particularly in rural China, female school enrolments were much lower than those of males, and that this adversely affected women's employment opportunities. He also stated that women were further disadvantaged because they were not paid the same as men for equal work. Also, because many women had been laid-off from their jobs in northeast China, due to factory closures and cutbacks, many of these women had been forced to enter the sex industry as a means of survival (Interviewee E 2003, pers. comm., 27 August).

Hence, while both Interviewees C and E were aware of the effects gender has on HIV/AIDS vulnerability, neither their particular organizations, nor any other organizations responsible for HIV/AIDS prevention and treatment campaigns at the time, incorporated gender into their programmes or education campaigns. Interviewee A, who was a Senior Programme Officer for an overseas aid agency (2003, pers. comm., 21 August), offered two possible reasons for this oversight. Firstly, she believed a gendered response was not a major component of China's HIV/AIDS strategy because 'gender issues are generally addressed by the All China Women's Federation (ACWF) or the Regional Women's Commission (RWC)' (Interviewee A 2003, pers. comm., 21 August). Secondly, at the time of fieldwork, ordinary Chinese women among the general population were not widely recognized or targeted as being vulnerable to HIV transmission (Interviewee A 2003, pers. comm., 21 August). Therefore, according to Interviewee A, because women among the general population were not regarded as a vulnerable group it made little sense to organizations such as hers to engender their HIV/AIDS prevention strategies.

However, if we consider Interviewee A's first response, it would appear that the ACWF and RWC have unintentionally 'marginalized' women in discussions on HIV/AIDS vulnerability among organizations responsible for HIV/AIDS prevention and treatment campaigns because these organizations do not want to interfere with the role of the ACWF and the RWC. This reluctance could in part be because of the historical background of the ACWF. This organization was one of the first mass organizations formed by the Chinese Communist Party following the 1949 Liberation and was the impetus for the social, legislative and policy changes aimed at improving the status of women in the 1950s. While it was temporarily disbanded during the Cultural Revolution, the organization was fully reformed in 1978 and since that time it has continued its earlier work on improving the status of women in China through legislative and social change (Howell 2003). Therefore, the ACWF has had a monopoly on women's issues in China for much of China's post-Liberation period.

While there has been an expansion of women's groups and organizations since the reform and opening of China in 1978, it is significant to note that the ACWF has remained an important ally for these groups (Lee and Regan 2009), and the strongest women's organization in China due to its political legitimacy and sway in the political structure (Howell 2003). Therefore, Interviewee A's reasons for the lack of consideration of gender in official responses to HIV/AIDS in China demonstrates that there are serious impediments which need to be addressed. It would seem there is a reluctance to either tackle gender issues by non-ACWF organizations as they may perceive a turf war conflict, or simply because they feel that such issues are best handled by the ACWF. Whatever the reason, because such organizations are reluctant to incorporate gendered responses into their HIV/AIDS prevention and treatment campaigns women have been marginalized in the mainstream responses to HIV/AIDS in China even though international experience has repeatedly demonstrated that if they are left unresolved, gender vulnerabilities to HIV transmission fuel HIV epidemics.

However, Interviewee A did state that should the epidemic move into the 'rampant prevalence' period, these groups (meaning women in the general population not belonging to any of the traditional 'high-risk' groups) would receive more attention from organizations like hers. Thus, it would appear some organizations do believe gendered responses may be necessary in the future. Nonetheless, the reluctance of international organizations like Interviewee A's to incorporate gendered responses was concerning as in many AIDS-stricken countries, especially those in Sub-Saharan Africa, women among the general population have been found to be at substantial risk of contracting HIV through non-commercial heterosexual intercourse (UNAIDS, UNFPA and UNIFEM 2004: 1–2). As stated above, much of this vulnerability stems from social, cultural, economic and political factors that often reflect gender inequality and this chapter now turns to an examination of these in the context of women in the PRC.

2.2 Sexual and Reproductive Health Knowledge

Accurate knowledge about HIV/AIDS, including the prevention and transmission of HIV, is an essential part of an adequate response to HIV/AIDS. However, surveys conducted by some INGOs have revealed that as much as 20–40% of China's population has no knowledge of HIV/AIDS at all (Park 2003: 54; UNAIDS 2002: 43). While recent figures suggest this has changed and that 'basic'[5] HIV/AIDS awareness is in the vicinity of between 74.5% and 85.1% for urban and rural residents and migrant workers, there still remain pockets of the population who lack accurate HIV/AIDS knowledge and awareness (Ministry of Health of the People's Republic of China 2010: 7). One of the reasons often cited for this lack of knowledge is that due to China's size and regional variances in language dialects, country-wide HIV/AIDS education campaigns are difficult to conduct. Interviewee F (2003, pers. comm., 9 September), the Division Director of a government organization that examines HIV/AIDS related issues, confirmed this when she stated 'because China is so large… not everyone knows about AIDS [and] the information has not spread to very remote areas, [therefore] more work will be done there'. These factors seriously complicate the dispersal of accurate HIV/AIDS knowledge, and are a key area that the Chinese government must overcome to effectively respond to China's growing HIV/AIDS epidemic. However, there also exists a range of other reasons for the poor levels of HIV/AIDS knowledge in China.

The reform and opening period, which began in the late 1970s, loosened societal attitudes and views on sexual issues in China, and this resulted in an increase in premarital sex and societal acceptance of premarital sex (Qian et al. 2004; Wu et al. 2007). A study by the Sex Sociology Institute of the People's University of China found that in people over 40 years of age, 45.7% of men and 24.1% of women reported they had engaged in premarital sex. However, for the 25–29 year old age bracket, rates were significantly higher with 72.2% of men and 46.2% of women reporting they had engaged in premarital sex (Xia 2004: 14). Even though premarital sex is occurring, sex education and the supply of contraceptive devices to young, unmarried people remains a contentious issue.

Interviewee C (2003, pers. comm., 22 August) stated that sex education was an important topic in China and that there had been much debate over when young people should be taught about sexual health, with some sections of Chinese society arguing that the university level was the most appropriate time for formalized sex education. There was also growing debate over abstinence-based sex education as opposed to sex education that promotes 'safer sex', such as using condoms, with the proponents of the abstinence-based sex education style hoping to see a return to 'traditional morality' (Xia 2004: 15). In the meantime, no real steps have been made in implementing a comprehensive sex education curriculum into Chinese schools. As a result, many university students in the PRC have 'alarmingly low' levels of AIDS knowledge and self-perceived risk (Wu et al. 2007: 683), reflecting the need for a national sex education curriculum. This is concerning as HIV in China is most prevalent among people in the 20–29 year old age bracket, with this group accounting for 56% of China's overall HIV/AIDS cases (Ma et al. 2009: 249). However, these rates of infection are unsurprising when one considers that surveys of university students have found that only 15% of those who were sexually active reported

---

[5] However, there was no indication of what 'basic' knowledge meant and whether a basic knowledge reflected accurate and appropriate knowledge on how HIV could be prevented.

100% condom use in their sexual encounters during the year prior to the study (Ma et al. 2009: 256).

For many young unmarried people in China, the lack of accurate knowledge on 'safer sex' has been a contributing factor in them engaging in unprotected sex, which easily facilitates the transmission of STIs, including HIV, as well as increasing rates of unintended pregnancy. Although young unmarried people can access contraceptive services in China, information and advice about contraception is somewhat limited. This is because the National Family Planning Programme only targets married couples for the delivery of contraception information and devices. Furthermore, studies conducted in rural and urban Shanghai found that when premarital sex resulted in pregnancy, most pregnancies were unintended, and were usually because the couple had not used contraceptives (Qian et al. 2004). Surveys conducted on confidence levels when purchasing condoms found that only 44.3% of women compared to 85.5% of men felt confident buying condoms (Ma et al. 2009: 257). Clearly, even though premarital sex has become more commonplace and generally more acceptable, a comprehensive sex education programme and easy, more accepted access to reliable barrier methods of contraception are needed if optimum health outcomes are to be achieved.

Another key factor in this discussion is how condoms are perceived by Chinese society. With the resurgence of STIs in China, and the need to promote condoms effectively as a means of preventing STIs, condoms have undergone a name change from *bi yun tao*, or 'avoid pregnancy sheath', to *an quan tao*, or 'safety sheath'. The change reflects the dual role of condoms in preventing conception, but also as a means of preventing the transmission of STIs/HIV (Yuan et al. 2003: 17). Interviewee F acknowledged this change, adding that her organization stressed '…using condoms is beneficial for men and women, from the point of view of health, because men and women will both benefit from the[ir] use' (2003, pers. comm., 9 September). However, a recent study has reinforced that condoms are still primarily perceived by some university students as pregnancy prevention rather than protection against STIs/HIV. The study found that 95% of respondents identified condoms as protection against pregnancy while only 30–41% regarded them as protection against STIs/HIV (Ma et al. 2009: 256). Clearly, condoms are a necessary part of an effective HIV prevention strategy so it is imperative that their role in STI prevention is stressed and encouraged in the Chinese situation.

Thus, even with the name change, condom use in China remains low. This is alarming to epidemiologists because of the role of condoms in preventing STIs/HIV, particularly for women. A study by Xia in 2002 found that 75.1% of male respondents were unwilling to use condoms in their sexual relations because they found them to be 'troublesome', to decrease male sexual pleasure, as well as too expensive. In addition, many unmarried men preferred not to use condoms because they felt their 'sexual and reproductive ability' was proven if their partners became pregnant (2004: 22). Furthermore, many men continue to view their sexual relationship with their wife as procreation, whereas sexual pleasure is derived from commercial sex workers. Therefore, condoms within marriage are not considered appropriate and they are rarely used, regardless of some men having multiple sexual partners (Chen 2008).

Interviewee B (2003, pers. comm., 22 August), a Programme Officer for an overseas aid agency, believed that women could be vulnerable to STIs from their partners because 'there is no such dialogue [safer sex] between husband and wife or partners'. Furthermore, she concluded that in south-west China for instance, promotion of condom use in sexual relationships was absolutely necessary because the main route of HIV infection for men there has been IDU and for women, it was through heterosexual intercourse 'within the family, within marriage, it's not through commercial sex workers' (Interviewee B 2003, pers. comm., 22 August). Increasing condom usage rates among the general population is further complicated because many Chinese women use intra-uterine devices (IUDs) or have had surgeries such as tubal ligation or hysterectomies to avoid further pregnancies, causing condoms to be viewed as unnecessary.[6] Therefore, Interviewee B believed that it was imperative condoms be promoted as a sexual health device within marriage and committed relationships in addition to persons engaging in premarital sex or infidelity.

While promoting condom use among the general population was also identified as a necessity by Interviewees D and C, work is needed on promoting 100% condom use among commercial sex workers in both their commercial and non-commercial sexual relations. In China, condom use among sex workers is also extremely low with only 10% of sex workers surveyed at various locations reporting that they always used condoms, and close to 50% of sex workers reporting that they had never used a condom with a client (Kanabus 2004). This is not surprising considering many sex workers lack adequate HIV/AIDS information in the first instance and secondly because condom use in sexual exchange generally involves a 'discount' due to both decreased sensitivity and male sexual pleasure. Therefore, the economic burden faced when insisting on condom use in the commercial sex exchange means that for many sex workers condom use is not a viable or desirable economic option.

In addition, low rates of HIV/AIDS and STI knowledge has meant that many sex workers do not believe they are at risk of contracting HIV. This clearly indicates a continuing lack of HIV prevention knowledge in an important 'high-risk' group, which increases the likelihood of the transmission of HIV among sex workers and their clients (Kanabus 2004). Furthermore, other sex workers who wanted to use condoms in the commercial sexual exchange were prevented from doing so because they lacked 'the power to insist on the use of condoms with their clients' (Thompson 2004). In most instances, it is the client who decides whether or not a condom is used in commercial sexual exchange, again reflecting the disempowered status sex workers face (Kanabus 2004). Hence, poor HIV/AIDS awareness and female disempowerment facilitates such 'high-risk' behaviour, and this situation reinforces the need for widespread public education campaigns to better educate the entire Chinese population on HIV/AIDS prevention and risk. This is particularly pressing considering that commercial sex is the leading contributing factor for the transmission of HIV through heterosexual intercourse (Hong et al. 2009). However, such an

---

[6]The National Population and Family Planning Commission of China reports that 38.24% of Chinese women have undergone sterilization and 45.51% have IUDs (Zhao 2001).

education campaign must contain accurate and appropriate messages about HIV/AIDS and HIV prevention.

2.3 Stigma, Discrimination and Self-perceived Risk

Early state media representations of HIV/AIDS negatively affected HIV/AIDS knowledge in China, and how PLWHA were received by society and by the medical profession. Interviewee D (2003, pers. comm., 27 August) stated that when the state media initially discussed HIV/AIDS, it was portrayed as 'the enemy' and that media reports were largely focused on scaring people about the virus. Furthermore, Interviewee D believed that these early representations greatly contributed to the stigma and discrimination of PLWHA in China. This argument was reinforced by Dikötter, who claimed that AIDS was initially described in official discourse as an 'evil from abroad', and that it was widely believed that the 'superior immune system' of the Chinese, combined with their 'Neo-Confucian values', would mean that HIV/AIDS would not infect the general population but would largely remain limited to homosexual men and sex workers who serviced foreign clients (1997: 78–79). Such beliefs became accepted by Chinese society and have influenced how both the virus and PLWHA are perceived.

In addition to stigma and discrimination, these early representations of HIV/AIDS have also led to many people falsely believing that they are not at risk from contracting HIV if they do not belong to one of the above-mentioned groups. This false sense of security was reflected in the section on 'Self-perceived risk of contracting HIV/AIDS' in a study conducted by the Futures Group (2004: 17). This study explored the levels of HIV/AIDS knowledge among respondents and their attitudes and behaviours towards AIDS related issues. The study found that 78% of those surveyed believed themselves to be at 'low-risk' of contracting HIV/AIDS, and that the main reason for such a belief was because very few of the respondents (2%) reported that they knew of a PLWHA or a person who had died from AIDS. Therefore, because they themselves had not known anyone affected by HIV/AIDS, their perception of the virus was that it is something that affects the 'other' or that it only affected 'degraded people' (Futures Group 2004: 17). Consequently, because they did not fit either category, they believed themselves to be of little risk of contracting HIV/AIDS.

Self-perceived risk has also been skewed by the government's HIV/AIDS prevention policies, which have long been focused on 'high-risk' groups. It can be argued that current prevention strategies actually put women at risk because they stress partner reduction over condom use as an effective way to avoid HIV transmission. The 'one partner' or 'faithfulness' prevention messages, which teach both men and women to protect themselves against HIV transmission by limiting the number of partners they have to one, has been described by UNAIDS as lulling people into a 'false safety' (UNAIDS 2002: 44). Surveys that have been conducted in China among traditional 'low-risk' groups such as married women, who do not engage in any of the traditionally recognized 'risky practices' conducive to HIV transmission, have found that most women believe that limiting the number of partners they have to one is much better protection against HIV transmission than using condoms (UNAIDS 2002: 44). However, such a measure is dependent upon their spouse having a negative status upon the commencement of the relationship, and not engaging in practices that may cause them to contract HIV for the duration of the sexual relationship.

Furthermore, the 'one partner' campaign ignores the fact that for many women in the developing world who have contracted HIV/AIDS through heterosexual intercourse, the source of their transmission was their only sexual partner, usually their husband.[7] Often these women were unaware of their husband's HIV+ status, and in other cases, whereby they knew their husband was HIV+, they were unable to say no to sex or insist on condom use due to the unequal gender-based power relations within the relationship. In a study of Chinese women who contracted HIV from their husbands, none of the women interviewed were aware of their husband's HIV+ status prior to their own diagnoses. In addition, one husband commented that he felt women 'had little choice if their husbands insisted they do so [have sex], inasmuch as the fact that "we are still married" legitimized their sex' (cited in Zhou 2008: 1119). Therefore, the government sponsored campaigns in China that primarily focus on individuals reducing 'risky practices' or limiting the number of sexual partners they have to one, are out of step with reality. Instead, HIV/AIDS prevention campaigns also need to focus on providing easily accessible sexual and reproductive health information for both men and women, and making condoms available and accessible to all sexually active persons. They should also aim to empower women and challenge the negative gender stereotypes and biases attributed to both men and women that heighten their vulnerability to HIV transmission.

2.4 Gender Stereotypes and Patriarchal Views in the PRC

Worldwide, women's vulnerability to HIV/AIDS is further heightened in societies where women are expected to be passive towards sex. While China was, traditionally, very much a society whereby passivity was expected of women in sexual matters, after 1949 this situation was widely believed to have altered because of Mao's proclamations about female equality as well as the belief that the 'smashing' of class

---

[7]Surveys conducted in Africa reveal that 60–80% of HIV positive women, who contracted HIV from sexual intercourse, reported that their only sexual partner was their husband. Another study, which was conducted in India, another region where HIV/AIDS is growing at an alarming rate, reveals that 91% of HIV positive women surveyed, who had contracted HIV from sexual intercourse, also reported that their only sexual partner was their husband (Feinstein and Prentice 2000: 22). These findings support the results of an earlier study conducted in 1989 which also found the majority of HIV positive women who had contracted HIV through heterosexual intercourse, had also contracted HIV/AIDS from their only sexual partner, their husband. The researchers in this instance concluded that often 'condom use was more effective in preventing HIV infection than was limiting the number of partners' (Berger and Vizgirda 1993: 62).

difference would lead to the eradication of outdated sexual stereotypes regarding men and women. However, patriarchal views still permeate Chinese society and overall Chinese men retain their position of gender privilege, often reflected in the power dynamics of heterosexual relationships.

The One Child Policy is one of the main factors in increasing female insecurity in contemporary China, particularly within the marital unit. Since its introduction, there has been a strong resurgence in son preference, especially in the rural areas where sons play an important role in continuing the family lineage, contributing to the family labour force and their filial duty to provide for their parents in old age (Croll et al. 1985; Croll 2000; Chan et al. 2002). In some areas of China, the re-emergence of son preference has caused there to be strong pressure on women to give birth to a son and failure to do so can lead to domestic violence and even divorce. This is because women are wrongfully blamed over the sex of the child due to poor knowledge on the biological determinants of the sex of the fetus and also because it is believed to be 'the duty of a Chinese wife to bear a son to continue the family name' (Chan et al. 2002: 427).

In her discussion of son preference and the resultant violence against women who give birth to daughters, Croll provided several accounts of incidences whereby a husband committed acts of domestic violence against his wife after she bore a daughter (2000: 78–80). The ACWF has found that *reported* cases of domestic violence occur in approximately 30% of Chinese families, with 32.5% of abused women being beaten around four times per month (Xinhua 2000). Female suicide rates are also high in the PRC, reflecting female insecurity there. Of the total number of female suicides worldwide, 56% occurred in China (Renwick 2002: 383). In addition, while the urban rate of female suicide is estimated to be in the vicinity of 15.9 per 100,000 women, in rural areas the figures have reached 78.3 per 100,000 women, clearly demonstrating a rural/urban divide in female suicide rates in China (HRIC, cited in Renwick 2002: 383). A report by the BBC echoed these findings, and stated that many rural women are highly successful in their suicide attempts because they used pesticides and rat poisons to commit suicide (BBC 2002).

If gender-based violence such as domestic violence is viewed as an acceptable factor in preserving gender relations in the home, it can substantially increase women's vulnerability to HIV transmission. In societies where there exists 'a cultural ethos that violence is a valid means of solving inter-personal disputes' (Whelan 1999: 11), such as in the domestic spheres, women may avoid discussing the use of condoms or fidelity issues with their partners for fear of violent response. The fear of violent retribution was identified by women from a range of countries such as Guatemala, Jamaica and Papua New Guinea as being the reason why they did not try to negotiate condom usage with their sexual partners (Feinstein and Prentice 2000: 24). Women's vulnerability to HIV/AIDS is heightened by male aggression because it can often be linked to the occurrence of sexual coercion, non-consensual sex and sexual violence against women. For many women, decisions about their sexual behaviour are denied to them because they are forced into sexual intercourse against their will. This is applicable both inside and outside of relationships. In such instances, condom usage is unlikely, so women's vulnerability to HIV transmission is increased (Irwin et al. 2003: 31). Therefore, the accounts given above of high rates of domestic violence and female suicide demonstrate that there are a great number of women in the general population who are facing increased HIV vulnerability due to their unhealthy domestic environment.

The traffic of women in China is also fuelling female vulnerability to HIV transmission, and is most prolific in Sichuan and Guizhou. Interviewee A (2003, pers. comm., 21 August) attributed this to the fact that these two provinces 'have a high number of poor farmers and unemployed' so they sell women for financial rewards. Interviewee A also stated that the 'traffic of women in China is generally restricted to marriage, whereas trafficking outside of China is generally for prostitution'. In saying this, the interviewee believed that the traffic of women, while bad, would not increase the likelihood of HIV transmission because the women were sold as 'brides', not sex workers (Interviewee A 2003, pers. comm., 21 August). The belief that trafficked 'brides' are not particularly vulnerable to HIV transmission was also shared by Interviewee E (2003, pers. comm., 27 August). However, this belief demonstrates a serious lack of understanding of human trafficking as members of the trafficking gangs sometimes rape the women, regardless of them being trafficked as 'brides' or as sex workers. Furthermore, prospective husbands are sometimes allowed to have intercourse with the women before purchasing them, in order to decide which woman will become their 'bride' and also so that they can bargain the price of the woman (*South China Morning Post*, cited in Jaschok and Miers 1994: 264). Clearly, the rape of these women by numerous men, including their 'husband', increases their vulnerability to HIV transmission. In addition, the likelihood that their 'husband' will contract HIV from them or from other women he 'sampled' is also heightened if he does not already carry the virus. Hence, it is a very serious misconception that the traffic of women in China as 'brides' will have little impact on the HIV/AIDS epidemic there.

Equally alarming is the view held by some segments of Chinese society that 'as long as they [men] have the money, buying a wife or child is their own affair' (Li Zhongxiu, cited in Jaschok and Miers 1994: 265). Again, this kind of attitude illustrates the low status that many women (and children) continue to occupy in Chinese society and the patriarchal factors that heighten their vulnerability to HIV/AIDS. In addition, it is widely predicted that the sale of women in China is set to continue to expand because from a purely economic standpoint, buying a trafficked bride can be far cheaper than paying a dowry (Song, cited in Jaschok and Miers 1994: 265). Also, the skewed sex ratios that have resulted from the introduction of the One Child Policy and resultant resurgence of son preference have seen men far outnumber women in many areas of China (Edwards 2000: 75). It has been estimated that by 2029, there will be 30 million more males than females in the 20–49 year age bracket due to sex selective abortion and the neglect of girl children in China (Chan et al. 2002: 429). Due to the gender imbalance it is unlikely that these men will be able to find a bride to marry legally and they will increasingly turn to bride trafficking as the solution, making it a crime that is likely to soar over the next few decades, alongside prostitution.

While the Chinese government has not ignored this situation, and the Public Security Bureau often detects and arrests human traffickers, trafficking is difficult to police as the number of women trafficked yearly is believed to be in the vicinity of tens of thousands. They are primarily abducted from poor regions in Guizhou, Sichuan and Yunnan Provinces (Woodman and Ho, cited in Hughes et al. 1999). Further complicating this issue is the fact that many women who have escaped their 'husbands' have not received assistance because some authorities also have sympathy toward men who have been unable to find brides. As a result, women who escape their situation are often returned to their 'husbands' by authorities. Villagers also assist in the trafficking of women either by ignoring the problem, or by helping to buy women. In fact, it has been reported that one remote village collectively purchased women with the intention of soliciting them from their homes (Woodman and Ho, cited in Hughes et al. 1999). The traffic of women constitutes a serious potential bridge for HIV transmission to the general population and again reflects a heightened vulnerability, in terms of both HIV transmission and human insecurity, for Chinese women.

Another factor identified by Interviewee C as compounding the situation of women's vulnerability to HIV transmission was the migration of rural workers to the cities for work. She stated that although many male migrant workers are married, they leave their wives behind and often engage in 'risky practices' in the cities, such as IDU, procuring sex workers, and infidelity. Generally, the men return to their homes once a year, during which they engage in sexual activity with their spouse, usually without using condoms. The interviewee further stated that even if the woman may suspect her spouse of having engaged in 'risky practices' while away, many women are unable to insist that their spouse use a condom (Interviewee C 2003, pers. comm., 22 August). In addition, for many rural women, labour migration can heighten their vulnerability to HIV transmission because it removes them from the economic support and protection nets that exist in their home villages, making them easy targets to be lured or forced into prostitution. In fact, a large number of China's sex workers are migrant women (Thompson 2003) and they sometimes display higher risk behaviour than non-migrant sex workers, in part due to low education levels and poor HIV/AIDS awareness, which increases their likelihood of contracting HIV (Hong et al. 2009). Many migrant women have also become the victims of sexual harassment and sexual violence, which also increases their vulnerability to HIV transmission.

While conservative estimates suggest the number of sex workers in China is approximately three million (Thompson 2004) to four million (Harding 2000), scholars such as Professor Pan of People's University of Beijing believe the figure to be much higher when the numbers of women who engage in 'casual or infrequent transactional sex' are included (cited in Thompson 2004). It has also been reported by UNAIDS that the Public Security Bureau estimates the number of sex workers in China could be as high as six million (UNAIDS 2002: 65). Jeffreys states that government authorities in China have called prostitution a 'widespread and growing problem' (2004: 83).[8] Thus, a conservative estimate of four million sex workers demonstrates that a considerable number of Chinese women are vulnerable to HIV infection through prostitution.

---

[8] For further reading, see Jeffreys (2004).

The illegal nature of prostitution in China is a major barrier to HIV/AIDS advocacy for sex workers and continues to exacerbate the vulnerable status of sex workers. Interviewee D (2003, pers. comm., 27 August) stated that organizations like hers could give HIV prevention information to sex workers, without arresting them, because it was not a government organization. If workers from the government organizations identified sex workers, she stated that they were required to report them because of the illegality of prostitution. After being reported, the identified sex worker would then face detention in a rehabilitation centre. While there are debates in China as to whether or not prostitution should be decriminalized or legalized so as to allow INGOs, NGOs and government organizations to legally provide STI prevention knowledge and services to sex workers, the rehabilitation system does currently offer an opportunity to reach this vulnerable group with HIV/AIDS prevention information. However, Interviewee D (2003, pers. comm., 27 August) stated that this was not occurring, even though the organization she worked for had been trying to launch programs that linked 'HIV/AIDS prevention education into the rehabilitation programs of these centres'. Furthermore, without adequate help to overcome their economic insecurity, upon release from these centres many women actually returned to prostitution. Thus, she stated, an important opportunity was being missed.

There is concern however, over the contradiction in the government's response to prostitution, which sees sex workers targeted by interventionist programs, not those soliciting the prostitutes. This obvious gender bias is in part fuelled by the extant view in China that those selling sex always come before those buying sex. This view is problematic in that one could argue that it is demand that drives provision; however at a very basic level it punishes the sex worker as the guilty party in the commercial sex exchange and not the solicitor. It also means that many of the men who solicit prostitutes are left out of the targeted commercial sex HIV prevention strategies although they are clearly a 'high-risk' group (Chen 2008). If they are married or have other sexual encounters outside of the commercial sexual exchange, they are also a possible 'bridge' population who have the potential to transmit HIV into the general population.

Chen (2008) argues that the failure of the Chinese government to adequately respond to this contradiction reflects that there is an urgent need in China for recognition of the important role men play in safer sexual practice, a responsibility that is continually being thrust onto women. In fact, recent campaigns by the ACWF reportedly 'exposed' 27.25 million women across China to HIV/AIDS prevention and awareness knowledge. However, there was no discussion of if/how men were also given this important knowledge or if they were made aware of how their actions can impact on the HIV vulnerability of their spouses (SCAWCO and UNAIDS 2007). Considering the unequal gender-based power relations discussed above, it is unlikely that these types of measures will have much success as men and women both need to be involved in such advocacy programs. To neglect the involvement and importance of men serves to increase women's vulnerability while at the same time proportioning responsibility to women for their own HIV safety, something that is simply unachievable for many women.

2.5 The Health System and Government Responses

The failure of the rural health system is also exacerbating the vulnerability of Chinese women to HIV/AIDS. Approximately 60% of rural women are now showing symptoms of having untreated RTIs or STIs (Interviewee C 2003, pers. comm., 22 August), both of which increase their susceptibility to HIV through sexual transmission (Jolly and Ying 2003: 2). The figures on STIs clearly indicate that behaviours conducive to the transmission of HIV/AIDS, such as unprotected intercourse, are becoming more widespread. However, rural healthcare facilities continue to be inadequate, and therefore information on HIV/AIDS and prevention of the virus is not reaching rural men and women (Interviewee C 2003, pers. comm., 22 August). In addition, many rural women are not targeted for information dissemination due to the official belief that these women fall into the 'low-risk' category due to their marital status and individual behaviour. In light of the discussion above, this overly simplistic classification of who is or is not 'at risk' is substantially heightening women's vulnerability to HIV. Considering the changing face of China's HIV/AIDS epidemic in the current era, the failure of the government to have a comprehensive gendered response to the burgeoning AIDS epidemic in the PRC may result in the government ineffectively responding to HIV/AIDS. Chen (2008) warns that this could lead to an increase in stigma and discrimination against women as their HIV+ rates increase and may further exacerbate women's insecurity.

When critiquing the privatization of health care in China, Interviewee D (2003, pers. comm., 27 August) stated that prior to the 1990s, the health system in rural China was much better because 'bare foot doctors and health workers were active in even the most remote areas'. However, after the dismantling of government sponsorship, the rural healthcare system was left in ruins, with only expensive private doctors available to meet the health care needs of the rural population. Another problem with the provision of health care is that the government does not regulate STI facilities. In fact, some STI clinics are now being rented out to private practitioners. While this can benefit PLWHA, because it reduces the possibility of their HIV+ status being leaked,[9] it also causes prices to rise and patient care tends to decline (Interviewee C 2003, pers. comm., 22 August). Therefore, the privatization of essential services such as the health industry has seen medical services fall out of the economic reach of many poorer families or individuals. This compounds Chinese women's vulnerability to HIV because it limits the ability of both men and women to manage their sexual and reproductive health.

Another difficulty identified by Interviewee D (2003, pers. comm., 27 August) was that organizations like hers lacked adequate funding both to run programs as well as to support PLWHA. She stated that because most PLWHA in China are rural poor, education on lifestyle, proper diet and medication was in vain as 'many [patients] can't follow these instructions because they live in poor conditions in

---

[9]Clinics that are not privately owned are often linked to a person's work unit so their HIV+ status is sometimes leaked to colleagues and employers.

rural China, where their income is just enough to feed their families'. However, with better funding, HIV/AIDS prevention and treatment campaigns could help PLWHA with the costs of living and medications, making their lives better (Interviewee D 2003, pers. comm., 27 August). Interviewee F (2003, pers. comm., 9 September) also identified funding as a problem for HIV/AIDS prevention and treatment. She stated that sometimes her organization wanted to carry out pilot projects, but because they were given insufficient funding they were unable to run the projects. Clearly, without the funding to properly test pilot programmes or institute nation-wide campaigns, HIV/AIDS prevention in China will continue to be hindered.

On the other hand, the introduction of the 'Four Frees and One Care' policy in 2003 has seen a positive change in the government's funding response to China's AIDS epidemic. The 'Four Frees' provided by the policy include government funded schooling for AIDS orphans, drug therapy for PLWHA, prevention of MTCT and voluntary counseling and testing (VCT). The 'One Care' component refers to care and economic assistance for people afflicted with or affected by HIV/AIDS (Cao et al. 2006: 520). However, by the government's own admission, the implementation of this policy has been uneven (National Center for AIDS/STD Prevention and Control 2006: ii), so while it is certainly a step in the right direction, it is not fully operational as it will require a great deal of cooperation between all levels of government and assistance by civil society before it can really meet its objectives. It should be acknowledged that China has been injecting more funds into HIV/AIDS prevention and treatment strategies since 2003. The 2009 update by UNAIDS and the World Health Organization reported that there had been a threefold increase in funding by China in the period between 2003 and 2006 demonstrating stronger commitment from the government (UNAIDS and WHO 2009).

The incorporation of civil society into HIV/AIDS prevention was an issue also identified by Interviewee B (2003, pers. comm., 22 August). She stated that the solitary nature of the MOH in combating HIV/AIDS in China means that it is effectively tackling HIV/AIDS by itself. While the enabling environments for HIV transmission include diverse fields such as employment and public security, Interviewee B stated that there was no cooperation between the Ministry of Public Security (MPS) and the MOH, a point which Chen believes has led to;

> tensions, and sometimes contradictions, between the goals of public policies and the methods of policy practice, such as the conflict between public security (law enforcement) policies relating to sex work and public health policies for the prevention of HIV/AIDS (2008: 185).

Furthermore, issues pertaining to commercial sex workers and IDUs, which were handled by the MPS, also did not involve input from the MOH. This is quite possibly the reason why HIV/AIDS prevention advocacy programs have still not been uniformly implemented in all rehabilitation centres for IDUs and sex workers.

Interviewees C and F both believed that education campaigns aimed at the general population could be a valuable way to disperse HIV/AIDS information. They stated that efforts like the Severe Acute Respiratory Syndrome (SARS) mass media education campaigns would be a major step in changing people's beliefs about HIV/AIDS and increasing knowledge and public awareness of the virus and how it is transmitted. After the cessation of SARS, the Chinese government did shift its focus to HIV/AIDS, and education campaigns on HIV/AIDS have been undertaken. Therefore, unlike previous efforts, top leaders in government have demonstrated they are serious in their response to HIV/AIDS. While this signals a positive change, unfortunately the gender issues that contribute to HIV/AIDS vulnerability do not appear to be an integral component of these campaigns, so their overall effectiveness is doubtful. In addition, gender inclusive campaigns would also need to be supported with active steps at both the government and grassroots level to reverse the continuing unequal social, political and economic structures that disempowered Chinese women, which have been shown to heighten their vulnerability to HIV/AIDS. However, Beijing's reluctance to support the development of an unrestrained civil society in China makes this unlikely.

In the United Nations report *HIV/AIDS: China's Titanic Peril* (2002), China's political system was identified as possibly the most sensitive obstacle to tackling HIV/AIDS in the PRC. This was because the central government has long appeared uncomfortable with the emergence of organizations that are independent of the government and especially the free flow of information that such organizations may facilitate (UNAIDS 2002: 69–82). Yet, while the central government may fear that the emergence of civil society could contribute to a breakdown in the Chinese Communist Party's authority in China, civil society participation and the free flow of information are not only good governance when responding to HIV/AIDS epidemics, but international experience has proven them to be essential elements in a state's response to HIV/AIDS. Therefore, until the central government is willing to allow greater autonomy among the various NGOs and INGOs operating in China, it is unlikely that the Chinese response to HIV/AIDS will make any real inroads in the prevention of HIV transmission – and even less so in terms of gender-specific issues such as the human insecurities that increase women's vulnerability to HIV/AIDS.

2.6 Conclusion

When determining women's vulnerability to HIV transmission, female human security, or more aptly their 'insecurity', is an important factor. The status of many women in China, and the privileged position accorded to Chinese men, strongly indicates that Chinese women face a heightened vulnerability to HIV transmission. While many of these vulnerabilities are similar to women elsewhere in the world and certainly are not unique to China, they attest to the interplay of the unequal status accorded many Chinese women due to their sex, their disempowered status within society, unequal gender-based power relations both within the domestic and public arenas, and the patriarchal norms and attitudes that influence all of the above. By overlooking the many social, cultural, economic and political factors that contribute to HIV/AIDS vulnerability and transmission of the virus, particularly those faced by women, China has a long way to go before Chinese women are protected from HIV transmission. Given that HIV/AIDS heightens human insecurity, the stage is set for Chinese women (and men) to face an insecure future if the Chinese government does not fully implement international best practice, meaning a gendered response, into its overall HIV/AIDS response.

Acknowledgments The author would like to thank Professor Donald McMillen, Dr Rosemary Roberts and an anonymous reviewer for their insightful comments and suggestions.

References

BBC. (2002 November 26). HIV hits women hardest, *BBC News World Edition*. http://news.bbc.co.uk/2/hi/health/2516273.stm. Accessed 2 Jan 2003.
Berger, B., & Vizgirda, V. (1993). Prevention of HIV infection in women and children. In F. L. Cohen & J. D. Durham (Eds.), *Women, children and HIV/AIDS* (pp. 60–82). New York: Springer.
Cao, X., Sullivan, S., Xu, J., & Wu, Z. (2006). Understanding HIV-related stigma and discrimination in a "blameless" population. *AIDS Education and Prevention, 18*(6), 518–528.
Chan, C., Yip, P., Ng, E., Chan, C., & Au, J. (2002). Gender selection in China: Its meanings and implication. *Journal of Assisted Reproduction and Genetics, 19*(9), 426–430.
Chen, L. (2008). Gendering China's strategy against HIV/AIDS: Findings from a research project in Guangdong Province. *Feminist Economics, 14*(4), 183–211.
Croll, E. (2000). *Endangered daughters: Discrimination and development in Asia*. London: Routledge.
Croll, E., Davin, D., & Kane, P. (1985). *China's one-child family policy*. Hampshire: Macmillan.
Dikötter, F. (1997). A history of sexually transmitted diseases in China. In M. Lewis, S. Bamber, & M. Waugh (Eds.), *Sex, disease and society: A comparative history of sexually transmitted diseases and HIV/AIDS in Asia and the Pacific* (pp. 67–84). London: Greenwood Press.
Edwards, L. (2000). Women in the People's Republic of China: New challenges to the grand gender narrative. In L. Edwards & M. Roces (Eds.), *Women in Asia: Tradition, modernity and globalisation* (pp. 59–84). Ann Arbor: University of Michigan Press.
Feinstein, N., & Prentice, B. (2000). Gender and AIDS Almanac. http://data.unaids.org/topics/Gender/genderandaidsalmanac_en.pdf. Accessed 18 Feb 2003.
Futures Group. (2004). AIDS crisis impending: Research on knowledge, attitudes and behaviours related to HIV/AIDS in China. http://www.futuresgroup.com/Documents/CHN2003Survey.pdf. Accessed 27 Aug 2004.
Gill, B., Huang, Y., & Lu, X. (2007). Demography of HIV/AIDS in China: A report of the task force on HIV/AIDS Center for Strategic and International Studies, Washington: CSIS. http://csis.org/files/media/csis/pubs/070724_china_hiv_demography.pdf. Accessed 18 July 2009.
Harding, L. (2000). India is new loser in Asian AIDS epidemic, *The Guardian*. http://www.guardian.co.uk/international/story/0,3604,230527,00.html. Accessed 20 Feb 2003.
Hayes, A. (2005). AIDS, bloodheads and cover-ups: The "ABC" of Henan's AIDS epidemic. *Australian Quarterly: Journal of Contemporary Analysis, 77*(3), 12–16.
Hong, Y., Li, X., Yang, H., Fang, X., & Zhao, R. (2009). HIV/AIDS-related sexual risks and migratory status among female sex workers in a rural Chinese country. *AIDS Care, 21*(2), 212–220.
Howell, J. (2003). Women's organizations and civil society in China. *International Feminist Journal of Politics, 5*(2), 191–215.
Hughes, D., Sporcic, L., Mendelsohn, N., & Chirgwin, V. (1999). The factbook on global sexual exploitation. http://www.catwinternational.org/factbook/China%20and%20Hong%20Kong.php. Accessed 19 Feb 2005.

Irwin, A., Millen, J., & Fallows, D. (2003). *Global AIDS: Myths and facts. Tools for fighting the AIDS pandemic*. Cambridge: South End Press.

Jaschok, M., & Miers, S. (1994). Traditionalism, continuity and change. In M. Jaschok & S. Miers (Eds.), *Women and Chinese patriarchy: Submission, servitude and escape* (pp. 264–267). London: Zed Books.

Jeffreys, E. (2004). Feminist prostitution debates: Are there any sex workers in China? In A. McLaren (Ed.), *Chinese women – living and working* (pp. 81–102). New York: Routledge Curzon.

Jolly, S., & Wang, Y. (2003). Key issues on gender and HIV/AIDS in China. http://www.genie.ids.ac.uk/docs/jolly_aidschina.doc. Accessed 17 June 2003.

Kanabus, A. (2004). HIV & AIDS in China. http://www.avert.org/aidschina.htm. Accessed 1 Feb 2005.

Lee, T. L., & Regan, F. (2009). Why develop and support women's organizations in providing legal aid in China? Women's rights, women's organization and legal aid in China. *Journal of Contemporary China, 18*(61), 541–565.

Ma, Q., Ono-Kihara, M., Cong, L., Pan, X., Xu, G., Zamani, S., Ravari, S. M., & Kihara, M. (2009). Behavioural and psychosocial predictors of condom use among university students in Eastern China. *AIDS Care, 21*(2), 249–259.

Ministry of Health of the People's Republic of China. (2010). China 2010 UNGASS country progress report (2008–2009). http://data.unaids.org/pub/Report/2010/china_2010_country_progress_report_en.pdf. Accessed 9 Apr 2010.

National Center for AIDS/STD Prevention and Control. (2006). 2005 update on the HIV/AIDS epidemic and response in China. http://www.unchina.org/unaids/2005-China%20HIV-AIDS%20Estimation-English.pdf. Accessed 1 Jan 2006.

Park, A. (2003). China's secret plague: How one US scientist is struggling to help the government face up to an exploding AIDS crisis. *Time, 15*(49), 48–54.

Qian, X., Tang, S., & Garner, P. (2004). Unintended pregnancy and induced abortion among unmarried women in China: A systematic review. *BMC Health Services Research, 4*(1). http://www.pubmedcentral.gov/articlerender.fcgi?tool=pmcentrez&artid=333425. Accessed 20 Jan 2005.

Renwick, N. (2002). The 'nameless fever': The HIV/AIDS pandemic and China's women. *Third World Quarterly, 23*(2), 337–393.

SCAWCO, & UNAIDS. (2007). A joint assessment of HIV/AIDS prevention, treatment and care in China (2007). http://www.un.org.cn/public/resource/a24f2886ef699b0a64637e9ba91b58d6.pdf. Accessed 3 May 2010.

Thompson, D. (2003). HIV/AIDS epidemic in China spreads into the general population. http://www.prb.org/Template.cfm?Section=PRB&template=/ContentManagement/ContentDisplay.cfm&ContentID=8501. Accessed 27 June 2004.

Thompson, D. (2004). China's growing AIDS epidemic increasingly affects women. http://www.prb.org. Accessed 1 Feb 2005.

UNAIDS. (2002). HIV/AIDS: China's titanic peril. http://www.unaids.org/whatsnew/newadds/AIDSChina2001update.pdf. Accessed 26 Mar 2003.

UNAIDS, UNFPA, & UNIFEM. (2004). Women and HIV/AIDS: Confronting the crisis. http://www.unfpa.org/upload/lib_pub_file/308_filename_women_aids1.pdf#search='unaids%2C%20unfpa%20%26%20unifem'. Accessed 17 Sep 2004.

UNAIDS, & WHO. (2009). AIDS epidemic update 2009. http://data.unaids.org/pub/Report/2009/JC1700_Epi_Update_2009_en.pdf. Accessed 24 Apr 2010.

UNDP. (1995). Redefining security: The human dimension. *Current History, 94*(592), 229–236.

Whelan, D. (1999). Gender and HIV/AIDS: taking stock of research and programmes. http://www.unaids.org/html/pub/publications/ircpub05/jc419gendertakingstock_en_pdf.pdf#search='gender%20and%20hiv%2Faids%3Ataking%20stock%20of%20research%20and%20programmes'. Accessed 10 Aug 2003.

Wu, Z., Sullivan, S., Wang, Yu, Rotheram-Borus, M. J., & Detels, R. (2007). Evolution of China's response to HIV/AIDS. *Lancet, 369*, 679–690.

Xia, G. (2004). *HIV/AIDS in China*. Beijing: Foreign Languages Press.
Xinhua. (2000). Ban on family violence urged in China, China Guide. http://www.chinaguide.org/english/2000/Aug/560.htm. Accessed 30 July 2002.
Yuan, J., Xu, Y., Jiang, T., & Huobao, Xu. (2003). *Modelling the impact of the legal and policy environment on HIV/AIDS in China*. Beijing: UNDP China.
Zhao, B. (2001). Quality of care of reproductive health in China today. http://www.npfpc.gov.cn/en/rhpro.htm. Accessed 17 May 2005.
Zhou, Y. (2008). Endangered womanhood: Women's experiences with HIV/AIDS in China. *Qualitative Health Research, 18*(8), 1115–1126.

Chapter 3
From National Security to Human Security: Population Policy Shifts in Vietnam

Kathleen A. Tobin

3.1 Context

For more than a decade, regional strategists have given more serious attention to the value of human security over national security when attempting to shape the futures of post-conflict societies. Rethinking traditional approaches has lent far more credence to programs intended to meet human needs as a way to insure long-range peace and civility; and, sole reliance on military buildup and high level diplomatic chess play as means to protect national interests has waned. The transition has not been a smooth one, or clear, with each country undergoing unique shifts based on historical and contemporary circumstances. Vietnam is an important place to consider because of the severity of its experiences in the last half century, and the swiftness of social and economic changes in the past 15 years. Essential to Vietnam's story is an address of population and parallel issues and policies as they relate to security. Demographics tend to shape human and national security concerns, and courses of action taken affect people's lives. Upon closer examination of Vietnam's population trends, interests, and directives, we get a better sense of where security approaches have shifted, and where human security challenges persist.

The end of the Second Indochina War/American War in 1975 ushered in new policies, including those addressing population. In a little over a decade, the Vietnamese government would initiate an era of reform, affecting both human security and population policies. The transition from national to human security approaches in Vietnam as they relate to population can be best understood by examining: (1) migration, (2) reproductive rights, (3) food production and the environment, and (4) minority rights. The levels of transition in each area are not yet clear, nor are the intentions of state and non-state actors clear. Nonetheless these issues play essential roles in the broader study of population policy and human security,

K.A. Tobin (✉)
Purdue University Calumet, Hammond, IN, USA
e-mail: tobin@purduecal.edu

a fundamental address of each can illustrate both successes and limitations in the process.

3.2 Principles of Human Security

The emphasis on human security emerged largely as the result of two recent historical shifts. First, the Cold War had served to sustain a focus on national security between the superpowers and among their allies. As it came to an end, the nearly constant threat of nuclear war subsided, and ideological polarization of the world diminished. Greater authentic attention could be paid to meeting human needs in post-colonial regions without endangering the geo political balance dictated by the superpowers. Second expanding globalization empowered non-state actors – both local and transnational – to address human needs beyond the framework of national security. Critics argued that globalization advanced development in ways that threatened individuals' access to a living wage, adequate health care, and clean drinking water. At the same time, transnational human security advocates intensified their efforts to meet those needs by using tools enhanced by globalization (Amouyel 2006).

In *Human Security, Concepts and Implications*, Shahrbanou Tadjbakhsh and Anuradha M. Chenoy define the idea as "the protection of individuals from risks to their physical or psychological safety, dignity and well-being." They add, "An environment that is said to provide its members with human security is one which affords individuals the possibility to lead stable, self-determined lives." These statements accurately reflect the general focus on "freedom from want and freedom from fear" as defined by the 1994 United Nations Development Program (UNDP) report, and on "the freedom of future generations to inherit a healthy environment," as UN Secretary-General Kofi Annan later articulated. According to Annan, "Human security can no longer be understood in purely military terms. Rather, it must encompass economic development, social justice, environmental protection, democratization, disarmament, and respect for human rights and the rule of law." Very importantly, human security issues encompassed considerations for protection not only on national and international levels, but also on regional, local, and individual levels (Tadjbakhsh and Chenoy 2007; McRae and Huberts 2001; den Boer and de Wilde 2008; UNDP 1994; Annan 2001).

While many policy analysts agree on the essence of human security principles, not all agree on their fundamental purpose or the responsibility for implementation. Some perceived this new approach as a step needed to protect the primary interest, national security. For example, if poverty and hunger persist, agitation within the population might intensify, resulting in increasing levels of unrest leading to revolution. Or, such conditions might weaken the state, allowing for outside intervention and occupation. On the other hand, some argued that meeting human needs should be an end in itself. Securing public health, ample food supplies, safe housing, etc., should remain the focus regardless of state or international interests. With regard to implementation, the imposition of human security principles by the state or international governing organizations is regarded as a "top-down" approach. A "bottom-up" approach, or "human security from below," recognizes and often expects people to address their own issues, while taking into consideration that they might need support. To those advocates, freedom from want and freedom from fear would more effectively be addressed by the people themselves. Conflict remains between those suspicious of state motives in security matters, and those insistent that the state is the only entity capable of establishing and protecting human security.

Mary Kaldor embraces a "bottom-up" approach in *Human Security: Reflections on Globalization and Intervention*, noting that concepts such as "partnership" and "local ownership" already understood in development policies should be a "given" in creating security policies. She also places a high value on maintaining a "regional focus" in human security matters. Where national borders, for example, had acted as critical factors in state and military security issues, they need not when it comes to human security. Cultures, environments, employment opportunities, and human beings cross borders, so attempting to confine human security issues within boundaries would be unrealistic. This is true in the case of Vietnam where the interests of ethnic minorities ignore national borders. Many of Vietnam's environmental and economic concerns are inextricably linked with those of Laos and Cambodia, and, to a degree, China (Kaldor 2007).

When examining development shifts in Vietnam's contemporary history, acknowledging the character and influence of "bottom-up" approaches is crucial. As the nation has opened itself to greater communication from the outside, donor nations have sought to inform change through extended support of Non-Governmental Organizations. These efforts were designed to build, sustain and expand civil society activities there, many of which might affect migration, labor, birth rates, and so on. Reaction from the Vietnamese people has followed – some of it critical – as the intentions of non-Vietnamese organizations have been questioned. Still, the roles that civil society have played, at the very least in paralleling sweeping changes in Vietnam, continues to gain significant attention by researchers and policymakers (Gray 1999).

3.3 Background

The unique historical position of Vietnam is analogous to discussions of its human security issues. Since the Colonial Period from the end of the nineteenth century to the end of French colonial rule in 1954, the Vietnamese had become accustomed to the state playing a primary role in addressing social and economic needs of the population. While other post-conflict or developing nations might question the state's capacity, potential, or motives in providing for the people, the Socialist Republic of Vietnam was founded largely on this basis. The victory of socialism served to lay the groundwork for a human security approach that could not have gained any ground before or during the military and Cold War conflicts. The Cold War had sharply defined the battle over Vietnam and its people in the 1950s and

1960s with "national security" lying at the heart of arguments originating in France, China, the Soviet Union, and the United States, as well as Vietnam.

Today, Vietnam is a country of 85 million people, the second largest population of any nation in the Southeast Asian region. Still largely an agricultural society with a majority of its people living in rural areas, Vietnam is experiencing rapid urbanization. Its cities, primarily Hanoi and Ho Chi Minh City are growing quickly, and are now among the most densely populated metropolitan areas in the region. The economy is growing and shifting, as the country expands integration with the global market. However, the benefits of that growth are not enjoyed by all Vietnamese. The new Vietnam faces additional challenges in meeting the needs of its changing population. And many of those challenges are rooted in its history.

Population policies in Vietnam's past most often focused on spatial location and migration. Colonial rule from 1858 to 1954 was marked by tight restrictions on migration, with the French generally attempting to tie particular groups of people to certain places. Movement was allowed only rarely, and it was always highly supervised. The French also maintained control by undermining local village autonomy throughout Indochina. The onset of the First Indochina War in 1945 spurred mass migration, with some 50,000 fleeing to China between 1946 and 1948. The 1954 Geneva Accords marking French withdrawal and partitioning North and South Vietnam pending elections also allowed for civilians to move freely during a 300-day grace period. As a result, between 130,000 and 140,000 supporters of the Viet Minh national liberation front (both civilian and military) subsequently moved north of the border, where its power base lay. At the same time, approximately 930,000 civilians and 120,000 military personnel moved south. Of the migrants moving south, 98% were ethnic Vietnamese, and 85% were Catholic. Historically, overpopulation in the north had urged migration to the less populated south. However, the civil conflict intensified the desire to move, encouraging more Vietnamese to take advantage of the opportunity to migrate. Motives included family reunification following the pullout of French troops, belief among Catholics that they could practice religion more freely in the non-Communist South, and general fear among the comparatively wealthy who had collaborated with the French in the years preceding the Geneva Accords (Salemink 2003; Stocking 1991; Breman 1987; Hickey 1982; Robinson 1998; Wiesner 1988; Luong 1959).

In October of 1955, the Catholic Ngo Dinh Diem became President of the Republic of Vietnam (South Vietnam), and quickly initiated the social engineering of population designed to consolidate control through relocation. Resettlement programs of both North and South Vietnam moved tens of thousands into the Central Highlands – a strategic border area. The region had been inhabited largely by ethnic minorities who were viewed as less patriotic, and less loyal to the nationalist cause on either side. Resettlement was viewed as creating a "safety valve" for overcrowded urban areas and a means to expand the Vietnam presence through population growth along the border. In addition, it would generally keep the population under control and separate peasants from the influence of national liberation Viet Cong guerrillas which had gained strength since the Geneva Accords. In order to escape resettlement, many fled to growing cities, particularly Saigon and DaNang.

By 1962, Diem responded to Viet Cong penetration of the South by creating a "strategic hamlet program" modeled after British counter-insurgency efforts in Malaysia. "Operation Sunrise" moved villagers to fortified areas and then burned their villages. An estimated 4–8 million had been moved by 1963 when Diem was assassinated. The American War, or Second Indochina War, compounded migration problems, with more than half of the South Vietnamese population displaced in the years between 1954 and 1975. As the country was reunified into the Socialist Republic of Vietnam at the end of the war, the United States government quickly implemented evacuation plans. By the 1980s, the extensive fleeing of refugees was brought under control by an "Orderly Departure Program," through which millions were relocated to North America and Western Europe (Robinson 1998; Hickey 1993; U.S. Congress 1975).

The war caused demographic imbalances in all parts of Vietnam. In the 10 years between 1965 and 1975, an estimated 800,000–1,200,000 Vietnamese died. Civilian casualties were high, including those among women and children. However, as with all wars, men were killed in greater numbers creating demographic imbalances. Census data from 1979 indicated there were only between 78 and 90 men for every 100 women among those born before 1954. In addition, large tracts of forest and farmland were destroyed, much through the use of Agent Orange, as were industrial and transportation centers in the North, due to U. S. bombing. War itself is often considered a means of population control, but for the Vietnamese a responsive policy was needed to help rebuild and restructure the country (Luong 2003; Hirschman et al. 1995; Gough 1990; Lewallen 1971).

The government of the Socialist Republic of Vietnam also used resettlement as a means of economic and political control. Many of those residing in southern cities were moved to the New Economic Zones in the Mekong Delta and the Central Highlands, with 50 million still living in the delta areas and 25 million in the highlands. In addition, northerners moved south in search of land and to help influence changes in ideology (Huy and Kendall 2003). In addition to developing spatial location programs, the new government expanded access to birth control. Historically, nations had promoted pro-natalism following wars by encouraging parenthood and prohibiting contraceptives in order to rebuild the population. A primary example is found in the case of France following the First World War. This was not the case with Vietnam. The North Vietnamese government had endorsed family planning as early as 1963, an indication of changing attitudes in the post-World War II socialist world. This comparatively early endorsement may account for lower fertility than in Catholic-influenced South Vietnam of the 1960s. Fertility in both areas declined sharply during the Second Indochina War, a natural trend during military conflict. After family planning efforts extended to South Vietnam in 1975, fertility declined more rapidly than in the North. But this was not achieved through the efforts of the Vietnamese government alone. The United Nations Fund for Population Activities and the Population Council supplied the country first with Intra Uterine Devices (IUDs) and then with Norplant implants and injectables, as well as condoms and sterilization (Shapiro 1996). These two developments, (1) resettlement as an economic development and job distribution measure, and (2) family planning rather than pro-natalist programs, indicate a shift away from traditional national security practices long before the 1990s.

3.4 *Doi Moi* and Human Security

In 1986, the Vietnamese government introduced the era of *Doi Moi*, a new period of "renovation" or "renewal" which placed a high value on individualism, privatization, and integration into the global economy. Critics of the Vietnamese socialist system argued that it had not served the needs of the people well, that the economy stagnated and poverty levels remained high. As a response, *Doi Moi* was designed to restructure the nation's economy, much as *perestroika* would for the Soviet Union. This transition from a state-controlled economy to one inclusive of local autonomy and social perspectives from abroad would influence new human security measures, as well. However, in neither of these areas was the state prepared to cede responsibility easily. Many who embraced human security approaches during the 1990s tended simultaneously to embrace a policy shift from a state-based to a societal-based framework (Truong et al. 2006). But it proved difficult in a socialist Vietnam, where on various levels the state and society had been considered one. Protection of the individual as essential to the social good had become the responsibility of the state. Critics of the failed system urged decentralization as a way to ensure economic opportunity and democratic civil society measures which would ultimately benefit more of the population.

Western leaders, most notably U.S. President Bill Clinton, encouraged Vietnam's entrance into the Association of Southeast Asian Nations and the World Trade Organization as necessary steps in paving the way for more society-driven political processes. Critics of neo-liberalist policies, however, warned that transitioning to a free market economy might help some gain financially, but that subsequent changes in the political process might be implemented by new-found wealth in order to maintain and protect it. Prospective international investors would look to security issues as they had in other regions, with the protection of their investments foremost. Whether civil peace and non-violence were achieved through national security policy or human security measures did not matter to them, as long as they could do business. Human security advocates warned, however, that a rapid transition toward decentralization and privatization, including the closing of stable, state-owned enterprises, might well lead to social hardships among laid-off workers. If plans for human security were to genuinely address human want and human fear, the economic transition could well be at odds with it. Economists of all persuasions might argue for human security either at the front end in influencing policy, or as the ultimate goal. However, businessmen themselves were generally interested only in doing business (Lizee 2002; Koh 2001a).

Some top-level Vietnamese and transnational policy makers sought to strengthen Vietnam's fragile foundation for rule of law, maintaining that a genuine protection of economic, social or individual rights was impossible without it. Many discussions centered on state and economic security rather than individual safety. Still, the persistence of voluntary associations, such as those of veterans, and civil society organizations in Vietnam during this period was notable, and deserves much more attention. Some were created and supported by the state as a way to keep abreast of popular demands. Women's organizations endorsed by the state, for example, were designed to articulate policies and programs in various regions of the country, and to relay concerns back to government officials. Other organizations have directly challenged the state to be more effective in protecting rights, while some have seen their missions as advancing rights beyond the purview of state sanction. The successes within this "bottom-up" approach are beginning to draw the attention of researchers (Lizee 2002; Koh 2001b).

3.5 Migration Today

Many of Vietnam's leaders today still maintain that government policies provide the only effective means to regulate migration and its consequences (Dang et al. 1997). But they ignore the fact that an authentic embrace of the free market, increased privatization, and new economic development would recognize peoples' access to employment and their desire to move in order to secure better jobs. In countries with long histories of open markets and the movement of people that comes with it, government policies have generally responded to particular needs, e.g. housing and infrastructure development in swelling industrial centers. However, in Vietnam, where the government had become accustomed to relocating people in order to suit the needs of the country, policy makers presumed that this process would continue. In much of Asia it had become common, for example, to dissuade or even prohibit people from moving into expanding urban centers, as a matter of economic and social stabilization. This has been the case in China, Indonesia, Thailand, Malaysia and the Philippines. During the Cold War, disparity in population density in Vietnam was viewed not only as an issue of socio-economics, but also of national security. Mid-twentieth century air warfare and nuclear proliferation had made urban areas exceptionally vulnerable. As a result, population policies of redistribution and rural resettlement were designed to counteract this through decentralization (Dang et al. 1997; Vietnam General Statistical Office 1991; Hardy 2003).

Resettlement and labor relocation put in place during the 1980s provided incentives such as transportation, housing, and basic necessities for people moving into less densely populated areas. However, the programs saw little success, due both to financial and practical issues. Lack of good wages, poor infrastructure and inadequate social services led to frustration, and many of the newly resettled moved from their new homes. As many as half of those sent to the new economic zones left in the first few years. To some extent, government labor location policies and the potential for market forces remained at odds with one another in the decade following the initiation of *Doi Moi*, as an essential component of an authentic free market is the free and spontaneous flow of labor. The transition toward a market economy resulted in greater unevenness of development among regions and provinces, spurring spontaneous migration. Furthermore, decollectivization of farmlands has influenced additional movement, as plots have been reallocated to individuals and their families (Dang et al. 1997; Banister 1993; Desbarats 1987).

The current level of voluntary spatial mobility and its relationship to economic transitioning are gaining increased attention among researchers. They are unique to modern history in Vietnam, and imply a shift toward the protection of individual freedoms outlined in human security prescriptive literature. However, greater emphasis might be placed on the relationship among freedom to move and freedom from fear and freedom from want among the general population. It is true that in the postwar period, Vietnam is a much safer place to live and the ability to choose a home where one feels safe and secure has increased. Still, one trend that remains a concern is the apparent growth in forced migration of women and children. There continues to be extensive trafficking across international borders of women and girls lured by promises of marriage or jobs (UNICEF 2001). In addition, recent studies of economic disparity suggest that even with free migration for better jobs, poverty continues to plague some sectors of the population.

3.6 Reproductive Choice

One key principle of freedom strongly supported by the United Nations is that of reproductive choice. Around the globe, proponents of family planning maintain that if a woman is to have economic equality, i.e. equal access to full compensation and satisfactory employment, she must have control over her own reproduction (Sen 2006). Where policy makers see large numbers of children in the less developed world as deepening the levels of individual family poverty, family planning programs are viewed as a way to alleviate problems. Some see an economic drain on an entire region or nation if family size is not controlled. And from a human security perspective, an individual's freedom from want may be sustained through access to contraceptives. When this is achieved simply through making birth control available, we see an authentic support for women's reproductive choice – a measure that parallels individual freedoms defined in recent human security documents.

In largely agricultural societies – and Vietnam remains largely agricultural – children are viewed as an economic benefit rather than a detriment. But a surge in population and expanding urbanization influenced change. If the state wishes to force a decline in population growth, it often does so through financial measures. This was the case in Vietnam. The government established a National Committee on Population Control and Family Planning in 1984, as severe shortages of arable land in densely populated regions threatened the country's future (Knudsen 2006). The Women's Union implemented family planning campaigns designed to improve population by persuading Vietnamese couples to follow a "one to two child" policy. Violators were threatened with a fine or pressure to have an IUD involuntarily implanted. Central to the movement was the idea that healthy families were essential for a healthy economy (Pettus 2003). Article 6 of Vietnam's fertility policy included the following:

> Families that have more than the allowed number of children (which includes the children they already have) must pay a housing or land rent calculated at a high price for the extra space they request.
>
> Henceforth, families with three children or more will not be permitted to move into the urban centers of municipalities, cities and industrial zones.
>
> Families that have more than the stipulated number of children must contribute social support funds, which include funds for education and health care and an increased contribution of socially beneficial labor [...]
>
> The state shall adopt regulations offering incentives to encourage persons to cease child bearing by means of vasectomies and tubal ligations.
>
> (Vietnam's New Fertility Policy 1989; Shapiro 1996)

There were additional incentives put into place in the workplace. For example, The Thanh Cong Textile Company in Ho Chi Minh City provided compensation equivalent to 200 kg of rice for sterilized women, while women bearing a third child were forced to forgo raises and promotions for a period of 3 years. Work and financial penalties for couples having more than two children were imposed throughout Vietnam by 1988. Enforcement was sporadic, but the message was clear. When availability is accompanied by incentives or disincentives in attempting to influence family size, as is often the case in the developing world and transitioning societies, we hear allegations of coercion (Hoa 1993; Bich 1999; Gammeltoft 1999).

In *Engendering Human Security: Feminist* Perspectives, Thanh-Dam Truoung illustrates the emphasis on a "working-mother" contract for Vietnamese women, reflecting women's contributions to the economy as well as their continuing role as bearers and nurturers of children. Demographic concerns at the turn of the twenty-first century kept the state watchful. First, it saw population growth putting strains on resource production. In addition, the female population remained slightly higher than the male population, a universal worry in the demography arena. Still, women appeared to play an equal role in economic production, with the new movement toward export-orientated industrialization appearing to be female-led. Where socialist Vietnam could promise health, wealth and happiness in a utopian future, the economic transition saw them as necessary for building a politically stable and internationally competitive society. Market reforms of the late 1980s urged the Women's Union assume new responsibilities for developing educational programs that would promote well-being among the Vietnamese people. As economic structures shifted from state frameworks to individuals, so did contraceptive education (Truong et al. 2006; Gammeltoft 2001; UNDP 2002; UNESCO 1989; Pettus 2003).

3.7 Food Production and the Environment

By the turn of the twenty-first century, Vietnam's concerns over the disproportionate relationship between population growth and food production had intensified. In addition, its sharp trend toward urbanization (with nearly one quarter of Vietnamese living in metropolitan areas by 1999) meant that fewer people were able to produce their own food for consumption. Though there had developed a new examination and emphasis on food security, *Doi Moi* placed a higher value on producing foodstuffs for the global market, and the government was giving high priority to exports. Rice production was high, but critics warned that it would eventually be needed to feed the domestic population. In addition, mass production and exportation of coffee and shrimp placed increase demands on energy and other resources. Rapid economic growth and increased consumption resulted in greater income disparities and environmental damage.

In some cases, the introduction of cash crops resulted in short-term economic gains, but resulted in the destruction of forests. Forestry itself has not been sustainable and is resulting in rapid deforestation and land degradation. In both cases, poorer ethnic minorities lack the skills needed to compete in these kinds of agricultural production and generally in the changing market economy. Their situation is worsened with lesser access to education and health care (DiGregorio et al. 2003; Huy and Kendall 2003; Freeman 1994; Sikor and O'Rourke 1996).

Deforestation did not begin under *Doi Moi*, but its expansion has forced new attention to its impact on long-term development and the environment. In addition to supporting livelihoods for many Vietnamese, the forests are essential to protecting the environment. They maintain ecological health by limiting erosion, protecting watersheds, reducing flooding and providing habitats for wildlife. Since the 1980s the Vietnamese government has undertaken an ambitious reforestation program. Large-scale reforestation of the 1990s farmers were encouraged to plant tree and fruit crops to support the development of agroforestry strategies at times to the detriment of local tree planting movements. Subsequent programs emphasized improved forest management, and incorporated the input of local people (Kelly et al. 2001; Panayotou and Naqvi 1996; Ha 1993; Rambo et al. 1995).

Oxfam International is paying close attention to the issue of climate change and its potential effects on Vietnam. Such international organizations praise the Vietnamese government for meeting its Millennium Development Goal of poverty reduction, bringing more than one third of its population out of poverty by 2006 (Oxfam 2008). Still, they warn of remaining challenges that could be worsened by climate change. Even recent strides in alleviating poverty may be jeopardized by severe flooding and drought, compounded with long term threats of sea rise. Community-led initiatives have mobilized the local population in the area disaster risk management designed to reduce vulnerability include rescue drills in case of flooding and typhoons. Many of the poor living in the most threatened provinces live in poorly constructed housing, and cannot swim. In response, locals have organized rescue team training to prepare for saving their villages in case of emergency. More long term community-based planning efforts address the need for researching and planting drought resistant and flood resistant crops, and in areas where the potential for sea rise poses a threat, they are considering more salt-resistant crops (Oxfam 2008; DFID 2008; UNDP 2007; VARG 2006).

Of more immediate concern is the recent escalation in China's dam building projects on the Mekong River. The Mekong is estimated as the eighth most significant in the world in water volume when measured at its end in Vietnam, where it flows into the South China Sea. More than 50% of Vietnam's agricultural contribution to its Gross Domestic Product is generated in the Mekong Delta, most of which stems from rice growing. China's dam operation causes immediate and severe changes in water flow, affecting fish stocks, cargo travel, silt accumulation, and irrigation for the population living downstream. While some have argued that the Vietnamese may benefit from desalination in the delta through man-made floods, critics suggest the overall environmental destruction is far greater. Vietnam has been equally criticized for its construction and operation of the Yali Falls Dam on the Se San, a tributary of the Mekong which flows through Cambodia. Intended to generate electricity in advancing Vietnam's development and growing population, it has been operating with unannounced releases of water, resulting in the death of at least 39 Cambodians, and the disruption of traditional fishing and agriculture, particularly among Cambodian ethnic minorities. Plans for six additional dams along the Se San are underway (Osbourne 2004).

3.8 Minority Rights

Ethnic diversity has played a critical role in Vietnamese history, and some observers blame it for the failures of socialist land reform in the 1950s and economic collectivization at the end of the Second Indochina War. They argue that broad-based changes are best implemented among homogeneous populations, and that land reform and collectivization measures are often resisted by indigenous who are culturally and historically tied to land in specific regions and to cultivation practices unlike those encouraged by modernization. In addition, collectivization becomes problematic when imposed by forces refusing to acknowledge the power of ethnic differences. When these are compounded by forced migration, or resettlement programs, human security advocates begin to pay closer attention to minority rights.

Today the cultures and cultural practices of Vietnam's ethnic minorities are endangered for a number of reasons. First, decades of war placed the population in constant fear of violence and displacement, obstructing the natural progression of cultural activities. Though the national government has generally supported the protection of minorities' culture, local officials have been reluctant to enforce protection. Transitioning to an industrializing and urbanizing society has threatened cultural practices, and in particular traditional farming and village life. Finally, a more modern Vietnam tends to marginalize minority culture as something backward and outdated. This is true particularly among urban Vietnamese youth (Thanh 2001).

While globalization may have facilitated the address of minority rights transnationally, some blame the trend itself for influencing new standardization of culture that is encroaching on even remote areas of the world. In Vietnam, radical socioeconomic transformation was tied to modern nations abroad. Intensive farming and forestry are expanding into areas populated by minorities. Factories and mines are taking power from cottage industries. Industrial centers and hydroelectric power stations in the highlands, a trans-Vietnamese highway, and the Hoa Binh dam have uprooted minorities, and threatened the way of life of those who remain. While some argue that the economic changes are improving the material conditions of minorities as well as the general population, the two groups have not benefited equally. Just over half of the population of the uplands is ethnic Vietnamese. Yet, nearly all of the country's minority groups still live in the hills and mountainous regions, with ten million ethnic minorities living in the Highlands alone. Comparatively rapid population growth is taxing the environment in the uplands, leading to food shortages and nutritional deficiencies. Dislocation has created obstacles to adaptation while increasing resource depletion, poverty and lack of cultural identity. While population density is still relatively low, pressure on nutritional and other resources is high. More than 40% of the uplands population is under 14 years old. The government has supported family planning, and many women have accepted it. But population will continue to grow, perhaps doubling again in the next 20 years (Van 2001; Rambo and Jamieson 2003).

One of the clearest cases of disparity between ethnic minorities and the Viet population is in levels of access to health care. Because much of the minority population is spatially as well as culturally marginalized, they are often located great distances from modern health care facilities. But more importantly, the public health issues they face in rural areas differ from those living in urban areas. First, economic transformation has changed the diets of those who had traditionally depended on subsistence farming of rice, beans, fruits and vegetables, with income supplemented through cash crops such as rubber and black pepper. *Doi Moi* has supported expanded coffee production in highlands areas, diminishing access to locally-produced and nutritionally-dense foods. In addition, poor sanitation (latrines are available, but not often used) and lack of potable water has contributed to the spread of disease. With cooking fuel shortages in the countryside, relatively few are committed to boiling water before consumption (Barrett et al. 2001; Gellert 1995).

3.9 Unintended Consequences and Next Steps

The state had anticipated that *Doi Moi* would expand the economy in the countryside through increased foreign investment in rural development. Instead, the vast majority – around 90% – of foreign investment came primarily into the cities of Hanoi and Ho Chi Minh City. This rapid development spurred greater movement into these two cities, supporting the common image of Vietnam as a pole with a rice basket at each end. In previous decades, the North had succeeded to some extent in spatial control of the population, by restricting excessive flow into Hanoi, and incenting people to remain in rural areas through successful agricultural collectivization programs. The South took less control of population movement, and experienced a rapid growth primarily in Saigon (Ho Chi Minh City) with the introduction of improved infrastructure and communications. The United Nations predicts that rapid urbanization will continue (Kilgour and Drakakis-Smith 2002; McGee 1995).

Though foreign investment and a growing industrial sector have drawn large numbers of Vietnamese from the countryside, in many cases, those migrants have been left unemployed. When "ideal" jobs are unavailable, many opt to work in the informal economy where they are considerably underemployed. Planners and urban policy makers have found it difficult to keep up with the rapid growth, which has resulted in environmental problems and inadequate housing. Public health problems have expanded as increasingly large numbers of people are dwelling in single apartments, and development has put pressure on urban water supplies. Increased sewage and industrial liquid waste is overtaxing systems nearly 80 years old. Cases of water-borne diseases such as malaria and diarrhea are on the rise. Insufficient unemployment exacerbates a myriad of problems connected to standard of living and have contributed to a rise in crime and prostitution. In addition, periodic setbacks in the new market economy have brought extensive layoffs – a situation that is new to Vietnam. Still, the United Nations and master planners in Vietnam predict that the urban population will continue to grow (Kilgour and Drakakis-Smith 2002; Drakakis-Smith and Dixon 1995; Van Arkadie and Mallon 2003).

Unless every sector of Vietnam's infrastructure becomes privatized, many problems need to be addressed by the government – if not at the national level, then at the municipal level. But it is the voluntary associations who are increasing pressure to have something done. Beyond state population policies, particularly with regard to migration/spatial location and family planning/reproductive rights, a growing number of individuals are making choices they feel can protect them from want and fear. And when that is not possible, due to larger market forces, economic development and agribusiness, a growing number are organizing in order to challenge the government to take action. Historical circumstances have shaped the population dynamics which exist today. But the unique relationship between Vietnam's government and its people, and the expectation that individual rights should be maintained as well as should the social good, may position the country to meet these challenges in ways unknown in other regions of the world.

References

Amouyel, A. (2006). What is human security? *Revue de Securite Humaine/Human Security Journal, 1*, 10–23.
Annan, K. A. (2001). Towards a culture of peace: Letters to future generations. http://www.unesco.org/opi2/lettres/TextAnglais/AnnanE.html/. Accessed 24 Apr 2010.
Banister, J. (1993). *Vietnam population dynamics and prospects*. Berkeley: University of California/Institute of East Asian Studies.
Barrett, B., Ladinsky, J., & Volk, N. (2001). Village-based primary health care in the central highlands in Vietnam. *Journal of Community Health, 1*, 51–71.
Bich, P. B. (1999). *The Vietnamese family in change: The case of the Red River Delta*. Surrey: Curzon Press.
Breman, J. (1987). *The shattered image: Construction and deconstruction of the village in Colonial Asia*. Amsterdam: Centre for Asian Studies in Amsterdam.
Dang, A., Goldstein, S., & McNally, J. (1997). Internal migration and development in Vietnam. *International Migration Review, 2*, 312–337.

den Boer, M., & de Wild, J. (Eds.). (2008). *The viability of human security*. Amsterdam: Amsterdam University Press.
Department for International Development. (2008). *Vietnam: Country assistance plan*. London: DFID.
Desbarats, J. (1987). Population redistribution in the Socialist Republic of South Vietnam. *Population and Development Review, 1*, 43–76.
DiGregorio, M. A., Rambo, T., & Yangisawa, M. (2003). Clean, green, and beautiful: Environment and development under the renovation economy. In H. V. Luong (Ed.), *Postwar Vietnam: Dynamics of a transforming society*. Singapore/College Park: Institute of Southeast Asian Studies and Lanham/Rowman & Littlefield Publishers.
Drakakis-Smith, D. W., & Dixon, C. J. (1995). Sustainable urbanization in Vietnam. *Geoforum, 1*, 21–38.
Freeman, D. B. (1994). *Doi Moi* policy and the small-enterprise boom in Ho Chi Minh City, Vietnam. *Geographical Review, 2*, 178–197.
Gammeltoft, T. (1999). *Women's bodies, women's worries: Health and family planning in a Vietnamese rural community*. Surrey: Curzon Press.
Gammeltoft, T. (2001). Faithful, heroic, resourceful: Changing images of women in Vietnam. In Kleinen John (Ed.), *Vietnamese society in transition: The daily politics of reform and change*. Amsterdam: Het Spinhuis.
Gellert, G. A. (1995). The influence of market economics on primary health care in Vietnam. *Journal of the American Medical Association, 273*, 1498–1502.
Goodkind, D. M. (1989). Vietnam's new fertility policy. *Population and Development Review, 1*, 169–172.
Gough, K. (1990). *Political economy in Vietnam*. Berkeley: Folklore Institute.
Gray, M. L. (1999). Creating civil society? The emergence of NGOs in Vietnam. *Development and Change, 4*, 693–713.
Ha, N. Q. (1993). *Renovation of strategies for forestry development until 2000*. Hanoi: Ministry of Forestry.
Hardy, A. (2003). *Red hills: Migrants and the state in the highlands of Vietnam*. Honolulu: University of Hawaii Press.
Hickey, G. C. (1982). *Ethnohistory of the Vietnamese central highlands*. New Haven: Yale University Press.
Hickey, G. C. (1993). *Shattered world: Adaptation and survival among Vietnam's highland peoples during the Vietnam war*. Philadelphia: University of Pennsylvania Press.
Hirschman, C., Preston, S., & Loi, V. M. (1995). Vietnamese casualties during the American war. *Population and Development Review, 21*, 783–812.
Hoa, N. T. (1993). *Female workers at Thanh Cong Textile company in the renovation process*. Paper presented at the Seminar on Family and the Condition of Women in Society. Ho Chi Minh City.
Kaldor, M. (2007). *Human security: Reflections on globalization and intervention*. Cambridge: Polity Press.
Kelly, P. M., Lien, T. V., Hien, H. M., Ninh, N. H., & Adger, W. N. (2001). Managing environmental change in Vietnam. In W. N. Adger, P. M. Kelly, & N. H. Ninh (Eds.), *Living with environmental change: Social vulnerability, adaptation and resilience in Vietnam* (pp. 35–58). London: Routledge.
Kilgour, A., & Drakakis-Smith, D. (2002). The changing economic and urban situation in Vietnam. In P. P. Masina (Ed.), *Rethinking development in East Asia: From illusory miracle to economic crisis*. Surrey/Copenhagen: Curzon Press and Copenhagen/Nordic Institute of Asian Studies.
Knudsen, L. M. (2006). *Reproductive rights in a global context: South Africa, Uganda, Peru, Denmark, United States, Vietnam, Jordan*. Nashville: Vanderbilt University Press.
Koh, D. (2001a). State-society relations in Vietnam: Strong or weak state? In D. Singh, A. L. Smith, & C. S. Yue (Eds.), *Southeast Asian Affairs* (pp. 369–386). Singapore: ISEAS.
Koh, D. (2001b). The politics of a divided society and Parkinson's State in Vietnam. *Contemporary Southeast Asia, 3*, 533–551.

Lewallen, J. (1971). *Ecology of devastation: Indochina*. Baltimore: Penguin.
Lizee, P. P. (2002). Human security in Vietnam, Laos, and Cambodia. *Contemporary Southeast Asia, 3*, 509–527.
Luong, Hy V. (2003). *Postwar Vietnam: Dynamics of a transforming society*. Singapore/Lanham: Institute of Southeast Asian Studies/Rowman & Littlefield Publishers.
McGee, T. G. (1995). The urban future of Vietnam. *Third World Planning Review, 3*, 253–277.
McRae, R., & Huberts, D. (Eds.). (2001). *Human security and the new diplomacy: Protecting people, promoting peace*. Montreal: McGill Queen's University Press.
Osbourne, M. (2004). *River at risk: The Mekong and the water politics of China and Southeast Asia*. Sydney: Lowy Institute for International Policy.
Oxfam International. (2008). *Vietnam: Climate change, adaptation and poor people, a report for Oxfam*. Hanoi: Oxfam International.
Panayotou, T., & Naqvi, N. (1996). Case study for Vietnam. In D. Reed (Ed.), *Structural adjustment, the environment, and sustainable development* (pp. 263–296). London: Earthscan Publications.
Pettus, A. (2003). *Between sacrifice and desire: National identity and the governing of femininity in Vietnam*. New York: Routledge.
Rambo, A. T., & Jamieson, N. L. (2003). Upland areas, ethnic minorities, and development. In Hy V. Luong (Ed.), *Postwar Vietnam: Dynamics of a transforming society* (pp. 139–170). Singapore/Lanham: Institute of Southeast Asian Studies/Rowman & Littlefield Publishers.
Rambo, A. T., Reed, R. R., Le Cuc, T., & DeGregorio, M. R. (Eds.). (1995). *The challenges of highland development in Vietnam*. Honolulu: East-West Center.
Robinson, W. C. (1998). *Terms of refuge: The Indochinese exodus & the international response*. London: Zed Books.
Salemink, O. (2003). One country, many journeys. In H. Van Nguyen & L. Kendall (Eds.), *Vietnam: Journeys of body, mind and spirit* (pp. 20–51). Berkeley/New York/Hanoi: University of California Press/American Museum of Natural History/Vietnam Museum of Ethnology.
Sen, G. (2006). Reproductive rights and gender justice in the neo-conservative shadow. In W. Truoung & A. Chhachhi (Eds.), *Engendering human security: Feminist perspectives*. London: Zed Books.
Shapiro, D. (1996). Women's employment, education, fertility, and family planning in Vietnam: An economic perspective. In B. Kathleen (Ed.), *Vietnam's women in transition*. New York: St. Martin's Press.
Sikor, T. O., & O'Rourke, D. (1996). Economic and environmental dynamics of reform in Vietnam. *Asian Survey, 6*, 601–617.
Stocking, G. W. (Ed.). (1991). *Colonial situations: Essays on contextualization of ethnographic knowledge*. Madison: University of Wisconsin Press.
Tadjbakhsh, S., & Chenoy, A. M. (2007). *Human security, concepts and implications*. New York: Routledge.
Thanh, T. N. (2001). The intangible culture of the Vietnamese minorities: Questions and answers. In O. Salemink (Ed.), *Viet Nam's cultural diversity: Approaches to preservation* (pp. 121–126). Paris: United Nations Educational, Scientific and Cultural Organization.
Truong, T.-D., Wieringa, S., & Chhachhi, A. (Eds.). (2006). *Engendering human security: Feminist perspectives*. London: Zed Books.
U.S. Congress. Senate. Committee on the Judiciary. (15, 25, and 30 April 1975). *Indochina Evacuation and Refugee Problems, Part II: The Evacuation. Hearings before the Subcommittee to Investigate Problems Connected with Refugees and Escapees*. Washington, D.C.: U.S. Government Printing Office.
United Nations Children's Fund. (2001). *Children on the edge: Protecting children from sexual exploitation and trafficking in East Asia and the Pacific*. Bangkok: UNICEF.
United Nations Development Programme. (1994). *Human development report*. New York: UNDP, Oxford University Press.
United Nations Development Programme. (2002). *Gender differences in the transitional economy of Vietnam*. Hanoi: UNDP.

United Nations Development Programme. (2007). *Terms of reference for technical assistance to conduct the eleventh PEP case-study: Linkage of poverty and climate change.* Hanoi: UNDP.

United Nations Educational, Scientific and Cultural Organisation Regional Office. (1989). *The status of women in Vietnam.* Bangkok: UNESCO.

Van Arkadie, B., & Mallon, R. (2003). *Viet Nam: A transition tiger?* Canberra: Asia Pacific Press at the Australian National University.

Van Dang, N. (2001). Preservation and development of the cultural heritage. In O. Salemink (Ed.), *Viet Nam's cultural diversity: Approaches to preservation* (pp. 33–62). Paris: United Nations Educational, Scientific and Cultural Organization.

Van Huy, N., & Kendall, L. (Eds.). (2003). *Journeys of body, mind and spirit.* Berkeley/New York/Hanoi: University of California Press/American Museum of Natural History/Vietnam Museum of Ethnology.

Van Luong, B. (1959). The role of friendly nations. In R. A. Lindholm (Ed.), *Vietnam: The first five years, an international symposium* (pp. 48–53). East Lansing: Michigan State University Press.

Vietnam General Statistical Office. (1991). *Statistical data of Vietnam: 1986–1991.* Hanoi: Statistical Publishing House.

Vulnerability and Adaptation Research Group. (2006). *Linking climate change adaptation and disaster risk management for sustainable poverty reduction, Vietnam country study.* European Union: VARG.

Wiesner, L. A. (1988). *Victims and survivors: Displaced persons and other war Victims in Vietnam, 1954–1975.* New York: Westport.

Chapter 4
Irregular Migration in Thailand: New Possibilities for Anti-Trafficking and Development Programs

Jennryn Wetzler

4.1 Introduction

Despite the differing definitions and efforts addressing it,[1] the notion of human trafficking unites an increasingly globalized set of risks. Human trafficking is inextricably linked to a wide variety of social vulnerabilities, including the spread of HIV/AIDS, sexual violence, poverty and unequal wages, gender inequality, lack of access to health care, education, and land resources. The processes and effects of human trafficking jeopardize humans' economic, food, personal, health, and community securities: five out of the seven essential securities delineated in the United Nation's 1994 Development Report. Despite wide-ranging and related risks, efforts to combat trafficking tend to be narrower in focus. Because these ongoing vulnerabilities are perpetuated by limited policies, enforcement, and protection efforts, they easily blossom into wider social threats. Problems of gendered poverty, lack of family planning, and the spread of HIV/AIDS or STDs, once confined to the vulnerable populations of irregular migrants, spread longitudinally through generations. Vulnerabilities arising from irregular migration are inextricably linked to human trafficking issues. With the example of Thailand, this study evaluates the broader vulnerabilities and exploitative conditions of irregular migration to the sex and labor trades. Discussion suggests that the dominant trafficking paradigm in effect is often ahistorical and non-culturally specific, ignoring the global economic pulls, while classifying people as either victims or traffickers. The trafficking paradigm

---

[1] Given the variety of sources addressing human trafficking, defining the phenomenon takes different forms. The two most common definitions come from the United Nations and the US. The US definition is accessible in the Trafficking in Persons Report. The UN's "Protocol to Prevent, Suppress and Punish Trafficking In Persons" provides a background for comparison for US policies.

J. Wetzler (✉)
Department of State, Bureau of International Information Programs, Washington, DC, USA
e-mail: wetzlerjm@state.gov

highlights a small section within the larger range of migration and labor exploitation and only a limited time-span of exploitation (during transit and at the destination) to fight. Remaining beyond the paradigm's range of focus are the extensive forms of insecurity actually inextricable from the insecurities associated with conventional human trafficking. The time-span of exploitation exists before and after the duration of "trafficking" or transit to Thailand, and migration is more often voluntary.

This study asserts that Thailand has made considerable progress in addressing human trafficking concerns over the last two decades, providing model anti-trafficking policies for the global community. While some of the policies remain unrealized, the Thai government has engaged in many effective anti-trafficking initiatives, collaborating with non-government organizations (NGOs).

Second, while Thai anti-trafficking policies produce many successes in their scope of expertise, many larger migration concerns remain unaddressed. These concerns are inextricably related to trafficking concerns yet exist beyond the scope of anti-trafficking policies. Furthermore, despite considerable anti-trafficking efforts, Thailand arguably approaches broader migration concerns through traditional law enforcement and still hosts equally considerable human security vulnerabilities among trafficked populations or those vulnerable to trafficking. However, if anti-trafficking efforts collaborate more closely with community development efforts, they could alleviate a wider range of trafficking concerns. Thailand's indirect development efforts, such as improving access to education, income generation projects, promotion of condom use and family planning campaigns, and empowering vulnerable populations, have significantly improved defenses against trafficking and its ills. Development efforts have been effective because people do not have to qualify as trafficking victims to receive necessary support. Furthermore, development efforts tend to address the contexts impelling irregular migration and the agency of the people traditionally considered victims, rather than emphasizing the limited time-span of exploitation to fight and people to save.

Using the dominant paradigm of trafficking alone affords a myopic lens to alleviate the continuum of vulnerabilities of forced and unforced migration into Thailand's sex and labor trades. Using the case of street children, this study asserts that addressing these remaining vulnerabilities requires integrating anti-trafficking efforts with development projects; the combination could better combat vulnerabilities entangled with trafficking, providing holistic problem solving to the amalgamated problems.

4.2 Migration Vulnerabilities and Human Insecurities

Before understanding Thailand's anti-trafficking efforts, one must first understand the context of labor migration and the resultant human insecurities. Our contemporary era of technological, cultural, and economic globalization has increased the venues for people's migration. Increased global migration has become both a symbol of freedom and a reminder of global insecurities.

Thailand's geographic location and its dominant economy in Southeast Asia make it a source, transit, and destination country for trafficking and labor migration. Thailand holds social "push" and "pull" factors of its main cities' social and financial capital, impelling migration to and within national borders. Migrants from neighboring countries and within national borders flock to Bangkok, Chiang Mai, and Pattaya, among other cities and border towns, looking for work or merely curious to see the world beyond their local villages.

While migration offers unparalleled possibilities for most people, many undocumented migrants face a different reality of increasingly limited options. Migrants often cross national borders in search of work without the required visa and passport documentation—often unable to afford the financial costs or processing time. Impelling their migration are common vulnerabilities, including gender inequalities, poverty, political situations of instability, or the incursion of extensive human rights abuses. Continued vulnerabilities extending beyond the traditional anti-trafficking paradigm's focus include migrants' limited access to land, political representation, heath care, and education, and child migrants' particular experiences.

Without traditional documentation and means for getting work, migrants follow the unlawful trajectory of undocumented migration by default. Often they must avoid traditional law enforcement, and lacking legal protection or representation makes them increasingly vulnerable to exploitative conditions at work. Despite these vast experiences of exploitation, many migrants still chose Thai labor and sex work and repeated migration. While many of the irregular migrants are not forced to migrate, their experience of exploitation remains unrecognized. One easily recognizes how vulnerable irregular migrants like Burmese refugees are to the risks associated with trafficking and forced labor, yet very few of the populations qualify as "trafficked."

The trafficking paradigm directs a spotlight of attention on a sliver of the larger process of irregular migration patterns, focusing on irregular migrants' forced or coerced experiences in transit and at their destinations for labor. Like a searchlight overexposing one section of a crowd, the trafficking paradigm isolates forced migration and labor from its surrounding context and the momentum impelling it.

4.3 The Spotlight on Trafficking

To understand human trafficking in Thailand, an understanding of US and Thai definitions of trafficking as well as Thailand's anti-trafficking efforts is necessary.

4.3.1 The US and Thai Trafficking Definitions

The US arguably leads funding and enforcement of global anti-trafficking initiatives (see US Department of State's Office to Monitor and Combat Trafficking in Persons 2010). As a result, most countries, including Thailand, publically recognize

US-determined guidelines for anti-trafficking measures. "Human trafficking" has become a "buzz word" in a variety of international development efforts; it has origins in the United Nations Protocol to Prevent, Suppress and Punish Trafficking in Persons and the US Department of State's Office to Monitor and Combat Trafficking in Persons. The US Office to Monitor and Combat Trafficking in Persons states that trafficking is:

> "A) sex trafficking in which a commercial sex act is induced by force, fraud, or coercion, on in which the person induced to perform such an act has not attained 18 years of age; or B) the recruitment, harboring, transportation, provision, or obtaining of a person for labor services, through the use of force, fraud, or coercion for the purpose of subjection to involuntary servitude, peonage, debt bondage, or slavery". (US Department of State's Trafficking in Persons Report 2008)

The Trafficking in Persons (TIP) reports maintain the assumption that trafficked and exploited people are *victims*, evidenced in the language used to describe vulnerable populations. In addition to solidifying the label of victimhood for trafficked people in discourse, the Office to Monitor and Combat Trafficking in Persons collaborates with anti-trafficking policies, which further reinforce these definitions and preconceptions.[2]

The Thai law similarly addresses trafficking by defining the activity as doing any of the following for the purposes of exploitation[3]:

> (1) procuring, buying, selling, vending, bringing from or sending to, detaining or confining, harboring, or receiving any person, by means of the threat or use of force, abduction, fraud, deception, abuse of power, or of the giving money or benefits to achieve the consent of a person having control over another person in allowing the offender to exploit the person under his control; or (2) procuring, buying, selling, vending, bringing from or sending to, detaining or confining, harboring, or receiving a child; is guilty of trafficking in persons. (Trafficking in Persons Act B.E. 2551. 2008: Chap. 1 Sect. 6)

According to Thai and US guidelines, a person under 18 years old may be considered "trafficked" regardless of the question of force or coercion. According to the Thai conception of trafficking, smugglers assisting undocumented migrants to their destination arguably categorize as traffickers.[4] While Thai and US guidelines present a broad area of focus for anti-trafficking efforts, these policies face considerable criticisms.

---

[2] The US Congress's Trafficking Victims' Protection Act (TVPA) corresponded to the TIP reports. The TVPA faces criticism for victimizing trafficked people as well as prostitutes. According to the Council on Foreign Relations Symposium on Human Trafficking, this definition is unclear, creating funding vulnerabilities for those involved in multiple anti-trafficking programs. The reauthorized act, or TVPRA, prevents human rights and public health nongovernmental organizations (NGOs) from comprehensively serving all trafficking victims. The reauthorization of the TVPA in 2003, for example, prohibited anti-trafficking funding from the State Department for any organization promoting, supporting, or advocating the legalization or practice of prostitution. (Global Fund for Women 2006).

[3] According to Thailand's Anti-Trafficking In Persons Act B.E. 2551 (2008), exploitation is defined as "seeking benefits from the prostitution, production or distribution of pornographic materials, other forms of sexual exploitation, slavery, causing another person to be a beggar, forced labour or service, coerced removal of organs for the purpose of trade, or any other similar practices resulting in forced extortion, regardless of such person's consent".

[4] The UN's Protocol to Prevent, Suppress and Punish Trafficking in Persons details a similar definition of trafficking to Thailand.

At the same time, one cannot conflate the definitions of trafficking with subsequent anti-trafficking efforts—rather one should be wary of the limited trajectory these definitions place on anti-trafficking efforts (LSCW 2005b: 87).

The US trafficking paradigm and resultant anti-trafficking efforts face criticisms concerning migrant vulnerabilities to which the paradigm is not sensitive. By isolating trafficking from the rest of migration, anti-trafficking policies risk oversimplifying the roles of traffickers, recruiters, and workers. US policies' roles for victims and perpetrators do not allow for more ambiguous situations, such as when people in the sex trade later become traffickers. Trafficking is not a static phenomenon,[5] nor is it sensitive to gendered differences.[6] The term "trafficking" often becomes a gendered issue, reenforcing gender stereotypes about agency and victimhood. Female migrants are labeled as trafficking victims, while male migrants willfully travel with help from smugglers. Finally, the catch phrase also deters the focus from the interrelated and entrenched forms of exploitation, which exist in irregular migration outside of trafficking.[7]

In particular, isolating "human trafficking victims" as separate from the rest of the irregular migrant population is cited as counterproductive to limiting overall trafficking-related insecurities.[8] Many anti-trafficking organizations impose policies and "rehabilitation programs" upon the irregular migrants, based on assumptions of helplessness. International anti-trafficking organizations such as International Justice Mission face criticism for past brothel raids, which force sex workers to move to shelters with religious rehabilitation programs opposing their previous beliefs or repatriate them to the countries from which they deliberately left. Brothel raids in general have been criticized for ignoring the trafficked persons' needs (Unmacht 2003: 1). Finally, many international anti-trafficking efforts may traumatize trafficked people through additional measures of interrogation for prosecution.[9] While there are undoubtedly victims, the model of assuming victimhood curtails anti-trafficking efforts' potential effectiveness and limits the number of possibilities

---

[5] UNICEF (2003, p. 7) cites that trafficking is not a static phenomenon—rather it exists along a continuum of migration causes.

[6] LSCW reminds readers that the experience of irregular migration and trafficking is different for men and women. While Cambodian men accumulate debt to pay smugglers in the source province, Cambodian women accumulate debt to the employer at the destination, or through debt bondage (2005b: 46).

[7] LSCW states that "trafficking in Cambodia, as in other countries, has become synonymous with brothel-based sexual exploitation of women and children, forced and coerced to migrate by unscrupulous traffickers or known persons. This has resulted in a major focus in this particular component of trafficking, meaning that other forms of trafficking have largely been ignored, e.g. trafficking into domestic work, marriage, fishing, fish processing and other industries. Furthermore, it has lead to a grave misconception that men migrate and women are trafficked…" (2005a: 13).

[8] Pearson et al. (2006, p. xxvi) of the International Labor Organization (ILO) cite that, "Despite the plethora of organizations supposedly working against trafficking in Thailand, organizations do not seem to be effectively targeting or assisting migrants in these sectors in these geographical areas… with the exception of the NGOs who facilitated this research".

[9] Anti-trafficking efforts can include repeated interrogation concerning circumstances of trauma such as rape or assault for prosecution purposes.

to interrupt cycles of vulnerabilities. Policies blanketing the variety of these irregular migrants' experiences with the single policy to address human trafficking cannot accurately respond to the differences and complexity in migration patterns.

4.3.2 Thailand's Governmental and Legal Anti-Trafficking Efforts

Fortunately, the Royal Thai government has worked to address the complexity of human trafficking, as well as its reputation with the US Office to Monitor and Combat Trafficking in Persons, through a number of different channels, i.e., collaboration with NGO's, international NGO's, establishing Memorandums of Understanding (MOU) with regional neighbors about labor migrants, and through national development and legal initiatives. Thailand has ratified 14 International Labor Organization conventions protecting the rights of child workers (Pearson et al. 2006: 6). While Thailand has responded to the US "Trafficking In Persons" global standards, the Royal Thai government also acknowledges situational challenges particular to Thailand.

While the US TIP report defines trafficked persons as victims,[10] Thailand seems to officially recognize the agency of irregular migrants in several policies.[11] Thailand also hosts a variety (and large quantity) of rehabilitation centers and programs to empower trafficked people.[12] The Thai Health Ministry, e.g., has created welfare and vocational training centers for women, training approximately 7,000 women and girls per year.[13] Thailand might well offer the most number of reintegration and rehabilitation programs and assistance for trafficking survivors worldwide.

While Thailand hosts governmental and legal support structures, it also host a number of tangential development initiatives, which actually help anti-trafficking goals. Unlike the dominant anti-trafficking agenda, these programs do not view trafficked people as victims and often address the larger contexts of exploitation before a specific time frame of forced migration or labor. Thailand legally recognizes the paramount challenges poverty (and its migration and labor byproducts) poses to its

---

[10] According to Article 3 of the UN's Protocol to Prevent and Suppress Trafficking in Persons, "The consent of a trafficked victim is deemed irrelevant where any of the means described in the definition is present. If the victim is a child (below 18 years old), the recruitment, transportation, transfer, harboring or receipt of a child for the purpose of exploitation will be considered 'trafficking in persons' even if it does not involve any of the means described above".

[11] Thailand's Immigration Act B.E. 2522 (1979) provides example.

[12] Other initiatives include the Kredakkan Protection and Occupation Development Centre in Nonthaburi Province, the Reception Home for boys in the Nonthaburi Province, the Narisawat Protection and Occupation Development Center in Nakhon Ratchasima Province, the Development and Education Program for Daughters and Communities Centre (DEPDC) in Chiang Rai and the Child Protection and Development Center (CPDC) in Pattaya.

[13] For further details on trainings, see the Coordinated Mekong Ministerial Initiative against Trafficking (COMMIT) (2004).

human security and the need for people-centered development.[14] The goals for people-centered development provide methods to actualize the anti-trafficking agenda's ideals; yet, most development efforts remain categorically separate.

The Thai government also acknowledges the complexity of irregular and undocumented migration in variety of laws. Exemplifying this, Thailand's Labor Protection Act provides a good basis for workers' protections, despite the fact that certain categories of workers are exempt from protection. Those categories exclude the arguably more exploited trades such as domestic work, fishing, and agriculture (Pearson et al. 2006: xxvii). Those laws elicit arguably limited results for most migrants.

Despite the seeming open-mindedness in its legal and policy frameworks, Thailand's dominant method for addressing migration concerns is through the traditional means of law enforcement. The Thai law enforcement faces considerable criticism for exploiting undocumented migrants and accepting bribes for illegal issues ranging from border control to child sex tourism (see Immigration and Refugee Board of Canada 2007). A further challenge Thailand's law enforcement poses is within the sex trade; because prostitution is illegal in Thailand, many sex establishments must also bribe policemen; sex workers are also subject to police rape. Additionally, prostitutes cannot register for any system of regulation, recognition for oversight, or work-related health-care coverage (Asia Watch 1993: 75–77).

Finally, while Thailand legally recognizes the impetus for migration, its only lawful options for irregular migrants are repatriation or criminalization; both choices do not target root causes of migration and can cement vulnerabilities. Because the majority of people involved in Thailand's sex and labor trades migrated deliberately for work, removing them from their income sources creates financial instability and further entrenches the indebtedness that impelled their migration in the first place. Unregistered women and girls from neighboring countries who have willfully migrated or been trafficked into the sex industry remain targets for arrest and deportation, despite the provisions in Thailand's memorandums of understanding (MOUs) with neighboring countries (like Cambodia) warding against such actions (LSCW 2005b: 60). Clearly, there is a difference between the ideals promoted in Thai policies and the reality for migrants.

Thailand's legal and governmental efforts focus beyond conventional limits of the human trafficking paradigm. Thai policies are well positioned to help a wider range of interrelated migration problems. Thailand hosts extensive rehabilitation, reintegration, and empowerment initiatives for trafficked people. Yet, the methods for enforcing official efforts addressing migration still lie with law enforcement. Many migrants still face police exploitation of their vulnerable positions, e.g., rape, robbery, and enforced bribery (See Asia Watch 1993). Furthermore, Thailand faces the threat of sanctions if it does not conform to the annual US TIP's reports' anti-trafficking norms.

---

[14]The Ministerial Meetings Concept Paper on "Human Agenda: Partnership for Human Security" demonstrates the legal recognition of poverty and migration's human security challenges. (Human Security Network, 2009).

4.4 Beyond the Scope of Anti-Trafficking Efforts

Rather than simple divisions between trafficked victims and irregular migrants, or the timeframe of exploitation in travel and work abroad, there seems to be a spectrum of exploitation and agency among actors in the process of migration. The majority of migrants struggle to relocate, and reports such as the ILO's suggest migrants not see themselves as passively victimized or forced by processes of migration (Pearson et al. 2006: 6). Often, the situation of exploitation in Thailand is an improvement over the greater exploitation or conditions of poverty or political instability migrants face in their home countries. Anti-trafficking efforts must address source vulnerabilities impelling migration.

The following examples detail the interrelated vulnerabilities and exploitation migrants experience, some of which qualify as trafficking, and many of which remain classified as irregular migration. No matter what the classification, exploitative experiences overrule undocumented migrants' human rights and limit avenues of free choice.

4.4.1 Poverty and Unstable States Impelling Migration

Migrants often choose Thailand, given the country's relative economic prosperity and political stability in the region. Many of Thailand's sex workers willingly come from impoverished homes in neighboring countries or from Thailand's Esarn province. For Burmese migrants coming from the dictatorial military regime of Burma, life in Thailand is better. Simon Baker relates his Burmese interviewees' claims that even conditions in a sex establishment on the Thai border can be better than conditions in Burma (Baker 2007: 25). Most people choose to migrate, but the resulting conditions they face in transit and at their destination vary. For anti-trafficking efforts to best address the exploitation in these cases, the efforts must understand the reasons migrants are moving in the first place.

4.4.2 Gender Norms and Gendered Poverty Impelling Migration

Apart from the exploitative conditions associated with poverty and political regimes, unequal gender norms in home countries also impel migration. According to the Legal Support for Children and Women (LSCW), gendered migration to Thailand remains inextricable from women's role in traditional Southeast Asian society.[15]

---

[15] Women's worth is contingent upon their virginity; girls who have been raped, lost their virginity to a boyfriend and migrated with a broken heart, or women who have been tricked into working in a brothel often "decide" to leave Cambodia to work in the sex industry. Additionally, work in the sex industry is considerably more lucrative than other jobs in the service industries, factory, or farm work (LSCW, 2005a).

Gender inequalities also limit girls' continued access to education, which, in turn, limits future employment and empowerment possibilities. Traditional female responsibilities coupled with impoverishment make girls drop out of school and enter the work force earlier. The lack of education and impoverishment increases girls' vulnerabilities to trafficking and prostitution. LSCW cites that, "Good women are not supposed to have sexual feelings, desires, or knowledge about sex, thus sexual knowledge is prohibited, creating vulnerabilities – particularly for young girls when they leave home and migrate" (2005b: 22). Cultural values of women's sexual naivety coupled with women's lack of education and early entrance in the work force makes them particularly likely to seek income in the sex trade. Exemplifying this, the vast majority of sex workers in Cambodia's Koh Kong province are functionally illiterate (LSCW 2005b: 24). Cultural norms arguably narrow many migrant women's choices to prostitution, while some chose it despite alternatives.

While many female migrants enter the sex trade lacking awareness or access to other financial possibilities, one cannot assume that the majority of sex workers or other laborers are forced. Responding to *todtan bunkhan*, a Thai tradition of indebtedness or gratitude, many children must pay to their parents; daughters often enter the sex trade as the fastest route to pay off their families' debts (Baker 2000: 19). Simon Baker finds evidence of this in Mai Sai, stating that, "All of the sex-workers in Mae Sai I talked to had decided to undertake this work. They were not sold, trafficked, or tricked into prostitution" (2000: 2). Research and informal conversations with sex workers confirmed that many *chose* to work in Pattaya in the sex trade (See Cahn 2009). While one cannot claim the majority of sex and labor workers have been trafficked in Pattaya, many chose sex jobs or high-risk jobs because they offer the highest pay.[16] Given the very limited economic options within mainstream professions, many people chose the sex trade; some out of economic necessity and some out of a material desire for the higher wages. The average wages in Pattaya's service industries range between 3,500 Baht and 6,500 Baht or between 99 and 185 USD per month. Women in the sex trade claimed to make between 15 and 57 USD and more per night.[17]

Regardless of women's reasons for entering the sex trade, gender inequalities, lack of awareness and education, and conditions of poverty lead to their greater exploitation and sexual violence in sex work, as well as other labor trades. LSCW cites "the causes of trafficking are applicable to both men and women, but women are faced with an additional vulnerability that stems from social discriminatory practices" (LSCW 2005b).[18] For example, Cambodian women and girls, who often

---

[16]Further exemplifying the free choice in the sex trade, the mamasans, or older women, in Pattaya managing the sex trade in a bar or entertainment place facilitate business for sex workers rather than forcibly pimping them to customers.

[17]Prices are based on a 35.22 Baht/1 USD exchange rate of February 14, 2009. For similar price quotes, see McGeown (2007).

[18]LSCW cites discriminatory practices particular to Cambodian women and girls, but the cultural example applies to broader Southeast Asian gender migration patterns as well (2005b: 14).

work in the worst forms of labor in Thailand and at home, reflect their low status in Cambodian society (LSCW 2005b: 14).

Without efforts addressing gender equality, education, equal wages, and increased income possibilities, large populations of women and young girls remain at a heightened risk of being trafficked into the sex trade. Yet, the dominant anti-trafficking paradigm does not include gender equality training or education for origin communities (in community-sensitive terms) (LSCW 2005b: 28).

4.4.3 Additional Vulnerabilities

Aside from the circumstances in the communities from which they originate, most irregular migrants face conditions of exploitation during their migration and work as well. Burmese refugees and hill tribe people experience extreme challenges during migration and work. Women's experiences are often more extreme. The Physicians for Human Rights (PHR) reports that at least one million Burmese are living in Thailand, and the vast majorities are undocumented migrants. "[They] often must find the resources to pay bribes to authorities on both sides of the border to avoid detention; job brokers or other types of smugglers may facilitate this passage, and often a debt is owed" (PHR 2004: 2). PHR reports that as undocumented migrants, many women and girls have been trafficked by police and border and immigration officials, who enjoy "virtual impunity in Thailand, despite a highly praised national legal framework and prioritization of the issue by the current Thai government" (PHR 2004: 3). Additionally, the threat of deportation often keeps women in extremely exploitative conditions (PHR 2004: 2). According to the PHR, "women and girls trafficked into the sex industry suffer particularly harsh and endangering abuse: beatings, sexual assault, and unsafe sex practices by traffickers, commercial sex venue owners, clients, [etc.]" (PHR 2004: 3). Many of these Burmese receive little or no pay and endure dangerous forced labor, physical confinement, sexual abuse, employers confiscating essential documentation, and repeated trafficking (PHR 2004: 3). Finally, women are more often responsible for children. The case of Burmese refugees in Thailand represents one end of the spectrum of trafficking and migration but provides good example. Aside from gendered differences in migration, the majority of all Burmese refugees categorize as irregular migrants, with no legal rights or assistance such as that provided to trafficked people.[19]

Once at their destination, irregular migrants often do not qualify for legal support afforded to trafficked people yet face the same human insecurities associated with trafficking, i.e., exploitation by law enforcement, including robbing migrants, lack of representation in decision-making bodies, as well as limited or no access to health

---

[19]The vast majority of Burmese refugees and hill tribe people are denied refugee status. To qualify for refugee status in Thai law, Burmese refugees must be able to demonstrate the immediate threat, from which they flee, among other factors.

care, land rights, legal rights, or education (ibid: 2). Migrants also face continued sexual violence, gender inequalities, poverty, and unequal wages (LSCW 2005b: 21). The International Labor Organization's 2006 study of almost 400 of Thailand's laborers found that on fishing boats, 20% of males claimed they were "forced to work" and were 15–17 years old. Sixty percent of live-in domestic workers were not allowed to leave the house for recreation or receive visitors, and 82% worked more than 12 h per day. Almost half of the laborers in the fishing industry worked more than 12 h per day as well.[20] While each of these cases exemplifies exploitation at the work destination, some cases do not qualify as trafficking per se.

One of the main constraints for migrants' choices and vulnerabilities to future exploitation is their lack of personal identification and documentation. Once Burmese women and girls enter Thailand without work or residency documentation, they face heightened discrimination and human rights violations. Lack of identification for hill tribe communities limits their ability to buy land, open bank accounts for example. Baker asserts that, "It creates poverty, limits education and increases the risk of children becoming victims of child prostitution" (2000: 23). According to PHR research, "stateless hill tribe women or girls are afforded long-term shelter, but denial of citizenship [which] limits their opportunities for education, work or independent living, and they end up in a kind of limbo in state custody" (2004: 3). Clearly the Burmese and hill tribe populations' vulnerabilities are similar—especially the women's experience; addressing those vulnerabilities requires an equally connected approach, sensitive to the gendered differences. These heightened risks and insecurities pose greater threats to the larger community, e.g., entrenched poverty and the spread of HIV/AIDS.

4.4.4 *The Particular Case of Street Children*

One of the often overlooked populations facing particular vulnerabilities is that of street children. Without alternative guidance or education available, family structure or lawful possibilities for employment, or fluency in Thai (for some), street life reinforces children's high-risk behaviors. Street children are particularly susceptible to the sex trade.

Trafficking researchers targeting street children estimate that Pattaya hosts about 1,500–2,000 homeless and impoverished children per year (Personal communication, January 18, 2008a, Conversations with a representative from the Pattaya Orphanage). Children, migrating from Thailand's Northeast provinces, Cambodia, Burma, Laos, and Vietnam, search for work with family members or alone. Options for legal work for children below 18 are limited. Thai labor laws stipulate children aged 15 and older are eligible to work in limited settings—non-hazardous work environments between the hours of 6 am and 10 pm generally and

---

[20] About half of employers across all sectors agreed with the statement that "we should lock migrants in at night to make sure they don't escape" (Pearson et al. 2006: xviii).

with notification to the labor inspector (Labor Protection Act B.E. 2541 1998: Chap. 4). Without documentation, children cannot register for work, eliminating the option of labor inspector notification. Once workers are 18 years old, or legally adult, they have more options. Most migrant and local street children are left with more unlawful venues for financially sustaining themselves than lawful ones. The child rehabilitation center at which I worked recognized these limitations for young laborers and aimed to help the most vulnerable of them. Only one of the 29 inhabitants was 18.

While child labor laws ideally protect the human rights of child workers, there are a variety of ways in which these laws and their enforcement methods increase risks for children. First, many employers do not register child workers and avoid accountability for work conditions that violate the child labor laws. Many industries hiring irregular migrant children often retain hazardous conditions or unlawful working hours, the fishing industry being an example. Furthermore, child migrants often come from contexts with more lax child labor standards. In fact, child labor laws in Thailand's neighboring countries, Laos, Burma, and Cambodia face criticism for their lax laws, interpreted to be widespread child labor abuses.[21] It is no wonder children hope for greater work possibilities in Thailand's cities like Pattaya and are willing to endure more hazardous conditions. The cultural contexts from which they originate, coupled with the limited legal options street children face in Thailand, seem to funnel them into illegal work of the sex trade.

Also limiting street children's lawful options is the lack of education possible to street children. The Thai education system remains expensive, requiring students to buy books, uniforms, and food—street children and impoverished children from Pattaya's slums are most likely to drop out of school, limiting both lawful employment options and guidance and access to role models.

Pattaya hosts community development organizations like the Redemptorist Center, Mercy Center, Fountain of Life Children's Center, the Pattaya Street Kids' Project, and the Child Protection and Development Center, which offer vocational training and remedial education to Pattaya's children. However, the annual influx of migrant children exceeds these programs' capacities. Furthermore, the lack of legal protection for street children compounds their vulnerabilities. According to a local Thai social worker, the majority of pedophiles in Pattaya can simply bribe police when they face conviction of child sexual abuses (Personal communication, January 15, 2008b, Conversations with a Pattaya social worker and police informant).[22] Police offer little and inadequate responses in areas known for child sex tourism.

---

[21] The Cambodia Human Rights report (section 6d) cites that 15 year olds can engage in non-hazardous labor, not affecting school attendance, and 18 year olds can engage in any labor; yet, over half the population of children between 5 and 17 were employed in a wide range of hazardous and non-hazardous activities. Only a third of the number of children employed was over 14.

[22] Current estimates of pedophiles in Pattaya range from 150–200 people annually. However, these numbers are subject to change and reevaluation and are not supported by empirical data.

For example, according to conversations with a prostitute, police generally ignore trade that occurs before 9:30 pm along Dogdan beach, next to Pattaya (Personal communication, October 7, 2008c, Conversations with a prostitute). Without adequate law enforcement, Thailand's many anti-trafficking policies cannot be effective. With corrupt and exploitative law enforcement, Thailand's trafficking scene gains momentum.

The combined factors of Thailand's work being illegal for children under 15, home countries with traditions of vast child labor abuses, the prevalence of child migration without documentation, and limited access to education and role models make viable income or empowerment virtually impossible. Young migrants face additional odds against getting legal work due to the lack of fluency in Thai, lack of family structures, and lack of police protection. Simon Baker asserts that "children who come from dysfunctional families and are living on the streets, hill-tribe children, and children from neighboring countries are still at risk of being exploited in the sex trade. If services are not provided to assist these children, they will continue to sell sex to survive" (Baker 2007: 144). Similarly, street children in Pattaya often enter the sex trade voluntarily but with few other options open to them.

A final factor contributing to street children's sex work relates to their lack of support structure. Child migrants have limited access to education or legal work and often end up working in bars, where they are vulnerable to pedophiles. Many of Pattaya's street children exhibit addictive behaviors, such as video gaming or glue sniffing. Pedophiles often seek children in Pattaya's video arcades, knowing street children will sell sexual services to support their addiction. Children in Pattaya's 17 slums are also at risk of sexual abuse and trafficking by foreign pedophiles who often "groom" poor families to gain older family members' trust for unsupervised access to the children. Video gaming and family life in Pattaya's slums may seem like strange vulnerabilities, but they exemplify how street children's limited support systems lead them to higher risk lifestyles.

While street children selling sex match the definition of trafficked persons, fully addressing their particular needs would require empowerment efforts to reach them before their entry to the sex trade. Post-trauma rehabilitation and empowerment efforts are valuable, but to curb Pattaya's street children from entering the sex trade initially, efforts should target the factors motivating their choices, which are unstructured living environments as well as educational and financial opportunities. Preventatively helping street children to limit their risks of being trafficked would require community development initiatives, as well as enforced labor laws, additional income generating choices, and reforms with law enforcement. More vested collaboration between these agents could ideally create additional lawful possibilities for street children's financial and emotional empowerment, as later explored.

The remaining differences between Thailand's legal and policy ideals and reality of continued migrant vulnerabilities are clear. Ideally, future collaborative efforts between the government and development efforts could synthesize migrant experiences with those policies.

4.4.5 These Vulnerable Populations Pose the Greatest Threats to the Broader Society

The continued security threats, despite Thailand's extensive efforts, demonstrate how connected human trafficking is to other social insecurities and the need to address the said insecurities holistically. No country can be secure when its neighbors are not; similarly, a community as a whole faces threats of spreading insecurities when its most vulnerable members are insecure. The weakest links in Thai society do pose the greatest threats for the regional human security. The sex trade remains a clear vehicle for the weakest links spreading security threats. It facilitates the international spread of STDs such as HIV/AIDS as rapidly as the return flight to one's home country after vacation.[23]

Those without economic options or resources for education or skills training, such as impoverished women, refugees and other undocumented migrants, and street children are more likely to increase the risks for everyone.[24] Each of these vulnerable populations poses considerable social risk, in turn. The spread of HIV/AIDS and perpetuation of high-risk activities including trafficking represent a couple of those social risks. In turn, HIV/AIDS creates subcultures of orphans and street children, perpetuating the cycle of instability and vulnerabilities.

Finally, an area of great vulnerability is with street children. The current law enforcement does not curb the risks street children face, as they remain particularly vulnerable to the sex trafficking, HIV/AIDS, and other forms of physical and sexual abuse. Without effective support, the children are also more likely to spread their high-risk norms to future generations.[25] These subcultures, such as those related to the child sex trade, reinforce and perpetuate the cycle of social threats and vulnerabilities.

Without appropriate and comprehensive policies addressing all of the risks associated with migration and the sex and labor trades, experiences of exploitation will grow further entrenched. Human trafficking and the related social threats will continue.

---

[23] While most sex workers receive regular medical checkups, this does little to eliminate the global spread of diseases without regular condom use.

[24] As demonstrated, there is an increased chance of spreading HIV/AIDS among the most vulnerable Burmese communities in Thailand. Burma's instability also breeds other problems; the majority of methamphetamines are manufactured and trafficked from Burma. Finally, the traditions of gender inequalities compound risks for women in migration and sex work. They are often sexually abused, raped, and trafficked into the sex industry.

[25] Lacking family support structures, education, and other resources, and often developing addiction problems to cope, this population often engages in higher risk behavior, making them more vulnerable to trafficking, HIV/AIDS, as well as sexual abuse. Older street children often lead younger generations of siblings into the same lifestyle. Often, these young adults are also more likely to have children of their own without the means to support them, perpetuating the same lifestyle and vulnerabilities to future generations. On Chiang Mai, Baker notes that, "Thai and foreign tourists, in turn, attract street children, as they are able to earn a livelihood by begging, selling flowers, or selling their bodies" (Baker 2007: 142–144).

4.5　What's Next? The Need for Development

If Thailand, a country with model anti-trafficking policies still faces trafficking-related insecurities, what does this mean about the anti-trafficking paradigm? Perhaps the diversity of exploitative experiences migrant populations face cannot be subsumed under the "trafficked" label. Perhaps the label cannot encompass all of migrations' complexities and related concerns without losing meaning. While the "trafficked" label and its accompanying anti-trafficking measures might not be appropriate to address all migration concerns, the vulnerabilities still exist. Migrant exploitation must be better addressed.

There are several unrelated development efforts in Thailand, which have indirectly alleviated some of the trafficking-related insecurities, HIV/AIDS, gendered violence, and poverty being examples. These efforts do not maintain the same limits in scope as the anti-trafficking paradigm and holistically address related vulnerabilities associated with trafficking. Unlike the dominant anti-trafficking agenda, these programs do not view trafficked people as victims and often address the larger contexts of exploitation beyond a specific timeframe of forced migration or labor.

The Population and Community Development Association (PDA) provides one example of a holistic approach to development. PDA addresses health, financial empowerment, family planning, and education in low-resource communities. PDA's work instigated a demographic "revolution" where the average number of children per family dropped from seven to less than two (Baker 2000: 8). Largely attributed to PDA's national condom and birth control campaigning, Thailand's HIV/AIDS rate significantly dropped as well.[26] In a country known for its sex trade, the effective condom campaign has been critical. Lowered birth rates are attributed as one dominant cause for decline in child prostitution (Baker 2007: 7–10). PDA has also addressed one of the vulnerabilities HIV-positive citizens face—the lack of employment opportunities.[27] Combining lowered birth rates with additional empowerment efforts helps at-risk populations limit their vulnerabilities. PDA has also empowered local governments and individual families to keep their children in school, decreasing the likelihood of their entering the sex trade.[28]

Furthermore, Baker asserts that, "As the Thai Ministry of Public Health expands its anti-retroviral medication program for all people who need it, the number of HIV/AIDS orphans is likely to drop, and so will the number of children forced into the sex industry because of this problem" (Baker 2007: 144). While this policy operates in isolation from PDA's efforts, both initiatives clearly target the same cause.

---

[26] According to the PDA website (2010), "The current number of infected people new stands at more than 1,000,000. If this problem was not tackled, it was predicted that by the year 2000 there would be between 2 and 4 million infected persons".

[27] The business branches of PDA offer some of the few sources of employment for HIV-positive individuals. The Cabbages and Condom's restaurants try to accommodate the individual's needs, as well.

[28] Baker affirms that, "With greater wealth and smaller families, children are increasingly unlikely to enter into prostitution" (Baker 2007: 143).

If anti-trafficking initiatives collaborated with these two efforts, the risk of HIV/AIDS could be further controlled.

Clearly, Thailand identifies and addresses its particular risks and root causes associated with human trafficking and migrants' entangled vulnerabilities with HIV/AIDS and poverty being at the forefront of the countries' operations. Yet, those efforts emphasize community development, individual empowerment, and remain tangential to the human trafficking agenda.

While the anti-trafficking spotlight highlights a more limited crowd of exploited migrants, and traditionally targets a more limited time frame of exploitation, community development initiatives strengthen community defenses against most forms of exploitation, trafficking included. Until combined efforts work with law enforcement to thoroughly address the source problems creating and perpetuating the symptoms of poverty, limited education, health care, and migration into often exploitative trades, there will always be "human trafficking" in Thailand.

4.5.1 Weaving Street Children into the Fabric of Acceptable Society

The need for increased collaboration between community development and anti-trafficking efforts is clear. Such collaboration could take a variety of forms.[29] Further addressing the vulnerabilities street children face as possibilities for collaboration and social growth represents a valuable example.

If the US and Thai anti-trafficking initiatives held Thailand's law enforcement more accountable for limiting street children's vulnerabilities, perhaps police would prosecute more pedophiles. Synthesizing anti-trafficking resources with the goals and resources of international development programs, local community programs such as museums and tourism activities might help empower street children's particular situation. Collaborative programs could encourage apprenticeship programs with local businesses. For example, street children could work in conjunction with the MIT-initiated "One Laptop Per Child" program and contribute to Thailand's hospitality industry through volunteer service or through the creation of sellable artisan crafts. With increased collaboration between the traditionally separate sectors, street children's particular situations of vulnerability could be used for their individual and communal empowerment.

---

[29] Thailand's street child development organizations are collaborating with international prevention and prosecution efforts against child sex offenders. Resulting from such collaborations, Thailand will be part of a new international registry for sex offenders by the time this book is published.

4.6 Conclusion

Irregular migration and its related vulnerabilities represent a variety of human insecurities particular to our contemporary, globalized era.[30] Using the example of Thailand, this discussion has suggested that addressing the wide insecurities of irregular migration seems to require an equally broad scope of focus.

Thailand's anti-trafficking efforts and related migration and labor have broadened their scope. Yet, the methods of traditional enforcement do not share the same ideals. Thai law enforcement faces accusations of robbing migrants, indirectly encouraging child sex tourism, and exploiting and sexually abusing prostitutes. Thai law enforcement's approach to migration often perpetuates those forms of exploitation.

Fortunately, seemingly successful development efforts in Thailand have furthered the anti-trafficking agenda while maintaining a more holistic approach. Such indirect empowerment and community development initiatives coupled with traditional anti-trafficking efforts might alleviate the insecurities in a more effective, holistic way than direct anti-trafficking efforts alone.

To more effectively address the vulnerabilities sex and labor migrants face, it may be important to evaluate the contexts of street children and their choices in addition to adult migrants and laborers. One possibility for development and anti-trafficking efforts synthesis would be providing alternative economic and educational opportunities for these most vulnerable migrant populations. A new blend of efforts rather than maintaining the traditionally distinct approaches might offer a more cohesive set of solutions to their high-risk and vulnerable lifestyles.

While this study targeted the challenges of street children as areas for potential progress in particular, there are areas for further collaboration between anti-trafficking and development initiatives as well.

Additional suggestions include:

- If Thailand will maintain its trajectory of progress, it must further actualize government policies, declarations, MOU's, and laws addressing migration concerns. Aside from direct anti-trafficking initiatives, addressing the underlying factors of social instability remains crucial to development and limiting insecurities. Such factors include poverty, gender equality, and access to education, political stability, as well as political and legal protection.
- In particular, recognizing the refugee status of more Burmese migrants and giving them access to resources such as health care is essential. Currently, the only way migrants have access to Thailand's 30-Baht universal health care plan is if they are registered for work. Unfortunately, the majority of job categories dominated by migrants are not part of the registry, according to the PHR. If Thailand does not recognize the refugee status of more Burmese

---

[30]Those vulnerabilities include exploitation by law enforcement, poverty and gendered poverty in source countries and gendered migration, lack of representation, heath care, land rights, legal rights, lack of education, perpetuating high risk behaviors, and the spread of HIV/AIDS.

migrants, and the worker status of other migrants, the government should at least enable more undocumented migrants to register for the work they are already doing. The registry should include more work venues. While employers of migrant workers have complained about the costs of registering migrants, there is significant evidence that the "costs are ultimately borne by the migrants and are usually recouped by employers through salary deductions" (Pearson et al. 2006: xxv).

- Thailand should also offer more economic options for HIV-positive citizens. While PDA has provided a good model of financially empowering HIV-positive citizens; its policy is not the norm. Without financial alternatives, HIV-positive people are more likely to turn to the sex trade, despite the greater risk of spreading HIV/AIDS. A further measure to decrease the spread of HIV/AIDS might entail Thailand legalizing or at least enforcing systems of regulation for prostitution. Regulation could provide safety measures, better access to healthcare, and more legal protection against sex workers' vulnerabilities to rape, sexual assault, exploitation by law enforcement, and legal representation. Decreasing sex workers' vulnerabilities bolsters the broader society's vulnerabilities to the spread of HIV/AIDS.
- Furthermore, migrant laborers need stronger political representation particularly from the Ministry of Labor. The ILO recommends collaboration between development organizations working with migrants and the Ministry of Labor, and the further development of Thai labor and trade unions.
- More of Thailand's vulnerable populations of migrant workers need access to education.

Thailand would better address the context of exploitation and migrant vulnerabilities through the mentioned policies, which each require increased collaboration among fields. In addition: increased collaboration with international and domestic anti-trafficking efforts, development and government could improve the effort's accountability, and integration with all initiatives targeting migration concerns. For example, Thai law enforcement would not be able to violate memorandums of understanding, human rights, and participate in trafficking. A united focus of anti-trafficking efforts, holistic community development, and law enforcement might best address the broad range of vulnerabilities people face in irregular migration.

References

Baker, S. (2000). The changing situation of child prostitution in northern Thailand: A study of Changwat Chiang Rai. http:www.childtrafficking.com/Docs/baker_2000_changing_situation_child_prostitution_thailand_5.pdf. Accessed 15 Jan 2009.

Baker, S. (2007). *'Child labour' and child prostitution in Thailand: Changing realities* (Studies in contemporary Thailand, Vol. 18). Bangkok, Thailand: White Lotus.

Cahn, D. (2009). The trade of Asia's girls, New America Media, 26 March. http://news.newamericamedia.org/news/view_article.html?article_id=beb218c449d15c9a3f1874230c3d320d. Accessed 10 Sep 2010.

Cambodia Human Rights Report (n.d.). Status of child labor practices and minimum age for employment. Section 6d. http://www.ncbuy.com/reference/country/humanrights.html?code=cb&sec=6d. Accessed 15 Jan 2009.

Coordinated Mekong Ministerial Initiative against Trafficking (COMMIT). (2004). Thailand country paper, Senior Officials Meeting 1. United Nations Conference Center, Bangkok, Thailand.

Global Fund for Women. (2006). Symposium on human trafficking, In collaboration with the Council of Foreign Relations' Women and US Foreign Policy Program, New York, 6 May. http://www.cfr.org/publication/10603/us_foreign_policy_and_women_symposium.html. Accessed 20 May 2010.

Human Security Network. (2009). Human agenda: Partnership for human security, Ministerial Meetings Concept Paper. http://www.humansecuritynetwork.org/docs/bangkok_concept-e.php. Accessed 15 Jan 2009.

Immigration Act, B.E. 2522 (1979). Thailand, 30 May. http://www.unhcr.org/refworld/docid/46b2f9f42.html. Accessed 10 July 2010.

Immigration and Refugee Board of Canada. (2007). Thailand: Police corruption particularly in the state of Udon Than, THA102694.E. http://www.unhcr.org/refworld/docid/47d6547dc.html. Accessed 16 May 2010.

Labor Protection Act B.E. 2541. (1998). Chapter 4, Child Labor. http://www.unicz.it/lavoro/THAI_LPA(98).htm#c5. Accessed 15 Jan 2009.

LSCW (Legal Support for Children and Women). (2005a). Needs assessment and analysis of the situation of Cambodian migrant workers in Klong Yai District, Trat, Thailand. Migrant Support Project. http://www.lscw.org/images/situational_analysis_for_web.pdf. Accessed 27 May 2010.

LSCW (Legal Support for Children and Women). (2005b). Gender analysis of the patterns of human trafficking into and through Koh Kong Province. http://www.lscw.org/images/lscw_research_gender.pdf. Accessed 15 Jan 2009.

McGeown, Kate. (2007). Life as a Thai sex worker. BBC News, 22 February. http://news.bbc.co.uk/2/hi/asia-pacific/6360603.stm. Accessed 10 Sep 2010.

PDA (Population and Community Development Association). (2010). Online website. http://www.pda.or.th/eng/aids_aware.asp?Menu=01. Accessed 4 July 2010.

Pearson, E. et al. (2006). The Mekong challenge, underpaid, overworked and overlooked: The realities of young migrant workers in Thailand. International Programme on the Elimination of Child Labour, International Labour Organization (ILO), 1: 1–145. http://www.ilo.org/public/english/region/asro/bangkok/child/trafficking/buildingknowledge/publicationsresearch.htm. Accessed 27 May 2010.

PHR (Physicians for Human Rights). (2004). No status: Migration, trafficking & exploitation of women in Thailand. Boston, MA. http://www.phrusa.org/campaigns/aids/pdf/nostatus.pdf#search='trafficking%20in%20women%20thailand. Accessed 15 Jan 2009.

The Anti-Trafficking in Persons Act B.E. 2551 (2008). http://www.baliprocess.net/files/Thailand/1.%20trafficking_in_persons_act_b.e%202551%20(eng.).pdf. Accessed 23 May 2010.

UNICEF (United Nations Children's Fund). (2003). Rapid assessment on child labour employment in the border area between Thailand and Cambodia, Srakaew, Chantaburi and Trad Province, Bangkok.

Unmacht, E. (2003). Cambodia Brothels under threat. BBC News, 7 May. http://news.bbc.co.uk/2/hi/asia-pacific/3007761.stm. Accessed 15 Jan 2010.

US Department of State. (2008). Trafficking in persons report 2008. http://www.state.gov/g/tip/rls/tiprpt/2008/. Accessed 10 July 2010.

US Department of State. (2010). Office to monitor and combat trafficking in persons. http://www.state.gov/g/tip/. Accessed 10 Sep 2010.

Watch, A. (1993). *A modern form of slavery: Trafficking of Burmese women and girls into brothels in Thailand*. New York: Human Rights Watch.

Chapter 5
Security in Labor Migration in the Philippines: National Honor, Family Solidarity, and Migrants' Protection

Asuncion Fresnoza-Flot

5.1 Introduction

The question of labor migration has been dividing the Philippine society since the 1970s: the economic gains, "brain drain", labor exploitation, and health problems induced by migration constitute some of the most important issues that preoccupy the country. The considerable number of reported crimes and abuse against Filipino migrants, especially women (that have exceeded male migrants in numbers in the 1990s), has triggered social debates concerning the impact of migration on human security. The recent wave of Filipino mother breadwinners has also raised concerns about its social costs on family members left in the country, particularly children (Asis et al. 2004; Wolf 1997). As one of the most important and organized migratory phenomena in the world, Filipino overseas migration has been a popular object of empirical and theoretical studies in the domain of social sciences, both in the Philippines and in many receiving countries (See Choy 2003; Mozère 2004; Ogaya 2004). However, the question of human security in the Filipino migration context remains an underexplored area.

This chapter attempts to fill a gap in the literature by addressing the issues of labor migration and its relation to human security from the perspective of the state and of non-state actors in the migrants' sending country: the Catholic Church, non-governmental organizations (NGOs), and the media. This resembles the "portfolio diversification" approach (involving many actors in a given society) to human security proposed by Hampson et al. (2002): here, I use this approach to demonstrate how the state and non-state actors in the Philippine setting define human security in the context of migration.

Since the independence of the Philippines in 1946, Filipinos have emigrated massively towards nearly all countries in the world. This post-colonial migratory phenomenon is very intense with regards to the annual number of emigrants

A. Fresnoza-Flot (✉)
Université Paris Diderot, Paris 7, France
e-mail: afresnoza@hotmail.com

concerned, and is composed of men and women of all ages, professions, civil statuses and social classes. Characterized by a collective conscience of their historical and cultural connection to the Philippines, Filipino migrants overseas form a "community" in a permanent or "provisional diaspora¹" (Barber 2000: 399) that is the third largest in the world after the Chinese and Indian ones. According to estimations published by the Commission on Filipinos Overseas (CFO 2008), there are about 8.7 million Filipino migrants abroad, compared with 34 million Chinese and 20 million Indians (Ong 2009; Zhang 2006). The Filipino migration is a part of a global movement of people from developing countries to developed countries in response to labor demand, notably in the service sector. It can also be considered as the direct result of the 1974 institutionalization of labor migration by the Philippine state to counter its economic problems. The nature of the Filipino migration attests to the plurality of ways taken by Filipino migrants in managing to go out of their country in order to secure a better future for themselves and for their families, to escape from their problems at home or simply to fulfill their dream of traveling around the world. The opportunities they see abroad contrast with the social precariousness they undergo in the Philippines, where a large part of the state's budget goes to pay its external debt and the "care resources" (Parreñas 2005) are drying down, notably in the areas of health, education and housing. This shows that human migration and human security are "interlinked and immutable" (Graham 2000: 185).

The analysis presented in this chapter comes from a larger study I conducted in 2006 and 2007 among Filipino migrant mothers in France and their family members left in the Philippines (Fresnoza-Flot 2008). The materials I examined for this chapter included books, academic journals, newspapers, television programs, documentaries, movies, and even short articles published by migrant NGOs and made available on the Internet. I start with a discussion of the way human security has been defined and used in the academic literature, notably in the context of migration. I then move to the main section of the chapter, in which I examine the varying viewpoints of the state and of non-state actors in the Philippine society in order to find out how they define the migrants' human security. To conclude, I reflect on the emerging definition of human security in the Philippine context and ponder on the social stakes of the Filipino migratory movements.

5.2 Human Security in the Context of Migration

The concept of human security and its definition have been a subject of intense scholarly discussions since 1994 when it appeared in the United Nations Development Programme (UNDP) report, as this concept shifted the referent object

---

¹ The term "diaspora" originally meant the forced movement of Jews from their homeland and their subsequent quest for home driven by a collective memory of their past; however, this term is also used nowadays to describe other movements of people from their homeland, whether voluntary or forced.

of security from states to groups and individuals within society. Human security is defined as "safety from such chronic threats as hunger, disease and repression" and "protection from sudden and hurtful disruptions in the patterns of daily life – whether in homes, in jobs or in communities" (UNDP 1994: 23). This definition has been criticized as "extraordinarily expansive and vague" (Paris 2001), "incoherent" and "too wide to use" (Alkire 2003) among others, resulting in a strong call in the field of social sciences to find a way to define it clearly and precisely, in order to better gain empirical significance.

Within the literature on security studies and international relations, human migrations (particularly irregular ones) have been viewed as threats to the receiving countries' national identity, economic condition, social cohesion and peace and order situation (Gallissot 1985; Poku and Graham 2000; Weiner 1993). In brief, migration in relation to security is often highlighted through the perspective of the receiving countries, and rarely from the viewpoint of the sending countries (Graham 2000). As Bigo (2002) argues, "the articulation of migration as a security threat continues" nowadays. Such focus on state security completely overlooks the effects of migration on the human security of the migrants themselves. In the case of irregular migration, topics such as human trafficking, labor exploitation and abuses are well discussed in the migration literature (Koser 2005). Irregular migrants usually work "underground" and concentrate in the service, manufacturing and agricultural sectors. The irregular migration status of these migrants limits their spatial and professional mobility. Moreover, they have no access to the social security system in their receiving country, and those separated from their families left in their country of origin experience difficulties to maintain intimate family relations over geographic distance (Cohen 2000; Fresnoza-Flot 2009). The situation of irregular migrants can be taken as an example of "human insecurity", as they have no access to rights or to the means of securing their health, legal status, etc. As Alkire (2003) argues, "the vital core that is to be secured" comprises "a minimal or basic or fundamental set of functions related to survival, livelihood and dignity", and "the institutions that undertake to protect human security will not be able to protect every aspect of human well-being, but at very least they will protect this core" (p. 24). Following this logic, the migrants' sending countries appear to have an important duty to protect them, which is why some non-state components of the Philippine society try hard to motivate the government to promote its migrant citizens' rights. In this case, human security appears to be closely linked to human rights.

Given the multidimensionality of human security, this chapter considers it as "a social construct" that possesses "different meanings in different societies" (Baldwin 1997 cited in Davies 2000). In the Philippines, human security has been continuously constructed and reconstructed by the interactions between the state and non-state actors. Various events affecting or directly implicating migrants (e.g. trafficking, labor exploitation, abuse) have influenced these interactions. As we will see, the emerging understanding of "human security" in the country turns out to be compatible with the definition proposed by the UNDP in 1994.

5.3 The Ambivalent Attitude of the Philippine State Towards Migration

The states establish the frameworks based on which migrations are judged legitimate or not, and these frameworks produce concrete effects on the life of all migrants, whether legal or illegal (Sindjoun 2005). In the case of the Philippines, the continuous massive emigration of Filipino migrant workers considered as "modern heroes" in their country would not have been possible without the support of the Philippine government, for which this movement represents the principal source of foreign currencies. Despite reported cases of violence against Filipino migrants, the Philippine state continues to promote labor migration while trying to preserve the national honor embodied in its women population – two preoccupations that may appear contradictory.

For a long time, the Philippine state has regarded the exportation of Filipino workers as a "temporary solution" to its economic problems as their remittances sustain the country's foreign currency reserves, currently equivalent to 45,764.36 million US dollars (IMF 2010). The government uses this money to pay its importations and to settle its foreign debt. Migration also benefits many branches of the local economy, such as telecommunication, banking, real estate, transportation, and retail industry. Since the beginning of the 1970s, the amount of Filipino migrant remittances sent from abroad has increased tremendously: from 103 million USD in 1975 to 16.4 billion USD in 2008. The economic benefits generated by the exportation of Filipino labor abroad are so important that the government has become a prisoner of a system heavily dependent on migration.

To understand better the Philippine state's position concerning labor migration in relation to human security, let us start with an examination of its efforts since its institutionalization of emigration in 1974. These efforts reflect its ambivalent attitude towards labor migration: on the one hand, the government aims to encourage the emigration of its citizens to maximize its economic gains (even if it means making its migrant citizens more vulnerable to abuse and exploitation), but on the other hand, it intends to preserve the nation's honor and reputation abroad that appears to be particularly embodied in its women citizens, and to secure the well-being of its migrants. Analysis of these government actions suggests that, from the point of view of the state, human security in migration translates into free choice of employment type and place, elevated social position, efficient access to employment opportunities abroad as well as to social structures (health, education) both abroad and in the Philippines, and finally, safety from all forms of violence.

5.3.1 Promoting Migration and Maximizing Profit

In 1974, the administration of Ferdinand Marcos (1965–1986) introduced in the Labor Code of the Philippines a migratory program to address the country's unemployment problem and facilitate Filipino's access to jobs abroad (presidential decree

442, article 17). Within the context of this program, the government established infrastructures to manage the deployment abroad of Filipino workers, deregulated the local market of recruitment and placement of these workers, engaged in the valorization of Filipino migrants' economic contributions, and provided migrants with social and civic rights. All these actions were intended to promote labor migration and to maximize the benefits the government could obtain from it.

The establishment of migration infrastructures started with the founding of two agencies: the Overseas Employment Development Board and the National Seamen Board. In 1982, these two government bodies were fused into one agency that still exists today, the Philippine Overseas Employment Administration (POEA). This agency is responsible for the protection, promotion and direction of the migration market (including the deliverance of permits to private recruitment agencies, regulators and adjudicators). Then, in 1977, the government created the Welfare and Training Fund for Overseas Workers that later became the Overseas Workers Welfare Administration (OWWA[2]). It provides migrants with cultural services, social security, as well as judicial, social, employment and remittance transfer assistance. This agency installed in 24 countries obliges Filipino migrants and their foreign employers to pay an annual membership fee that aliments its funds used to finance various services to migrants and their families (such as affordable real estate loans, professional training, and health insurance[3]). These migration infrastructures have allowed the Philippine government to secure control of its labor outflow towards other countries.

However, in 1978 the Philippine government started to pursue a very different path characterized by the progressive deregulation of its labor export industry, both as an attempt to invigorate it and to follow the liberal guidelines of the International Monetary Fund and the World Bank. As a result, legal and illegal private recruitment and placement agencies of OFWs (Overseas Filipino Workers) flourished. The collapse of the dictatorial government of Marcos in 1986 did not put an end to this economic logic as Marcos' successor Corazon Aquino (1986–1992) showed renewed determination to promote labor migration. On the contrary, under the Fidel Ramos administration (1992–1998), migration was only viewed as an "alternative source of employment opportunities" (Alcid 2003), transforming the role of the state from the one of a promoter to the one of a simple administrator of the Filipino migratory movements towards foreign countries. The Migrant Workers and Overseas Filipinos Act of 1995 purported to uphold the rights and welfare of migrant workers and their families, but actually set in motion the deregulation of the state's labor export industry.

---

[2] In 1980, the Welfare and Training Fund for Overseas Workers became the Welfare Fund for Overseas Workers under Presidential Decree no. 1694 of President Marcos. It was renamed in 1987 Overseas Workers Welfare Administration by the Executive Order no. 126 of President Aquino.

[3] Branches of OWWA can be found in Europe (England, Switzerland, Italy, Spain and Greece), in Asia (Hong Kong, Singapore, Japan, Brunei, South Korea, Malaysia and Taiwan), in the Middle East (Saudi Arabia, Qatar, Kuwait, Israel, United Arab Emirates, Bahrain, Oman, Lebanon and Jordan), in the United States (Washington), and in the North Marianas Islands (Saipan).

This law projected that the said deregulation would be achieved within 6 years after its promulgation. Within the context of deregulation, "the migration of workers becomes strictly a matter between the worker and his foreign employer" (section 29 at the Act), which makes Filipino migrant workers more vulnerable to exploitation and reduces their capacity to defend their rights as workers. During the administration of Joseph Estrada (1998–2001), the state continued its promotion of labor migration, whereas his successor Gloria Arroyo (2001–2010) launched a so-called "Labor Export Program" aiming to deploy one million of Filipino migrants annually.

Despite the advertised liberalization of the Filipino labor market, the Philippine government maintains its control of this market (and notably the migrants' remittances) through various political and economic infrastructures, which points to a contradiction between its political discourse and its economic priorities. The deregulation of the Philippine labor export industry has resulted to an annual increase in the number of deployed Filipino labor migrants abroad and of the amount of remittances they send to the country, but there has been a concomitant increase in the number of reported crimes, diseases (including HIV contamination) and mental disorders among migrants. The consequences of the state's liberalization strategy are obviously heavy in terms of the human security of Filipino migrants.

Aside from the establishment of migration infrastructures and the liberalization of its labor export industry, the state launched a series of programs of social valorization of Filipino migrants' economic contributions, which somehow elevates these workers' place in the Philippine society. These programs convey the message that migration provides a sort of social security, which drives more people to migrate abroad. These programs include the "Operation Homecoming" that was introduced in 1973 to attract Filipino migrants back home by offering them certain privileges such as access to entry visa and to discounted flights, and expedited treatment of their immigration and custom requirements (Lawless 2005). Another program, called "Balik Scientist" (*balik* means return in Tagalog) was introduced in 1975 to encourage Filipino scientists abroad to return to the country and bring their expertise and know-how. Since 1975, about 300 scientists and engineers have registered to participate to this program, and for the period 2007–2010 the Department of Science and Technology planned to attract 100 participants (Salazar 2007). In 2007, the government inaugurated the National Reintegration Center for OFWs (NRCO) to tackle the "brain drain" issue and the social costs of migration. The NRCO has started various programs for migrant returnees and their families, which allows the government to confront the criticism that it concentrates more on the deployment of Filipino workers abroad than on the well-being of migrant returnees and on job creation to avoid re-emigration. Other gestures of recognition from the government towards its migrants include: the declaration of the year 2000 as the year of Filipino migrant workers,[4] celebration of the month of December of each year as "the OFW month", and presidential welcome of migrant returnees in the international airport

---

[4] The Presidential Proclamation no. 243 signed by former president Estrada on 8 February 2000 formally recognized the economic role played by Filipino migrant workers abroad.

of the country. However, these gestures can also be interpreted as an effort to maximize the migrants' input into the national economy: for instance, the choice of December for celebrating the migrants was not innocent, as it is during this month that the largest amount of remittances is sent to the country to provide for Christmas and New Year gifts. This shows well how the government succeeded in "domesticating the *balikbayan*" (Rafael 1997) and how it indirectly encouraged more labor emigration. The easy entry and sojourn in the Philippines accorded to Filipino migrants and the privilege to spend their money at tax-free shops valorize undoubtedly emigration in the eyes of the wider Filipino public, as migration has become associated with money and buying power on the one hand, and with professional skills and elevated social status on the other hand.

Socially securing its migrant citizens abroad represents another strategy that the Philippine government has adopted to make labor migration more attractive to its population. This shows how it considers the present migration of its citizens: a temporary stay abroad that will end up with a definitive return to the country. Providing social protection to migrant workers has also reinforced the government's influence over its migrants widely spread around the world, an action that deterritorializes the Philippine nation-state within the context of globalization. The Philippine state keeps following its migrants in diaspora as they "conduct economic, political, social, and cultural transactions that are essential for the maintenance of the home state's survival" (Basch et al. 2003: 269–270). In line with this objective, the Philippine state has demonstrated an interest in improving its migrants' social rights (i.e., access to work and to social security) in the Philippines and in receiving countries. The state also tries to provide its migrants with easier access to labor markets abroad through bilateral agreements with their receiving countries; until now, however, the government only succeeded to forge such agreements with 13 countries[5] (Go 2007). In yet another measure, the Philippine Social Security System (SSS[6]) was opened in 1973 to Filipino migrants through voluntary membership (Shinozaki 2005). Seventeen branches of the SSS are now found in 13 countries where the grand majority of Filipino migrants are concentrated.[7] In 2001, the SSS introduced the Flexi-Fund Program for Filipino migrants abroad and for persons benefiting from migrant remittances. Membership to the ordinary SSS program is needed to subscribe to this new program that serves at the same time as

---

[5] They were the Commonwealth of Northern Marianas Islands, Indonesia, Iraq, Jordan, Kuwait, Libya, Norway, Papua New Guinea, Qatar, Sweden, Switzerland, Taiwan and United Kingdom.

[6] There are two systems of social security in the Philippines: the Government Service Insurance System for government employees and the Social Security System for those who work in the private sector. These institutions provide provisions in case of sickness, handicap, retirement and death.

[7] The branches are in Hong Kong (China), Taipei (Taiwan), Brunei Darussalam and Singapore in Asia; Riyadh, Jeddah and Al-Khobar (Saudi Arabia), Kuwait, Abu Dhabi (United Arab Emirates) and Doha (Qatar) in the Middle East; Rome and Milan (Italy), London (England) and Paris (France) in Europe; San Francisco and California (United States); and Sydney (Australia).

savings and tax-free pension plans. The monthly payment for the Flexi-Fund stops at the age of 60, and compensation for death or handicap can be versed to subscribing migrants or their heirs in the form of monthly pension, one-time cash payment or a combination of the two. Hence, subscribing both to the regular and Flexi-Fund programs of the SSS ensures double coverage for the migrant worker and his family. However, given that membership to SSS is voluntary and that SSS branches are only found in a handful of the 200 receiving countries of OFWs, only 515,762 of about eight million Filipino migrants in the world are SSS members and only about 16,000 have subscribed to the SSS Flexi-Fund program (Dumlao 2006). In particular, undocumented Filipino migrants and those who live in countries that do not have yet bilateral social security agreement with the Philippines are left out of the system. The government was only able to forge bilateral social security agreements with nine receiving countries of Filipino migrants.[8] Another governmental measure was the creation of the Insurance and Health-Care Program under the OWWA covering disability, natural or accidental death, as well as funeral expenses. However, this insurance covers migrant members only during the duration of their work contract abroad, and several administrative obstacles have to be overcome before one can receive money from it.

Furthermore, in order to legitimize its conception of Filipino migrants as Filipino citizens, the government has granted them civic rights: the right to vote on 13 February 2003[9] and the right to double nationality[10] on 17 September of the same year. In order to participate in the 2010 national elections in the Philippines, 589,830 Filipino migrants registered in Philippine embassies and consulates abroad (Suarez 2009). As for double nationality, about 43,000 Filipino migrants have taken advantage of this law to retain or regain their Filipino nationality since 2003 (Ortiz 2007).

The Philippine government's extension of social and civic rights to Filipino migrants stems from a logic of maximization of the economic benefits it obtains from this population. Following the example of China, the Philippines encourage Filipino migrants abroad to return to the country to invest their financial capital and their know-how. Simultaneously, the government continues to promote a deregulated labor migration that nourishes the whole country, while acknowledging, at least in discourse, the necessity of increased protection of OFWs.

---

[8] The nine countries are Austria (since 1982); England, Northern Ireland, Spain, and France since 1989; Canada since 1997; Switzerland and Belgium since 2001; and South Korea since 2005.

[9] This is made possible by the signing of the Overseas Absentee Voting Act of 2003 by President Arroyo.

[10] The Citizenship Retention and Re-acquisition Act allows Filipino migrants to retain or reacquire their Filipino nationality when becoming nationals of another country. Under this law, Filipino migrants can now acquire foreign nationality and still be able to invest in commerce, to acquire properties and to reside in the Philippines.

5.3.2 Preserving the National Honor

> In his *note verbale* to the Greek Foreign Ministry, Philippine Ambassador Norberto Basilio said the definition of "Filipineza" in the recently published dictionary of modern Greek was an insult to Philippine women and was far from its literal translation, "Filipino lady." He urged Greek authorities to call the matter to the attention of the dictionary's compiler, George Babiniotis, so the latter can make the necessary correction. "In this dictionary, the definition of 'Filipineza' or a Filipino lady was stated not only to mean a woman from the Philippines but also a domestic worker from the Philippines or a person who performs non-essential auxiliary tasks," Basilio said in his note dated July 27.
>
> (Asian Political News, 10 August 1998)

Earlier, the Philippine government had already protested against the definition of "Filipina" as "domestic" in the Oxford English dictionary in 1989. These incidents put into light the way the Philippine government tries to defend its "national honor" embodied in the women of the nation. As Oishi (2005) argues, women "symbolize a nation's dignity and constitute the foundation of nationalism and national identity" and this explains why "the public tends to be more sensitive to their abuse and exploitation than to that of men" (p. 100). Following this reasoning, all forms of violence inflicted by "foreigners" on Filipino migrant women tarnish the dignity of the country, and the government must thus exert all-out efforts to preserve it. To do so, the Philippine government has not only relied on verbal or written protests, but has also taken initiatives to protect the rights of its migrants, specifically women, and to develop their skills (which also facilitates their migration overseas).

In order not to acquire an image of a "country of domestic workers" that would be considered an insult to the "national identity" of the Philippines, the government has started to concentrate on the improvement of Filipino migrants' qualifications, notably seamen and migrant domestic workers. For example, the Department of Labor and Employment has proposed Management Level Courses to maritime engineers wanting to raise their qualifications (presently, only one third of Filipino seamen hold officer positions in the global maritime industry). Reinforcing Filipino seamen's position in the global market can be interpreted both as a strategy to make the Philippines appears as a country of strong, male, qualified migrant workers, and as a response to the increasing demand for ship officers in the world.

Concerning Filipino migrant women domestic workers, the POEA launched in December 2006 a body of reforms aiming to improve their working conditions in their receiving countries and to protect them against abuses and exploitations. These reforms specifically intended to professionalize paid domestic work by developing the skills and competences (linguistic, technical, etc.) of migrant Filipinas before their departure. The proposed changes included the augmentation of the minimum salary for domestic workers from 200 to 400 USD, the instauration of a minimum required age of 23, the prohibition of placement fees subtracted from the migrant's salary abroad, and a mandatory evaluation of competence (with qualifying trainings for those who fail the evaluation three times in a row[11]). It also became mandatory for migrants to follow an introductory training on the language and culture of their country of destination prior to their departure. To complete these reforms, the government introduced a new term to refer to migrant domestic workers – the Household Service Workers. This terminology aims to favor the emergence of a new Filipino domestic worker figure as a skilled worker trained to take charge of household chores at her employer's home abroad. This contrasts with the current stereotype of Filipino domestic workers as modest, obedient, and subservient.

Moreover, the government has started to tackle the problem of violence committed against Filipino migrants, notably women. Following the mysterious death in Japan of Maricris Sioson in 1991, the condemnation and execution in Singapore of Flor Contemplacion in March 1995, and the imprisonment of Sarah Balabagan in September 1995 in the United Arab Emirates, the Philippine government finally ratified in November 1995 the UN "International Convention on the Protection of the Rights of all Migrant Workers and Members of their Families". In 2002, under the pressure of various organizations defending migrant rights, the government carried out a campaign against human trafficking that notably concerned women and children, and ratified the "Anti-trafficking in Persons Act" in 2003. Moreover, the Philippine senate approved in 2006 two conventions of the International Labor Organization: the convention no. 97 on "Migration for Employment" that promotes well organized recruitment of migrant workers and the convention no. 143 on "Migrations in Abusive Conditions and the Promotion of Equality of Opportunity and Treatment of Migrant Workers" that aims to avoid the trafficking of migrants and to punish those involved in it. The government also resorts to intergovernmental lobbying to prevent the execution of Filipino migrants condemned to death in foreign countries. Through these efforts, the government tries to prove to the Filipino public and to the international audience that it is exerting efforts to protect its migrant citizens in the world.

Another reaction of the government to the increasing number of crimes committed against Filipino migrants was to forbid completely the deployment abroad of Filipino domestic workers in 1988 and the emigration of "mail-order brides" in 1990. Under the Ramos administration, the government discouraged in 1999 the emigration of domestic workers by suspending it for certain countries like Kuwait, Saudi Arabia and Singapore. The government apparently did not exert much effort to implement this, probably since domestic workers are the most sought-after laborers abroad and represent thus an important source of foreign currencies for the country. All these measures not only failed to stop the migration of Filipino women, but also reinforced the illegal market of emigration. In general, the laws and measures adopted to protect Filipino migrants are not well respected and do not efficiently protect their rights and security. For instance, the illegal recruitment of

---

[11] A person who has never worked as a domestic helper in the Philippines or in foreign countries and who wishes to take up this type of work abroad needs to follow the "Household Services Course" organized by the Technical Education and Skills Development Authority.

migrant workers continues and despite the life imprisonment promised to violators, nobody has ever received yet this sentence. We observe here an important gap between the symbolic practices of the state (such as new laws for the protection of migrants) and what is happening at present in the Philippine society.

5.4 The Philippine Non-state Actors' Diverse Views on Emigration and Human Security

The increase in the number of women migrants since the beginning of the 1990s has triggered an increase in the number of Filipino transnational families, the members of which are spread around the world but maintain links to one another through various means of communication and transportation. Such families have existed since the beginning of the 1970s when the government launched its labor export program that led to a "masculine" Filipino migration towards the Middle East; however, this migratory phenomenon did not provoke a public reaction as strong as the one observed today. The recent emigration of Filipino mothers to work abroad while leaving their families in the Philippines has engendered numerous debates focusing on the future of the Filipino family and on the effects of mother's migration on children left behind.

The diversity of positions of non-state actors concerning the migration of Filipino men and women, as we will see in this section, reflects the values and global ideologies that dominate the Philippine society. The Philippine Catholic Church mainly emphasizes the preservation of the family, the NGOs working for the cause of migrants call for more legal protections, while the Philippine media rally for the safety of Filipino migrants, particularly women, and for the safeguarding of the family throughout the migration process. What is evident here is the central place occupied by the family as a basic social institution that the whole society relies on: it is for and through their families that Filipino men and women migrate. This is why Philippine non-state actors associate human security in migration to the maintained unity of the family.

5.4.1 Migrate, But Preserve the Family: The Position of the Philippine Catholic Church

> Man has the right to leave his native land for various motives – and also the right to return – in order to seek better conditions of life in another country.
>
> (Pope John Paul II, Laborem exercens 1981)

This sentence illustrates clearly the position of the Catholic Church on labor migration: a human right to be respected. However, Pope Jean-Paul II underlined that "emigration in search of work must in no way become an opportunity for financial or social exploitation" and that the rights of migrant workers must be promoted in both their sending and receiving countries. This position of the "Holy See"[12] finds its echo in the Philippines, as can be observed in the official discourses and activities of the Philippine Catholic Church. Since the emigration boom in the Philippines, this institution has been very active in protecting the well-being of the migrants and their families, and in controlling the social behaviors of women as depositories of the nation's honor.

Recognizing the economic contributions of migrants to their household and to their country, the Catholic Bishop Conference of the Philippines (CBCP[13]) declared in 1987 every first Sunday of Lent the "National Migrants Sunday". In a pastoral letter, the CBCP explained its support to the Filipino migratory phenomenon but warned the public about the negative factors accompanying migration: "exploitation, broken families, moral degradation, solitude and other psychological sufferings" (1988). Given the mounting problems of violence perpetrated against Filipino migrants, the CBCP issued again in 1995 a second pastoral letter on Filipino migration from where it reiterated the cost of labor migration: "loss of life, loss of human dignity, moral degradation, or a broken family" ("Comfort my people, comfort them" 1995). In the same letter, the CBCP criticized also the government's "liberal" attitude towards migration: "the first duty of Filipino diplomacy is the protection of its citizens and not the facilitation of the activities and business of government functionaries". This active involvement of the CBCP in upholding the interests of migrants attests its important role in the Philippine society. For instance, it played a major role in toppling down Marcos' dictatorial government in 1986 and the Estrada administration in 2001.

In 1955, the CBCP created the Episcopal Commission for the Pastoral Care of Migrants and Itinerant People (ECMI)[14] to respond to the needs of migrants and their families. Moreover, the CBCP has deployed priests and missionaries abroad to take care of Filipino migrants' moral and social needs. Every 2 years, the ECMI gathers all its Filipino missionaries in the world to discuss various issues concerning migration, family, religion, etc. (De Leon 1998). Each of these meeting results in a declaration passed to the government to attract attention on the migrants' social problems in need of immediate solutions. In addition to the Catholic Church, other Christian churches[15] in the Philippines represented by their organization founded in 1963, the National Council of Churches in the Philippines, are also interested in the well-being of migrants. This council conducts various programs to help migrants abroad and their families in the Philippines.

Like the Vatican, the Philippine Catholic Church emphasizes the vulnerable position of migrant women. It calls the government to adopt laws and programs to

---

[12] It refers to the central government of the Roman Catholic Church.

[13] It is an organization representing the Catholic episcopacy of the Philippines.

[14] This commission was established before the founding in Rome of the Pontifical Council for the Pastoral Care of Migrants and Itinerants in 1988.

[15] For instance, the Baptist, Methodist, Lutheran, Anglican and Ecumenical churches.

protect them, and also warns the society about the undesirable impacts of the migration of mothers who become separated from their families in the Philippines. In 2005, the CBCP published another pastoral letter for the 19th celebration of "National Sunday of Migrants" under the theme "With Mary, the migrants and their families find life in the Eucharist". The personage of Mary, mother "instrument of salute", is utilized to symbolize on the one hand the Filipino mothers who migrate abroad to sustain their families, and on the other hand the hope that this feminized migration offers something good to the migrant families and to the nation. This popular image serves as a model to follow for women migrants as it conveys the values of maternal sacrifice, devotion to the family and conjugal fidelity.

Hence, human security in migration means for the Church the safeguarding of the family, the preservation of the dignity of women, and the respect of the migrants' human rights. The last two definitions obviously converge with that of the state, but it is not the case of the first one since the state continues to promote labor migration without taking specific measures to address its impacts on the family.

5.4.2 The NGOs' Calls for More Protection of the Migrants

During the 1986 revolution against the Marcos' dictatorial regime, the active participation of NGOs played an important role and marked the beginning of their growing social visibility. Taking into account the large number of NGOs in the country, estimated somewhere between 50,000 and 100,000 (NGO-JICA 2006), the Philippines can be considered as one of the countries in the world having the most dynamic "civil society". One very visible action of these NGOs is their intense lobbying to the government, notably concerning the human security of Filipino migrant workers.

Since the later part of the 1980s, Filipino NGOs have acted as a sort of verifier, examiner and critic of the government's actions concerning labor migration. NGOs play a role in empowering Filipino migrants in the Philippines and even in their receiving countries, as they guarantee "[…] the needs and rights of globalized workers [to be] more broadly recognized and ultimately attended to" (Ball and Piper 2002: 1030). They gather data on the living condition of migrants and their families, diffuse them to inform the public and call for immediate action from the government. About 41 NGOs work in the Philippines for the cause of Filipino migrants (SMC 1997), and some of them build networks with other groups to effectively design and implement programs and activities directed to migrants. The Philippine Migrants Rights Watch (PMRW), for instance, is a network of nine groups established in 1995 "[…] to encourage the recognition, protection and fulfillment of Filipino migrants' rights - both in the Philippines and abroad during the entire migration process" (PMRW 2004). Another example of a network of NGOs is the Network Opposed to Violence against Migrant Women, composed of 16 group members that work specifically to support women migrants.

In addition, almost all the local NGOs working for migrants' interests are linked more or less to one another or with organizations or public institutions of the country.

They also weave networks with NGOs founded by Filipino migrants abroad to effectively lobby the government for the approval of bills or international conventions on migration. Thus, NGOs serve as a way for migrants to communicate their insecurities to their sending country. One good example of this is the *Kapisanan ng mga Kamag-anak ng Migranteng Manggagawang Pilipino, Inc.* founded in 1983 and represented by migrant workers' families. This NGO is an active member of eight national NGO networks and two international ones, as well as partner of 50 migrant NGOs, governmental organizations, support and pressure groups in the world. The signing in 1995 of the UN "International Convention on the Protection of the Rights of all Migrant Workers and Members of their Families" and of the bill for the protection of Filipino migrant workers abroad are also the results of NGO lobbying.

The emergence of local NGOs established by non-migrants and migrant returnees or those still abroad is directly related to the multiplication of violence committed against migrants, notably women, and the passivity of the government to protect them. For these NGOs, human security in migration boils down to legal protection of the migrants' rights. Indeed, if we compare the protection of Filipino migrants' rights today and during the 1980s and 1990s, most visible improvements result from NGOs' efforts.

5.4.3 The Philippine Media's Plea for the Safety of Women and the Safeguarding of the Family

The existence of nearly nine million Filipino migrants and their continuous spreading around the world have attracted a lot of attention from the Philippine media (whether in print, on the radio, on TV, in movie theaters or in the Internet). By reporting on the migrants' situation, the Philippine media have succeeded in portraying Filipino migrants, notably women, as "sacrificial victims" and "heroes" who therefore need legal protection and social recognition.

For the last 20 years, the principal newspapers of the Philippines and television programs have presented Filipino migrants abroad simultaneously as victims (of violence, exploitations, abuses, accidents, negligence, etc.) and as modern heroes (for their economic contribution to the country), following the government's discourse. These representations intensified after the execution of Flor Contemplacion that strongly increased the public awareness of the living condition of Filipino migrants abroad. With the feminization of Filipino migration in the 1990s, the Philippine media have focused on the situation of Filipino migrant women and of their families living in the country by emphasizing the sacrifices of the former for the benefit of the latter. The local media also frequently report on the negative effects of women's migration on their families: marital infidelity, family separation, incest, drug addiction of certain children left in the country, etc.

Many Filipino films are devoted to the theme of migrant Filipinas: either the lives of real migrants, such as "Maricris Sioson story – Japayuki" (by Joey Romero 1993), "the Flor Contemplacion story" (by Joel Lamangan 1995) and "the Sarah Balabagan story" (by Joel Lamangan 1997), or fictions such as "Anak" (by Rory Quintos 2000), and "Caregiver" (by Chito Rono 2008). The sufferings of migrant Filipinas have become a popular object of attention in the local movie and television industries, which mirrors the way the Philippine society looks at its women population as the bastion and guardian of the country's honor. Hence, local media have contributed significantly to the image building of human security in migration as encompassing the safeguarding of migrants, especially women, from all forms of violence, and of families from all forms of threats to their unity. However, this portrayal of migrants in the local media as "sacrificial" citizens has now started to change: the government's promotion of the country as a good investment place and the incentives offered to migrants to invest in the country have motivated the Philippine media to focus on success stories of Filipino migrants, notably in the domain of business.

5.5 Conclusion

Careful examination of the position of the Philippine state and of non-state actors shows that diverse opinions concerning migration in relation to human security converge around a central theme: the continuation of labor migration while assuring migrant workers' security through protection of their rights, especially those of women. For the state, the migrants' human security appears to mean not only their protection from all forms of violence and exploitation throughout the migration process, but also their freedom to choose their job type and place of work (among the ones offered to them by the deregulated labor export industry), their elevated social position, and their easy access to available resources and social structures in both their country of origin and their country of immigration. For non-state actors, the emerging discourse on human security highlights the respect of human rights, the preservation of the country's honor embodied in Filipino women, and the protection of the family against the undesirable effects of emigration.

Nowadays, the obvious social stakes of the Filipino labor migration are the preservation of the nation's honor and the future of the Filipino family. The former can be realized by providing more legal protection to migrant women, whereas the latter seems a more complicated issue since it involves a social unit considered to be private. The emergence of motherless families due to migration has become a real preoccupation in the Philippine society, which emphasizes the keystone role of women in the preservation of traditional family values. This is observable in the way various components of the Philippine society, and especially the Catholic Church, react to the migration of Filipino women by emphasizing the challenge it imposes on family unity. This migratory phenomenon has indeed created a sort of "public sympathy" for the families of mothers working abroad that gained an image of social "insecurity" and of vulnerability to familial problems caused by migration. At this moment, no concrete political solutions have been implemented by the government to buffer the "undesirable" impacts of migration on the Filipino family, neither have formal social structures been established to assist migrants' family members left in the country (e.g. by providing care for the children and the elderly). As this chapter shows, the need to safeguard the family is what differentiates the viewpoints of the state and of the non-state actors. With the global economic crisis that started in 2008, Filipinos now seem even more ready to emigrate than before, irrespective of whether their migration path is secured or not. For them, emigrating remains the only accessible solution to confront the social and economic insecurity they experience.

References

Alcid, M. L. (2003). Overseas Filipino workers: Sacrificial lambs at the altar of deregulation. In E. Ostergaard-Nielsen (Ed.), *International migration and sending countries: Perceptions, policies and transnational relations* (pp. 99–118). New York: Palgrave Macmillan.

Alkire, S. (2003). "A conceptual framework for human security," CRISE Working Paper, University of Oxford. http://www.crise.ox.ac.uk/pubs/workingpaper2.pdf. Accessed 10 Dec 2008.

Asian Political News (1998 August 10). Philippines blasts 'Filipina' entry in Greek dictionary. http://findarticles.com/p/articles/mi_m0WDQ/is_1998_August_10/ai_53000395. Accessed 22 Jan 2008.

Asis, M., Huang, S., & Yeoh, B. (2004). When the light of the home is abroad: Unskilled female migration and the Filipino family. *Singapore Journal of Tropical Geography, 25*(2), 198–215.

Baldwin, D. (1997). The concept of security. *Review of International Studies, 23*, 5–26.

Ball, R., & Piper, N. (2002). Globalisation and regulation of citizenship – Filipino migrant workers in Japan. *Political Geography, 21*(8), 1013–1034.

Barber, P. (2000). Agency in Philippine women's labour migration and provisional diaspora. *Women's Studies International Forum, 23*(4), 399–411.

Basch, L., Schiller Nina, G., & Blanc Cristina, S. (2003). *Nations unbound: Transnational projects, postcolonial predicaments, and deterritorialized nation-states*. New York: Routledge.

Bigo, D. (2002). Security and immigration: Toward a critique of the governmentality of unease. *Alternatives: Global, Local, Political, 27*, 63–92.

CBCP. (1988). "On the occasion of national migration day," Catholic Bishop Conference of the Philippines. http://www.cbcponline.net/ecmi/letters/On%20the%20Occasion%20of%20National%20Migration%20Day.htm. Accessed 19 Jan 2008.

CBCP. (1995). "Comfort my people, comfort them," Catholic Bishop Conference of the Philippines. http://www.cbcponline.net/ecmi/letters/COMFORT%20MY%20PEOPLE,%20COMFORT%20THEM.htm. Accessed 22 Jan 2008.

CFO. (2008). "Stock estimate of overseas Filipinos," Commission on Filipinos Overseas. http://www.cfo.gov.ph/pdf/statistics/Stock%202007.pdf. Accessed 14 Mar 2008.

Choy, C. (2003). *Empire of care. Nursing and migration in Filipino American history*. Quezon City: Ateneo de Manila University Press.

Cohen, R. (2000). 'Mom is a stranger': The negative impact of immigration policies on the family life of Filipina domestic workers. *Canadian Ethnic Studies, 32*(3), 76–88.

Davies, R. (2000). 'Neither here nor there?' The implications of global diasporas for (inter)national security. In D. T. Graham & N. K. Poku (Eds.), *Migration, globalisation and human security* (pp. 23–46). London: Routledge.

De Lorenzo, L. (1998). Filipino ministry overseas. *Panawagan, 10*(1), 2.

Dumlao, D. (2006). SSS wants mandatory membership of OFWs. *Philippine Daily Inquirer, 27*(June), B3.

Fresnoza-Flot, A. (2008). *Migration, genre et famille transnationale: l'exemple des mères migrantes philippines en France* [Migration, gender and transnational family: The example of Filipino migrant mothers in France]. Ph.D. Thesis in sociology. Université Paris Diderot – Paris 7, Paris.

Fresnoza-Flot, A. (2009). Migration status and transnational mothering: The case of Filipino migrants in France. *Global Networks, 9*(2), 252–270.

Gallissot, R. (1985). *Misère de l'antiracisme: racisme et identité nationale, le défi de l'immigration [Misery of antiracism: Racism and national identity, the challenge of immigration]*. Paris: Arcantère.

Go, S. (2007). "Asian labor migration: The role of bilateral labor and similar agreements," Regional Informal Workshop on Labor Migration in Southeast Asia. http://www.fes.org.ph/2007%20conferences/reading%20and%20presentations/Stella%20Go's%20Paper.pdf. Accessed 24 Oct 2007.

Graham, D. (2000). The people paradox: Human movements and human security in a globalising world. In D. T. Graham & N. K. Poku (Eds.), *Migration, globalisation and human security* (pp. 185–214). London: Routledge.

Hampson, F. O., Daudelin, J., Hay, J., Reid, H., & Martin, T. (2002). *Madness in the multitude: Human security and world disorder*. Ontario: Oxford University Press.

IMF. (2010). Philippines. International reserves and foreign currency liquidity, international monetary fund. http://www.imf.org/external/np/sta/ir/phl/eng/curphl.htm. Accessed 30 Apr 2010.

Koser, K. (2005). Irregular migration state security and human security, Global Commission on International Migration. http://www.gcim.org/attachements/TP5.pdf. Accessed 17 Feb 2009.

Lawless, R. (2005). Philippine diaspora. In M. Ember, C. R. Ember, & I. Skoggard (Eds.), *Encyclopedia of diasporas: Immigrant and refugee cultures around the world* (pp. 244–253). New York: Springer.

Mozère, L. (2004). Des domestiques philippines à Paris: un marché mondial de la domesticité défini en termes de genre [Filipino domestic workers in Paris: A world market of domesticity defined in gender terms]. *Journal des Anthropologues, 97–98*, 291–319.

NGO-JICA. (2006). NGOs in the Philippines. History of civil society in the Philippines, Japan International Cooperation Agency. http://jica-ngodesk.ph/PhilippineNGOs/#4-2. Accessed 25 Jan 2008.

Ogaya, C. (2004). Social discourses on Filipino women migrants. *Feminist Review, 77*, 180–182.

Oishi, N. (2005). *Women in motion: Globalization, state policies, and labor migration in Asia*. California: Stanford University Press.

Ong, J. (2009). Watching the nation, singing the nation: London-based Filipino migrants' identity constructions in news and karaoke practices. *Communication, Culture & Critique, 2*, 160–181.

Ortiz, M. (2007). Former Filipinos reacquiring Philippine citizenships, say BI, Philippine Daily Inquirer. http://globalnation.inquirer.net/news/breakingnews/view_article.php?article_id=101690. Accessed 15 Jan 2008.

Paris, R. (2001). Human security: Paradigm shift or hot air? *International Security, 26*(2), 87–102.

Parreñas, R. (2005). *Children of global migration: Transnational families and gendered woes*. California: Stanford University Press.

PMRW. (2004). What is PMRW? The Philippine Migrants' Rights Watch. http://www.pmrw.org/. Accessed 23 Jan 2008.

Poku, N., & Graham, D. (2000). Introduction. In D. T. Graham & N. K. Poku (Eds.), *Migration, globalisation and human security* (pp. 1–8). London: Routledge.

Pope John Paul II. (1981). Laborem Exercens, Scalabrini Migration Center. http://www.smc.org.ph/religion/laborem.htm. Accessed 22 Jan 2008.

Rafael, V. (1997). Your grief is our gossip: Overseas Filipinos and other spectral presences. *Public Culture, 9*(2), 267–291.

Salazar, T. (2007). "For Balik scientists, home is where the heart is," Philippine Daily Inquirer. http://globalnation.inquirer.net/news/news/view_article.php?article_id=112398. Accessed 15 Jan 2008.

Shinozaki, K. (2005). 'For the sake of the family'? Exploring the nexus between Philippine's social security and overseas employment policies. *F-Gens Jaanaru, 4*, 103–111.

Sindjoun, L. (2005). "Introduction. Éléments d'analyse relationnelle des migrations et des transactions entre état et individu [Elements of relational analysis of migrations and transactions between state and individual],". In L. Sindjoun (Ed.), *État, Individus et Réseaux dans les Migrations Africaines [State, individuals and networks in African migrations]* (pp. 5–16). Paris: Karthala.

SMC. (1997). "Philippines. Directory of NGOs for migrant workers in Asia," Scalabrini Migration Center. http://www.skyinet.net/~smc/ngodir.htm. Accessed 23 Jan 2008.

Suarez, E. (2009). "Qualified OFWs, seamen voters reach 589,830," *Manila Bulletin*. http://www.mb.com.ph/articles/234467/qualified-ofws-seamen-voters-reach-589830. Accessed 20 Dec 2009.

UNDP. (1994). *Human development report*. New York: Oxford University Press.

Weiner, M. (1993). Security, stability and international migration. In M. Weiner (Ed.), *International migration and security* (pp. 1–35). Colorado: Westview.

Wolf, D. (1997). Family secrets: Transnational struggles among children of Filipino immigrants. *Sociological Perspectives, 40*(3), 457–482.

Zhang, K. (2006). Recognizing the Canadian diaspora. *Canada Asia Commentary, 41*, 1–13.

Part II
Regional Approaches to Human Security and Policy Implications

Chapter 6
Insecurity Within and Outside the State: The Regional and Local Dynamics of Environmental Insecurity in the Mekong

Duncan McDuie-Ra

6.1 Introduction

Environmental security has become perhaps the most prominent of the seven aspects of human security conceived by the United Nations Development Program (UNDP) in 1994 (UNDP 1994). As environmental issues have risen in importance in global politics environmental security has become a cornerstone of thinking and policy making in the spheres of development, security, and international cooperation. Despite the strong rhetorical commitment to environmental norms from governments, international organizations, and various non-state actors, environmental degradation continues to produce insecurity for vast numbers of people, and East Asia is no exception. This chapter examines the dynamics of environment insecurity in the Mekong region; specifically in the lower Mekong states of Cambodia, Lao People's Democratic Republic (Lao PDR hereafter), and Vietnam. The region has been selected owing to the extent of environmental change occurring in the last 20 years as post-Cold War economic, political and social relationships have transformed the region. The Mekong provides a compelling example of the various extra-regional and intraregional dynamics shaping the production of environmental insecurity at the inter-state, national, and local levels.

In examining these dynamics this chapter argues that environmental insecurity poses four interlinked challenges to the conceptual and material bases on which human security is commonly understood. First, closer analyses of which forms of environmental insecurity are acted upon and which are marginalized suggests that certain environmental issues have more visibility than others regardless of their impact on insecurity. Second, environmental insecurity is the result of a number of political, social, and economic dynamics that are transnational in origin but

D. McDuie-Ra (✉)
University of New South Wales, Sydney, Australia
e-mail: d.mcduie@unsw.edu.au

experienced locally, requiring a contextually driven understanding of the locations where insecurity is produced and experienced. Thirdly, politicizing and addressing environmental insecurity depends upon a range of actors and the state, though important, should not necessarily be prioritized, thus actors both within and outside the state become crucial. Lastly, politicizing environmental insecurity is vital, but further attention needs to be paid to the complex configurations within which different actors, particularly non-state actors, operate in making the diverse experiences of environmental insecurity visible.

This chapter begins by examining the rise of environmental security within the human security and critical security discourses and the relationship between environmental security and the prominence of environmental issues in global politics. The second section examines the extra-regional and intraregional dynamics that have produced environmental insecurity in the lower Mekong states of Cambodia, Lao PDR, and Vietnam. The third section identifies four local catalysts of environmental insecurity emanating from these extra-regional and intraregional dynamics: hydropower, deforestation, changing land relations, and mining. The fourth section discusses the uneven impacts of environmental insecurity at the local level. The fifth section uses these examples to demonstrate the four conceptual and material challenges posed by environmental insecurity. The chapter concludes by stressing that although events of the last two decades have deepened peace and regional integration in East Asia, insecurity has not vanished but taken different forms.

6.2 The Rise of Environmental Insecurity

Environmental security, or more accurately its absence referred to here as environmental insecurity, describes the insecurities experienced by groups and individuals from environmental degradation (Dyer 2001; Graeger 1996). The concept of environmental security emerged from three crucial turns in thinking about politics, security, and development during the 1990s. The first was the inclusion of environmental security in the normative agenda of human security most widely publicized by the UNDP in their 1994 *Human Development Report* (1994: 24). The UNDP report focused on threats to the environment, particularly concerning access to water, land use and deforestation, pollution, and natural disasters, and linked these threats to increased poverty as both a cause and symptom of environmental change at the global and national levels (1994: 29–30). This drew the concept of environmental security into discussions and policy agendas on sustainable development, social justice, and international peace and security. Most of these discussions have since been embodied in the *Millennium Development Goals* and subsequent global and national initiatives aimed at their implementation (Pronk 2005).

The second was the so-called 'critical turn' in security studies in the 1990s epitomized by a questioning of the 'meaning and production of security.' (Dunne and Wheeler 2004) Critical security has been defined as both a reconstructive project that seeks to construct and operationalize alterative approaches to security and a deconstructive project that seeks to expose the limitations and implications of conventional security discourse and policy (Burke and McDonald 2007: 4–5). In doing so the critical security school identified the following limitations of conventional security thinking: (i) the state can be a cause of insecurity and does not always act to protect the interests of its citizens (and especially non-citizens), (ii) security has been conceptualized from a masculine perspective, ignoring the role of women and the impact of conflict on women, (iii) by maintaining the state as the referent object of security, conventional security is very limited in dealing with a wider range of non-state and non-military threats that can occur from within and outside states, (iv) conventional security is constructed and reconstructed by politics and relies upon notions of otherness to classify threats to the state and its citizenry, and (v) by extension critical security aims to emancipate individuals and communities from security priorities externally imposed (Booth 1991). Environmental security has become a key component of this as it challenges conventional security thinking, enabling new thinking about the complex causes of insecurity and opens the provision of security to a more diverse set of actors.

The third was the rise in environmental politics at the global, regional, and national levels from the 1970s and growing concern about the impacts of climate change (Kimble 2005; Williams 2005). Environmental concerns have become integrated into the operations of a range of actors from transnational corporations, multilateral development banks, international organizations, and governments (Clapp 2005; Lipschutz 2005). This has corresponded to the 'opening up' of many of these same actors to civil society actors (Utting 2006); long considered the chief purveyors of environmental politics allowing environmental non-governmental organizations (NGOs), epistemic communities, social movements, and other civil society actors more influence in global agenda setting. In effect, environmental issues have become normalized in everything from trade negotiations (Barkin 2005) to peace building (Lidén and Eneström 2005).

In the decade and a half since the UNDP report popularized the concept, and at a time where 'going green' is a practice adopted, at least rhetorically, by every conceivable entity from government ministries to oil companies, the environment has become one of the key issues in international relations, development, and security. Environmental issues have become the main signifier of a broader security agenda ensuring that even obstinate states and institutions recognize the importance of the environment for a more secure world. Yet does this enable a more complete understanding of the ways environmental degradation causes insecurity for different groups, communities and individuals? In other words, does the increased mainstreaming of environmental issues at the global and national levels enable a more complete understanding of the environmental insecurity experienced by people in their everyday lives? Analyzing environmental insecurity in a particular location, in this case the lower Mekong states, raises a number of challenges to the standard approach taken on environmental insecurity by scholars, organizations, and policy makers. Before these challenges are extrapolated a breakdown of the dynamics of environmental insecurity in the lower Mekong region will be given.

6.3 Dynamics of Environmental Insecurity in the Mekong

Environmental insecurity in the lower Mekong states is produced through three extra-regional dynamics and four intraregional dynamics. Extra-regional refers to dynamics originating and/or linking the lower Mekong states to East Asia and beyond. Intraregional refers to dynamics taking place at the national level in the lower Mekong, between the governments in the region, and within each state. While this section identifies regional dynamics it is not intended to strip states of their agency, rather the aim is to locate these states in different contexts and relationships driving economic, political, and social changes; changes that produce environmental insecurity for different groups and individuals.

6.3.1 Extra-Regional Dynamics

There are three main extra-regional dynamics: foreign investment, institutional integration and the adverse impacts of environmental movements. These will be discussed briefly in turn.

Foreign investment in Cambodia, Lao PDR, and Vietnam has been increasing over the last two decades as these governments have attempted to open their previously centralized socialist economies to international markets. This has both direct and indirect implications for environmental insecurity. Directly, investment has provided capital boosts for more intense exploitation of natural resources. Indirectly, increased openness leads to changes in production, consumption, and the use of natural resources. While natural resource extraction has long been a driver of economic growth in East Asia, changes over the past two decades have accelerated extraction in the Mekong states and exposed natural resources to more investors and more potential markets. Public and private investment from China, Japan, South Korea, Malaysia, Singapore, and Thailand has changed the way natural resources are utilized, valued, and degraded in the lower Mekong (Oehlers 2006). Links between private business interests in different parts of the East Asia, and between these networks and governments has also had an indirect impact on environmental degradation, especially in states where the influx of foreign capital is relatively recent, poorly regulated, and where natural resources are relatively plentiful (Freeman 2001; Jacobs 2009; Thongpakde 2001; Varis et al. 2008). As these linkages thicken the likelihood of further environmental degradation increases. Furthermore, bilateral development aid from China, Japan, and South Korea, as well as Australia and Europe, has created an enabling environment for investment in infrastructure, much of which is necessary for economic development and access to health care and services, but which also increases the likelihood of environmental degradation as access to previously remote areas becomes easier. This is not to argue that regional integration, cooperation, development aid, and transnational investment lead to environmental degradation by default, nor that the intention of such flows of capital is to exploit the environment *per se*; the casual links are not predetermined.

However, given the value of the region's natural resources, the desire for investment by governments, and the facilitating role of development aid, environmental degradation is reality of regional integration.

Second, increased cooperation and integration through formal institutions and regimes has had an indirect impact on environment insecurity. The expansion of ASEAN, the creation of the Greater Mekong Subregion (GMS), and the involvement of the Asian Development Bank in development projects has impacted on the environment. The construction of intra-regional highways, transnational hydropower projects, and increased cross border trade have normalized environmental degradation as a necessary, though often 'manageable', part of economic growth, development, and regional prosperity (Gunn 2008). This type of cooperation opens up new areas of the lower Mekong that were previously less accessible, and while often greatly benefitting certain groups within these states, this places new pressures on the environment. Cooperation must be compared to the divisions of the Cold War particularly given the lower Mekong states were isolated from the rest of Southeast Asia and much of greater East Asia during that time, though the degree of isolation is contestable (Walker 1999).

Thirdly, the success of environmental NGOs and social movements in other parts of East Asia has led to a shifting of intensive resource extraction to other locations, including the lower Mekong states (Simpson 2007). As environmental issues such as dams and deforestation have become heavily contested in neighboring states, particularly Thailand (Darlington 1998; Foran and Manoram 2009), central governments have introduced more stringent regulations and have decentralized the management of natural resources to local governments and communities. This type of regulation has taken longer to develop in the lower Mekong states, particularly as civil society and local environmental movements are less autonomous, though efforts at decentralization of natural resource management have taken place in some locations (Fujita and Phengospha 2008; Manivong and Sophathilath 2007; Pellini and Ayres 2007). Despite these well intended nascent measures, decentralization of natural resource management is in transition in all three states.

6.3.2 Intraregional Dynamics

There are four main intraregional dynamics producing environmental insecurity in Cambodia, Lao PDR, and Vietnam: economic liberalization, the formation of the GMS, the Mekong River Commission (MRC), and broader social changes.

First, all three states are transition states adopting economic liberalization to varying degrees and subject to both small-scale and large-scale development projects aimed at accelerating economic growth. All three states have high levels of poverty, variously defined, despite the difficulties of accurate measures in Cambodia and Lao PDR (Kaosa-ard 2003). In order to increase national revenue all three states are in the process of liberalizing parts of their economies and shifting from subsistence to commercial agricultural and industrial production. The embedded legitimacy of economic growth at the regional level and within national political cultures throughout the region places enormous strain on the environment. As Rwabizambuga (2007) argues, the links between development the environment and human security are strong in such contexts. This is not to suggest that environmental degradation did not occur in these states prior to the present era of integration, indeed the impacts of the Indochina Wars, massive displacement of populations, post-conflict rebuilding, and socialist modernization projects have all had major environmental impacts. What is different in the Mekong states presently is the opening of land borders, both between these three states, and between these states and the rest of East Asia, particularly Thailand and China. This has increased access to previously remote areas and the natural resources within. The extent of environmental degradation varies considerably within these states; however it can be assumed at the very least that communities within these states are facing a changing environmental scenario when compared to previous decades.

Second, all three states are part of the GMS. The GMS is a transnational political and economic arena comprising of six states that share the Mekong River: Cambodia, China, Lao PDR, Myanmar, Thailand, and Vietnam. It also refers to the regional programs and initiatives instigated by these states and international organizations, particularly the Asian Development Bank and the MRC, and increasingly by civil society actors from within and outside the GMS, focusing on governance of common resources and creating stronger inter and intra state linkages (Dore 2003; Masviriyakul 2006; Poncet 2006). While the expansion of the Association of South East Asian Nations (ASEAN) institutionalized the political realignment of Southeast Asia in the post-Cold War era, the GMS exemplifies a deeper regional integration more reflective of the dynamics of globalization, particularly in terms of economic development and transnational investment (ADB 2006; Theeravit 2003). The GMS has become a locus for foreign direct investment, and this has had a major impact on the three states in question as all three receive foreign direct investment from within Southeast Asia (and the GMS), particularly Malaysia and Thailand, and from Northeast Asia, particularly Japan, South Korea, and China (ADB 2006: 49–51). Investment patterns are uneven, domestic regulations on ownership vary in each state, taxation rules differ, and reform processes are at different stages (ADB 2006: 44–5). However the formation of the GMS has facilitated the process of economic, and hence environmental, transformation. In March 2008, the triennial meeting of the GMS was held in Vientiane, capital of the Lao PDR, with a focus on deepening regional integration through public-private partnerships in the above mentioned sectors. In short, the GMS provides a platform for inter and intra-regional economic integration; integration that has major implications for environmental insecurity.

Thirdly, all three states are part of the MRC along with Thailand. The MRC was established in 1995 to manage and preserve natural resources. The MRC builds upon two older agreements, the Mekong Commission 1957–1978 and the Interim Mekong Committee 1978–1995 both of which faced multiple obstacles during the Indochina wars and the Cold War divide (Jacobs 2002). The main aim of the MRC is to orchestrate cooperation between governments in the areas of development, ecological protection, and sharing of water resources (Jacobs 2002: 360). The MRC is based on natural resource management, a seemingly innocuous concept, but in practice the agreement is a forum for pursuing the joint utilization of the region's environment to serve state interests; interests that can be at odds with different communities within the respective states. As Fox and Sneddon argue, intraregional water sharing agreements such as the MRC may espouse the language of environmentally aware sustainable development but in practice are largely 'vehicles to promote the developmental goals (e.g., hydroelectricity production and irrigation expansion) of their signatories.' (2007: 239- brackets in original) While this may decrease the likelihood of environment related conflict between states it does not guarantee that such utilization will not produce environmental insecurity for groups, communities, and individuals at the local level. Furthermore, it makes the reversal or alteration of projects that have been agreed upon by all four governments far more difficult. This is particularly salient when viewed in the context of the GMS discussed above, a forum through which the same governments are pursuing investment in the natural resources the MRC is 'managing' (Ratner 2003).

Fourthly, all three states are undergoing social changes that have an impact on the environment and typify changes that have taken place throughout the East Asian region. The emergence of a new elite and a growing middle class has increased demand for consumer goods, cars, and electricity, all with direct and indirect impacts on the environment (Sinh 2003), particularly with regard to electricity (read hydropower in the Mekong) water provision, and land availability. Urban migration has placed increased pressure on urban infrastructure and access to services, while migration to neighboring countries, particularly Thailand, and farther afield has changed local demographics, preferences, and aspirations contributing to broader social changes (Harima et al. 2003; Kaur 2010; Muntarbhorn 2005). In addition the governments of the three lower Mekong states, seeing the value of remittances and repercussions for local labor markets, are all attempting to promote their migrant labor force through new legislation and regulation (Harima et al. 2003: 233–6). Urban migration and the intensification of export-oriented agriculture has had an impact on rural communities and pushed those left behind further into the margins of agrarian production and in certain cases increased their dependency on the environment for their livelihoods. Again, this is not to pass negative judgment on such changes, but merely to note the ways they contribute to the production of environmental insecurity.

6.4 Forms of Environmental Insecurity

These dynamics produce environmental degradation that leads to environmental insecurity. Accounting for all the incidences of environmental degradation in Cambodia, Lao PDR, and Vietnam is well beyond the scope of this chapter. Instead, four main forms of degradation emanating from the extra-regional and intraregional dynamics discussed above are identified: hydropower, deforestation, changing land relations, and mining. These will be discussed briefly in turn.

6.4.1 Hydropower

Hydropower has underpinned the national and regional development agenda in the Mekong. Data on the actual number of hydropower dams planned in Cambodia, Lao PDR and Vietnam is constantly being revised (Yu 2003). Bakker's 1999 estimates show 60 dams being planned in the Lao PDR, 36 in Vietnam, and 17 in Cambodia (1999: 214). Recent data from the MRC indicates that the number of dams planned in Lao PDR has not changed, but the number in the other two states is slightly less (MRC 2008), indicating that there has been no major shift in the development strategy in the region over the past decade. Hydropower dams are often rationalized as providing much needed electricity, irrigation, flood control, a source of foreign exchange gained from the export of power to neighboring countries, and as fostering cooperation between states sharing water resources (Fox and Sneddon 2007). Indeed with vast hydropower potential the Lao PDR has been described as the 'Battery of Southeast Asia' by governments, investors, and donors (IRN 2008). Large dam construction is embedded in the politics and economics of the region and is difficult to contest (Käkönen and Hirsch 2009), though civil society actors have had success in modifying and cancelling particular projects (Hirsch 2001). Despite their popularity amongst governments and aid donors, large hydropower dams produce environmental insecurity in a number of crucial areas: water quality, flooding, land loss, livelihood loss and/or alteration, displacement, resettlement, and inadequate compensation, embodied in the Nam Theun II project in the Nakai plateau of Lao PDR (Lebel et al. 2009; Jönsson 2009). Furthermore indirect impacts include deforestation after road construction to dams, displacement for road construction and transmission lines, higher population pressure on remaining agricultural land and fisheries, increased completion in labor markets from displaced populations, and changing migration patterns to both urban and rural areas (Tar 2003; Pech and Sunada 2008).

6.4.2 Deforestation

Deforestation in these three states is not a new phenomenon. Centuries of migration into upland areas, changes in agricultural methods, colonial timber production, the use of exfoliates during the Indochina Wars, ongoing civil conflict, and socialist modernization have all played a role in shaping the forest ecology in the region (Berhe 2007; Donovan 2003). In recent decades, the regional dynamics discussed above, particularly increased regional integration and trade, foreign investment, and the decline of the timber industry in Thailand, have led to an acceleration of deforestation in Cambodia, Lao PDR, and Vietnam. It is estimated that in 2003 the lower Mekong Basin had lost 69.2% of its original forest cover and was losing forest cover at a rate of 0.5% per year (Rowcroft 2008: 213). Other factors are also important; rapid urbanization and population growth, changes in land use particularly the promotion of export cash crops, displacement, and the power accorded to ministers and local officials involved in forestry all have an impact. Deforestation produces environmental insecurity in a number of ways; erosion, flooding, loss of livelihoods, loss of supplementary food and income, loss of fuel sources, and potential conflict within and between communities and between communities and local authorities over forest rights and revenue (Nguyen 2008). As Heinimann et al. (2007) point out, it is not only deforestation of primary forest that affects local populations, but the degradation of secondary forest has a major impact on communities and individuals as it plays a more immediate role in their livelihoods. As will be discussed below this affects some communities more than others.

6.4.3 Changing Land Relations

Changes in land use abound in the lower Mekong. The 'dual transition' from subsistence farming to more diverse agricultural production in these countries and from command economies to more liberalized market economies has led to substantial changes in the ways land is owned, used, and distributed (Lee 2003; Rerkasem 2003; Rowcroft 2008). Rubber, cassava, sugarcane, corn, palm oil, cashews and eucalyptus are all being produced for export in the three countries (Rutherford et al. 2008: 4). This produces environmental insecurity in a number of ways: land acquisition often leads to displacement and/or major disruptions to lives and livelihoods, new patterns of land ownership give access to larger and more powerful economic and political interests which can lead to less sustainable use of land and natural resources, the gradual replacement of subsistence agriculture with commercial agriculture has implications for the sustainability of land and the environment, the active discouragement of shifting or swidden cultivation by governments and international development agencies forces many communities to take up alterative livelihoods with no access to land or forests, and new structures of land relations lead to intra-rural migration and shifts from community land use to landlordism creating more precarious livelihoods for many (Hughes 2008; Rerkasem 2003; Sekhar 2007). Commercial agriculture has also heightened the unsustainable exploitation of secondary forest produce (or non-timber forest products) and better links to markets in other parts of East Asia have increased incentives for local people and business interests to work together to exploit secondary forest resources.

6.4.4 Mining

Mining has increased in the region, mainly as a result of foreign direct investment from Chinese and Australian mining companies and favorable conditions created by host governments, particularly in the Lao PDR (ADB 2006: 20). Thus far mining in the three countries has concentrated on bauxite, gold, copper, iron, zinc and coal (Rutherford et al. 2008: 23–5, 38–9, 50–2). Mining produces environmental insecurity directly in the land that is being mined, which is also linked to displacement and resettlement, but also indirectly by polluting soil and watercourses, often due to inadequate waste disposal. Mine sites are usually cleared of forests, new roads are constructed to mining areas, and the local economy must readjust to both the influx of workers to mining areas and the change in livelihoods in local food and agricultural markets. Wealth from mining is rarely shared by those most affected by its operations, and land rarely recovers permanently changing the ecology in different locations. It is important to note that many individuals from local communities in affected areas work at mine sites, creating new fissures amongst communities and between pro and anti mine groups.

6.5 Uneven Impacts of Insecurity

Environmental insecurity is not experienced in the same way by all groups, communities, and individuals within each state. Environmental insecurity is felt disproportionately by the poor in both urban and rural areas, those living in marginal geographic areas, ethnic minorities, and women. The poor are often dependent upon a sustainable environment and access to natural resources for their livelihoods, nutrition, and health, and are generally more likely to experience insecurity from environmental degradation (Dasgupta et al. 2005). In the lower Mekong states, a range of poverty indicators reveal that a far greater number of the poor reside in rural areas and are dependent on natural resources, whether these indicators measure monetary income, access to food, or purchasing power (Kaosa-ard 2003). Furthermore, the rural and urban poor are often exposed to greater health risks from pollution, poor quality water, and poor quality soil. Yet conceptualizing those affected as a single category 'the poor' overlooks the differentiated impact of environmental insecurity within different locations. In other words, 'the poor' are not a distinct identifiable group within the region or within each of the three states. Rather, among affected peoples or within affected locations the poorer members of the community are usually least capable of bearing the costs of environmental insecurity.

The current phase of environmental degradation in the region is increasingly being located in marginal geographic areas such as border areas, upland areas, and areas populated by ethnic minorities (Lee 2003). This is not to suggest that these are the only areas where environmental insecurity is experienced, however, given the opening of borders between the Mekong states and Thailand and China, as well as the increase in foreign investment in natural resources in the region, areas that were previously peripheral, isolated, or buffers between former rival governments are now being opened up for development. In addition, environmental degradation is accelerating in these areas as decades of relative isolation kept natural resources distant from large-scale extraction. Many of the communities inhabiting these regions are already marginalized from the social, political, and economic mainstream in their respective states (Lestrelin and Giordano 2007; Quang 2004). In all three states examined here ethnic minorities populate border areas and upland areas, both of which are subject to government interventions aimed at enabling these regions to 'catch up' to the rest of the country. In certain cases, such as among Hmong and Khmu communities in the Lao PDR (Lee, 2003; Ovesen 2004) and Hmong and Tai speaking communities in Vietnam (Corlin 2004), this has involved the commercialization of biodiversity, enforced resettlement, and forced adoption of settled agriculture, though often compensation has been paid these programs have not been consistent (Evrard and Goudineau 2004).

Environmental insecurity is experienced in different ways along gender lines. As women are usually more involved in food production and provision, the gathering of fuel and secondary forest produce, and the collection and provision of water, environmental insecurity has a major impact on gendered labor and social roles. Women are often more marginal in local organizations and local government bodies and thus are not always able to make their experiences of insecurity visible (Howell 2006). Resettlement creates new insecurities and again these have gender dimensions, particularly as women still have the responsibilities they carried in their previous community, but must now adapt to a new location where access to resources may be limited, the population pressures may be greater, and new social relations create new asymmetries of power that displace previous social orders. Migration has significant impacts on livelihoods, labor, and social networks which creates new burdens on migrants but also on family members remaining behind. Women face new insecurities when male family members move away from areas where the environment has been degraded as their workload and responsibilities increase. However, women also migrate to work in the labor markets in urban areas and larger towns, while some migrate abroad, particularly to Thailand. In many cases women migrants work for low wages, work in more precarious occupations, and have fewer outlets for support increasing their insecurity.

6.6 The Challenges of Environmental Insecurity

As can be seen above, environmental insecurity in the Mekong raises a number of challenges for scholars, policy-makers, and activists. These will be discussed in turn.

6.6.1 The Utility of the Environment as a 'Security' Issue

The first challenge is the discord between the ways environmental insecurity is experienced and the ways it has been defined; shaping which environmental issues are made part of policy agendas and which are marginalized. As Elliot points out, the majority of the literature on environmental security adopts one of two positions: the role of environmental degradation in producing armed conflict and thus threatening the security of states, the 'modified realist position', and the role of environmental degradation in jeopardizing sustainable livelihoods and thus threatening the security of individuals and communities, the 'human security position' (Elliot 2007: 137–8). This affects the ways environmental insecurity is defined, identified, and acted upon, which can be vastly different to how it is experienced.

The 'modified realist position' is problematic as it implies that environmental degradation causes insecurity *only* when it leads to violent conflict, especially between peoples from different states and/or nationalities. In doing so this perspective excludes the more common causes of insecurity caused by environmental degradation that might not ever lead to violent conflict yet produce insecurity for vast numbers of people in their everyday lives.

The 'human security position' raises a different set of problems that are more difficult to see. By embedding environment security within the human security discourse environmental degradation must compete for political and policy space with other forms of human insecurity. Some will be ignored and excluded, while others will be politicized and acted upon (McDuie-Ra 2009). In particular contexts certain insecurities may be more materially or politically lucrative, or less controversial, less complicated and thus more amenable to policy agendas. This does not always pose a problem when there are adequate resources to address each, but in contexts where resources are limited such as the Mekong states, actors advocating different issues compete with each other for legitimacy and political recognition. Furthermore different aspects of insecurity can also compete at the local level such as economic insecurity, which may lead a group of people to support a mine for example, and environmental insecurity which may lead another group to oppose the same mine (McDuie-Ra 2007). In such cases the realization of human security for one group in that location produces insecurity for another group.

6.6.2 Reconsidering Space

The very concept of environmental security forces scholars and policy makers to rethink national frames of reference in identifying the production and experiences of insecurity. In other words, while it may be analytically convenient to set out the threats posed by 'environmental insecurity in Cambodia' for example, examining environmental insecurity at the national level gives a limited view of both the causes of degradation and the unevenness of its impacts.

The prevalence of environmental degradation within and across international borders forces a reconsideration of state boundaries and state sovereignty. Viewing the region as a series of interlinked ecosystems relocates cites of insecurity both within and outside international borders. For example, the lives and livelihoods of many of the peoples (and governments) of the lower Mekong region are interlinked and dependent on the management of a river system that transcends conventional notions of borders and sovereignty. In the context of poverty, privatization, and commercialization these states are being linked to each other, to other states in the

Mekong region, to donors and investors in the wider East Asian region, and farther afield. Thus Cambodia, Lao PDR, and Vietnam cannot be viewed as just states, or just states in the Mekong subregion, they are linked to other regions and other patterns of commerce, trade, and development that are beyond state boundaries.

The question of space is not, however, simply one of elevating environmental security to regional or extra-regional levels. Environmental insecurity is experienced in different ways and to different degrees by groups, communities and individuals within existing state borders, particularly at the local level. The term 'local' is not used as a substitute for 'national' when compared to 'international' or 'global', rather 'local' refers here to political and social spaces existing at the sub-national level as defined by the peoples that constitute said spaces. Such a space can be limited in size and scale, such as a particular community centered on a village or number of villages or an urban locality. Local can also refer to a political and social space extending across provinces, federal states, autonomous regions or other sub-national units. In other words, the local need not be defined by existing and distinct administrative units.

At the local level a single form of environmental degradation may affect different groups and communities in different ways. For example, in the province of Attapeu in the Lao PDR deforestation has been increasing as roads have improved and as the border to Vietnam has opened to commercial traders giving timber merchants better access to forests. Deforestation affects different groups and individuals in different ways depending on whether forest products are part of their livelihoods, whether a community or family collect forest products to supplement their diet or their income, whether any family members have gained employment in the timber industry, whether their livelihoods depend on trade or service provision for the timber industry, whether they have been displaced by new roads into the area, whether they own stall in the market that has benefitted from better transportation links (Rigg 2006).

Examining environmental insecurity suggests that there are no clear boundaries between these different spatial zones, nor are linkages necessarily formed in a linear manner. Environmental insecurity allows us to view these spatial zones as mutually constitutive; and factors causing environmental insecurity emanate from both within and outside the state. The impacts of environmental insecurity are often experienced most acutely at the local level, yet the causes of insecurity are often generated outside local spaces, and in East Asia a great deal of environmental degradation has transnational causes. Similarly, degradation may have local origins but have impacts far beyond the local area, even crossing international borders, as downstream communities along the Mekong know all too well.

6.6.3 Reconsidering Actors

The value of environmental security as both a concept and an analytical framework for shaping political agendas and policies lies in the possibility that people, not states, can identify the sources of their insecurity. Thus identifying environmental insecurity can come from a number of sources and allows security to be realized in a number of contexts, not solely at the level of the state (McDonald 2002: 293). Indeed, the state is not necessarily the actor most capable of, or indeed willing to identify and politicize environmental insecurity at the local level. Environmental insecurity in the lower Mekong states has rarely led to conflict between states. While there have been tensions around water issues, particularly between Vietnam and Cambodia, transnational environmental issues and natural resource management has been characterized by cooperation over conflict, embodied in the MRC. As the legitimacy and survival of governments in all three states is dependent on continued economic growth and rapid development, there is little prospect that they will take environmental insecurity into consideration where it threatens this legitimacy. That is not to say they will not adopt environmental safeguards and impact assessments, particularly when working in partnership with aid donors and foreign investors (Dore 2003). Yet it is unlikely that governments will act upon any cause of environmental insecurity that challenges economic growth and threatens foreign investment without sustained pressure from non-state actors politicizing insecurity.

6.6.4 Politicization: Opportunities and Constraints

Non-state actors have a crucial role to play in identifying, politicizing, and addressing environmental insecurity in the region. However, the ability of non-state actors to politicize the causes of environmental insecurity should not be assumed and analysis must focus on both opportunities and constraints for politicization. In effect non-state actors work in three main configurations in the Mekong states, each with different agential capacities.

The first configuration is comprised of international organizations and formalized international civil society organizations engaged in development activities of various kinds. This ranges from international and regional development banks to United Nations agencies and programs, to large NGOs. Virtually all actors involved in this configuration uphold environmental norms and follow environmental procedures such as environmental impact assessments. In many instances actors in this configuration are compromised from politicizing experiences of environmental insecurity caused by partner governments and donors. Their continued presence in host states depends upon satisfying funding objectives and on the permission of host governments, thus their potential for challenging projects that lead to widespread environmental insecurity is limited. Many of these organizations engage directly with governments in these three states and with inter-governmental organizations and international organizations, what Dore refers to as 'track 3' diplomacy in the region (2003). They are often better equipped to identify and resolve environmental insecurity at the transnational level, as with tensions over the Se San dam between Cambodia and Vietnam. While such engagements are welcome on the one hand, these engagements privilege particular types of actors that are formalized and 'seen' at the regional and national levels, empowering international actors which may not have the best knowledge of the intricacies of environmental insecurity at the local level. Even when they work in partnership with local civil society actors the different capacities of resources and expertise mean that local experiences of insecurity are unlikely to be filtered up through the first configuration in any systematic manner; though that is not to say it will not occur from time to time.

The second configuration involves formalized civil society organizations from Cambodia, Lao PDR and Vietnam which have varying degrees of autonomy and work in partnership with international actors and often their own national governments. Actors in this configuration, while nominally 'closer' to the locations where environmental insecurity is experienced, have a limited capacity to challenge the status quo. In a very general sense, studies of civil society in each of these states characterize them in very different ways; vibrant but dependent in Cambodia, dormant and/or co-opted by the state in Lao PDR, and participatory but state-controlled in Vietnam (Hughes 2007; Landau 2008; Vasavakul 2003). In order to be chosen to work in partnerships these organizations must ensure that their approach reflects that of their financiers and partners. Despite being staffed and often headed by nationals from the country in question, professional requirements mean that the staff are generally drawn from the social and political elite, limiting their understanding of development needs of people from other class and ethnic groups, and ensuring they have an embedded interest in maintaining the broader status quo least their positions be threatened. In the case of Lao PDR and Vietnam, legal restrictions and registration requirements make it difficult for these organizations to challenge the state and still be eligible to work in partnerships with foreign donors. Those that do mount a challenge can be harassed by the state or co-opted by different ministries and state sponsored organizations. Furthermore, many of these organizations depend upon political patronage for networking and survival leaving a very limited scope for politicizing environmental insecurity.

The final configuration is grassroots actors that are more deeply involved in communities at the local level. This includes formalized NGOs and philanthropic groups, but also more informal social movements, unions, community groups, religious organizations, networks of activists, collectives, village councils and traditional institutions. Such actors can be more participatory and inclusive than other actors enabling a more diverse set of voices to emerge in defining and politicizing environmental insecurity. Ironically, they are not always distant from the state, particularly in Lao PDR and Vietnam, but often their local legitimacy gives them a degree of autonomy that formal organizations don't have. Such actors are perceived to have a greater knowledge of the issues affecting communities and individuals at the local level and are able to utilize knowledge that is otherwise marginalized to address insecurity. Despite this, actors in this configuration are often isolated in spaces beyond the local. When invited to participate with actors from the first and second configurations, they are often minor partners as they lack the professional knowledge and expertise in the language of civil society and international organizations. This is particularly true for grassroots actors from ethnic minorities that may not speak the language of dominant ethnic groups or have to face discrimination and stereotypes in their quest to politicize their insecurity. Furthermore, for many of these organizations and their members the costs of involvement can be high, such as forgoing work to attend workshops, raising the ire of local officials and powerbrokers, and risking cooption into the agendas of more powerful actors. Thus while these organizations may have deeper knowledge of environmental insecurity, their ability to voice this knowledge and to be 'seen' at the national and regional level is limited.

Political patronage can provide opportunities for politicization at the local level, especially at the level of district or regional government. This should not be underestimated or necessarily unwelcomed. However this can also lead to constraints for grassroots actors who are not well connected to local powerbrokers. Add to this scenario ethnic difference between government officials and certain communities, systematic corruption in local natural resource governance, and the exclusion of women and young people from many of the relationships of patronage politics and further constraints become evident.

If non-state actors are to become effective in politicizing environmental insecurity, the opportunities and constraints that constitute the configurations in which they operate must be taken into careful consideration. A blanket assumption that the existence of non-state actors will somehow ensure that insecurities are politicized, addressed, and hopefully alleviated is unhelpful and unrealistic. In the lower Mekong those most able to politicize environmental insecurity are those with closest contact with the actors that produce insecurity, limiting which insecurities are politicized, addressed and alleviated.

6.7 Conclusion: The Challenges of Politicizing Insecurity

Environmental insecurity raises a number of challenges. It forces analysts, activists, and policy makers to rethink both conventional security and the grafting of the environment into existing security frameworks. It also allows a rethinking of the competing and even contradictory cleavages within the human security discourse. It forces a reconsideration of the spaces where environmental insecurity is produced and experienced, but also where it is politicized and where attempts are made to alleviate it. In doing so it forces a reconsideration of the actors capable and indeed willing to act on experiences of environmental insecurity beyond the inter-state level and a questioning of which experiences of insecurity these actors are able to 'see'. The different actors involved in producing and addressing environmental insecurity in direct and indirect ways allow the complex configurations of actors operating within and outside the state to be rendered more visible and also more open to critical scrutiny. The assumption that the presence of non-state actors, especially NGOs, will keep states and other actors 'on their toes' with regards to environmental degradation must be examined more critically and the question of which causes of environmental insecurity are politicized and why must be continually asked. The argument presented here is that many of the groups, communities, and individuals experiencing severe environmental insecurity have few opportunities to voice their insecurity, despite the ubiquity of environmental norms, agreements, and assessments.

In Cambodia, Lao PDR and Vietnam extra-regional and intraregional political, economic, and social dynamics produce environmental insecurity in different ways. As the relative peace between states in the Mekong and in East Asia has removed the conventional insecurities faced by states, for many groups and individuals insecurity has increased as rapid changes have taken place, especially to the environment. This environmental insecurity is produced, experienced, politicized and addressed in spaces within and outside the state and by state and non-state actors. Identifying how these dynamics produce environmental insecurity, identifying the uneven impacts of insecurity, and identifying the opportunities and limitations of the political configurations capable of addressing insecurity is crucial to comprehending and acting upon the challenges posed by environmental degradation.

References

Asian Development Bank (ADB). (2006). *The Mekong region: Foreign direct investment*. Manila: ADB.
Bakker, K. (1999). The politics of hydropower: Developing the Mekong. *Political Geography, 18*(2), 209–232.
Barkin, J. S. (2005). The environment, trade and international organizations. In P. Dauvergne (Ed.), *Handbook of global environmental politics* (pp. 334–347). Cheltenham/ Northampton: Edward Elgar.
Berhe, A. (2007). The contribution of landmines to land degradation. *Land Degradation and Development, 18*(1), 1–15.
Booth, K. (1991). Security and emancipation. *Review of International Studies, 17*(4), 313–326.
Burke, A., & McDonald, M. (2007). Introduction: Asia-Pacific security legacies and futures. In A. Burke & M. McDonald (Eds.), *Critical security in the Asia-Pacific* (pp. 1–24). Manchester: Manchester University Press.
Clapp, J. (2005). Transnational corporations and global environment governance. In P. Dauvergne (Ed.), *Handbook of global environmental politics* (pp. 284–297). Cheltenham/Northampton: Edward Elgar.
Corlin, C. (2004). Hmong and the land question in Vietnam: National policy and local concepts of the environment. In N. Tapp, J. Michaud, C. Culas, & G. Y. Lee (Eds.), *Hmong/Miao in Asia* (pp. 295–320). Bangkok: Silkworm Books.
Darlington, S. (1998). The ordination of a tree: The Buddhist ecology movement in Thailand. *Ethnology, 37*(1), 1–15.
Dasgupta, S., Deichmann, U., Meisner, C., & Wheeler, D. (2005). Where is the poverty-environment nexus? Evidence from Cambodia, Lao PDR, and Vietnam. *World Development, 33*(4), 617–638.
Donovan, D. (2003). Trading in the forest: Lessons from Lao history. In L. Tuck-Po, W. De Jong, & A. Ken-ichi (Eds.), *The political ecology of tropical forests in Southeast Asia: Historical perspectives* (pp. 72–106). Kyoto/Melbourne: Kyoto University Press/Trans Pacific Press.
Dore, J. (2003). The governance of increasing Mekong regionalism. In M. Kaosa-ard & J. Dore (Eds.), *Social challenges for the Mekong* (pp. 405–440). Chang Mai: Social Research Institute.
Dunne, T., & Wheeler, N. (2004). 'We the peoples' contending discourses of security in human rights theory and practice. *International Relations, 18*(1), 9–23.

Dyer, H. (2001). Environmental security and international relations: The case for enclosure. *Review of International Studies, 27*(3), 441–450.
Elliot, L. (2007). Harm and emancipation: Making environmental security 'critical' in the Asia-Pacific. In A. Burke & M. McDonald (Eds.), *Critical security in the Asia-Pacific* (pp. 121–135). Manchester: Manchester University Press.
Evrard, O., & Goudineau, Y. (2004). Planned resettlement, unexpected migrations and cultural trauma in Laos. *Development and Change, 35*(5), 937–962.
Foran, T., & Manoram, K. (2009). Pak Mun dam: Perpetually contested? In F. Molle, T. Foran, & M. Käkönen (Eds.), *Contested waterscapes in the Mekong region: Hydropower, livelihoods, and governance* (pp. 55–80). London: Earthscan.
Fox, C., & Sneddon, C. (2007). Transboundary river basin agreements in the Mekong and Zambezi basins: Enhancing environmental security or securitizing the environment? *International Environmental Agreements, 7*, 237–261.
Freeman, N. (2001). The rise and fall of foreign direct investment in Laos, 1988–2000. *Post-Communist Economies, 13*(1), 101–119.
Fujita, Y., & Phengospha, K. (2008). The gap between policy and practice in Lao PDR. In C. P. Colfer, G. R. Dahal, & D. Capistrano (Eds.), *Lessons from decentralization: Money, justice and the quest for good governance in Asia-Pacific* (pp. 117–132). London/Sterling: Earthscan.
Graeger, N. (1996). Environmental security? *Journal of Peace Research, 33*(1), 109–116.
Gunn, G. (2008). Laos in 2007: Regional integration and international fallout. *Asian Survey, 48*(1), 62–68.
Harima, R., Varona, R., & DeFalco, C. (2003). Migration. In M. Kaosa-ard & J. Dore (Eds.), *Social challenges for the Mekong* (pp. 225–262). Chang Mai: Social Research Institute.
Heinimann, A., Messerli, P., Schmidt-Vogt, D., & Wiesmann, U. (2007). The dynamics of secondary forest landscapes in the lower Mekong basin. *Mountain Research and Development, 27*(3), 232–241.
Hirsch, P. (2001). Globalisation, regionalisation, and local voices: The Asian Development Bank and re-scaled politics of environment in the Mekong region. *Singapore Journal of Tropical Geography, 22*(3), 237–251.
Howell, J. (2006). Gender and civil society. In H. Anheier, M. Glasius, & M. Kaldor (Eds.), *Global civil society* (pp. 38–63). London/Thousand Oaks/New Delhi: Sage.
Hughes, C. (2007). Transnational networks, international organizations and political participation in Cambodia: Human rights, labor rights and common rights. *Democratization, 14*(5), 834–852.
Hughes, C. (2008). Cambodia in 2007: Development and dispossession. *Asian Survey, 48*(1), 69–74.
International Rivers Network (IRN). (2008). *Power surge*. Berkeley: IRN.
Jacobs, J. (2002). The Mekong River Commission: Transboundary water resources planning and regional security. *The Geographical Journal, 196*(4), 354–364.
Jacobs, J. (2009). Planning for change and sustainability in water development in Lao PDR and the Mekong river basin. *Natural Resources Forum, 20*(3), 175–187.
Jönsson, K. (2009). Laos in 2008: Hydropower and flooding (or business as usual). *Asian Survey, 49*(1), 200–205.
Käkönen, M., & Hirsch, P. (2009). The anti-politics of Mekong knowledge production. In F. Molle, T. Foran, & M. Käkönen (Eds.), *Contested waterscapes in the Mekong region: Hydropower, livelihoods, and governance* (pp. 333–356). London: Earthscan.
Kaosa-ard, M. (2003). Poverty and globalization. In M. Kaosa-ard & J. Dore (Eds.), *Social challenges for the Mekong* (pp. 81–108). Chang Mai: Social Research Institute.
Kaur, A. (2010). Labour migration in Southeast Asia: Migration policies, labour exploitation and regulation. *Journal of the Asia Pacific Economy, 15*(1), 6–19.
Kimble, M. (2005). Climate change: Emerging insecurities. In F. Dodds & T. Pippard (Eds.), *Human and environmental security* (pp. 103–114). London/Sterling: Earthscan.

Landau, I. (2008). Law and civil society in Cambodia and Vietnam: A gramscian perspective. *Journal of Contemporary Asia, 38*(2), 244–258.

Lebel, L., Sinh, T., Bach, G., Po, S., Suong, T., Ahn, L., & Van Truc, D. (2009). The promise of flood protection: Dikes and dams, drains and diversions. In F. Molle, T. Foran, & M. Käkönen (Eds.), *Contested waterscapes in the Mekong region: Hydropower, livelihoods, and governance* (pp. 282–306). London: Earthscan.

Lee, K. (2003). Social challenges for Lao PDR. In M. Kaosa-ard & J. Dore (Eds.), *Social challenges for the Mekong* (pp. 109–122). Chang Mai: Social Research Institute.

Lestrelin, G., & Giordano, M. (2007). Upland development policy, livelihood change and land degradation: Interactions from a Laotian village. *Land Degradation and Development, 18*(1), 55–76.

Lidén, A., & Eneström, A.-K. (2005). The Peacebuilding Commission: Linking security and development. In F. Dodds & T. Pippard (Eds.), *Human and environmental security* (pp. 17–26). London/Sterling: Earthscan.

Lipschutz, R. (2005). Environmental regulation, certification and corporate standards: A critique. In P. Dauvergne (Ed.), *Handbook of global environmental politics* (pp. 218–232). Cheltenham/Northampton: Edward Elgar.

Manivong, K., & Sophathilath, P. (2007). *Status of community based forest management in Lao PDR*. Bangkok: RECROFT.

Masviriyakul, S. (2006). Sino-Thai strategic economic development in the greater Mekong subregion (1992–2003). *Contemporary Southeast Asia, 26*(2), 302–319.

McDonald, M. (2002). Human security and the construction of security. *Global Society, 16*(3), 277–295.

McDuie-Ra, D. (2007). Owning the environment: Ethnicity, development, and civil society. *Asian Ethnicity, 8*(1), 44–59.

McDuie-Ra, D. (2009). *Civil society, democratization and the search for human security: The politics of the environment, gender, and identity in India*. New York: Nova Science.

Mekong River Commission (MRC). (2008). *Draft programme document: Sustainable hydropower programme*. Vientiane: MRC.

Muntarbhorn, V. (2005). *The Mekong challenge: Employment and protection of migrant workers in Thailand*. Bangkok: International Labor Organization.

Nguyen, & Tan, Qunag. (2008). The household economy and decentralization of forest management in Vietnam. In C. P. Colfer, G. R. Dahal, & D. Capistrano (Eds.), *Lessons from decentralization: Money, justice and the quest for good governance in Asia-Pacific* (pp. 187–210). London/Sterling: Earthscan.

Oehlers, A. (2006). A critique of ADB policies towards the greater Mekong sub-region. *Journal of Contemporary Asia, 3*(4), 464–478.

Ovesen, J. (2004). The Hmong and development in the Lao People's Democratic Republic. In N. Tapp, J. Michaud, C. Culas, & G.Y. Lee (Eds.), *Hmong/Miao in Asia* (pp. 457–476). Bangkok: Silkworm Books. Jan.

Pech, S., & Sunada, K. (2008). Population growth and natural-resources pressures in the Mekong river basin. *AMBIO: A Journal of the Human Environment, 37*(3), 219–224.

Pellini, A., & Ayres, D. (2007). Community participation in local governance in Cambodia: Learning from the village networks approach. *Development in Practice, 17*(3), 404–409.

Poncet, S. (2006). Economic integration of Yunnan with the greater Mekong sub region. *Asian Economic Journal, 20*(3), 303–317.

Pronk, J. (2005). Globalization, poverty and security. In F. Dodds & T. Pippard (Eds.), *Human and environmental security* (pp. 71–102). London/Sterling: Earthscan.

Quang, V. D. (2004). The Hmong and forest management in Northern Vietnam's mountainous areas. In N. Tapp, J. Michaud, C. Culas, & G. Y. Lee (Eds.), *Hmong/Miao in Asia* (pp. 321–334). Bangkok: Silkworm Books.

Ratner, B. (2003). The politics of regional governance in the Mekong river basin. *Global Change, Peace & Security, 15*(1), 59–76.

Rerkasem, K. (2003). Uplands land use. In M. Kaosa-ard & J. Dore (Eds.), *Social challenges for the Mekong* (pp. 323–346). Chang Mai: Social Research Institute.

Rigg, J. (2006). Forests, marketization, livelihoods and the poor in the Lao PDR. *Land Degradation and Development, 17*(2), 123–133.

Rowcroft, P. (2008). Frontiers of change: The reasons behind land-use change in the Mekong basin. *AMBIO: A Journal of the Human Environment, 37*(3), 213–218.

Rutherford, J., Lazarus, K., & Kelley, S. (2008). *Rethinking investments in natural resources: China's emerging role in the Mekong region*. Phnom Penh/ Copenhagen/ Winnipeg: Heinrich Böll Stiftung Cambodia/ WWF Denmark/ International Institute for Sustainable Development.

Rwabizambuga, A. (2007). Environmental security and development. *Conflict, Security & Development, 7*(1), 201–225.

Sekhar, N. (2007). Traditional versus improved agroforestry systems in Vietnam: A comparison. *Land Degradation and Development, 18*(1), 89–97.

Simpson, A. (2007). The environment – Energy security nexus: Critical analysis of an energy 'love triangle' in Southeast Asia. *Third World Quarterly, 28*(3), 539–554.

Sinh, B. T. (2003). The cultural politics of development and environment in Vietnam. In M. Kaosa-ard & J. Dore (Eds.), *Social challenges for the Mekong* (pp. 371–404). Chang Mai: Social Research Institute.

Tar, C. M. (2003). Fishing lots and people in Cambodia. In M. Kaosa-ard & J. Dore (Eds.), *Social challenges for the Mekong* (pp. 347–370). Chang Mai: Social Research Institute.

Theeravit, K. (2003). Relationships within and between the Mekong region in the context of globalization. In M. Kaosa-ard & J. Dore (Eds.), *Social challenges for the Mekong* (pp. 49–80). Chang Mai: Social Research Institute.

Thongpakde, N. (2001). Impact and implications of ASEAN enlargement on trade. In M. Than & C. Gates (Eds.), *ASEAN enlargement: Impacts and implications* (pp. 45–79). Singapore: ISEAS.

United Nations Development Program (UNDP). (1994). *World Development Report 1994*. New York: Oxford University Press.

Utting, P. (2006). Introduction: Reclaiming development agendas. In P. Utting (Ed.), *Reclaiming development agendas: Knowledge, power, and international policy making* (pp. 1–24). Basingstoke: Palgrave Macmillan/ UNRSID.

Varis, O., Keskinen, M., & Kummu, M. (2008). Mekong at the crossroads. *AMBIO: A Journal of the Human Environment, 37*(3), 146–149.

Vasavakul, T. (2003). From fence-breaking to networking: Interests, popular organizations, and policy influences in post-socialist Vietnam. In B. Kerkvliet, R. Heng, & D. Koh (Eds.), *Getting organized in Vietnam: Moving in and around the socialist state* (pp. 25–61). Singapore: ISEAS.

Walker, A. (1999). *The legend of the golden boat: Regulation, trade and traders in the borderlands of Laos, Thailand, China and Burma*. Honolulu: University of Hawaii Press.

Williams, M. (2005). Knowledge and global environmental policy. In P. Dauvergne (Ed.), *Handbook of global environmental politics* (pp. 402–416). Cheltenham/ Northampton: Edward Elgar.

Yu, X. (2003). Regional cooperation and energy development in the greater Mekong sub-region. *Energy Policy, 31*, 1221–1234.

Chapter 7
The Association of Southeast Asian Nations (ASEAN) and Climate Change: A Threat to National, Regime, and Human Security

Alfred Gerstl and Belinda Helmke

7.1 Introduction

In the last decade, severe natural disasters such as the Boxing Day Tsunami of 2004 or Cyclone Nargis in 2008 have claimed the lives of hundred of thousands of people and caused severe economic damage throughout Southeast Asia. The rising number of natural catastrophes directly or indirectly caused by climate change, e.g., typhoons in the Philippines, floods in Thailand and Vietnam, or droughts in the Mekong Delta, has further illustrated the vulnerability of the Southeast Asian societies to changing environmental conditions. Despite the fact that governments have become less climate change skeptical in the last years (Francisco 2008), they still refuse to commit to robust adaptation policies. Being an intergovernmental organization, the policies of the Association of Southeast Asian Nations (ASEAN) mirror the consensus of its members. ASEAN's influence in shaping the climate change agenda is thus heavily constrained.

In a region where security has traditionally been defined as national security and where the neorealist ASEAN Way values of sovereignty, noninterference into domestic affairs and (limited) intergovernmental cooperation prevail (Emmerson 2008a), climate change poses not only a new factual but also a conceptual threat. Since the end of the Cold War, the political, scholarly, and media focus has shifted from the ideological East-West rivalry and traditional inter-state wars to new nontraditional and human security threats. Underdevelopment, poverty, the trafficking of people, weapons and drugs, organized crime, terrorism, the spread of mass diseases, and not least environmental degradation have been identified as new threats (Nishikawa 2009).

A. Gerstl (✉)
University of Vienna, Vienna, Austria
e-mail: alfred.gerstl@univie.ac.at

B. Helmke
University of Sydney, Sydney, Australia
e-mail: belinda.helmke@syd.edu.au

What these threats have in common is that they cannot be dealt with by military means alone or even at all, that they are mostly transnational and that they affect the state, the regime, the economy, and individual citizens alike. In particular, in regard to environmental risks individuals or communities of individuals are very often the most vulnerable: be it that they are direct or indirect victims of the multiple short-term and long-term impacts of extreme weather events or that they are the main bearers of the social costs of adaptation to climate change (IPCC 2007).

The resolution of human security threats is a major task for the elites in Southeast Asia. How determined and serious ASEAN is in resolving such hazards needs to be analyzed on a case-by-case basis. In this chapter, we aim to ascertain how ASEAN frames the threat of climate change and which mitigation and adaptation strategies it promotes on a regional level. Theoretically, this study is based on the constructivist Copenhagen School (Buzan et al. 1998), empirically on an analysis of climate change-related ASEAN resolutions and declarations as well as the respective policies of Singapore and Indonesia. We claim that ASEAN copes with human security threats such as climate change, underdevelopment, or migration because it perceives them as real *security* threats – to the state, the regime, the economy, and the individuals. To address human insecurity not only discursively but to tackle it more efficiently is a rational political decision of the mainly output-orientated Southeast Asian states (cf. Caballero-Anthony 2004: 160). Failure to deal with hazards that have a direct impact on the safety, security, and well-being of millions of people could endanger the legitimacy of their regimes, triggering political unrest. Accordingly, the argument here is that the stronger focus on human security in ASEAN's security discourse represents not a fundamental conceptual or policy shift but a logical evolution of the neorealist interpretation of politics of the Southeast Asian regimes. The governments have realized that they have to be at least perceived as being concerned about human insecurity.

Yet, there remain conceptual and political tensions between human and state security, i.e., national and regime security, which make it difficult to implement the holistic notion of human security. Due to state-centrism and output legitimacy, the very concept of human security represents a political challenge in Southeast Asia. Human security is a security, political, and democratic concept alike, with a strong individual connotation (UNDP 1994: Chap. 2; Gerstl 2010a). The implementation of a notion of human security that encompasses human rights and democracy can therefore have adverse effects on the regime security of the region's nondemocratic states.[1] Empowered people become aware of their need for human rights, political participation, and an open political discourse (Sen 1999a, b). The Southeast Asian governments, however, we claim, realize that both implementing the holistic concept of human security and not addressing human security can have negative repercussions on their regime stability. Therefore, they have "ASEANized" and depoliticized

---

[1] The authors concur with the Freedom in the World Index 2010 which labels Indonesia as the only "free" democracy in Southeast Asia. The Philippines, Malaysia, Singapore, and Thailand are regarded as partly free, Brunei, Cambodia, Laos, Myanmar, Vietnam as not free (cf. Freedom House 2010; Köllner 2008).

human security, i.e., framed it under the ASEAN Way values and diminished the political dimension through an emphasis on social and human development (Gerstl 2010b: Chap. 2). We argue that the Association's climate change policies reflect both this fragmented notion of human security and a narrow understanding of energy security that is primarily concerned with securing access to energy resources.

This chapter starts with an analysis of how ASEAN has securitized and framed climate change and which mitigation and adaptation strategies the organization promotes on a regional level. It examines ASEAN's climate change "speech act" consisting of the Association's Charter (ASEAN 2007a), its climate change related resolutions and declarations as well as of Singapore and Indonesia's climate change policies. It then discusses ASEAN's emerging notion of human security and relates it to its climate change approach. It will thereby explore the political and conceptual conflicts between state-centric national and individual human security. Subsequently, it examines two case studies for cooperation to cope with climate change, the Trans-ASEAN Gas Pipeline Infrastructure Project and transboundary haze in Indonesia. The chapter will conclude that human and regime security do not have to be contradictory.

7.2 Climate Change: A Comprehensive Human Security Threat

The International Panel of Climate Change (IPCC 2007), the Stern Review (2006), and the Asian Development Bank (ADB 2009) claim that Southeast Asia will be more severely affected by the direct and indirect negative impacts of climate change than other world regions. Yet these assessments also stress Southeast Asia's huge potential for effective adaptation and mitigation measures (ADB 2009: 26). While adaptation refers to actions taken in response to changes in climate, be they actual or expected, with the aim of reducing vulnerabilities and strengthening resilience, mitigation means taking concrete measures to reduce the causes of climate change, notably limiting greenhouse gas emissions. Adaptation measures can aim either to reduce the negative repercussions or to take advantage of the effects of climate change.

Whether or not directly caused by climate change, the increased number of cyclones and earthquakes in the last years has demonstrated Southeast Asia's vulnerability to environmental risks. Lower crop yields causing food insecurity, rising sea levels, heat waves, the spread of human diseases or environmentally induced migration are indirect consequences of a failure to adapt to climate change. Notably the horrific tsunami in 2004 and the devastating Cyclone Nargis in Myanmar in 2008 demonstrated that the people can be more affected by human insecurity than the state, regime, or economy. Despite tremendous achievements in poverty reduction and an overall increase of socioeconomic development in the last three decades, large parts of the Southeast Asian populations, in particular in Indochina, remain poor and often politically marginalized, making them even more vulnerable to environmental risks.

Climate change is a fact. Yet its negative repercussions on human security can be politically and discursively either exaggerated or minimized (cf. Pettenger 2007). Moreover, even though environmental hazards do clearly pose threats to national and individual security, the exact linkages between climate change and security are complex. Accordingly, similar to human security, environmental security is a broad and still contested theoretical approach that is difficult to conceptualize (Vogler 2008). The emerging consensus posits that climate change has the potential to weaken state and civil society actors, thus increasing the vulnerabilities of the Southeast Asian societies to various nontraditional security threats (Jasparro and Taylor 2008; cf. Barnett 2007). Paul J. Smith, for instance, correctly claims that climate change can stifle or undermine economic development, thus increasing poverty. He argues: "Climate change, rather than being a direct 'root cause' of terrorism, acts instead as an overarching destabilizing element that fosters the enabling for non-state actor terrorist groups" (Smith 2007: 271).

7.2.1 ASEAN's View of Climate Change

According to the Copenhagen School, a security actor has to convince a target group through a "speech act" that a certain threat poses an existential danger to a certain referent object. Once successfully securitized, the issue is regarded as standing above traditional politics, thus extraordinary measures can be applied to resolve the problem in a faster and more efficient manner (Emmers 2007). Due to the political and discursive dominance of the governments – they possess "the capabilities to make securitization happen" (Floyd 2007: 41) – this analysis focusses on the "speech act" of the political leaders (heads of government and state, environmental ministers, senior diplomats). Consequently, ASEAN's declarations, resolutions, and agreements as well as Singapore's and Indonesia's policies in the realm of the environment will be examined.

The analysis of ASEAN's climate change "speech act" demonstrates that the members of the Association remained for a very long time climate change skeptics. They also downplayed the role of human behavior in the acceleration of climate change. Therefore, the Association could only achieve a consensus on framing climate change as a comprehensive security challenge. ASEAN regards climate change and specific effects such as global warming and haze as a threat to human as well as national, regime, and economic security. Yet the regimes primarily frame it as a challenge to regime security (ASEAN 2007b, c), as its adverse economic impacts can undermine economic development. The latter is, together with nation-building, crucial for their output legitimacy (Gerstl 2008: 120). Failure to resolve the threat of climate change could thus undermine the elites' hold on power.

Today, however, all ten ASEAN member states have formulated national climate change policies and have established ministries or agencies that specifically deal with environmental problems (ADB 2009: 215). Nevertheless, on a regional level, there is still a lack of coordination and cooperation in tackling climate change.

The Association clearly locates the primary responsibility on a national rather than a regional level (ASEAN Secretariat n.d.).

One reason for this is that climate change is a comparatively new threat, thus collaboration to cope with this problem is untested – unlike in many other political, economic, and security affairs in which ASEAN has since the end of the Cold War and in particular since the Asian Financial Crisis (AFC) of 1997/1998 successfully deepened its cooperation, even including the ASEAN plus three (APT) partners China, Japan, and South Korea. The main political hindrances for a robust regional environmental cooperation are the respective policies and different threat perceptions of the member states. A consensus among ASEAN on adaptation policies is difficult to achieve as climate change affects all Southeast Asian nations, yet they face different concrete threats, e.g., rise in sea levels, deforestation, flooding, or drought. The political will, economic capabilities, and adaptive capacities for coping with these problems vary also considerably among the ASEAN-10. Moreover, unlike in other policy areas such as trade, organized crime, and counter-terrorism until 2009, no ASEAN member had assumed a leadership role in advocating robust adaptation measures. Not surprisingly, collaborative actions in the realm of environment and in particular common efforts to tackle climate change are still elusive in Southeast Asia. The lack of cooperation also means that the Southeast Asian governments miss out on international funding, know-how, and technology transfer (ADB 2009: 208).

Only since the United Nations Climate Change Conference of Parties (COP) 11 in Montreal in November/December 2005 has the need for Southeast Asia as a region to mitigate and adapt to climate change been discussed more seriously (Francisco 2008; Greenpeace 2007; cf. ASEAN 2009a, b). While all ASEAN members, except Brunei, have signed and ratified the Protocol, being developing nations they have, as so-called non-Annex I countries, no legally binding obligations to reduce their carbon emissions under the Kyoto Protocol. As the wording of the tenth Informal ASEAN Ministerial Meeting on the Environment in Bangkok from September 2007 (ASEAN 2007b) shows, the Association remains very cautious. This is despite of the international attention ASEAN and notably Jakarta have attracted due to Indonesia's role as host of the Bali Climate Conference in 2007.

With their verbs frequently in the subjunctive, the ASEAN politicians noted that the Southeast Asian countries are "experiencing extreme weather events that could be due to the impacts of climate change" (ASEAN 2007b). Even though they proposed to conduct more research on the specific vulnerabilities in Southeast Asia and increase information exchange, to commission regional and country studies is a *desideratum*. To assess the specific risks, vulnerabilities and financial costs of climate change, though, would only be the crucial first step to identifying and subsequently implementing adaptation strategies. The next step must be, according to a critical ADB report, raising public awareness and "the mainstreaming (of) climate change adaptation in development planning, i.e., making it an integral part of sustainable development, poverty reduction and disaster risk management strategies" (ADB 2009: xxvi).

In recent years, the Southeast Asian leaders have become aware that economic development rests on the sound management of natural resources and social equity (Glover and Onn 2008; ASEAN 1997). One very visible negative impact of the rapid economic growth in Southeast Asia is uncontrolled urbanization. In the "Cool ASEAN – Green Capitals" initiative (November 2009), ASEAN attempts to address this issue caused by rural–urban migration, which is a result of both the development of the major urban centers and the lack of economic opportunities in the countryside.

Considerable political achievements were made at the Singapore Summit in November 2007. The ASEAN Climate Change Initiative (ACCI), the ASEAN Declaration on Environmental Sustainability, and the Singapore Declaration on Climate Change, Energy, and Environment were endorsed by the ASEAN leaders. The ACCI is, *inter alia*, an instrument for the member states for information exchange and consultation on the impacts of climate change. Very optimistically, the ASEAN Secretariat (2009) describes the ACCI as means to strengthen Southeast Asia's capacity for mitigation and adaptation efforts. Ideally, the initiative will also serve as platform for finding a common ASEAN position in international fora. In the two declarations from 2007, the Association promises increased regional and international collaboration to reduce air and water pollution, increase the management of forests, and strengthen its efforts to promote sustainable development and pledges support for the United Nations Framework Convention on Climate Change (UNFCCC) and the Kyoto Protocol.

In its new Charter from 2007, ASEAN defines as one of its purposes (Chap. 1, Art. 1, § 9) "to promote sustainable development so as to ensure the protection of the region's environment, the sustainability of its natural resources, the preservation of its cultural heritage and the high quality of life of its peoples." Surprisingly, this is the only reference to the environment in the whole document; climate change is not even mentioned once.

At the institutional level, ASEAN seems to have made more progress in coping with climate change. For instance, it has established regular meetings of the ASEAN environment ministers and, since 1997, with their counterparts from China, Japan, and South Korea under the ASEAN plus three umbrella. There are also regular meetings of senior diplomats and experts such as the new ASEAN Working Group on Climate Change (AWGCC). In the lead-up to the Kyoto Conference in Bali in December 2007 and the Copenhagen Climate Change Conference (COP15) in December 2009, the ASEAN Secretariat has prominently advertised its workshops with politicians and climate change experts. Within the ASEAN Socio-Cultural Community Department of the ASEAN Secretariat, the Association has also created an Environment Division. Thus the administrative tools for a more robust adaptation approach would appear to be in place.

7.2.2 ASEAN at COP15

The Singapore Declaration on Climate Change, Energy, and Environment has a special political and declamatory relevance: all East Asian Summit partners, i.e., the ten ASEAN members, China, Japan, South Korea, India, Australia, and New Zealand, in other words, developing and developed nations alike, signed this document.

Its focus is on improving energy efficiency and the use of cleaner energy. The Declaration, though, also stresses that "any actions to tackle global environmental issues should take into account diverse national and regional circumstances in accordance with the principle of common but differentiated responsibilities, as well as our respective capabilities" (ASEAN 2007c). The major political shortcoming is that even though the parties promised a reduction of greenhouse gas emissions, they refused once again to commit to numerical targets.

The ASEAN plus three countries reiterated these positions at the 15th UN Climate Change Conference in Copenhagen from 7 to 18 December 2009. The global political and media focus rested mainly on China and India which opposed the ambitious political aims of the European Union (EU) and Australia. Not for the first time, both countries, two main global polluters, took a hard stance. They also strictly opposed binding legal commitments and emission cut targets for developing nations. However, they also promised to cut back on greenhouse gas emission through improved energy efficiency to limit global warming to a maximum increase of two degrees Celsius over pre-industrial times (Walsh 2010). In particular Beijing's arguments were in line with its traditional emphasis on the right to development.[2]

Similarly to Beijing and New Delhi, ASEAN paid lip service to the Kyoto Protocol and the UNFCCC. ASEAN also demanded financial and technical support from the First World in the struggle against global warming (Powell 2009; UN 2009; ASEAN 2007b). Overall, the ASEAN leaders seemed happy to play second fiddle on the international stage to China and India, two crucial political and economic partners. This is despite ASEAN being a major CO2 emitter, if the problem of deforestation in Southeast Asia, where approximately 16% of the world's tropical rainforests are located, is included into the emission statistics. Thus ASEAN's position on climate change and its refusal to implement stronger regional actions should have been even more closely scrutinized by the international media and NGOs (Greenpeace 2009a, b). The next section will highlight the limits and the potential for increased multilateral collaboration in Southeast Asia.

7.3 Regional Cooperation in the Realm of Environment: Energy Security and Haze

In Southeast Asia, regional cooperation is still intergovernmentally steered, yet ASEAN can add further value to intergovernmental collaboration through its efforts to coordinate and harmonize the respective policies of its member states and increase

---

[2] Already in the human rights debate in the early 1990s, many East Asian governments have highlighted the economic and social rather than the political rights. At the World Conference on Human Rights in Vienna in 2003, Indonesia, Singapore, and China argued that political rights are a luxury that can only be afforded once a country has reached a certain stage of development. Beijing stressed the right to development which is in the state-oriented East Asian region a right of the governments, not the individuals (cf. Tatsuo 1999 and Donnelly 1999).

the sharing of best practice. Eventually, the Association could create regional legal frameworks in the realm of climate change as it did in case of counter-terrorism (Gerstl 2010b). Yet, when it comes to concrete collaboration, a bilateral approach or cooperation within an inner circle seems more promising. While the problem of haze where Indonesia as the main polluter collaborates with Singapore and Malaysia is an example of a trilateral approach, the so-called Trans-ASEAN Gas Pipeline Infrastructure Project (TAGP) is an illustration for an ASEAN-wide approach. Before addressing these cooperation efforts, Singapore and Indonesia's climate change policies will be briefly examined.

7.3.1 Singapore's and Indonesia's Climate Change Policies

As a small and vulnerable city state, lacking most basic resources, e.g., it has to import its water and most agricultural products from Malaysia; Singapore's future is highly dependent on a clean and safe environment. Yet the government, led by the People's Action Party (PAP), only began to take from 2005 on a more proactive stance, culminating in the National Climate Change Strategy of 2008 (Hamilton-Hart 2009). Its main aim is to encourage a more sustainable use of energy and to reduce the carbon-emission-intensity of its economy. Even though it did not lead to any legal commitments, Singapore's accession to the Kyoto Protocol in 2006 can be regarded as a major boost for research and development in the city state as it enabled it to participate in the global Clean Development Mechanism (Lin 2007). Economic and fiscal incentives remain the major driving forces for investments in green technology: Singaporean companies have invested heavily in research in renewable energy technologies, eyeing China as a promising export market. Though, Natasha Hamilton-Hart (2006) critically claims that the Singaporean government has learned the language of the international environmental discourse opportunistically – and that in reality, the Lion city's climate change policies had changed only minimal. In a more recent assessment, she criticizes the PAP regime for refusing to agree on binding emission cut targets. The government stresses the special situation of Singapore as a small, but highly urbanized and industrialized city that has only limited capabilities for reducing its carbon gas emissions (Hamilton-Hart 2009: 28–29). Yet while the tiny nation is indeed not a major polluter on a global scale, a stronger leadership role would be crucial to commit its hesitant ASEAN partners to an active fight against climate change.

Indonesia is both a major contributor to climate change – due to peatland degradation, loss of rainforests, and forest fires, it is the third largest CO_2 emitter – and a victim of its impacts. Already the Suharto regime has stressed that the response strategy needs to be developed in the broader context of stability, economic growth, and equity (Government of Indonesia 1999: 1–3). Jakarta which has ratified the Kyoto Protocol in 2004 has, similarly to many other developing countries, on paper sound environmental policies; the problem, however, is the lack of enforcement, in particular in regard to policing illegal logging (PEACE 2007: 7–8). Even though Jakarta has started reforestation projects, Indonesian farmers are not likely to benefit sufficiently from international schemes such as the planned Reducing Emissions from Deforestation in Developing countries (REDD) (Chiew 2009: 362–363).

At the G8 summit in 2009, President Susilo Bambang Yudhoyono broke new ground when he announced that his country plans to cut emissions by 26% by 2020 from "business as usual" levels. If the international community would support this scheme, he claimed Indonesia could even reach a 41% reduction. This aim is to be achieved through curbing emissions from deforestation, changes in land use, and new investments in green energy, notably geothermal energy (Fogarty 2009; SMH 2009). In November 2009, the Ministry of Finance further specified the economic and fiscal instruments and incentives to curb greenhouse gas emissions, among them a carbon gas tax on fossil fuel and a decentralized regional incentive mechanism for land use and the forestry sector (Ministry of Finance 2009). Similar to the promotion of human security, Jakarta now plays a leadership role in combating climate change in Southeast Asia.

7.3.2 Multilateral Cooperation: Energy Security

The Singapore Declaration of 2007 closely relates the issue of energy security – which is a *sine qua non* for further economic development – to all adaptation and mitigation strategies in Southeast Asia. As in most Southeast Asian nations an "'economic first' mindset" (Hamilton-Hart 2006: 381) prevails, despite paying lip service to sustainable development, the political focus rests on economic growth and energy security (ASEAN 2007a, c). In 2002, ASEAN agreed on realizing the Trans-ASEAN Gas Pipeline Infrastructure Project, which has been discussed since the 1990s. The TAGP aims to connect all ten ASEAN member states and eventually energy-hungry China, making it one of the largest energy networks in the world. The optimistic expectation within the Association is that this project shall promote economic development and increase energy security, while at the same time contributing to the mitigation of climate change (ASEAN 2002a). Yet, as Benjamin K. Sovacool (2009: 486) convincingly argues, ASEAN's concept of energy security is very narrow. It is based on the priority of securing access to energy resources but does not take into account the political and socioeconomic differences or the varying degrees of respect for human rights and the environment among the ASEAN-10. He claims that without a holistic notion of energy security, the establishment of the TAGP could make the fast developing nations of Singapore, Malaysia, and Indonesia economically – and eventually politically – dependent on Myanmar or a currently politically unstable country such as Thailand.

7.3.3 Trilateral Cooperation: Deforestation and Transboundary Haze

Southeast Asia is blessed with forests and forestry resources, yet deforestation is a major problem in Indonesia, Thailand, Malaysia, and Vietnam. Deforestation leads to a loss of biodiversity and changes in water regulation and microclimate, causing droughts and landslides. In general, the individual Southeast Asian governments and ASEAN have failed to address this problem (ADB 2009: 107–109). One exception in ASEAN's pattern of limited cooperation in environmental issues is the forest fires in Indonesia that cause haze. Haze is a transboundary environmental and health problem, caused both by climate change and direct human activities, which severely affects Indonesia as well as Singapore, Malaysia, and Thailand. Due to these severe transnational ramifications, ASEAN has already since the 1990s aimed to resolve this problem.

The main responsibility for tackling haze rests with Indonesia. That country, which possesses about one tenth of the world's rainforests, has due to rampant logging and burning the highest deforestation rate in the world, toppling even Brazil. Since 1982, haze has been an annual problem, though it was never worse than in 1997, the year of the outbreak of the Asia Financial Crisis, and in 2006 (ADB 2009: 45). It has caused losses of up to US $5–$6 billions as offices and schools had to be closed for days in Singapore and parts of Malaysia. The health of millions of peoples was affected, and also tourism suffered (Karim 2008). Interestingly, both the authoritarian Suharto regime and the democratic government of President Susilo Bambang Yudhoyono apologized for the government's inactions and promised strong measures. In reality, though, due to still widespread corruption and the lack of enforcement capabilities of the Indonesian authorities, not much progress has been made to stop illegal logging (Tay 2008; Greenpeace 2010).

Haze is an example that ASEAN has started to acknowledge that even though the problem originates in a sovereign member country, due to its transnational impacts both the member country and the organization have a responsibility to tackle the problem (Qadri 2001). This is a cautious evolution from the strict notion of sovereignty to a form of conditional sovereignty. Since 1990, ASEAN has gradually increased transnational cooperation to resolve the threat of haze. Regular meetings and plans of action evolved, first, into the Regional Haze Action Plan (RHAP, December 1997) and then, the ASEAN Agreement on Transboundary Haze Pollution (Haze Agreement; ASEAN 2002b), a binding treaty, in force since November 2003. However, so far the main polluter Indonesia has not ratified it (as of July 2011), due to opposition in the parliament. In addition to these plans of action and a variety of meetings, ASEAN has established instruments to facilitate information exchange about haze, *inter alia*, an informative website on regional fire and haze hotspots.[3] Yet, a more efficient early warning system is required (ADB 2009: 108).

Overall, though, even despite the Association's institutional and political activism in tackling haze, collaboration has been mainly achieved on minilateral level, e.g., among Indonesia, Singapore, and Malaysia as the most affected parties. As early as 1997, Jakarta agreed to a collaboration plan under the RHAP. While Indonesia bears the main responsibility for mitigation of forest fires and haze, Malaysia is concerned with prevention and Singapore with monitoring activities

---

[3] For more information see http://haze.asean.org.

(Qadri 2001: xvi.). In practice, however, Indonesia must take much stronger actions to end illegal logging. More practical is the new multilevel approach that allows Singaporean and Malaysian authorities to deal directly with their counterparts on provincial level in Jambi and Riau in Sumatra (Tay 2008).

The main problem of ASEAN's cooperation approach and its attempt to create legal cooperative frameworks in general, though, is the organization's lack of legal and political enforcement capabilities. Even after Jakarta's possible admission to the Haze Agreement, a fundamental change in the country's policies is unlikely. This is because the Agreement is a "soft law" document, making not very far-reaching suggestions, and that, similar to all other ASEAN treaties, cannot sanction noncompliance.

Despite all these shortcomings, ASEAN's "speech act" in regard to haze reveals interesting principles that can guide the organization in its struggle against climate change: first, the respect for sovereignty but with the condition that threats arising in one country must not negatively impact on neighboring states; secondly, the notion of differentiated responsibilities between member countries.

7.4 The Depoliticization and "ASEANization" of Human Security

7.4.1 ASEAN's Fragmented Version of Human Security

Theoretically and conceptually, ASEAN seems to be well suited to combating the new nontraditional threats that affect the peoples in the region. Already in the late 1980s, earlier than other regional organizations, ASEAN had adopted the notion of comprehensive security, realistically including traditional and nontraditional threats. Moreover, it has acknowledged the need for increased transnational collaboration to cope with these challenges, for instance in the ASEAN Regional Forum (ARF). An effective trigger for a deeper collaboration in Southeast Asia since the early 1990s was, firstly, a perceived power vacuum in the Asia-Pacific with the prospect of a power rivalry between Japan and China (Gerstl 2008). Secondly, major catalysts for closer collaboration were the Asian Financial Crisis of 1997/1998, the Severe Acute Respiratory Syndrome (SARS) epidemic in 2003, the tsunami in 2004, and Cyclone Nargis in 2008. Subsequently, ASEAN has also addressed the broad cluster of organized crime, mainly drug and people smuggling, money laundering, and terrorism, thereby aiming to strengthen national law enforcement capabilities and to establish a common legalistic framework as a basis for increased minilateral and regional cooperation (Gerstl 2009; Karim 2008; ASEAN 2007d). These various human security threats can also be regarded as crucial catalysts for the furthering of a more people-oriented understanding of security in the region (Gerstl 2010a).

Even though, as Jörn Dosch (2008: 62) claims, this new notion has already changed the perception of and response to security challenges, there remain question marks in regard to ASEAN's framing of human security and its implementation of this concept. Tellingly, the ASEAN Charter (ASEAN 2007a) fails to clarify its security concept. "Human security" and "nontraditional security" are not even mentioned, let alone defined (Emmerson 2008b: Table 1.1). Yet, on the other hand, the Charter takes a positive view of the ASEAN Way principles, notably sovereignty and noninterference. The ASEAN People's Assembly (APA) and the Solidarity for Asian People's Advocacy (SAPA) have criticized these conceptual and political shortcomings. As the Charter illustrates, the organization has not fully endorsed the individual and democratic aspects of human security, and regional cooperation remains in too many vital areas of human security limited to verbal declarations rather than concrete collaboration. One reason is the lack of consensus among the ASEAN-10 on a catalogue of the most challenging human security threats (Nishikawa 2009). Yet, even in regard to tackling commonly defined threats such as organized crime and terrorism, there remains a lot to be done to implement a robust regional response (Gerstl 2009; Grabowski et al. 2009; Emmers 2003).

The main reason for ASEAN's reluctance to highlight human security more prominently in its "speech act," however, are the potentially negative politically repercussions of this concept on regime security. On one hand, the Southeast Asian elites are still mostly concerned with their own safety and security. On the other hand, they have acknowledged the existence of new nontraditional threats and thus adopted a comprehensive view of security. Arguably, ASEAN has combined neorealism with a constructivist notion of security.

Constructivism, notably the Copenhagen School, has been at the forefront of broadening and deepening the traditional understanding of security after 1989/1991 (Buzan et al. 1998; Caballero-Anthony 2008; Emmers 2003). Even though ASEAN's comprehensive notion of security converges with the School's view, there remain some distinct specifics of the Southeast Asian security discourse. Due to the preponderance of sovereignty, noninterference and regime legitimacy, comprehensive – and even human – security has a strong state-centric rather than individual dimension in Southeast Asia (Acharya 2006: 249; Caballero-Anthony 2004: 160–163). Thus, the stronger focus on more people-oriented security in the official Southeast Asian security discourse is not a fundamental conceptual or political shift but rather a logical evolution of the neorealist political understanding of the regimes and a means to secure their legitimacy. To identify human security threats, to address them discursively, and, finally, to tackle them more efficiently is thus a rational political act. However, there remain considerable political and conceptual tensions between human and national security (Peou 2009; Chandler 2008; Evans 2009; Kerr 2007; Floyd 2007; Paris 2004; Lodgaard 2000).

In response to human security threats such as organized crime and terrorism, ASEAN has developed a specific, fragmented concept of human security that it also applies to framing climate change. In order to insulate themselves from political criticism from the opposition and the civil society, the governments prefer to depoliticize and "ASEANize" a securitized threat. "Depoliticization" means that a threat is portrayed as to be discussed from a technical or scientific perspective; consequently, it has to be resolved by "neutral" experts rather than politicians. "ASEANization" can be defined as the framing of a policy within the ASEAN Way values, i.e., sovereignty, noninterference, and consensual decision-making.

Like depoliticization, "ASEANization" is both a method and a deliberate political action. For the governments, to securitize, depoliticize, and "ASEANize" human security (or a security threat in general) is a rational decision to promote regime stability. In regard to human security, rather than stressing the human rights and democratic aspects of this concept, ASEAN puts emphasis on the provision of socioeconomic and human development; the eradication of poverty; the implementation of long-term reforms in the economic, social, and education sectors; and the requirement of a broad, inclusive but nonpolitical dialogue with all stakeholders (Gerstl 2009; ASEAN 2007a, b). This approach can foster regional cooperation, as it is easier to achieve consensus on a nonpolitical matter. From a normative point of view, though, a successful regional promotion of a fragmented version of human security that emphasizes regime over individual security is debatable (Gerstl 2010a).

7.4.2 Hand in Hand? Human Security Versus State Security in Southeast Asia

The concept of a more people-oriented notion of security remained, unlike that of state and regime security, a largely insignificant one until the end of the Cold War (Jackson 2007). While the following decades brought many additions to the area of human rights legislation, the state ("national security") remained at the core of security concerns. Defending the state from external military threats was viewed as the key concern of governments. The United Nations Development Program's 1994 Human Development Report (HDR) was the first to define the concept of human security. The immediate aftermath of the Cold War witnessed the highest number of violent conflicts in the international system since 1946. The majority of these conflicts, however, were (and still are) internal in nature, including violent unrest in many so-called failing and failed states. The report claims that peace is not possible "unless people have security in their daily lives" (UNDP 1994: 1), arguing that security has a specifically human aspect to it and that the security of people can only be achieved through development, not arms. Human security, indeed, challenges a purely neorealist view of security (Acharya 2008; Kerr 2007).

The HDR (Chap. 2) lists seven threats, which must be considered under human security: economic, food, health, environmental, personal, community, and political security. While the first four aspects address nonmilitary threats, the latter deal with protection from violence and conflicts as well as the human rights dimension. These two clusters of human security are widely referred to as "freedom from want" (the nonpolitical dimension) and "freedom from fear" (the political/conflict dimension). Proponents of the broad "freedom from want" school, as reflected in the HDR, focus on threats arising from underdevelopment, equating human security with a wide range of both violent and nontraditional threats. Consequently, this approach is close to human development (Thakur 2006; Gasper 2005). The narrow approach prefers a sharper focus, arguing that human security is foremost about the protection of citizens from violence and conflict (Human Security Centre 2005).

While the notion of human security should ideally complement national security, many states, particularly non-Western ones, view the two concepts as conflicting (cf. Acharya 2008; Kerr 2007; Gasper 2005; Alkire 2003). The reasons for this are two-fold. First, in the developing world, state, and regime security are often inseparable, though they must not be confused: what is in the interest of the regime, i.e., the ruling elites may not always be in the interest of the state – or the citizens. While a successful implementation of human security increases the individual security in these countries – and thus regime legitimacy – due to the democratization effects of human security, their regime security might be undermined. Especially, as in many cases, the state is the main perpetrator of violence. Acknowledging that the protection of citizens from this violence is the core aspect of human security challenges the regime itself. Consequently, a majority of Southeast Asian states, like many other developing nations, were anything but pleased when the International Commission on Intervention and State Sovereignty (ICISS) argued that the protection of human rights, through outside intervention if necessary, was a duty of the international community (Helmke 2008). If a state was unwilling or unable to protect its population from suffering serious harm, "the principle of nonintervention yields to the international responsibility to protect" (IDRC 2001: ix).

Second, many Southeast Asian countries have not yet succeeded in nation-building and socioeconomic development. Thus, they have not achieved what they view as security from external threats and interferences. Democracy and human rights are still too often seen as a luxury which can only be considered once the welfare and security of the territorial integrity and political independence of the state and nation-building have been achieved (Tatsuo 1999: 34–37). The fact that human security is people- and not state-centered implies that it is of lesser appeal to authoritarian regimes. Consequently, Southeast Asian states favor the broad over the narrow school approach to human security.

Even though ASEAN could, today, politically not afford to condemn and dismiss a military intervention such as Hanoi's ousting of the genocidal *Khmer rouges* regime in Cambodia in December 1978 as a violation of the principles of sovereignty and territorial integrity, ASEAN's methods of stopping severe human rights violations in the region are still inadequate (Bercovitch 2008). The Association has stayed well away from considering peacekeeping or humanitarian intervention as the *ultima ratio* for safeguarding human security in case a regime oppresses or even kills its own citizens (cf. Helmke 2008; 2010). With the exception of the pivotal role played by ASEAN in the UN-led Cambodia mission in 1991–1993, it has been noticeably reserved about mounting a peacekeeping operation or even intervening politically when human security is at risk in a member country, as it was and is today in Myanmar. The other remarkable exception was East Timor in 1999. Indonesia was pressured by the international community, especially the United States, to agree to an armed intervention led by Australia and subsequently authorized by the UN Security Council. Unlike NATO's action in Kosovo, the International Force East Timor (INTERFET) was "a permissive, not uninvited, humanitarian intervention" (Dee 2001: 19; cf. Taylor 1999).

Since then, ASEAN's conflict management discourse has matured, reflecting ideas for lower-level humanitarian interventions. Under the label "constructive engagement" and "enhanced interaction," promoted by Jakarta, ASEAN attempts to play a proactive role in preventing the collapse of a regime. For this, it advocates, *inter alia*, a dialogue with political opponents and the civil society, the strengthening of the rule of law and developmental assistance (Caballero-Anthony 2009: 67–70; Kuhonta 2008; Sukma 2008). Even though this approach has failed in the case of Myanmar, the Association has not considered a forceful intervention (Kyaw 2008). While ASEAN has not subscribed to the potentially military protection of human security, another regional organization, the African Union (AU), has. In Article 4 (h) of the Constitutive Act, framed in 2000 in the aftermath of "Kosovo," the AU states its right "to intervene in a Member State pursuant to a decision of the Assembly in respect of grave circumstances, namely: war crimes, genocide, and crimes against humanity." Yet, the state-centric AU has proved reluctant to intervene beyond peacekeeping in the name of this right.

Highlighting sovereignty and noninterference, the ASEAN Political-Security Community (APSC), one of three pillars of the Asian Community, rests on cooperative, not collective security. Accordingly, the 2003 Bali Concord II (Art. 2) rejects the idea of creating "a defense pact, military alliance or a joint foreign policy" among ASEAN states. Yet while ASEAN as a unitary actor may not be on the verge of implementing specific measures to keep, let alone make peace on behalf of human security, individual states, e.g., Indonesia and the Philippines, are increasingly embracing the peacekeeping idea (Helmke 2009).

Having itself experienced a surprisingly successful democratization process, Indonesia among ASEAN states became the most vocal, though a nonconfrontational advocate of democracy for the region. In the context of its democratic spirit and hope that the APSC will reflect and encourage that process, Jakarta suggested the formation of a regional peacekeeping force. In 2004, however, ASEAN froze this proposal, citing differences in military capacity and doctrine among member states as reasons not to proceed. In consequence, the idea of creating a regional peacekeeping training center under the auspices of the ASEAN Regional Forum has not been realized. According to M.C. Abad Jr. (2003), Assistant Director of the ASEAN Secretariat, the embrace and establishment of peacekeeping operations is highly dependent on the political system of member states. Not surprisingly, authoritarian regimes are much more reluctant to even discuss this idea. However, if the democratization trend persists over the next few years, Donald K. Emmerson is optimistic that Jakarta might "draw more support from fellow members for enlisting regionalism, carefully and cautiously, in support of democracy in a reasonably 'liberal' form – or in support of human rights, better governance, and the rule of law without reference to the contentious 'L' word" (Emmerson 2008b: 54).

The most likely test case for ASEAN's adoption of a holistic notion of human security will be Myanmar. The human rights violations committed by the Burmese junta in the last 20 years have not triggered a strong political response from ASEAN. The only exception was the demonstrations in August/September 2007 which the regime cracked down brutally. The then ASEAN Chair Singapore urged Myanmar to cooperate with the United Nations, and the criticism from Jakarta and Manila was comparatively harsh. Yet, when the junta, diplomatically supported by Beijing, emphasized the principles of sovereignty and noninterference, the Association backed off.

In 2008, ASEAN scored in it its view a huge political success as it was able to provide disaster relief after Cyclone Nargis in 2008 in areas that were closed to Western relief agencies. Yet, the political price was high: ASEAN refrained from criticizing the regime for violating its responsibility to protect (R2P). In the end, the Association's depoliticized intervention played in the hands of the junta; ASEAN did not even promote its fragmented, nonpolitical version of human security (cf. Emmerson 2008b: 40–47). In the foreseeable future, it remains unlikely that ASEAN as an organization will vocally pressure Myanmar to halt human rights violations and introduce democratic reforms (Kyaw 2008: 186). The reason is that neither the junta nor human insecurity in that country threatens the other ASEAN members in a military sense; the only negative impact is that Myanmar's membership strains ASEAN's relations with the United States and the European Union.

While Myanmar will remain a thorny issue, addressing nontraditional threats is something which many Southeast Asian governments can imagine more readily. Transnational and regional cooperation on economic and environmental issues threatens the political integrity and territorial independence less than the issue of halting political violence does. However, cooperation in the realm of climate change is also limited in Southeast Asia. The reason is that the Association views it through the lens of its fragmented notion of human security and its narrow interpretation of energy security.

7.4.3 A More Realist View of Climate Change: Pressures to Adapt

It seems that in the security rectangle of national, human, environmental, and energy security, national security for ASEAN remains the strongest concern. Yet, the evolution of the Association's climate change "speech act" and its institutional adjustments show that ASEAN has increasingly become aware of international criticism of its lack of action. ASEAN, however, is not only under political pressure from the European Union, Japan, Australia, and even the US to reduce carbon gas emissions but also from China and India to oppose the far-reaching Western proposals (Ehrenfeld 2009). At the first meeting of the ASEAN leaders with President Obama in November 2009, in the Declaration "Enhanced Partnership for Enduring Peace and Prosperity," the two sides "agreed to strengthen our collaboration in both research on climate impacts and development and implementation of appropriate policies and measures" (ASEAN 2009a, b: paragraph 23). Furthermore, the increasingly vivid civil society in Southeast Asia demands credible actions from ASEAN to actively combat climate change (Ehrenfeld 2009). Demonstrations at the ASEAN Secretariat in Jakarta and the ASEAN Summit in Thailand (Greenpeace 2009a, b) have shown that many citizens feel uncomfortable with ASEAN's lack of action. Another hope for a more robust approach for ASEAN's climate change policies is Secretary-General Surin Pitsuwan. The academic and former Thai foreign minister is a credible advocate of human security who also promotes climate change measures (cf. ASEAN Secretariat 2009).

Indeed, the potential for increased mutual gains through collaboration in mitigation and adaptation in the region is huge. An example for successful transnational cooperation is the collaboration in the Greater Mekong Subregion between Vietnam, Laos, Cambodia, and China, facilitated by the ADB and Japan. Focused on common water management and energy production and distribution, a more comprehensive focus would yield even more results for the participants (Schmeier 2009). In the other parts of Southeast Asia, the prospects for collaborative actions to produce and better distribute clean and renewable energy are also promising. International cooperation is also increasing. In the joint statement of the first ASEAN – US Leaders' Meeting in Singapore in November 2009, for instance, the two parties "stressed that access to diverse, reliable, affordable, and clean energy is critical for sustainable economic growth, and agreed that accelerated deployment of clean energy technology and energy efficiency measures would diversify our energy supplies and strengthen our energy security" (ASEAN 2009a, b: paragraph 24).

Not to tackle climate change seriously means, in other words, that Southeast Asia would miss excellent business and technological opportunities. Under President Obama, Washington has started to subsidize green technology – as has the European Union for decades. Consequently, Simon Tay (2009) recommends, "Asians should try to latch on to these business opportunities and share technology with the US and other leading countries." In general, the ASEAN countries lag behind in the global trend toward adapting to climate change. One example is that Southeast Asia has not yet set up Clean Development Mechanisms (CDM) (Tay 2009). CDM allows developed nations to improve their carbon credit balance through investments in carbon emission projects in developing nations. The economic potential in the Certified Emission Reduction Units (CER) market is enormous, and so are the opportunities for technology and knowledge transfer.

To benefit from international cooperation and funding, the ASEAN countries will first need to commission more sophisticated national and regional assessment reports on the impacts of climate change and subsequently develop a cohesive policy response. A consensual regional approach is also crucial for ASEAN's international standing: The Association needs to speak with one voice to be heard. Due to its cooperation mechanisms that interlinks Southeast with Northeast Asia, ASEAN could perform the role of a good international citizen, if it manages to make Beijing and New Delhi more inclined toward committing to legal obligations in reducing carbon gas emissions.

7.5 Conclusion

Since 2005, a noticeable change in ASEAN's previously skeptical attitude toward climate change has occurred; the Singapore Summit in 2007 and the declarations issued in the run-up to the Copenhagen Climate Conference 2009 have confirmed this trend. The Association, though, still refuses to commit its members to concrete greenhouse gas emission targets. Thus, ASEAN risks losing out diplomatically and economically.

As the ASEAN members are affected to different degrees from climate change and have different economic and administrative capacities to adapt, the Association could not agree on strong common and concrete adaptation measures that need to encompass a broad set of environmental, economic, and social policies. Even in the realm of transboundary haze – identified as a severe threat by all member states – cooperation is limited to the three most affected countries.

However, as this chapter has argued, the main reason for the lack of cooperation is that ASEAN has framed climate change under its depoliticized and "ASEANized" notion of human security. Even though the Association has since the end of the Cold War adopted a more people-oriented notion of security, its understanding is still primarily based on the traditional neorealist state-centric view, enshrined in the ASEAN Way. The new human security lens is therefore primarily a means for the promotion of regime legitimacy. In addition, ASEAN members respond to climate change with measures that reflect a narrow interpretation of energy security, focused on securing access to energy resources.

Southeast Asia, though, has huge potential for adapting to climate change without undermining its economic growth (ADB 2009; Francisco 2008). A much more widespread use of renewable energy and increased energy and fuel efficiency would deliver the first positive results. The environmentally sound management of forests could play another key role in ASEAN's adaptation strategy. To stop deforestation and haze and promote reforestation and a sustainable forest management has priority (ASEAN Secretariat, n.d.), and carbon capturing by conserving forests is a promising approach (Tay 2009). Increased regional and international collaboration, not at least with First World countries, including technology transfer, would further strengthen Southeast Asia's resilience. Though, the ASEAN countries can also not avoid costly adaptive measures such as the building of new dams to protect villages from flooding or establishing sustainable regional energy infrastructures, e.g., in the Mekong Delta. In addition to global programs such as the Global Environment Facility (GEF) an own ASEAN adaptation fund that privileges the least developed ASEAN members is indispensable (Luci and Kabiling 2009; ADB 2009).

For all this, ASEAN has to further strengthen its collaboration to tackle climate change. A brief look at ASEAN's history, however, reveals that the Association has only deepened regional cooperation when it faced external pressures, be it the Vietnamese threat in the 1970s and 1980s or the end of the Cold War (Gerstl 2008: 121–123). Climate change might be the next existential challenge for the organization to which it *nolens volens* has to respond. The global concerns with climate change together with increasingly active environmental groups in the region have already pressured the Association to address this challenge more seriously. Yet even more promising is that Indonesia seems to assume the leadership role, both in human security and climate change. The sooner ASEAN starts to promote credible national and regional adaptation strategies under the umbrella of a non-fragmented, holistic human security concept, the sooner the human security of the citizens of Southeast Asia will improve. Human and regime security can be complementary. Due to their complexity, human security threats, and not least climate change, illustrate that the primary responsibility for guaranteeing human security rests with governments.

References

Abad, M. C. Jr. (2003). *Prospects for UN–ASEAN Cooperation in Conflict Management*, www.asean.org/14202.htm.

Acharya, A. (2006). Securitization in Asia: Functional and normative implications. In M. Caballero-Anthony, R. Emmers, & A. Acharya (Eds.), *Non-traditional security in Asia: Dilemmas in securitisation* (pp. 247–250). London: Ashgate.

Acharya, A. (2008). Human security. In J. Baylis (Ed.), *The globalization of world politics: An introduction to international relations* (4th ed., pp. 491–505). Oxford: Oxford University Press.

ADB (Asian Development Bank). (2009). *The economics of climate change in Southeast Asia: A regional review*. Manila: ADB.

Alkire, S. (2003). *A conceptual framework for human security*, Centre for Research on Inequality, Human security and ethnicity, (Working paper 2), University of Oxford.

ASEAN. (1997). *Ministerial understanding on ASEAN cooperation in rural development and poverty eradication*. http://www.aseansec.org/20320.htm. Accessed 29 Apr 2010.

ASEAN. (2002a). *The ASEAN Memorandum of Understanding (MoU) on the Trans-ASEAN Gast Pipeline (TAGP)*. http://www.aseansec.org/6578.htm. Accessed 8 May 2010.

ASEAN (2002b). *ASEAN agreement on transboundary haze pollution*. http://www.aseansec.org/pdf/agr_haze.pdf. Accessed 12 Dec 2009.

ASEAN (2007a). *The ASEAN charter*. Jakarta, Indonesia: ASEAN secretariat. http://www.aseansec.org/ASEAN-Charter.pdf. Accessed 13 Dec 2009.

ASEAN (2007b, September 5–7). *Media Release*. In 10th informal ASEAN ministerial meeting on the environment, 3rd Conference of Parties to the ASEAN Agreement on Transboundary Haze Pollution, 6th ASEAN Plus Three Environment Ministers Meeting, Bangkok. http://www.aseansec.org/20899.htm. Accessed 21 Jan 2010.

ASEAN (2007c). *Singapore declaration on climate change, energy and environment*. http://www.aseansec.org/21116.htm. Accessed 12 Dec 2009.

ASEAN (2007d). ASEAN Counter Terrorism Convention (ACCT). http://www.aseansec.org/19251.htm. Accessed 12 Dec 2009.

ASEAN (2009a, November 29). *Joint media statement of the special ASEAN ministerial meeting on Climate Change*. Hua Hin. http://www.aseansec.org/24076.htm. Accessed 21 Jan 2010.

ASEAN (2009b). *Climate change – rising to the challenge*. http://www.aseansec.org/23978.htm. Accessed 29 Dec 2009.

ASEAN Secretariat (n.d.). *Forest and climate change dialogue in ASEAN*. Jakarta: ASEAN secretariat. http://www.cbd.int/forest/doc/wscb-fbdcc-01/Sept3/asean-en.pdf. Accessed 20 Jan 2010.

Barnett, J. (2007). *Climate change and security in Asia: Issues and implications for Australia* (Policy Paper 9). Melbourne: The University of Melbourne.

Bercovitch, J. (2008). Third parties and conflict management in the context of East Asia and the pacific. In J. Bercovitch, K.-B. Huang, & C.-C. Teng (Eds.), *Conflict management, security and intervention in East Asia* (pp. 19–38). New York: Routledge.

Buzan, B., Wæver, O., & de Wilde, J. (1998). *Security: A new framework for analysis*. Boulder: Lynne Rienner.

Caballero-Anthony, M. (2004). Re-visioning human security in Southeast Asia. *Asian Perspective, 28*(3), 155–189.

Caballero-Anthony, M. (2008). Challenging change: Nontraditional security, democracy, and regionalism. In D. K. Emmerson (Ed.), *Hard choices: Security, democracy and regionalism in Southeast Asia* (pp. 191–217). Stanford: Stanford University Shorenstein APARC.

Caballero-Anthony, M. (2009). Southeast Asia's points of convergence on international intervention. In S. Peou (Ed.), *Human security in East Asia: Challenges for collaborative action* (pp. 61–76). New York: Routledge.

Chandler, D. (2008). Human security: The dog that didn't bark. *Security Dialogue, 39*(4), 427–438.

Chiew, H. (2009). Carbon hopes and landless farmers in Indonesia and Malaysia, *Contemporary Review, 291*(1694), 361–364.

Dee, M. (2001). 'Coalitions of the willing' and humanitarian intervention: Australia's involvement with INTERFET. *International Peacekeeping, 8*(3), 1–20.

Donnelly, J. (1999). Human rights and Asian values: A defense of 'Western' universalism. In J. R. Bauer & D. A. Bell (Eds.), *The East Asian challenge for human rights* (pp. 60–87). Cambridge: Cambridge University Press.

Dosch, J. (2008). Sovereignty rules: Human security, civil society, and the limits of liberal reform. In D. K. Emmerson (Ed.), *Hard choices: Security, democracy and regionalism in Southeast Asia* (pp. 59–90). Stanford: Stanford University Shorenstein APARC.

Ehrenfeld, Jon (2009, November 5). *The ASEAN stance at Copenhagen*. http://pisaspeak.wordpress.com/2009/11/05/the-asean-stance-at-copenhagen. Accessed 21 Dec 2009.

Emmers, R. (2003). ASEAN and the securitization of transnational crime in Southeast Asia. *The Pacific Review, 16*(3), 419–438.

Emmers, R. (2007). Securitization. In A. Collins (Ed.), *Contemporary security studies* (pp. 109–125). Oxford: Oxford University Press.

Emmerson, D. K. (Ed.). (2008a). *Hard choices: Security, democracy and regionalism in Southeast Asia*. Stanford: Stanford University Shorenstein APARC.

Emmerson, D. K. (2008b). Critical terms: Security, democracy, and regionalism in Southeast Asia. In D. K. Emmerson (Ed.), *Hard choices: Security, democracy and regionalism in Southeast Asia* (pp. 3–56). Stanford: Stanford University Shorenstein APARC.

Evans, P. M. (2009). Human security *in extremis*: East Asian reactions to the responsibility to protect. In S. Peou (Ed.), *Human security in East Asia: Challenges for collaborative action* (pp. 79–93). New York: Routledge.

Floyd, R. (2007). Human security and the Copenhagen school's securitization approach: Conceptualizing human security as a securitizing motive. *Human Security Journal, 5*, 38–46.

Fogarty, D. (2009, September 29). Indonesia CO2 pledge to help climate talks-greens, *Reuters*.

Francisco, H. A. (2008). Adaptation to climate change: Needs and opportunities in Southeast Asia. *ASEAN Economic Bulletin, 25*(1), 7–19.

Freedom House. (2010). *Map of freedom 2010*. Washington. http://www.freedomhouse.org/uploads/fiw10/FIW_2010_MOF.pdf. Accessed 12 May 2010.

Gasper, D. (2005). Securing humanity: Situating "Human security" as concept and discourse. *Journal of Human Development, 6*(2), 221–245.

Gerstl, A. (2008). The China factor in regional security cooperation: The ASEAN regional forum and the shanghai cooperation organization. *Austrian Journal of South-East Asian Studies (ASEAS), 1*(2), 73–99.

Gerstl, A. (2009). ASEAN im Krieg gegen den Terror: Sekuritisierung, Kriminalisierung, "ASEANisierung" und Depolitisierung des Terrorismus" [ASEANization and depoliticization of terrorism]. In M. Grabowski, H. Herold, & R. Jordan (Eds.), *Sicherheit kontra Menschenrechte. Antiterrorpolitik in Asien [Security versus human rights. Anti-terrorism policies in Asia]* (pp. 161–183). Bad Honnef: Horlemann.

Gerstl, A. (2010a). The changing notion of security in Southeast Asia. *Pacific News* Nr. 34, 4–8.

Gerstl, A. (2010b). The depolicitization and ASEANization of counter-terrorism policies in South-East Asia: A weak trigger for a fragmented version of human security. *Austrian Journal of South-East Asian Studies (ASEAS), 3*(1), 48–75.

Glover, D., & Onn, L. P. (2008). The environment, climate change and natural resources in Southeast Asia: Issues and challenges. *ASEAN Economic Bulletin, 25*(1), 1–6.

Government of Indonesia. (1999). *Indonesia: The first national communication on climate change convention*. Jakarta: Government of Indonesia.

Grabowski, M., Herold, H., & Jordan, R. (Eds.). (2009). *Sicherheit kontra Menschenrechte. Antiterrorpolitik in Asien [Security versus human rights. Anti-terrorism policies in Asia]*. Bad Honnef: Horlemann.

Greenpeace (2007, January 9). *ASEAN must focus on climate change, adaptation and mitigation*. http://www.greenpeace.org/seasia/en/news/greenpeace-asean-must-focus-o. Accessed 25 Jan 2010.

Greenpeace (2009a, March 1). *Greenpeace: Protection of ASEAN forests can deter climate change.* http://www.greenpeace.org/seasia/en/news/asean-save-forests-for-climate. Accessed 12 Jan 2010.

Greenpeace (2009b, *November 25*). *World leaders warned: 12 days left to avert climate chaos.* http://www.greenpeace.org/seasia/en/press/releases/greenpeace-activists-in-frontl. Accessed 11 Jan 2010.

Greenpeace (2010, January 26). *Greenpeace presents "World Cup of Forest Destruction" to SBY.* http://www.greenpeace.org/seasia/id/en/news/greenpeace-presents-world-cup. Accessed 27 Jan 2010.

Hamilton-Hart, N. (2006). Singapore's climate change policy: The limits of learning. *Contemporary Southeast Asia, 9*(1), 363–384.

Hamilton-Hart, N. (2009). Singapore's climate change policies and carbon emissions. *Innovation, 9*(1), 26–29.

Helmke, B. (2009). The absence of ASEAN: Peacekeeping in Southeast Asia. *Pacific News, 31*, 4–6.

Helmke, B. (2010). *Under attack: The challenge of recent state practice to the rules governing the international use of force.* London: Ashgate.

Helmke, B. (2008). *Under attack: The challenge of recent state practice to the rules governing the international use of force.* Ph.D. Dissertation, Macquarie University, Sydney.

Human Security Centre. (2005). *Human security report 2005: war and peace in the 21st century.* New York: Oxford University Press.

International Development Research Centre (IDRC). (2001). *The responsibility to protect. Report of the international commission on intervention and state sovereignty.* Ottawa: International Development Research Centre.

International Panel on Climate Change (IPCC) (Eds.) (2007). *Climate change 2007: Impacts, adaptation and vulnerability.* Contribution of working group II to the fourth assessment report of the intergovernmental panel on climate change, Report by Parry, M. L., Canziani, O. F., Palutikof, J. P., van der Linden, P. J., & Hanson, C. E. Cambridge: Cambridge University Press.

Jackson, R. (2007). Regime security. In A. Collins (Ed.), *Contemporary security studies* (pp. 146–163). Oxford: Oxford University Press.

Jasparro, C., & Taylor, J. (2008). Climate change and regional vulnerability to transnational security threats in Southeast Asia. *Geopolitics, 13*, 232–256.

Karim, M. S. (2008). Future of the haze agreement: Is the glass half empty or half full? *Environmental Policy and Law, 38*(6), 328–334.

Kerr, P. (2007). Human security. In A. Collins (Ed.), *Contemporary security studies* (pp. 91–108). Oxford: Oxford University Press.

Köllner, P. (2008). *Autoritäre Regime in Asien: Allgemeine Trends und jüngere Entwicklungen* [Authoritarian regimes in Asia: General trends and current developments] (GIGA *Focus* Asien No.12/2008), Hamburg: GIGA.

Kuhonta, E. M. (2008). Toward responsible sovereignty: The case for intervention. In D. K. Emmerson (Ed.), *Hard Choices: Security, Democracy and Regionalism in Southeast Asia* (pp. 293–313). Stanford, CA: Stanford University Shorenstein APARC.

Kyaw, Y. H. (2008). ASEAN's pariah: Insecurity and autocracy in Myanmar (Burma). In D. K. Emmerson (Ed.), *Hard choices: Security, democracy and regionalism in Southeast Asia* (pp. 151–189). Stanford: Stanford University Shorenstein APARC.

Lin, J. (2007). Singapore's climate change policies and carbon emissions. *Innovation, 9*(1), 26–29.

Lodgaard, S. (2000, December 8–9). *Human security: Concept and operationalisation.* Paper presented at the expert seminar on human rights and peace, Palais Wilson, Geneva.

Luci, Charissa M. & Kabiling, Genalyn D. (2009, October 21). *$5-billion ASEAN adaptation fund pushed.* Manila Bulleting Publishing Group. http://www.mb.com.ph/node/225814/5b-a. Accessed 29 Jan 2010.

Ministry of Finance. (2009). *Ministry of finance green paper: Economic and fiscal policy strategies for climate change mitigation in Indonesia.* Jakarta: Ministry of Finance and Australia Indonesia Partnership.

Nishikawa, Y. (2009). Human security in Southeast Asia: Viable solution or empty slogan? *Security Dialogue, 40*(2), 213–236.

Paris, R. (2004). Still an inscrutable concept. *Security Dialogue, 35*(3), 370–372.
Pelangi Energi Abadi Citra Enviro (PEACE). (2007). *Executive summary: Indonesia and climate change. Working paper on current status and policies.* Jakarta: PEACE, The World Bank and Department for International Development.
Peou, S. (2009). Introduction: Collaborative action problems in human security. In S. Peou (Ed.), *Human security in East Asia: Challenges for collaborative action* (pp. 61–76). New York: Routledge.
Pettenger, M. E. (Ed.). (2007). *The social construction of climate change: Power knowledge, norms, discourses.* Ashgate: Aldershot.
Powell, S. (2009, October 26). ASEAN demands emissions action, *The Australian*.
Qadri, S. T. (Ed.). (2001). *Fire, smoke, and haze. The ASEAN response strategy.* Manila: Asia Development Bank and ASEAN.
Schmeier, S. (2009). Regional cooperation efforts in the Mekong River Basin: Mitigating River-related security threats and promoting regional development. *Austrian Journal of Southeast-Asia Studies (ASEAS), 2*(2), 28–52.
Sen, A. (1999a). Human rights and economic achievements. In J. R. Bauer & D. A. Bell (Eds.), *The East Asian challenge for human rights* (pp. 88–99). Cambridge: Cambridge University Press.
Sen, A. (1999b). *Development as freedom.* Oxford: Oxford University Press.
Smith, P. J. (2007). Climate change, weak states and the "War on Terror" in South and Southeast Asia. *Contemporary Southeast Asia, 29*(2), 264–285.
Sovacool, B. K. (2009). Reassessing energy security and the Trans-ASEAN Natural Gas Pipeline network in Southeast Asia. *Pacific Affairs, 82*(3), 467–486.
Stern, N. (2006). The economics of climate change. London: Government Economic Service.
Sukma, R. (2008). Political development: A democracy Agenda for ASEAN? In D. K. Emmerson (Ed.), *Hard choices: Security, democracy and regionalism in Southeast Asia* (pp. 135–149). Stanford, CA: Stanford University Shorenstein APARC.
Sydney Morning Herald (SMH) (2009, December 7). *Copenhagen glimmer.* http://www.smh.com.au/opinion/blogs/greenlines/copenhagen-glimmer-update/20091207-kf5h.html. Accessed 8 Dec 2009.
Tatsuo, I. (1999). Liberal democracy and Asian orientalism. In J. R. Bauer & D. A. Bell (Eds.), *The East Asian challenge for human rights* (pp. 27–59). Cambridge: Cambridge University Press.
Tay, S. S. C. (2008). Blowing smoke: Regional cooperation, Indonesian democracy, and the haze. In D. K. Emmerson (Ed.), *Hard choices: Security, democracy and regionalism in Southeast Asia* (pp. 219–239). Stanford: Stanford University Shorenstein APARC.
Tay, S. S. C (2009). *ASEAN needs to step up its green efforts.* http://www.siiaonline.org/?q=programmes/commentary/asean-needs-step-its-green-efforts. Accessed 21 Jan 2010.
Taylor, J. G. (1999). *East Timor: The price of freedom.* Annandale: Pluto Press.
Thakur, R. (2006). *The united nations, peace and security: From collective security to the responsibility to protect.* Cambridge: Cambridge University Press.
United Nations (2009). *Copenhagen united nations climate change conference ends with political agreement to cap temperature rise, reduce emissions and raise finance, Press Release.* http://unfccc.int/files/press/news_room/press_releases_and_advisories/application/pdf/pr_cop15_20091219.pdf. Accessed 14 Jan 2010.
United Nations Development Program (UNDP) (Ed.). (1994). *Human development report 1994*, New York/Oxford: Oxford University Press.
Vogler, J. (2008). Environmental issues. In J. Baylis, S. Smith, & P. Owens (Eds.), *The globalization of world politics: An introduction to international relations* (4th ed., pp. 350–368). Oxford: Oxford University Press.
Walsh, B. (2010, 2 February). Climate accord suggests a global will, if not a way. *Time Magazine.* http://www.time.com/time/health/article/0,8599,1958234,00.html?xid=rss-topstories. Accessed 4 Feb 2010.

Chapter 8
Depoliticizing Natural Disasters to Enhance Human Security in a Sovereignty-Based Context: Lessons from Aceh (2004) to Yangon (2008)

Delphine Alles

8.1 Introduction: The Specificity of Natural Disasters Among the Other Components of Human Security

> The earthquake and tsunami disaster of 26 December 2004 have brought in their wake not only unprecedented loss of life and property, but more importantly laid bare our unpreparedness and our weaknesses in collectively addressing such large scale calamities.
>
> (Ong, March 2005)

In an unusual mea culpa, former ASEAN Secretary-General Ong Keng Yong half-admitted in March 2005 that the traditional security paradigm based on the protection of states' borders and sovereignty, which predominates in Southeast Asia's political culture, had proven unable to address such a large-scale nonmilitary drama. He further emphasized these comments in a September 2005 speech. As he was trying to highlight the lessons learned in the aftermath of the Tsunami in terms of regional cooperation and natural disasters management, Ong Keng Yong specifically stressed the need for cooperative and transnational mechanisms of prevention and immediate relief, as well as the fact that solutions to natural disasters had to be thought in the long run (Ong, September 2005). He thereby acknowledged that the Tsunami had shed light on the pitfalls of a regional security paradigm mostly focused on military threats, the preservation of state borders, noninterference and national sovereignty.

Encouraged by Ong Keng Yong's remarks, optimistic international and Southeast Asian advocates of human security hoped that from the tsunami's ruins would emerge the opportunity of replacing Southeast Asia's state-centered security paradigm with a new, people-centered approach. For the first time, an ASEAN leader was partially echoing the definition of human security. Theorized in 1994 by the

D. Alles (✉)
Sciences Po (Paris), Paris, France
e-mail: delphine.alles@gmail.com

United Nations Development Programme, this notion stresses the universal and people-centered nature of security, the interdependence of different factors of insecurity, as well as the fact that prevention is preferable to late intervention (UNDP 1994). Natural disasters, whose consequences ramify well beyond the category of environmental issues, epitomize the situations of "sudden and hurtful disruptions in the patterns of daily life" mentioned by the UNDP report. According to this documents' definition, human security encompasses seven main categories: environmental security is mentioned in parallel with economic security, food security, health security, personal security, community security and political security.

Despite an undeniable change of tone in Southeast Asia, it would have been somewhat optimistic to assume that the Tsunami would immediately unlock the regional leaders' reluctance toward an approach which focuses on individuals rather than states. The apparent comprehensiveness of the principle and the vagueness of its seven categories have attracted suspicion on the practical viability of human security (Owen and Burgess 2004). Moreover, despite the fact that former Thai Foreign Minister Surin Pitsuwan, who became Ong Keng Yong's successor at the General Secretariat of ASEAN in 2008, has been an early advocate of the paradigm,[1] most of the region's leaders remain reluctant to the idea of giving away the constituents of state sovereignty. Recognizing human security at the regional level would open a breach toward interferences in states' domestic affairs: For most of these recently independent Southeast Asian governments, the priority is, on the contrary, to limit external pressures on their sovereignty.

A reconciliation can however be envisioned in the area of natural disasters, which provides ground for the implementation of cooperative solutions at the supranational level without requiring a compromise with either national sovereignty or people's rights. Unlike the other threats to human security, which directly result from conscious policies or human intentions and can therefore not be addressed without political solutions, natural disasters happen randomly and do not directly result from human intentions. They allow for the implementation of politically neutral insurance-like mechanisms.[2] Conversely, the other components listed by UNDP necessarily entail a compromise whenever there is a difference between states' actions and any aspect of human security. This distinction between the political neutrality of the destructions caused by natural disasters and the political debates which can surface on the other threats to human security is crucial. In a region where a suspected intention of political interference can drive a government to reject outside

---

[1] As early as July 8th 1998, in his capacity as Foreign Minister of Thailand, during a seminar held for the 49th anniversary of the Thammasat University's faculty of political science (Bangkok), Surin Pitsuwan stated that "Perhaps it is time of ASEAN's cherished non-intervention principle to be modified. When a matter of domestic concern poses a threat to regional stability, peer pressure or friendly advice can help". It was the first declaration in this direction on the part of an acting minister of a prominent ASEAN member state.

[2] A distinction must be made between the proposed "insurance-like" system, whose goal is to aid, and the strict definition of an insurance mechanism which requires that the risk should be random, the loss should be definite and the insurer should be able to cover the loss.

support, singling out natural disasters would allow the implementation of supranational cooperation without compromising the sovereignty of states for which it is unacceptable. Singling natural disasters out of human security does not mean that the latter's objectives should be abandoned. On the contrary, it enables the implementation of faster responses without compromising on human rights, since these can be promoted by devoted institutions which can afford not to be constrained by humanitarian emergencies.

The evolution of the situation in Southeast Asia, between 2004 and 2008, illustrates the accuracy of this distinction. This chapter shows that the failure to respond to the tsunami in Aceh has enforced an evolution of the region's approach on natural disasters. A dramatic test case occurred when the Cyclone Nargis hit Myanmar[3] in May 2008, carrying consequences comparable in scale with the tsunami. Despite nonnegligible organizational flaws, the coordinated response to Nargis demonstrates that, between the two crises, lessons have been learned. Even more interesting is the instrumental role played by ASEAN in facilitating the access of humanitarian relief to the affected areas. The organization, which is often criticized for its commitment to the principle of noninterference in states' domestic affairs, has paradoxically proven more efficient than global organizations. Southeast Asia's most shielded regime was indeed better disposed toward the ASEAN than toward other international bodies, which were initially rejected on the grounds of their alleged tendency to blend political interventionism with humanitarian relief.

8.2 Aceh 2004: A Renewed International Attention to the Region, from Disaster-Relief to Disaster-Diplomacy

On December 26, 2004, off the coast of northern Sumatra, an earthquake with a magnitude comprised between 9.1 and 9.3 on the Richter scale generated a series of devastating tsunamis along the coastal areas of 14 countries bordering the Indian Ocean.[4]

An estimated total of 240,000 people have lost their lives in this disaster, in addition to nearly 50,000 missing, 125,000 injured and 1.7 million displaced people.[5] On top of the human casualties, considerable damage in infrastructures provoked the impossibility of using supplies of drinking waters and durably injured the local economies

---

[3] In order to avoid semantical disputes, the author wishes to clarify that she has chosen to follow the terminology employed by the United Nations and ASEAN, which use the term Myanmar rather than Burma, although the latter is preferred by various opposition groups and countries.

[4] This chapter focuses on the hardest-hit region of Aceh in North Sumatra, Indonesia. The tsunami was however a large-scale transnational disaster, which affected parts of India, Sri Lanka, Thailand, Bangladesh, Myanmar, Malaysia, the Maldives, the Seychelles, Madagascar, Somalia, Keynia, Tanzania and South Africa.

[5] Compilation of sources: Australian Government (Bureau of Meteorology), United Nations Development Program (Disaster Reduction Unit), UN News Center.

(ASEAN Virtual Information Centre 2005). In the province of Aceh only, the Indonesian government estimates nearly 130,000 deaths, 39,000 missing and over 500,000 displaced people (Doocy et al. 2005). Economic losses have been estimated to be close to US$5 billion, which roughly corresponds to 80% of the province's annual GDP (World Bank 2008). Most of the damages have affected fisheries, agricultural resources and facilities, small private enterprises, buildings, as well as the communication and telecommunication infrastructures (Saldanha et al. 2005). As a direct consequence, unemployment rose by about 20%, and the Acehnese economy shrunk by 30% in 2005, while poverty was undergoing a 50% surge (BRR 2005).

Within a few hours, the tsunami erased the very notion of national borders and demonstrated the limits of traditional security. It proved, if need was, that large casualties are far from being the preserve of inter-states military conflicts. The tsunami's long-term impact in several intertwined areas demonstrated the need for an integrated approach, which would be able to take into account the fact that environmental disasters can have repercussions on economic security, food security, health, but also political and personal security – especially for women and children, which were the most numerous victims of the disaster and were more vulnerable in its aftermath.

As one of the worst affected areas, Aceh has been the focus of an extensive international attention and relief efforts. The political situation of the North Sumatra province, which had been the theater of a secessionist rebellion since the 1950s, was an additional incentive for the international community to turn its attention and focus its efforts on Aceh.

8.2.1 *A Combination of Humanitarian and Political Concerns*

A convergence of global and local motives specifically contributed to the concentration of efforts on the North Sumatra province.

After the 9/11 attacks on the United States and the subsequent military interventions in Afghanistan and Iraq, Indonesia had attracted much attention as the most populous Muslim-majority country in the world. For an important donor like the United States, providing relief to Aceh was a way of demonstrating that they were not engaged on a war against Islam and an opportunity to improve their image in a part of the world where it had been seriously damaged. This logic was nonambiguously unveiled by US Secretary of State Condoleezza Rice, who mentioned in front of the US Senate's foreign affairs commission that the disaster had provided a "wonderful opportunity to show not just the US government, but the heart of the American people," adding that she believed it had paid great diplomatic dividends.[6]

At the time of the tsunami, Aceh was also the theater of an ongoing conflict between the Indonesian authorities and the Free Aceh Movement (GAM – Gerakan Aceh Merdeka). The rebels, mixing separatist and Islamist rhetoric, had been in

---

[6] As quoted by Agence France Presse, January 18, 2008.

conflict with the Indonesian Armed Forces (TNI – Tentara Nasional Indonesia) since the GAM's creation in 1976, and were the inheritors of the chronic struggle which had been harming the province since shortly after Indonesia's independence. Neither the agreement on a special autonomy status in July 2001 nor the implementation of martial law in May 2003 had been able to appease the rebels or calm down the movement. The peace talks between the government, the TNI and the GAM had resumed after the inauguration of President Susilo Bambang Yudhoyono in October 2005. The tsunami is believed to have triggered the search for a practical solution. It is indeed much likely that the disaster, by changing the priorities of the actors involved in the conflict and its resolution, had consequences on the short-term local political situation (details in Gaillard et al. 2008).

The tsunami also overemphasized the international attention to the region, and the peace process suddenly resurfaced on the international agenda. Between January and mid-July 2005, five rounds of discussions were organized in Helsinki, through the mediation of former Finnish President Martti Ahtisaari. Both sides agreed on a memorandum of understanding (MoU), which provided the platform for a normalization of the situation, the disarmament of the GAM as well as the organization of local elections. Five years later, despite a resurgence of localized tensions in the context of the Indonesian general election (International Crisis Group 2009), the situation can be considered relatively stable.[7]

Observers may interpret this successful post-disaster diplomacy as a positive side effect of the tsunami, which indeed proved instrumental in bringing the parties back to the negotiation table and driving them to find a way out of the conflict. However, from the point of view of sovereignty-preoccupied authorities, the involvement of external powers in both the reconstruction and the local political situation was noticed with a degree of concern. Notwithstanding the differences in the two countries' political situations, the determination to avoid such a conjunction of political and humanitarian agendas most probably resonated, 3 years later, in the initial decision of the Myanmar authorities to forbid the access of foreign relief teams and media to the areas affected by Cyclone Nargis (see Sect. 8.3).

8.2.2 From Humanitarian Response to Foreign Involvement

In December 2004 and January 2005, humanitarian emergency preceded over sovereignty concerns in the eyes of the Indonesian authorities, who immediately sought foreign assistance, both public and private, to help them cope with the immediate consequences of the disaster.

---

[7] In late February 2010, a terrorists training camp was uncovered by the Indonesian special forces in Aceh. It has been reported that the terrorists, coordinated by former Jemaah Islamiyah member Dulmatin, had no linkages with the independentist movement although they were expecting to recruit former GAM members deceived by the peace agreements (International Crisis Group 2010).

A few days after the disaster, an unprecedented movement of generosity was recorded among the civil societies worldwide. An estimated 300 international non-governmental organizations (NGOs) responded to the disaster, bringing about 2,000 foreign workers in addition to the thousands of Indonesians who came to help the Acehnese population. Although the exact total of individual contributions is impossible to determine, private donations have reached an estimated total of US$5–7 billion. Within a few weeks, an NGO called *Médecins Sans Frontières* (Doctors Without Borders) issued a statement stating that they had reached the level of donations they had targeted for the tsunami and suggesting that people should direct their generosity to other areas instead, which initially raised criticism on the part of other NGOs (Freschi 2010). The financial contributions from individuals, in fact, exceeded the absorption capacity of the organizations on the field, with the inconvenience that they favored a proliferation of inexperienced actors (Ville de Goyet and Moriniere 2006). They also acted as a disincentive for the organizations to coordinate their efforts: far from cooperation, rivalries between NGOs competing for the same areas of action have been deplored (Canny 2005), probably being the consequence of an excess of funds which did not incite them to pool resources and information.

In addition to this unprecedented mobilization of individual donors all over the world, extra-regional governments as well as non-affected neighboring countries began promising financial aid and sent assistance to the affected areas from Africa to Southeast Asia. A total of more than US$6 billion was pledged by foreign governments, including US$810 million from Australia (out of which US$760.6 million were directly promised to Indonesia); Germany pledged US$679 million, and Japan offered US$500 million (Pan 2005). The initial American contribution of US$35 million rose to US$ 350 million, while additional funds were promised to help the long-term support for the reconstruction of the coastal areas. On February 9, 2005, following a presidential demand, the US Congress agreed to increase the country's commitment to an unprecedented total of US$950 million.

Economic contributions were not the only type of foreign governmental assistance. Foreign military forces were also involved in the immediate recovery effort, erasing the classical theorem of national sovereignty – as well as the conventional regional security paradigm, according to which "Southeast Asians deal with Southeast Asia's problems" (Sukma 2005). The US Navy's seventh fleet began providing logistical and medical help as soon as January 1st, using several warships such as USS Abraham Lincoln carrier or the medical Mercy ships, in addition to a total of 70 navy ships and 90 aircrafts (Dille 2005). At the height of the relief operation, 15,000 troops were on the field. One thousand troops from the Japanese Self-Defense Forces, including 80 medical staff, also arrived on the field on January 25, in addition to Australian and Russian troops. Indonesia's neighbors also participated in the efforts, with 400 Malaysian police and military officers and 1,000 troops from the Singapore defense forces.

Realizing the extent of this divergence from the national sovereignty idea, the Indonesian authorities soon began to worry about the local consequences of this massive influx of foreign workers and, more importantly, troops. President Susilo Bambang Yudhoyono and Vice President Jusuf Kalla tried to reestablish control within a few weeks, declaring in mid-February that all foreign military personnel should leave the province not later than March 26 – with the exception of the troops of Indonesia's ASEAN neighbors and partners.

8.2.3 *A Trigger for the Evolution of the Regional Security Paradigm*

The deceiving role played by ASEAN as an organization, however, cannot be left unquestioned. As deplored by the organization's Secretary-General in the previously quoted speeches, ASEAN failed to provide a unitary response. Although these speeches demonstrate a new awareness provoked by the tsunami, it would be erroneous to claim that ASEAN ignored the existence of natural disasters and the urge to address them collectively prior to 2004. The regional organization was far from being empty of declarations of principles or initiatives in this field. Ong Keng Long himself bitterly recalled that a "Declaration on Mutual Assistance on Natural Disasters" had been signed as early as 1976, with the constitution of an experts' group (ASEAN 1976). An Internet-based earthquake and tsunami alert system had been established by ASEAN in 2000, but it had not been sufficiently developed (Huxley 2005). An "ASEAN Committee on Disaster Management" (ACDM) had been established in early 2003 to replace the previous experts group into a full-fledged committee. The ACDM, launched in May 2004 and reunited for the first time in December the same year, gathered the heads of national agencies responsible for disaster management and was supposed to assume overall responsibility for coordinating and implementing the regional activities. It had established an "ASEAN Regional Programme on Disaster Management" (ARPDM), whose task was to provide a framework for cooperation for the period 2004–2010. Featuring 29 activities organized in five areas of action, it included an "ASEAN Response Action Plan" and an "ASEAN Disaster Information Sharing and Communication Network" (ASEAN DISCNet). It was supposed to combine "regional activities covering cross-boundary issues and involving inter-country collaboration" and "regional activities in support of national activities".[8] Finally, less than a month before the disaster, ASEAN members had decided to set up a "regional agreement on disaster management and emergency response" – which was not given enough time to be implemented before the tsunami erupted (Ong, March 2005).

On paper, the necessity to prevent natural disasters and establish emergency response mechanisms was well understood and consensual among ASEAN members; the framework of action was supposed to exist, and the need for cooperation was acknowledged – which exacerbates the disappointment toward the absence of coordinated response. The tsunami did not reveal a necessity to act. Rather, it painfully

---

[8] ARPDM Activity Profile as described on the ASEAN Secretariat website, http://www.aseansec.org/18456.htm.

demonstrated the leaders' inability to implement the principles they had been calling for, as well as the practical failure of the organization in providing a coordinated response.

ASEAN's failure to act constituted a trigger for the creation of new mechanisms of assistance and prevention. A Special ASEAN Leaders' Meeting was immediately held in Jakarta, in order to discuss the coordination of international relief efforts and the creation of a region-wide early warning system. The ministers drafted a common ASEAN resolution for "Strengthening emergency relief, rehabilitation, reconstruction and prevention in the aftermath of the Indian Ocean tsunami disaster", which was unanimously adopted by the UN General Assembly on January 19, 2005, and allowed for the establishment and utilization of military and civilian personnel in disaster relief operations. Two important regional organs were also created: an ASEAN Humanitarian Assistance Center and the ASEAN Disaster Information Sharing and Communication Network. Additional steps have also been taken toward a regionally coordinated early warning system, through a center which was established in Thailand in order to prevent future disasters of this magnitude (Ministerial Meeting on Tsunami Early Warning Arrangements 2005).

It should, however, be positively observed that there was a degree of solidarity among ASEAN members. Neighboring countries, although they did not have the possibility of mobilizing important amounts of financial resources in comparison to Western or East Asian governments, were particularly helpful in providing manpower or goods. It can therefore be argued that ASEAN has created a framework within which bilateral cooperation was smoothed. Although the organization itself proved incapable of implementing a regionally coordinated response, the fact that ASEAN members have become used to working with one another has allowed for the intervention of Singaporean and Malaysian troops which, less than 40 years ago, were considered as rivals. Interestingly, when Indonesian Vice President Jusuf Kalla set a deadline on March 26 for foreign troops to leave the country, he specified that the deadline did not apply to ASEAN members (AFP 2005). The fact that ASEAN military forces were allowed to stay in Aceh while other countries had to call back their troops and equipment suggests that the regional organization had succeeded in improving mutual confidence among its member states. The declared commitment of ASEAN members to noninterference in each others' domestic affairs has probably contributed to this evolution since the Indonesian government did not consider the presence of neighboring armies as a threat to its national sovereignty and self-reliance. A similar line of reasoning probably guided Myanmar, in 2008, when it finally agreed to open its borders to an ASEAN-led relief mission.

Skeptical post-tsunami analyses insist on the fact that the "tsunami disaster was not to bring about a significant change with regards to the place of traditional norms in states' national security and foreign policy" (Sukma 2005). On a more positive note, it can be emphasized that the tsunami did demonstrate that states alone are not able to address such large scale and unexpected events. In the area of natural disasters, whose harmfulness is consensually recognized and which are not the result of human intentions or political actions, it is possible to implement cooperative mechanisms without infringing the principle of noninterference in political affairs. This specificity of natural disasters, as opposed to the other components of human security, has allowed ASEAN to play an important role in the attempts at implementing coordinated solutions in the aftermath of the Nargis cyclone.

8.3 Yangon, 2008: The Paradox of an Intervention Facilitated by ASEAN's Consensus on Noninterference

On May 2 and 3, 2008, less than 4 years after the tsunami, a category four cyclone, carrying 200 km winds, provoked colossal destructions in several Myanmar provinces, namely the Ayeyarwady delta, the former capital Yangon and parts of Bago division and Mon state. The extent of the devastations it left only compares to the tsunami. Low-lying coastal areas were hit by a 4-m high flood surge, which smashed thousands of houses and flooded huge areas of agricultural lands, tens of kilometers inland. According to the *Post Nargis Joint Assessment* conducted by ASEAN, the Myanmar government and the United Nations, 138,373 people died or remained missing. The actual death tolls have been estimated to be as high as 200,000 in addition to 800,000 displaced people and 2.5 million in need of aid. Total damages and future economic losses have been estimated to be as high as US$4 billion, which is equivalent to 21% of the country's 2007 GDP (74% and 57% in Ayeyarwady and Yangon, respectively) (Tripartite Core Group 2008). Considering the damages in the fishing sector, the destruction of the rice harvest and substantial damage to industrial parks, the economy will take a long time to recover.

The superposition of the humanitarian disaster to a particularly sensitive political context allows drawing a parallel with the Acehnese case, although the issues at stake were strictly different in nature. The fact that the Myanmar authorities' priority was to avoid external influences in the political process they were organizing in the country at the time of the disaster sheds light on their initial opposition to foreign interventions. Whereas the Indonesian government initially opened the countries' borders to foreign assistance in the context of the post-tsunami recovery efforts, the Myanmar junta initially rejected external interventions which were deemed suspect of being accompanied with political agendas. The role of ASEAN is particularly noticeable in this context: In addition to the fact that the organization's reaction shows that progress has been made since 2004 in terms of coordination, the fact that the Myanmar government began opening the access to the damaged areas only to an ASEAN-led mission shows that the organizations' decried principle of noninterference in political affairs has proved constructive in gaining the confidence and cooperation of its most shielded and suspicious member state. This tends to demonstrate that separating natural disasters from the other, more political dimensions of human security, can be a way of enabling more rapid and efficient responses in the affected areas. Since natural disasters are consensually detrimental and do not directly result from human decisions, this separation does not constitute an abandon of the promotion of the other components of human security: On the contrary, these can be promoted by openly political institutions without being constrained by the obligation to do tradeoffs with abusive governments when an immediate intervention is required to save lives.

8.3.1 Sources of the Authorities' Reticence to Foreign Interventions

The natural disaster occurred during a particularly sensitive episode for the Myanmar military junta. In the aftermath of the September 2007 monk's protests, the regime's activities had been confronted with renewed international criticism (Thawnghmung and Myoeg 2008). Despite a relatively fast return to "normalcy", as the junta managed to impose a stronger control on the opposition, the authorities were facing a sensitive situation as they were preparing the organization of a constitutional referendum. The referendum was supposed to be a step forward in the implementation of a "roadmap to democracy" which aims at installing a nominally democratic system with the organizations of elections in 2010 while securing the military's leading role. The referendum was supposed to take place on May 10, 2008, and the authorities insisted on going ahead with it despite the disaster. Although the polls were delayed to May 24 in the worst affected areas, the authorities did carry on and reported a bewildering 92.42% approval of the proposed constitutional reform (Xinhua 2008).

In this politically charged context, the humanitarian disaster was first and foremost addressed as a political hazard by the authorities, whose main preoccupation was to secure their control on the territories and population in order to ensure the highest possible rates of participation and success in the referendum. They were also anxious not to experience a remake of the 1960s, when an opposition movement led by former Prime Minister U Nu tried to mobilize support by touring the country with a religious caravan. This concern led to the arrest of nine people in mid-June 2008 for alleged "subversive activities" – or simply because they had been talking to the foreign media. Western governments and their allies in Asia, as well as international organizations and NGOs, were suspected of carrying hidden political agendas and supporting the opposition. As a matter of fact, they were encouraged in their suspicions by a conjunction of political moves and declarations prior to and after the disaster. At the end of April, Aung San Suu Kyi had been approved by the United States Senate as a recipient of the Congressional Medal of Honor for her struggle in favor of democracy in Burma. On May 5, she was officially conferred honorary citizenship by Canada. These moves contributed to reinforce the suspicion of a conjunction of humanitarian and political agendas (Selth 2008, 2009) when the United States urged the junta to accept a naval ship loaded with humanitarian relief supplies. The threat to use the responsibility to protect principle in order to force a humanitarian intervention by military means, raised by French Foreign Minister Bernard Kouchner, was rejected by the United Nations Security Council on May 7. However, it further raised the degree of paranoia in Naypyidaw, the capital of Myanmar.

8.3.2 The Inadequacy of the Government's Immediate Response

Despite several allegations in that sense, the lack of anticipation cannot be blamed on the military government since it had not been foreseen by any meteorological institute or specialized cyclone center (International Crisis Group 2008). The authorities, however, can be held responsible for the inadequacy of the immediate responses, their inability to implement basic measures which would have limited the consequences of the catastrophe and the obstacles they created for the humanitarian relief personnel.

The government immediately declared a national emergency for the five regions which had suffered from the cyclone and activated a Natural Disaster Preparedness Central Committee, under Prime Minister General Thein Sein and with the coordination of the Ministry of Social Welfare. However, a lack of communication between the central government and the local authorities dramatically hindered the efficiency of the response. Reports have denounced an insufficient coordination, irrational policy differences from one region to another with local officials providing different interpretations of the centralized orders, and the fact that bureaucratic controls were delaying every step, including the transportation of supplies to the affected zones. In addition to the fact that the authorities alone were obviously unable to provide enough relief aid and food, some local officials have been accused of selling or keeping a share of the relief supplies.

Despite the contrary allegations of media reports, the government did call for specific kinds of foreign assistance: On May 5, 2008, the Foreign Minister declared on a BBC broadcasted address that his country needed financial and material aid. The authorities made clear, however, that they would not allow foreign staff to enter the affected areas. They bluntly rejected the use of military helicopters from the US as well as the approach of French and British naval ships to the area, and refused permission for flights to use the Bathein military airport, which was closer to the theater of operations. Forty-eight international NGOs and ten United Nations agencies were already operating in Burma at the time of the cyclone and were therefore able to provide immediate relief. Some of them were already on the ground and managed to get access to the damaged areas (International Crisis Group 2008). Local NGOs have also apparently been able to work at the grassroots level, with the help of the local authorities and the contribution from local people (International Crisis Group 2008). However, as the army moved in to cordon off the affected zone, international staff members no longer had access to the field. The UN agencies and NGO workers who needed to get visas were not allowed into the country or were confined in Yangon during the first 2–3 weeks.

These restrictions and the junta's selectivity in the choice of "acceptable" aid provoked an outburst of international condemnations, crystallizing debates around the evocation of the "responsibility to protect" principle. It is only after the first round of the referendum, as could have been expected, that the situation began to evolve. During the 3rd week after the disaster, the authorities allowed regional medical experts as well as civilian helicopters, furnished by the World Food Program, to enter the delta. On May 21, 2008, UN Secretary-General Ban Ki Moon declared that only a quarter of the worst affected people received aid. Two days later, he managed to meet Senior General Tan Shwe and pledged in favor of the full access for foreign relief personnel. The success of this meeting, presented as a significant accomplishment for the United Nation's diplomacy, would probably not have been possible without the preliminary mediation of Myanmar's fellow ASEAN members.

The next section suggests that the organization's much decried principle of noninterference (Jones 2008) played a positive role in reassuring the junta and opening the country to foreign relief teams.

8.3.3 The Constructive Outcome of ASEAN's Noninterference Principle

Despite the fact that the Myanmar authorities never moved away from their radical defense of national sovereignty, ASEAN managed to play a positive role in the post-disaster recovery efforts. Ironically, the authorities' resolution to avoid external interventions and influences convinced them that it would be in their best interest to let ASEAN lead the relief efforts rather than the more interventionist extra-regional or global organizations (Honda 2008). Not only the absence of radical change of philosophy on this principle did not prevent the organization to implement some of the relief strategies it had imagined in the aftermath of the tsunami, but it is probably this very maintenance of the noninterference principle which led the Myanmar authorities to accept ASEAN's contribution.

The Aceh experience, in which ASEAN's failure to act constrained Indonesia to open its doors to external powers and led to an involvement of the European Union, most probably reinforced the argument. The threat of a forced international intervention based on the responsibility to protect principle, agitated at the United Nations before it was rejected by the Security Council, provided further incentive for the country's authorities to rely on ASEAN's assistance. During the days after the cyclone, Secretary-General Surin Pitsuwan called on ASEAN members to send relief to Myanmar, before calling on Myanmar's Minister of Foreign Affairs, Nyan Win, to allow ASEAN relief teams enter the country (see details in Amador III 2009). During the ASEAN foreign ministers' meeting, which was organized on May 19, 2008, the leaders agreed to set up an ASEAN Humanitarian Task Force to coordinate and lead the international response in the affected areas. This unprecedented initiative, built under the influence of long-time human security advocate and current Secretary-General Surin Pitsuwan, was a significant step toward the implementation of the coordinated responses. Despite its early reluctance, the junta realized that it would be in their best interest to accept this initiative. The fact that Indonesia (who was at the time a nonpermanent member of the United Nation's Security Council) had voted against the use of responsibility to protect on May 7, 2008, was an additional argument in favor of an ASEAN-led operation. Allowing ASEAN to take lead in the relief operation also provided a face-saving way of agreeing on opening the country, which had become unavoidable given the scale of the disaster.

This first breach into the nonintervention principle paved the way for the subsequent involvement of the United Nations, under the leadership of ASEAN, and facilitated the subsequent deliverance of visas for foreign relief teams. A Tripartite Core Group (TCG) was formed on May 31, 2008, gathering the Myanmar Government, ASEAN and the United Nations, as well as experts from the World Bank and the

Asian Development Bank. This TCG took charge of the Post-Nargis Joint Assessment (PONJA) in the framework of which 250 international experts – some of which had acquired their expertise during the post-tsunami reconstruction efforts – and volunteers were sent to the field in order to conduct a detailed assessment of the damages and needs. The PONJA report was published on July 21, 2008, evaluating the cyclone's consequences and assessing the response as well as the short- and medium-term needs (Tripartite Core Group 2008).

The TCG contributed in solving the administrative restrictions imposed by Myanmar's government on foreign workers during the first three weeks (International Crisis Group 2008), allowing UN Emergency Relief Coordinator John Holmes to conclude, on July 25, that "this is now a normal emergency relief operation" (Integrated Regional Information Network 2008). The TCG's mandate was prolonged for one more year in March 2009, demonstrating that it had successfully built confidence and established a working relationship between the three parties.

8.4 Conclusion: The Case for an Insurance-Like Mechanism to Address Natural Disasters in a Sovereignty-Based Context

The Indian Ocean tsunami and Cyclone Nargis have been the two most damaging disasters in Southeast Asia in the recent years. From Aceh in 2004 to Yangon in 2008, ASEAN members and leaders have consciously acknowledged that such transnational and dramatic events must be dealt with in a transnational way. They have realized that the region's traditional security paradigm, focused on the protection of national borders, is not sufficient to address such events – which can be as lethal as armed conflicts. Less than 4 years after the tsunami, far from his predecessor's confession of helplessness, ASEAN Secretary-General Surin Pitsuwan has observed that the organization had been "baptized" by Nargis. Referring to the organization's successful mediation, he added that a "new ASEAN" has emerged from the crisis (AFP, June 2008).

ASEAN members, however, are far from being ready to revise the principle of noninterference in each other's political affairs, which is one of the main constituents of the organization and remains a prerequisite to any international cooperation in the region.

Whereas pessimistic views consider that upholding this principle is an obstacle to any move toward a better protection of human security, the post-Nargis case suggests a different interpretation. The participation of Myanmar in ASEAN's institutions has enabled the junta to cooperate with the organization in a much more trustful way than it would have done with any other supranational body. If ASEAN was instrumental in opening Myanmar to international aid, it is paradoxically because of its noninterference policy, thanks to which the military government was better disposed toward the Southeast Asian organization than toward the allegedly "Western" international bodies, countries or NGOs.

This observation will not be satisfactory for advocates of a radical change of security paradigm. But as long as there is no agreement on the definition of the elements that should constitute the threshold basis of human security (Owen 2004), the paradigm will be considered with suspicion by states which prioritize domestic stability and national sovereignty. In a region characterized by its diversity, where sovereignty issues are sensitive and the wounds of a recent history of colonization and conflicts remain slow to heal, it is crucial to understand that attempts at forcing a new paradigm contra the governments' will are likely to be counterproductive.

The case of natural disasters, however, allows for a satisfactory resolution. Natural disasters are characterized by the fact that they are not the direct consequence of human intentions or political actions. They can therefore be singled out of the other dimensions of human security, which all call for political solutions and are therefore considered unacceptable by states opposed to political interferences in their domestic affairs. Distinguishing the political neutrality of natural disasters, from the unavoidable political debates on the other components of human security, presents the advantage of being satisfactory in terms of ethical principles as well as in terms of efficient results: By keeping away from negotiations and compromises, it allows for concrete actions to be implemented in a fast pace when an emergency situation requires them, without constraining the parties involved to abandon parts of their ethical or nationalist principles for the purpose of efficiency.

This approach, which seems to be compatible with the core principles of the ASEAN states, should provide enough grounds for the development of what is still needed in the region – an efficient early warning system and a transnational "ready to implement" response mechanism. If, in the context of the implementation of the ASEAN Charter, the organization pursues its move toward a more political orientation, this response mechanism could be implemented in the framework of an independent, transnational and voluntary insurance-like system.

References

AFP (Agence France Presse). (2005, January 17). *ASEAN troops in Indonesia's tsunami-hit Aceh to remain*. Kuala Lumpur: AFP.

AFP (Agence France Presse). (2008, June 17). *New ASEAN emerging from response to Myanmar cyclone: Surin*. Singapore: AFP.

Amador, J. S., III. (2009). Community building at the time of Nargis: The ASEAN response. *Journal of Current Southeast Asian Affairs, 28*(4), 3–22.

Association of Southeast Asian Nations. (1976). *ASEAN declaration on mutual assistance on natural disasters*. Manila: ASEAN. http://www.aseansec.org/1431.htm. Accessed 26 May 2010.

Association of Southeast Asian Nations Virtual Information Centre. (2005). *ASEAN's response to the tsunami disaster – issues and concerns: A special report*.

Badan Rehabilitasi dan Rekonstruksi NAD-Nias (BRR – Agency for the Rehabilitation and Reconstruction of Aceh and Nias) and international partners. (2005). *Aceh and Nias one year after the tsunami – the recovery effort and way forward* (Report). Indonesia: BRR. http://siteresources.worldbank.org/INTEASTASIAPACIFIC/Resources/1YR_tsunami_advance_release.pdf. Accessed 26 May 2010.

Canny, B. (2005, April 8). *A review of NGO cooperation in Aceh post earthquake/tsunami.* Geneva: Sponsored by the International Council of Voluntary Agencies (ICVA), http://www.humanitarianinfo.org/sumatra/reference/assessments/doc/other/ICVA-ReviewOfNGOCoordinationInAceh-080405.pdf. Accessed 26 May 2010.

Dille, P (2005, January 1). US 7th fleet first to provide naval support to Aceh province. *US Navy Today*, Washington DC (USA).

Doocy, S., Rofi, A., Burnham, G., & Robinson, C. (2005). *Tsunami mortality in Aceh province, Indonesia.* New York: United Nations' International Strategy for Disaster Reduction (UNISDR).

Freschi, L. (2010, January 20). *Too much of a good thing? Making the most of your disaster donations.* New York: Aidwatch. http://aidwatchers.com/2010/01/too-much-of-a-good-thing/. Accessed 26 May 2010.

Gaillard, J.-C., Clave, E., & Kslman, I. (2008). Wave of peace? Tsunami disaster diplomacy in Aceh, Indonesia. *Geoforum, 39*(1), 511–526.

Honda, M. (2008). *Disaster diplomacy and the dilemma of humanitarian intervention: The case of Myanmar/Burma in comparison with China.* Paper presented at the 3rd NTS-Asia annual convention – consortium of non-traditional security studies in Asia, Chinese Academy of Social Sciences, Beijing, China.

Huxley, T. (2005). The tsunami and security: Asia's 9/11? *Survival, 47*(1), 123–132.

Integrated Regional Information Network (IRIN). (2008, July 25). *Myanmar: Access is there, donors should respond generously, says Holmes.* Geneva: IRIN – Office for the Coordination of Humanitarian Affairs.

International Crisis Group. (2008, October 20). *Burma/Myanmar after Nargis: Time to normalize aid relations* (Asia Report No. 161). http://www.crisisgroup.org/home/index.cfm?id=5734. Accessed 26 May 2010.

International Crisis Group. (2009, March 23). *Indonesia: Big distrust in Aceh as elections approach* (Asia Briefing No. 90). http://www.crisisgroup.org/en/regions/asia/south-east-asia/indonesia/B090-indonesia-deep-distrust-in-aceh-as-elections-approach.aspx. Accessed 26 May 2010.

International Crisis Group. (2010, April 20). *Indonesia: Jihadi surprise in Aceh* (Asia Report No 189).

Jones, L. (2008). ASEAN's albatross: ASEAN's Burma policy, from constructive engagement to critical disengagement. *Asian Security, 4*(3), 271–293.

Ministerial Meeting on Tsunami Early Warning Arrangements. (2005). *Phuket ministerial declaration on regional cooperation on tsunami early warning arrangements.* Phuket, Thailand. http://www.gisthai.org/resource/tsunami/PhuketMinisterialDeclaration.pdf. Accessed 26 May 2010.

Ong K. Y. (2005a, March 3). *Leadership in Asia after tsunami.* Remarks delivered at the Asian leadership Conference 2005, Seoul, South Korea. http://www.aseansec.org/17302.htm. Accessed 26 May 2010.

Ong K. Y. (2005b, September 23). *Seven cardinal rules of regional partnership: Lessons from tsunami 2004.* Speech delivered at the Third Asia-Pacific Homeland Security Summit and Exposition, Honolulu, HI.

Owen, T. (2004). Human security – conflict, critique and consensus: Colloquium remarks and a proposal for a threshold-based definition. *Security Dialogue, 35*(3), 373–387.

Owen, T., & Burgess, P. (Eds.). (2004). What is human security?, *Security Dialogue, 35*(3), 347–387.

Pan, E. (2005, January 7). Tsunami disaster: Relief effort. *Backgrounder.* New York: Council on Foreign Relations, http://www.cfr.org/publication/7792/tsunami_disaster.html. Accessed 26 May 2010.

Saldanha, J. M., Carey, P. B., & Harriss-White B. (2005, June 11). *After the boxing day tsunami – Early warning, relief, reconstruction and peace process* (Report based on the workshop on post tsunami Asian countries organized by ABC, St Antony's college and SHE Department of International Development). London: University of Oxford.

Selth, A. (2008). Even paranoids have enemies: Cyclone Nargis and Myanmar's fears of invasion. *Contemporary Southeast Asia, 30*(3), 379–392.

Selth, A. (2009, February 15). Myanmar's fears of invasion: A strategic reality. *Opinion Asia.* http://opinionasia.com/MyanmarsFearsofInvasion. Accessed 26 May 2010.

Sukma, R. (2005). *Domestic and regional implication of Indonesian tsunami: The political and security dimensions.* Paper presented at the ASEAN Roundtable 2005: Implications on regional development and security, ISEAS, Singapore.

Thawnghmung, A. M., & Myoeg, M. A. (2008). Myanmar in 2007: A turning point in the "Roadmap"? *Asian Survey, 48*(1), 13–19.

Tripartite Core Group (Representatives of the Government of the Union of Myanmar, the Association of Southeast Asian Nations, and the United Nations). (2008). *Post-Nargis joint assessment.* http://www.aseansec.org/21765.pdf. Accessed 26 May 2010.

United Nations Development Program. (1994). Chapter 2: New dimensions of human security. In *Human development report 1994: New dimensions of human security.* New York: Oxford University Press.

Ville de Goyet, C. de, & Moriniere, L. C. (2006, July). *The role of needs assessment in the tsunami response.* London: Tsunami Evaluation Coalition (TEC), ALNAP. http://www.alnap.org/pool/files/needs-assessment-final-report.pdf. Accessed 26 May 2010.

World Bank. (2008, December 18). Four years after the tsunami, Aceh looks ahead. *News and Events, Feature Stories,* Washington DC: World Bank.

Xinhua. (2008, May 30). *Myanmar formally announces ratification of new constitution draft.* China: People's Daily Online.

Chapter 9
Human Health Threats and Implications for Regional Security in Southeast Asia*

James R. Campbell

9.1 Introduction

Health threats including infectious diseases, natural and man-made disasters and environmental change impact human populations worldwide, but they are especially challenging for vulnerable populations in many of the developing nations of Southeast Asia. These health security issues also represent non-traditional regional and global security challenges, which threaten human security more broadly in multiple, complex ways. In 1994 the United Nations Development Report included health security within its definition of human security, which it defined as, "…safety from such chronic threats as hunger, disease and repression, and protection from sudden and hurtful disruptions in the patterns of daily lives, whether in homes, jobs or communities"(UNDP 1994: 23). This is recognition that the traditional understanding of security as related to military and police issues is no longer adequate.

The most threatening of infectious diseases for developing countries in the region in terms of potential morbidity and mortality include malaria, tuberculosis and HIV/AIDS. These diseases are emerging as more dangerous, drug-resistant forms, particularly in less-transparent nations like Myanmar (Beyrer et al. 2006: e393). Moreover, many infectious diseases such as cholera are exacerbated during natural disasters, and incidence of vector-borne disease including malaria, dengue and Japanese encephalitis is increased through environmental change. While treatments for these diseases exist, the incidence remains inexplicably high among many populations in the region. One explanation for this sustained disease burden has been

---

*The views expressed in this chapter are those of the author and do not necessarily represent the views of the Asia Pacific Center for Security Studies, U.S. Pacific Command, the Department of Defense, or the U.S. Government.

J.R. Campbell (✉)
Asia-Pacific Center for Security Studies, Hawaii, USA
e-mail: campbellj@apcss.org

related to the widespread belief and practice of Buddhism in Southeast Asia. Many Buddhists believe that human suffering and hardships provide the catalysts for change and development. Delays in obtaining relief from illness may be a Buddhist stoic response to religious awakening (Young-Eisendrath 2002: 67). In addition, emerging diseases such as Severe Adult Respiratory Syndrome (SARS), Nipah virus and avian influenza create new, unpredictable challenges for national public health systems.

Natural disasters such as cyclones, earthquakes and tsunamis typically are catastrophic, short duration events that cause significant but focal loss of human life associated with extensive infrastructure damage. Despite their transitory initial impact, natural disasters generally compromise human security for extended periods, because they require long term redevelopment efforts to rebuild homes and businesses and re-establish essential government services.

Global environmental change occurs with a longer periodicity and greater persistence than other health threats, so the risks to humans are usually not as acute or as obvious as those posed by infectious diseases or sudden natural disasters. Changes in rainfall patterns alter the concentration and geographic distribution of insect vectors and animal reservoirs of human disease. Rising sea levels as a result of global warming threaten many island nations as well other nations with low elevation coastal zones (LECZ) worldwide. Of the ten countries worldwide that have the largest number of people living in a LECZ four are in Southeast Asia (Indonesia, Vietnam, Thailand, Philippines) (Earth Institute 2007). In addition to the risk of inundation, populations in low-lying coastal areas suffer loss of arable farmland and potable water through the effects of saltwater encroachment. These and other environmental events such as widespread annual flooding in Vietnam or the protracted drought in Australia reduce regional crop yields, which in turn affects food and nutritional security. In the United States, Australia and Europe, money, technology, and research and development enable adaptation to the effects of climate change on food security. Throughout much of Southeast Asia however, this capacity is lacking. In Vietnam for instance, economic development through agriculture, fisheries and forestry still relies directly on natural resources. Such dependence raises conflicts by placing added stresses on the environment such as deforestation, land degradation, flooding, water pollution, overfishing and waste, creating greater human security challenges for many of the country's poor (Ninh and Huy 2006: 10).

These three categories of health threats unfortunately do not always occur independently of each other; and complex interactions between simultaneous events can impose synergistic deleterious effects on susceptible human populations. This chapter examines the major human health threats, individually and as elements of a complex health security system, and relates them to human security in Southeast Asia and to the global security situation. Case studies are included to show how governmental failure to respond effectively to health challenges can compromise national and regional security. Additional case studies demonstrate best practices in preventing and mitigating negative health effects on human security and regional stability. Finally, this chapter argues that multilateral collaboration and cross-sectoral interagency cooperation are required for sustainable health security; and suggestions are offered for future research on the topic of health security in Southeast Asia.

9.2 Direct Effects of Human Health Challenges on Regional Security

According to the World Health Organization (WHO), health is not only the absence of infirmity and disease but also a state of physical, mental and social well-being (WHO 1946: 100). As disease incidence (the number of new cases of a particular disease within a population over time) increases, the burden on individuals, local health care systems and other government agencies increases. New or re-emerging infectious diseases, particularly diseases contracted from exposure to infected animals (zoonotic disease) such as SARS, Nipah virus and avian influenza spread quickly within a region, creating new, unpredictable crises for national public health systems. For biological and epidemiological reasons not fully understood, most of the new influenza viruses that spread globally each year originate in the Southeast Asian region. Yet treatments may not be equitably shared between countries, and international relations can quickly deteriorate. When Indonesia sought guarantees from the WHO that any vaccine against H5N1 influenza that was based on Indonesian strains of the virus would subsequently be made available to Indonesia at an affordable price, the WHO was unable or unwilling to convince the large pharmaceutical companies to provide such a guarantee (Current Concerns 2009). As a result Indonesia withheld critical virus strains from vaccine research and development, putting itself and the region at risk, for which it was rebuked by much of the international health community.

In 2005 the WHO updated and re-issued its International Health Regulations (IHR), which specifies mandatory infectious disease outbreak reporting requirements for the 194 state parties to the agreement. However the financial and technological burdens of increased disease surveillance inhibited compliance with the regulations among many of the low and middle income nations in the region. In future outbreaks, under authority of the IHR, the WHO may enter a country with regionally-placed teams of experts and supplement that nation's resources in order to protect global public health (WHO 2005). While the benefits of such a policy for regional and global public health are obvious, potential disputes involving state sovereignty create emerging threats to regional security. Diseases with pandemic potential are especially problematic to health security, with the additional potential to cause political unrest and civil disorder, deplete military forces, destabilize nations and contribute to state failure. These diseases also affect regional health security indirectly, through strategic impacts on important Asian neighbors like China. The most populous nation on Earth, China earned the enmity of the entire international health community for its dilatory response to the global outbreak of Severe Acute Respiratory Syndrome (SARS) in 2003 (Maclean 2008: 475). Because of the tremendous disparity between countries in planning and response capabilities for dealing with pandemics, in any global pandemic such as the H5N1 avian influenza outbreak developing countries in Southeast Asia will likely experience proportionately more morbidity and mortality than developed nations, due to limited access to any vaccines and anti-viral medications like oseltamivir (Tamiflu). Ill-will generated by such health inequity and perceived injustice could potentially damage international relations and impact regional stability.

In 2004 the Global Fund offered $100 million in grants to fight tuberculosis, malaria and HIV/AIDS in Myanmar. However in 2005, because of serious concerns about governance in that country and the unwillingness of the ruling military junta to respect the project's safeguards and performance-based grant implementation the funds were rescinded (Global Fund 2005). As a result these highly infectious diseases rampant in Myanmar have returned as imminent health security threats to neighboring countries. Border regions within Myanmar populated by ethnic minorities and marked by ongoing civil conflict suffer the highest national incidences of malaria. The ramifications for transnational health security are obvious, because regions within India, Bangladesh, Laos, Thailand and China that border Myanmar all have significantly higher incidences of malaria, tuberculosis and HIV/AIDS than other regions of those countries (Beyrer and Lee 2008: 2). Myanmar has one of the largest AIDS epidemics in Asia, and this can be as destabilizing as war. The age demographic affected most directly by AIDS includes the most productive segments of society, such as military and civil servants, business owners, teachers and parents. Higher mortality in these sub-populations results in an increased proportion of the young and the old, creating a less stable and more fragile social situation. By framing infectious diseases as a matter of national security with regional implications, governments and their people will be better prepared to handle sudden outbreaks that endanger human lives and threaten the existence and survival of nation-states (Caballero-Anthony 2005).

Another factor that destabilizes regional human security is the large number of the world's poorest people residing in Southeast Asia who lack access to essential medicines to treat these diseases, which argues strongly for health programs that emphasize prevention of disease. Besides the expense factor, this lack of access is also due to poor infrastructure, lack of technical assistance and uncertain quality of pharmaceuticals (International Dispensary Association 2009). The production, distribution and use of counterfeit medicines represent a thriving transnational crime in Southeast Asia. These fake drugs, either less than full strength or containing no drug at all, also are an increasing public health problem for the region, often with tragic results (Fernandez et al. 2008: 585, Newton et al. 2008: e32). Under-strength drugs are particularly insidious because they contain enough of the active compound to foil screening tests yet not enough to treat the disease, while at the same time the reduced potency accelerates the evolution of drug resistant strains of dangerous human pathogens.

Natural disasters such as cyclones, earthquakes and tsunamis typically are catastrophic, short-duration events that cause significant, immediate loss of human life. The Sumatra tsunami of 2004, generated by an earthquake that measured 9.0 on the Richter scale, caused an estimated 250,000 deaths in Indonesia, Thailand, Sri Lanka, and several other countries in the region (Thieren 2005: 81). The disastrous Cyclone Nargis that struck Myanmar in May 2008 is estimated to have caused over 100,000 immediate human fatalities (BBC News 2008). As infrastructure is often severely damaged in disasters, normal life is generally not possible until the government provides assistance to rebuild the community. Thus there is a critical linkage between the resilience of the people/community and the management of the built environment that serves those people and communities (Potangaroa et al. 2008: 57). Often, post-disaster settlement and shelter processes address only disaster-related change, and do not consider pre-existing vulnerabilities. The reasons for this are principally funding, capacity issues for organizations, and mandates, especially when organizations are officially invited by a host government to do specific post-disaster work. Yet disasters, even those involving a sudden-onset hazard, inevitably have multiple root causes, including poverty and conflict, which increase vulnerability to the hazard. If those root causes are not considered after the disaster, there is a danger that the same vulnerable state will be rebuilt, or that new vulnerabilities will be created (Kennedy et al. 2008: 24, Kennedy et al. 2007). Deaths and damage resulting from natural disasters and other large scale health emergencies are as much reflective of societal factors as of the naturally occurring event itself. They reveal major public health deficiencies, they may catalyze political violence, and they compromise human security through a lack of proper resources to respond to the disaster.

Direct environmental threats to health security include volcanic emissions, fires, and chemical exposures. These challenges cause acute negative human health effects, which require immediate action to prevent loss of human life. Longer duration environmental threats, often related to global climate change, include floods and droughts, air pollution and contaminated water supplies. Water issues in particular can be highly politicized, and compromise human security in more insidious ways. With every country seeking to satisfy its water needs from limited water resources, the potential for "water wars" between countries competing for the same water supplies is real. Singapore and Malaysia have endured a tense relationship over water rights since the 1960s, with Malaysian politicians periodically threatening to "turn off the tap" on Singapore's water supply, and Singapore flatly stating that if Malaysia reneged on its water treaty obligations there would be "consequences" – widely believed in both countries to mean immediate military action to restore its water access (Mauzy 2009). While this unquestionably is a political challenge for these two countries, should Singapore's water supply be interrupted, the direct (lack of drinking water, poor sanitation) and indirect (conflict) health consequences for impacted populations would be immediate and severe. According to UN Secretary-General Ban Ki Moon, speaking in 2007 on the occasion of World Water Day, "The consequences [of water shortages] for humanity are grave. Water scarcity threatens economic and social gains and is a potent fuel for wars and conflict." Of the 47 nations regarded as being either water stressed or water scarce in 2007, 25 are regarded as facing a high risk of armed conflict or political instability as a consequence of climate change (Smith and Vivekananda 2007: 3). Fortunately however, history shows that cooperation, not conflict, is the most common response to transboundary water management issues. Shared water resources may actually act as a unifying force to foster trust and promote peace. Over the last 60 years there have been more than 200 international water agreements worldwide and only 37 cases of reported violence between states over water (United Nations 2009). As 30 of these violent incidents were reported from the Middle East, where water supplies are often scarce, this may reflect the seriousness with which regional governments compete for limited water supplies and all that it means for health security for their nations.

9.3 Indirect Effects of Human Health Challenges on Regional Security

Besides the direct health effects of infectious diseases, natural disasters and environmental degradation there are complex secondary effects on human security. National development programs may be scaled back or stopped entirely in order to shift resources to control epidemics or respond to disasters. Disease outbreaks and other major health challenges compromise the ability of governments to provide basic services, and lack of basic services such as clean water and sanitation in turn further exacerbate health challenges, creating a reinforcing negative causal loop (Pegasus 2009) of human insecurity. Similarly, a negative causal loop exists wherein poverty causes ill health, and ill health leads to poverty. High infant mortality rates are often observed in countries where health security is compromised, and a high infant mortality rate has consistently been linked to state failures. Of countries whose infant mortality rates fall in the top quartile worldwide five (Laos, Cambodia, Papua New Guinea, Burma and East Timor) are found in the Southeast Asian region (CIA 2010). While there is no direct causal connection between infant deaths and ensuing political crises, infant mortality appears to be acting primarily as an indicator for the overall quality of material life. Like the canary in a coal mine, whose death indicates serious health risks to miners, high infant mortality serves as a powerful indicator of more broadly deleterious living conditions (Esty et al. 1999). Loss of confidence in government's ability to protect its people leads to civil unrest, refugee migrations into neighboring states, insurgencies and disruption of regional security. Domestic demographic changes including rural to urban shift and Internally Displaced Persons modify the resilience of populations in dealing with health challenges and reduce the ability of governments to ensure human security. Health problems also cause lost productivity, lost wages and medical expenses. These issues in turn highlight inequalities and may further contribute to social disorder.

Malnutrition and starvation continually plague many parts of the developing world. Food insecurity is a major contributing factor to human insecurity, and it unquestionably threatens regional and even global security. Shortages in 2007–2008 of food staples like rice and wheat, leading to soaring food prices, instigated violent protests from Pakistan to Mexico. Food riots can spin out of control and threaten State survival, particularly if they occur in countries where citizens already feel oppressed by authoritarian rule and rampant government corruption.

Famines represent the final stage in an extended process of deepening vulnerability and fracturing of social reproduction mechanisms (McMichael 2009). Rice is a staple for billions of Asians, and supplies of rice are at the lowest levels and the highest prices in over two decades. In Thailand, 55 of the kingdom's 76 provinces are suffering severe drought, including half of the key central rice growing provinces. 6 years of drought in Australia, a major supplier of rice to Southeast Asia, has reduced that country's rice crop by 98% (Kisner 2008; Bradsher 2008). Global stocks of wheat are at their lowest levels in 50 years, and today constitute less than 10 weeks worth of world consumption, according to the United Nation's Food and Agriculture Organization (Leake 2008). Many populations that formerly grew their own food have abandoned degraded land and left agriculture, moved to urban areas, and are now purchasing their food. The World Food Program is concerned that many potential food aid recipients who were not previously in the urgent category are being priced out of the food market, and are now in urgent need of direct food aid. The World Bank now believes that some 33 countries are in danger of being destabilized by food price inflation, while Ban Ki-Moon, the UN Secretary-General, recently asserted that higher food prices risk wiping out progress towards reducing poverty and could harm global growth and security (Clover 2008).

There are other approaches however for improving food security than providing direct food aid. With skyrocketing food prices and distribution costs, a better strategy than sending food aid to poorer countries may be to help farmers grow food domestically. According to the International Food Policy Research Institute, the Southeast Asian region has made significant headway since the Global Hunger Index (GHI) begin tracking food security nearly two decades ago (GHI 2008). Nonetheless the food security status of several Southeast Asian countries such as Indonesia, Myanmar, Vietnam and the Philippines is still classified on the GHI as serious, or even alarming in the case of Laos and Cambodia. Combating the food crisis is a complex challenge that will require international and multi-sectoral cooperation. This will involve more food aid for poor people; much greater investments in agriculture, especially the small farm sector; changes to biofuel policies; measures to calm global food markets; better data collection and improved monitoring of the food and nutrition situation in developing countries (von Grebmer et al. 2008).

Another aspect of food security is food safety. Food and water borne diseases caused by *Escherichia coli*, *Clostridium botulinum*, *Vibrio* spp., *Salmonella* spp. and other microbial pathogens are responsible for more than 600,000 deaths in Southeast Asia each year (WHO 2008). However unsafe food also imposes other, non-health consequences including significant economic impact both domestically and internationally. Developed nations concerned about food safety are reluctant to accept food products produced in Southeast Asia (Le 2007; QFF 2003), which constrains agricultural exports, further depresses local economies, and exacerbates social unrest. When local and national governments are unable or unwilling to deal in a sustainable way with these secondary effects of health security challenges, domestic stability can become threatened, posing spillover security threats for the region.

Global climate change impacts health security in less direct and more insidious ways. The unrelenting penetration and destruction of rainforests worldwide has led to exposure of humans to viruses and other microbes that otherwise would not have occurred. For example, an outbreak of Nipah virus in Malaysia occurred when pigs penned near fruit orchards contracted the virus from the droppings of bats, whose habitat had shifted as a result of deforestation. The infected pigs then readily transmitted the virus to their handlers (Lal 2007: vii). An emerging challenge in Southeast Asia is what may be termed "environmental migrants," representing individuals or even communities that choose or are forced to migrate as a result of environmental and climatic factors (Morton et al. 2008: 5). While governments and international donors more often concentrate on mitigating the effects of sudden disasters, gradual environmental degradation such as recurrent flood, protracted droughts and failing ecosystems can lead to migration as well. Protection of the environment includes cross-cutting issues, impacting every member of society. However the people who bear the brunt of the consequences of climate change are rarely consulted regarding their situation, their needs or possible options that may shape their future well-being.

9.3.1 *Case Study in Failed Policy, Programs and Practice: Myanmar, Cyclone Nargis*

In natural disasters, rapid response is essential to save lives at immediate risk and to prevent additional loss of life from post-disaster health challenges such as disease, starvation and environmental exposure. When Cyclone Nargis smashed into Myanmar on May 2, 2008, the full extent of the destruction was not immediately revealed and not likely even comprehended by the government. As word of the disaster spread regionally and soon globally, foreign nations and countless aid organizations rushed to provide goods and services to the beleaguered country. Despite the rapid and prodigious offerings of international aid, relief supplies and relief workers were initially stopped at the Myanmar border. To the consternation of donor nations and Non-Governmental Organizations (NGO), the government of Myanmar unconscionably restricted access to the country, particularly for aid workers and supplies from countries outside of the Southeast Asian region. In a clear manifestation of its xenophobia, the ruling military junta of Myanmar insisted that outside assistance was not needed, and that the national government had sufficient resources to respond to the disaster. Moreover, the government assured the international community that the situation inside their country was not nearly as serious as was being reported by foreign news agencies and aid organizations. Despite these claims by the government of Myanmar, the United Nations Office for the Coordination of Humanitarian Affairs (UNOCHA) estimated on 9 May 2008, 1 week after the disaster, that the death toll in Myanmar from Cyclone Nargis was between 63,000 and 101,000. The following week, on 16 May, the International Red Cross and the United Nations corroborated the OCHA estimate with their own report that the figure exceeded 100,000 (BBC 2008). Countries in the region and the international community were initially frustrated and soon outraged over the recalcitrance of the

Myanmar government, and its apparent indifference to the reality of the situation in terms of human insecurity.

In 2005 all member states of the United Nations reached consensus that states have a primary responsibility to protect their own populations and that the international community has a responsibility to act when these governments fail to protect their citizens. This is the principle of International Responsibility to Protect, or R2P (ICISS 2001). R2P states that "Where a population is suffering serious harm, as a result of internal war, insurgency, repression or state failure, and the state in question is unwilling or unable to halt or avert it, the principle of non-intervention yields to the international responsibility to protect" (Chia 2008). While the United States and some members of the European Union, including the United Kingdom, France, Germany, and Denmark did not rule out "humanitarian intervention" into Myanmar, the Association of South East Asian Nations (ASEAN) remained opposed to forced delivery of aid, because of sovereignty considerations and its fundamental adherence to non-intervention in the affairs of member states. Ultimately, conditions were negotiated under which foreign aid and foreign relief workers were granted access to Myanmar. However access was restricted to relief from ASEAN nations, whose resources were limited and whose capacity to provide urgent medical aid and recovery to avoid a health catastrophe was questionable. Expanded relief efforts did not begin in earnest for nearly 2 months after the cyclone hit, through U.N. agencies such as OCHA, the High Commissioner for Refugees (UNHCR) and the United Nations Children's Fund (UNICEF), plus the World Health Organization and numerous non-governmental organizations.

Much debate has occurred about the negative impacts of the delayed response and poor internal and external coordination by the Myanmar government. It appears probable that ineffective interagency coordination internally, compounded by the government's initial unwillingness to cooperate with outside agencies and non-ASEAN governments may have resulted in unnecessary and avoidable loss of human life in the days and weeks following the disaster. Moreover, from a geopolitical perspective, regional security was threatened. What began as a natural disaster and a domestic health security issue could have completely undermined ASEAN as a regional arbiter if extra-regional powers had decided to proceed with forced intervention.

9.3.2 *Case Study in Best Practices: China, Sichuan Earthquake*

Just 10 days after Cyclone Nargis devastated Myanmar, Sichuan China was hit by a magnitude 8.0 earthquake that leveled numerous towns and cities in the region and killed over 69,000 people. China is included in this chapter as an example because of its multi-factorial influence on its regional neighbors in Southeast Asia. Despite the widespread destruction, which disrupted most road and rail lines into the region, the response by the Chinese government was impressive, and dramatically different than the response by the Myanmar government to its cyclone disaster. The Chinese government, which acted quickly in the crisis, welcomed relief assistance from all countries throughout the world with an open attitude, invited and arranged foreign support for disaster relief in China, and offered direct access for contributions of equipment and materiel to the disaster areas through flexible policies (Wenjun and Ivy 2008). Local volunteers were mobilized effectively, and a unified response by all relevant agencies of the Chinese government including full utilization of the Chinese Army was implemented to provide disaster assistance. The US Agency for International Development/Office of Foreign Disaster Assistance (USAID/OFDA) as well as numerous NGOs were permitted immediate and full access to the region and were on site within days with relief supplies, specialized equipment and trained personnel. Despite multiple aftershocks in the ensuing hours and days following the initial quake, some as strong as 6.0, the government maintained a rapid, coordinated response and emphasized transparency in its actions and unrestricted access to the media. This proactive, open and collaborative response to the disaster mobilized international support and drew upon all relevant components of the Chinese government. China's response stood in sharp contrast to the uncoordinated and uncooperative response of Myanmar in Cyclone Nargis, and unquestionably served to limit further loss of life throughout Sichuan province.

9.4 Regional Cooperation on Health Security

Regional health security challenges require regional solutions, because globalization has increased the interdependency of neighboring states. In a globalized world, health security is an element of the international "commons" and thus may be considered a global public good, which Young defines as "lying wholly or largely outside the jurisdiction of any individual member of international society but of interest to two or more of them, or their nationals, as a valued resource" (Young 1997). In addition, health problems cannot be solved by Ministries of Health alone; sustainable solutions to health security problems require a holistic approach. Policymakers must recognize that providing resources in response to a health emergency invariably means shifting resources from other programs, with consequences for the other programs. Scrutiny of the root causes of health emergencies usually reveals additional issues of governance and rule of law, including corruption. So a whole of government strategy employing systems analysis is needed.

9.4.1 Case Study in Failed Policy, Programs and Practice: Fires and Air Pollution in Indonesia

For over 10 years Indonesia has been plagued by forest fires on the island of Kalimantan (Borneo), where forests have been cleared by purposeful and uncontrolled slash and burn techniques, in order to clear land for plantations and production of rice, palm oil and other agricultural products. Smoke from these fires spreads out from Indonesia, covering major shipping lanes like the Malacca Straits, and impacting air travel in the neighboring countries of Singapore and Malaysia. The resulting occurrences of haze currently rank among the world's worst air pollution episodes. The biggest problem of the fires in Indonesia was not the fire itself but the toxic smoke released. Air quality in Indonesia during these fires was many times worse than that of the most polluted cities of the world, and the polluted air affected the health of people living in neighboring countries (Field et al. 2009: 185). The health effects of this air pollution were significant, causing serious morbidity among residents of Indonesia, and seriously degrading air quality in Malaysia and Singapore (Heil and Goldammer 2001: 24). Despite regional complaints and international pressure, for over 10 years the Indonesian government appeared unable or unwilling to confront this serious health security problem, and the underlying causes of environmental mismanagement. As a result, relations between Indonesia and its neighbors deteriorated.

Civil society may consider fires as domestic natural disasters, and not fully appreciate the serious regional health security implications. As a result, governments and agencies in charge of fire and land management may not be held accountable. In 2002 Southeast Asian nations came together to create the ASEAN Agreement on Transboundary Haze Pollution (ASEAN 2002), which entered into force in 2003 with seven nations ratifying the agreement. This agreement was developed by government negotiators from the ASEAN nations, with the support of the ASEAN Secretariat and assistance from the United Nations Environmental Programme (UNEP). Importantly, indigenous knowledge and practices in fire prevention and management were sought and utilized, and public education programs were established. This act of improving health security governance through local involvement and regional engagement was a positive step forward, as local health professionals are often the most effective teachers. However quite noticeably, Indonesia was missing from the list of state parties ratifying the Agreement in 2002, and as of 2010 remains the only ASEAN nation yet to ratify it. This presents a difficult problem for the region since Indonesia is by far the biggest source of the fires and haze. Indonesia's ratification aside, the fact that the Agreement was even adopted is noteworthy in itself, given ASEAN's traditional penchant for non-legal, consensual decision-making and non-interference in member states' internal affairs (Tan 2005). ASEAN countries, particularly Malaysia, even attempted to rationalize Indonesia's lack of compliance on the basis that because the fires were exclusively on Indonesian territory, it was an internal problem best left to Indonesia to handle.

9.4.2 *Case Study in Best Practices: SARS and ASEAN*

In late 2002 the first case of Severe Adult Respiratory Syndrome (SARS) was reported in Hong Kong. Within 24 h the disease had spread to five other nations, and within 1 month it was reported on six continents. The disease affected over 8,400 people, killing 10% of those infected (WHO 2003). In an unusually quick response, Ministers of Health from ASEAN+3 (ASEAN plus Japan, China and Korea) met to craft a plan to stop the epidemic. Recognizing that the SARS epidemic was more than just a health security challenge, and that it threatened regional security more broadly, the ministers implemented a multi-sectoral response strategy, with high-level meetings involving labor, transportation, tourism, information and health. Within 2 months the Health Ministers were able to declare ASEAN as a SARS-free region, and note that ASEAN was the first area in the world with a coordinated, region-wide response to SARS (ASEAN 2003). With this official elimination of the health security threat, travel advisories to the region were lifted, enabling economic recovery to begin.

9.5 Opportunities for Regional Collaboration

Today health security is viewed within a more comprehensive regional security framework, and the more relevant referent for security is considered to be the individual rather than state sovereignty and territorial integrity. In addition to health security, this comprehensive security framework emphasizes the importance of other areas such as economics, energy, food supply and the environment, which often threaten individuals more on a daily basis. A people-centered view of security is necessary for national, regional and global stability. In employing multiple lines of effort to solve health security challenges, more holistic, whole of government security policies are developed. This also enables governments to leverage limited security resources more effectively, and develop mutually supportive approaches for international cooperation to expand regional health-security communities. In 2000 the World Health Organization established the Millennium Development Goals (MDG) (WHO 2010). These ambitious goals address global challenges in such areas as poverty and hunger, maternal and child health, and combating HIV/AIDS and other infectious diseases. The Millennium Development Goals Report (United Nations 2008a) details current success worldwide in achieving the MDG. Global progress has been variable, and reports for each Southeast Asian nation are available from the UNDP (United Nations 2008b, c).

Health issues receive greater attention from senior policy-makers when they constitute possible threats to international, regional, national and individual security, or potentially may affect the economic welfare of a country or region (Katz and Singer 2007: 233). However the historical record suggests that only in times of crisis does Southeast Asia grab the attention of international policy makers (Cossa et al. 2009). Negative effects on human security can be mitigated through regional recognition of the threat, new cooperative policies on surveillance and public health that emphasize an interagency approach, and new technologies. While infectious diseases clearly threaten human health, they also may raise opportunities for sustainable improvements in human security. Ancillary benefits include strengthening of institutional capacities and expanded security communities, leading to enhanced Southeast Asian regional security. The United Nation Development Programme (UNDP) created the Capacity for Disaster Reduction Initiative (CADRI), which focuses on capacity building through developing human resources, enhancing organizational capacity, and strengthening institutions that provide a framework for engagement between the state, the private sector, and civil society (UNDP 2007).

During regional health emergencies, countries may fail to cooperate with their neighbors. There are several potential reasons for such behavior. Governments may fear international scrutiny, stigmatization and potential negative effects on tourism, or they may feel the situation is within their own jurisdiction and capability. During the SARS outbreak of 2003 the epidemic spread throughout Southeast Asia and across the Pacific to North America. While disease reporting from many developing nations in Southeast Asia was unreliable at best, the Canadian city of Toronto cooperated fully with international health authorities in surveillance and mitigation of the epidemic in that city. Despite the Canadian government's aggressive and transparent efforts to control the outbreak, the WHO issued a travel advisory warning people to avoid travel to Toronto, with devastating effects on the city's hotel, restaurant and tourist industries. Even after the epidemic was over, it took more than a year for Toronto's economy to fully recover. The impact of an epidemic like SARS on regional and global economic stability is complex, because there are linkages across sectors and across economies in both international trade and international capital flows. The economic costs from a global disease such as SARS go beyond direct damages incurred in the affected sectors of the disease-affected countries. This is not just because the disease spreads quickly across countries through networks related to global travel, but also any economic shock to one country is quickly spread to other countries through the increased trade and financial linkages associated with globalization (Lee 2009).

In Southeast Asia, the "ASEAN Way" of non-interference and the preeminence of national sovereignty can delay or obstruct regional cooperation. This philosophy is written into the fundamental documents of ASEAN (ASEAN 1976), making it very difficult to gain consensus for humanitarian intervention in an epidemic or other health crisis under the terms of the International Responsibility to Protect, regardless of the security threat posed to regional neighbors or the rest of the planet. Plus, not all health challenges represent security concerns, and there is discomfort among some nations that approaching health challenges from the perspective of their effects on security may direct attention toward a few specific [infectious] diseases and susceptible populations, while other health problems and vulnerable groups will be ignored. Furthermore, characterizing a health issue as a security threat often results in it being addressed through programs and policies developed for law enforcement rather than public health. The result may be that a disproportionate emphasis is placed on assigning responsibility and levying sanctions to control the threat, as opposed to more traditional health models that identify and ameliorate risk factors and behaviors that contribute to the threat (McInnes and Lee 2006: 5). For many countries, disease and global health add to the uncertainty in developing foreign policy; a coherent regional strategy for

Southeast Asia may require a "bi-multilateralism" approach, involving a mix of bilateral and multilateral agreements.

9.5.1 Case Study in Failed Policy, Programs or Practice: The Asian Food Crisis

In the recent food crisis in Southeast Asia the negative impact of rising prices of rice, other food and petroleum products was exacerbated by the lack of regional cooperation. Thailand is the world's largest exporter of rice, and Vietnam and Cambodia also produce large quantities of rice. On the other hand, the neighboring Philippines is the biggest rice importer in the world, and Singapore and Brunei are also rice importers. Regional cooperation to assure rice supplies in Southeast Asia would likely have helped control price speculation in the market, enhancing food security in the region. Instead, rice producing countries unilaterally restricted rice exports within the region, causing widespread public panic and violent protests. ASEAN must take a more proactive leadership role in ensuring regional food security, and consider a shift at least on this issue away from the traditional informal understandings and voluntary arrangements, toward more legally binding agreements. A more unified and effective Southeast Asian policy on this critical component of regional security will also build public confidence in the ability of local and national governments to provide basic goods and services, while at the same time limiting the appeal and penetration of extremist groups. Such groups already ignore national boundaries and exploit popular grievances in order to recruit more members, foment insurgency and launch terror attacks in the region.

9.5.2 Case Study in Best Practices: Transboundary Water Management in Southeast Asia

The Mekong River Commission's (MRC) Mekong Programme is a regional cooperation program for the sustainable development of water and related resources in the Mekong basin (MRC 2010). Its goal is to achieve more effective use of water and related resources to alleviate poverty while protecting the environment. Developing the economic potential of the Mekong River system for food, domestic uses, power generation, transport and tourism is key to fighting poverty, improving health and increasing human security in the region. Through cooperation, planning and regional integration, MRC has implemented a sustainable plan for the region's long-term development. Furthermore, since water use does not recognize borders, it is also clear that for water related developments, regional cooperation at the scale of the entire basin including Cambodia, Laos, Thailand and Vietnam is essential. In addition, a dialogue mechanism has been set up with the two upstream countries

China and Myanmar. Development in one country may have consequences for security in another country, and investments in one sector may affect other sectors within a country. Therefore, there is a need for a joint water resources development program at basin scale, owned and managed by the riparian countries themselves, in close cooperation with the donor community, investment institutions and civil society (Cogels 2005).

9.6 Health Insecurity and the Roots of Conflict

More ominously, health challenges are also related to the roots of conflict and insurgency. To a great extent people will tolerate substandard housing, inadequate education and lack of job opportunities; however they are generally less tolerant of serious health security challenges. When people perceive their government as unwilling or unable to protect them, they seek other sources of support, and become vulnerable to extremists who promise near-term solutions.

The rapid emergence of HIV/AIDS in Southeast Asia particularly in Myanmar, and also including the large regional neighbor China, represents a serious challenge to national and regional security. In certain African nations AIDS has eliminated so many of the key productive members of society in the 25–45 year age group that the standard bell-shaped population age curve now shows a bimodal distribution, with primarily the elderly and the young left to fend for themselves (Stanecki 2000). AIDS orphans and unsupervised young people are particularly vulnerable to ideologues who may recruit them for terrorist activities, transforming a health security challenge into a true national security problem. In Southeast Asia, HIV is rapidly and efficiently spread through intravenous drug use, and via human trafficking in the sex trade. The epidemic, already severely impacting Myanmar, Thailand and Cambodia threatens to increase in incidence throughout the rest of Southeast Asia. This critical and imminent health threat to the region demands immediate, aggressive, cooperative action to limit the spread of this disease and protect regional security.

When the massive tsunami struck Sumatra in Indonesia in 2004, the devastation and loss of human life was almost unimaginable. No government could have been adequately prepared for such a disaster, and Indonesia cooperated with international donors and foreign governments offering aid. The government's response was remarkable because disaster aid was focused largely on Aceh, a province disrupted by a separatist insurgency for over three decades. The protracted conflict had also compromised economic, social and health security, creating conditions that maintained the roots of conflict. While the disaster was tragic in all respects, it formed the catalyst for substantive security changes in the province. In 2002, 48% of the population of Aceh had no access to clean water, 36% of children under the age of five were undernourished, and 38% of the Acehnese had no access to health facilities. The humanitarian emergency triggered by the tsunami provided a critical opportunity for change in Aceh. Following the tsunami, in the process of rebuilding virtually every element of society in Aceh, the government and its international partners *de facto* addressed many of these underlying causes of the insurgency. The tsunami provided a powerful and catalyzing shock; it produced a focus on common goals of relief, recovery and reconstruction; and it brought increased international attention (Renner 2006). The multinational and multi-sectoral response to the disaster was then able to introduce sustainable improvements in health security as well as socio-economic security.

9.7 Conclusions and Future Proposed Actions

Emerging infectious diseases represent transnational security threats that threaten regional health security. Because of modern rapid transportation systems, weak public health and primary health systems in many Southeast Asian nations permit potentially pandemic diseases to spread internationally and jeopardize global health security. Natural disasters disrupt normal life, threaten the health and well being of individuals, communities and nations, and may compromise regional security through loss of government infrastructure. Ecosystem degradation and environmental mismanagement negatively impact agricultural productivity and diminish food security. Internally displaced populations and refugees lacking adequate food for their families quickly lose confidence in their government's ability to protect them and become vulnerable to recruitment by violent extremists, exacerbating regional security problems. Rising sea levels due to global climate change pose an existential threat to small island nations and many coastal communities.

The case studies presented in this chapter clearly demonstrate that multilateral, multi-sectoral cooperation is mandatory for developing sustainable solutions for health security challenges. Multilateralism means increased participation at global, regional and sub-regional levels, and includes regional platforms like ASEAN, ASEAN+3, ASEAN Regional Forum and the Asia Pacific Economic Cooperation. Southeast Asian nations need to place higher regional priority on cooperative action in dealing with health security because these countries are geographically close, there is a high concentration of health security threats in the region, and there is a relatively high level of security interaction and interdependence. Best practices also require government cooperation and transparency as essential elements in responding to public health emergencies of international concern, and this also extends to general disease prevention and control. Other best practices include engaging local expertise in health security planning and in responding to health emergencies. Public health is fast becoming an independent marker for good governance.

In addition, original quantitative studies analyzing health security in Southeast Asian nations need to be conducted. Such work should include randomized sampling of populations to assess the most important health insecurities that they have objectively experienced or subjectively felt. A ranking scale should be developed that rates these health insecurities based on how serious a problem they are considered to be. Such studies must be strongly supported by ASEAN and by appropriate agencies of the World Health Organization such as the Global Health Security Initiative. Data from these studies will inform national and international stakeholders and help them to develop new public health policies, programs and practices to reduce health threats and improve Southeast Asian regional security.

References

ASEAN. (1976). Declaration of ASEAN Concord, Bali, Indonesia. http://www.aseansec.org/1216.htm. Accessed 14 Oct 2009.
ASEAN. (2002). ASEAN agreement on transboundary haze pollution. http://www.aseansec.org/agr_haze.pdf. Accessed 14 Oct 2009.
ASEAN. (2003). ASEAN is SARS free. http://www.aseansec.org/pis_sars.htm. Accessed 3 Nov 2009.
BBC News. (2008, May 16). Burma death toll jumps to 69,000. http://news.bbc.co.uk/2/hi/asia-pacific/7405260.stm. Accessed 17 Sept 2009.
Beyrer, C., & Lee, T. (2008). Responding to infectious diseases in Burma and her border regions. *Conflict and Health, 2*, 2.
Beyrer, C., Suwanvanichkij, V., Mullany, L., Richards, A., Franck, N., Samuels, A., & Lee, T. (2006). Responding to AIDS, tuberculosis, malaria, and emerging infectious diseases in Burma: Dilemmas of policy and practice. *PLoS Medicine, 3*(10):e393. doi/10.1371/journal.pmed.0030393. Accessed 4 Dec 2009.
Bradsher, K. (2008). A drought in Australia, a global shortage of rice. *New York Times*, April 17. http://nytimes.com/2008/04/17/business/worldbusiness/17warm.html. Accessed 1 Sept 2009.
Caballero-Anthony, M. (2005). Security threat from disease. http://search.japantimes.co.jp/cgi-bin/eo20050715a1.html. Accessed 20 Aug 2009.
Central Intelligence Agency. (2010). Country comparison: Infant mortality rates, The World Factbook. https://www.cia.gov/library/publications/the-world-factbook/rankorder/2091rank.html. Accessed 6 Feb 2010.
Chia, H. (2008). Crisis in Myanmar and responsibility to protect, Center for Strategic and International Studies. http://www.reliefweb.int/rw/rwb.nsf/db900sid/RMOI-7F53R6?OpenDocument. Accessed 6 July 2009.
Clover, C. (2008). Food shortages: How will we feed the world? http://www.telegraph.co.uk/scienceandtechnology/science/sciencenews/3340417/Food-shortages-how-will-we-feed-the-world.html. Accessed 1 Sept 2009.
Cogels, O. (2005). The Mekong programme, Mekong River Commission. http://www.mrcmekong.org/mekong_program_ceo.htm. Accessed 29 Dec 2009.
Cossa, R., Glosserman, B., McDevitt, M., Patel, N., Przystup, J., & Roberts, B. (2009). The United States and the Asia-Pacific Region: Security Strategy for the Obama Administration, Center for a New American Security, Washington, DC. http://www.cna.org/documents/CampbellPatelFord_US_Asia-Pacific_February2009.pdf. Accessed 18 Dec 2009.
Current Concerns. (2009). Fairness, transparency and equity in international public health. http://www.tlaxcala.es/pp.asp?reference=7836&lg=en. Accessed 16 Dec 2009.
Earth Institute. (2007). Countries at greatest risk from climate change impacts, Earth Institute News Archive. http://www.earth.columbia.edu/news/2007/story03-29-07.php. Accessed 6 Nov 2009.
Esty, D., Goldstone, J., Gurr, T., Harff, B., Levy, M., Dabelko, G., Surko, P., & Unger, A. (1999). State failure task force report, environmental change and security project report, Issue 5, SAIC. http://www.wilsoncenter.org/events/docs/Phase2.pdf. Accessed 22 Oct 2009.
Fernandez, F., Green, M., & Newton, P. (2008). Prevalence and detection of counterfeit pharmaceuticals: A mini review. *Industrial and Engineering Chemistry Research, 47*(3), 585–590.

Field, R., van Der Werf, G., & Shen, S. (2009). Human amplification of drought-induced biomass burning in Indonesia since 1960. *Nature Geoscience, 2*, 185–188.

Global Hunger Index in Full. (2008). *BBC News*. http://news.bbc.co.uk/2/hi/in_depth/7670229.stm. Accessed 4 Sept 2009.

Heil, A., & Goldammer, J. (2001). Smoke-haze pollution: A review of the 1997 episode in Southeast Asia. *Regional Environmental Change, 2*(1), 24–37.

ICISS (International Commission on Intervention and State Sovereignty). (2001). Responsibility to protect, Report of the International Commission on Intervention and State Strategy, Ottawa, International Research Centre. http://www.iciss.ca/pdf/Commission-Report.pdf. Accessed 6 July 2009.

International Dispensary Association. (2009). Core values. http://www.idafoundation.org/we-are/core-values.html. Accessed 16 Dec 2009.

Katz, R., & Singer, D. (2007). Health and security in foreign policy. *Bulletin of the World Health Organization, 85*(3), 233–234.

Kennedy, J., Ashmore, J., Babister, E., & Kelman, I. (2007). Post-tsunami transitional settlement and shelter: Field experience from Aceh and Sri Lanka. *Humanitarian Exchange Magazine, 37*. http://www.odihpn.org/report.asp?id=2879. Accessed 17 Sept 2009.

Kennedy, J., Ashmore, J., Babister, E., & Kelman, I. (2008). The meaning of 'Build Back Better': Evidence from post-tsunami Aceh and Sri Lanka. *Journal of Contingencies and Crisis Management, 16*(1), 24–36.

Kisner, C. (2008). Climate change in Thailand: Impacts and adaptation strategies, Climate Institute. http://www.climate.org/topics/international-action/thailand.htm. Accessed 1 Sept 2009.

Lal, S. (2007). *Emerging viral diseases of Southeast Asia*. Basel: Karger Publishers.

Le, L. (2007). Stink over Vietnamese food exports. *Asia Times*. http://www.atimes.com/atimes/Southeast_Asia/IL12Ae02.html. Accessed 22 Nov 2009.

Leake, J. (2008). Food shortages loom as wheat crop shrinks and prices rise. *The Times Online*. http://business.timesonline.co.uk/tol/business/industry_sectors/natural_resources/article3423734.ece. Accessed 1 Sept 2009.

Lee, J-W. (2009). Globalization and disease: The case of SARS, The Brookings Institution. http://www.brookings.edu/papers/2004/02development_lee.aspx. Accessed 3 Nov 2009.

Maclean, S. (2008). Microbes, mad cows and militaries: Exploring the links between health and security. *Security Dialogue, 39*(5), 475–494.

Mauzy, D. (2009). Water wars: Singapore versus Malaysia. Available online at: http://www.politics.ubc.ca/index.php?id=3436. Accessed 8 Dec 2009.

McInnes, C., & Lee, K. (2006). Health, security and foreign policy. *Review of International Studies, 32*(1), 5–23.

McMichael, P. (2009). The world food crisis in historical perspective. *Monthly Review, 61*(3). http://www.monthlyreview.org/090713mcmichael.php. Accessed 18 Dec 2009.

Mekong River Commission. (2010). http://www.mrcmekong.org. Accessed 29 Dec 2009.

Morton, A., Boncour, P., & Laczko, F. (2008). Human security policy challenges. *Forced Migration Review, 31*, 5–7.

Newton, P., Fernández, F., Plançon, A., Mildenhall, D., Green, M., et al. (2008). A collaborative epidemiological investigation into the criminal fake artesunate trade in South East Asia. *PLoS Medicine, 5*(2), e32. doi:10.1371/journal.pmed.0050032. Accessed 2 Oct 2009.

Ninh, N., & Huy, L. (2006). Climate change vulnerability: Challenges and opportunities in Indochina, *Global Change Newsletter* 67.

Pegasus Communications. (2009). Causal loop diagrams. http://www.pegasuscom.com/cld.html. Accessed 5 Dec 2009.

Potangaroa, R., Wang, M., & Chan, Y. (2008). Identifying resilience in those affected by the 2008 Sichuan earthquake. http://www.resorgs.org.nz/pubs.shtml. Accessed 17 Sept 2009.

Quick Frozen Foods International. (2003). New FDA food safety regulations in USA worry Thai exporters. *QFFI's Global Seafood Magazine, 45*(2), 40.

Renner, M. (2006). Aceh: Peacemaking after the tsunami, Worldwatch Institute. http://www.worldwatch.org/node/3930. Accessed 17 Sept 2009.

Smith, D., & Vivekananda, J. (2007). A climate of change: The links between climate change, peace and war. *International Alert*, (no vol).

Stanecki, K. (2000). The AIDS pandemic in the 21st century. http://www.usaid.gov/pop_health/aids/Publications/docs/aidsdemoimpact.pdf. Accessed 17 Nov 2009.

Tan, A. (2005). The ASEAN agreement on transboundary haze pollution: Prospects for compliance and effectiveness in post-Suharto era. *New York University Environmental Law Journal*, 13(3): 647–722. http://www3.law.nyu.edu/journals/envtllaw/issues/vol13/3/v13_n3_tan.pdf. Accessed 14 Oct 2009.

The Global Fund. (2005). Termination of grants to Myanmar, fact sheet. http://www.theglobalfund.org/content/pressreleases/pr_050819_factsheet.pdf. Accessed 1 Sept 2009.

Thieren, M. (2005). Asian tsunami: Death-toll addiction and its downside. *Bulletin of the World Health Organization, 83*(2).

UNDP (United Nations Development Programme). (1994). *Human development report 1994*. New York: Oxford University Press.

UNDP (United Nations Development Programme). (2007). Capacity for disaster reduction initiative. http://www.unisdr.org/cadri. Accessed 17 Nov 2009.

United Nations. (2008a). Millennium development goals report. http://www.undp.org/publications/MDG_Report_2008_En.pdf. Accessed 17 Nov 2009.

United Nations. (2008b). Delivering on the global partnership for delivering the millennium development goals, MDG Task Force. http://www.undp.org/mdg/MDG-GAP-TF-Report.pdf. Accessed 17 Nov 2009.

United Nations. (2008c). Tracking the MDGs: Country progress. http://www.undp.org/mdg/tracking_countryreports2.shtml. Accessed 17 Nov 2009.

United Nations World Water Day. (2009). http://www.unwater.org/wwd09/flashindex.html. Accessed 20 Sept 2009.

von Grebmer, K., Fritschel, H., Nestorova, B., Olofinbiyi, T., Pandya-Lorch, R., & Yohannes, Y. (2008). *Global hunger index: The challenge of hunger 2008*. Washington, DC: International Food Policy Research Institute.

Wenjun, Z., & Ivy, R. (2008). Sichuan earthquake and the Chinese response. *Architectural Record*. http://archrecord.construction.com/community/editorial/archives/0807.asp. Accessed 17 Sept 2009.

World Health Organization. (1946). Preamble to the Constitution of the World Health Organization as adopted by the International Health Conference, New York, 19–22 June, 1946; signed on 22 July 1946 by the representatives of 61 States (Official Records of the World Health Organization, no. 2) and entered into force on 7 April 1948.

World Health Organization. (2003). "Cumulative number of reported probable cases of SARS," Epidemic and pandemic alert and response. Available online at: http://www.who.int/csr/sars/country/2003_06_27/en/index.html. Accessed 3 Nov 2009.

World Health Organization. (2005). "Epidemic and pandemic alert and response," International Health Regulations. http://www.who.int/csr/ihr/en/. Accessed 10 Dec 2009.

World Health Organization. (2008). "The global burden of disease," 2004 Update. http://www.who.int/healthinfo/global_burden_disease/GBD_report_2004update_full.pdf. Accessed 17 Nov 2009.

World Health Organization. (2010). Millennium development goals. http://www.undp.org/mdg/basics.shtml. Accessed 17 Nov 2009.

Young, O. (1997). *Global governance*. Cambridge: MIT Press.

Young-Eisendrath, P. (2002). The transformation of human suffering: A perspective from psychotherapy and Buddhism. In P. Young-Eisendrath & S. Muramoto (Eds.), *Awakening and insight: Zen Buddhism and psychotherapy*. New York: Brunner Routledge.

Chapter 10
The Proliferation of Trading Agreements and Implications on Human Livelihood

Benny Teh Cheng Guan

10.1 Introduction – FTAs, One Too Many?

From the early 1950s until the late 1980s, the number of cumulative active regional trade agreements (RTAs) recorded by the World Trade Organization (WTO) did not even exceed 50. From 1992 onwards, the WTO recorded a more than fivefold exponential increase with a total of 271 agreements in force as of February 2010. The recent economic crisis that affected many parts of the world has not dampened the spirit of FTA proliferation as new RTAs notified in 2008 and 2009 continued to be strong (WTO Online 2010). Ignoring Indian economist and academic Jagdish Bhagwati's call as early as 1991 to exercise caution and weigh the negative impacts of FTAs, states have been engaging one another for FTAs in a competitive pace and are considering them as gateways to explore new economic opportunities in an effort to reduce overreliance on traditional trade partners.

In East Asia, 119 FTAs have been concluded or implemented so far out of a total of 227. This figure increases to 147 when three additional countries – India, Australia and New Zealand are brought into the ambit of the region (see Table 10.1). With more FTAs being proposed or negotiated, East Asia is fast becoming the center of world FTA activity. Not only are East Asian countries engaged in intra-regional agreements, they are proactively seeking new agreements with countries outside their region. One of the trends has been to move beyond major trading partners and seek partnerships with economically less significant but strategically important ones. Singapore, with the highest number of concluded FTAs at 20, has indeed been leading the pack. Unsatisfied with the slow pace of the ASEAN Free Trade Area (AFTA) that was set up in 1992 (Ramesh 2004), Singapore sought bilateral tie-ups with New Zealand, Japan, the United States (US), and the European Free Trade Association (EFTA) before expanding to include countries such as Jordan, India, Panama, and Peru. Similarly, Thailand has successfully

---

B.C.G. Teh (✉)
Universiti Sains Malaysia, Penang, Malaysia
e-mail: ben@usm.my

Table 10.1 Free trade agreement status by country (as of January 2010) (Source: Author's compilation from ADB-ARIC database)

Country	Proposed	Under negotiation	Concluded	Total
Brunei	4	1	8	13
Cambodia	2	1	6	9
Indonesia	6	2	8	16
Laos	2	1	8	11
Malaysia	3	6	10	19
Myanmar	2	2	6	10
Philippines	4	1	7	12
Singapore	5	9	20	34
Thailand	6	7	11	24
Vietnam	2	2	7	11
ASEAN	36	32	91	159
Japan	4	5	11	20
China	8	6	10	24
South Korea	8	9	7	24
ASEAN+3	56	52	119	227
India	12	10	11	33
Australia	6	6	8	20
New Zealand	4	2	9	15
ASEAN+6	78	70	147	295

Note: East Asia defined as ASEAN+3 countries

concluded bilateral trade agreements with Japan, Australia, China and New Zealand and is expanding its FTA circle by considering Pakistan, Bahrain, Chile, Peru, Mercosur, EFTA and most recently the European Union (EU). As for Malaysia, its first ever bilateral FTA was with Japan before concluding similar agreements with Pakistan, Chile and New Zealand. Despite its more reserved outlook, it is currently negotiating with Chile Australia, Turkey, EU and India.

Indeed, bilateralism has remained popular for its flexibility in yielding results over multilateral or regional frameworks that are much more complex in nature and time consuming. While most bilateral FTAs are concluded within a year or two, regional ones like the ASEAN-Japan FTA took four long years. Others such as the proposed East Asia Free Trade Area (EAFTA) or the Comprehensive Economic Partnership in East Asia (CEPEA) still remain on the chopping block. Despite the existence of an FTA agreement between ASEAN and China, India, Japan, Australia and New Zealand, and South Korea respectively, this has not stopped some of the more competitive ASEAN members from renegotiating with these countries to establish separate bilateral FTAs.

With such a plethora of bilateral and regional FTAs with differing rules of origins (ROOs)[1] crisscrossing and creating a complex web of unregulated connections, how should businesses be organized and economies be structured to

---

[1] For a list of the various rules of origins on concluded FTAs in East Asia, see Kawai and Wignaraja (2007).

yield maximum benefits for the citizen and enhance their livelihoods? Though the benefits of FTAs to the state and the people are not a zero sum game, they are often criticized as instruments promoting state's foreign policy without the proper in-depth assessment of how peoples' security could be impacted. Feasibility studies, which are often used as a benchmark for FTA negotiation, are useful only in highlighting the significance of wealth creation for the *entire country* and rarely effective in showing the direct impact on the welfare of citizens. The latter is seen as a domestic concern and is therefore left entirely at the responsibility of the state to manage.

Moreover, the fact that firms are organized regionally in East Asia and that states are more comfortable with bilateral agreements than regional/global ones shows that an FTA is more than purely economics. They have geopolitical and strategic values that not only help states position their economic competitiveness but also their foreign policy objectives. As clearly captured by Japanese researcher Naoko Munakata (2002), "East Asian countries talk about region-wide visions but they only act bilaterally". The counter argument that is often provided by states is that bilateral FTAs form the required building blocks to a region-wide FTA. This, unfortunately, is rhetorical since there are no blueprints or roadmaps put in place from the beginning to properly guide states in the proliferation process. With so many bilateral pacts in place, the Asian leaders have yet to come to an agreement on how a regional FTA should be realized, if it ever would be.[2] Left to their own decisions, bilateral FTAs have become a tool for states to compete for international trade and investment and to strategize in furthering their political goals.

In East Asia, it has become apparent that several factors such as the continued slow progress of the WTO Doha round, the rise of China and its creativeness towards FTAs, the preparedness of Japan to reduce its overdependence on multilateralism and the perceived shifting of US policy towards bilateralism have contributed to greater willingness of states to embrace the concept of FTAs. However, factors that influence states' decisions to identify and select their FTA partners have been less clear. Certainly, prioritizing countries in terms of trade volume is one important factor but its only one of numerous reasons. The next section divides the discussion into economic and political considerations to look at the factors that affect the selection process of partners. Following that, several case studies are highlighted for discussion to identify the differing perception on issues pertaining to FTA proliferation between states and societies. The last section concludes the chapter with some recommendations on ways to better secure the well-being of the people.

---

[2] The ASEAN+3 Economic Ministers (AEM+3) meeting in 2004 approved a proposal by China to set up an Experts Group to study the feasibility of EAFTA. The Group held 4 meetings between April 2005 and July 2006 before submitting their report to the AEM+3 meeting in August 2006. Senior officials were then tasked to study the recommendations in the report.

10.2 Factors Influencing FTA Partner Selection

To be certain, there is no uniformity in how states select their FTA partners. The selection of partners can be affected by domestic political strategies as well as foreign policy aims. Japan, for example, decided to engage Mexico to correct an imbalance in the trading of the automobile and electronics industries. Malaysia, on the other hand, could not engage Australia due to its foreign policy under Mahathir Mohamad. Political spats between the latter and Australia's Paul Keating as well as his successor John Howard prevented any possibilities of exploring cooperation in trade. Leadership changes in Malaysia, South Korea, Thailand and Indonesia have played decisive roles in generating a more favorable outlook towards FTAs.

While some countries exhibit clear FTA strategies, others may base their decisions on a case-by-case basis. Japan had at one point in time listed economic, geographic, political and diplomatic, feasibility and time-related factors as criteria for partner selection apart from maintaining conformity with WTO rules and keeping in mind the possible impact on domestic markets (MOFA 2002). For developing countries like Thailand, Indonesia, the Philippines and Malaysia, trade facilitation is not the only factor in prioritizing partners since investment and technical cooperation that can help achieve market expansion and higher competitiveness are deemed important. Choosing the right candidates could boost export growth, which is the prime driver of economic development in these countries.

Most of the issues affecting states' choices in bilateral partnerships are categorized into economic and political/strategic factors. They are, however, not mutually exclusive as politics and economics can no longer be separated with a clear distinction. Often involving both considerations, they weigh unevenly and changes over time due to adjustments in internal and/or external priorities.

10.2.1 Economic/Commercial Factors

The nature of FTAs as an 'economic tool' to expand trade and investment and integrate a country's market into the regional and global economies through gradual trade liberalization illuminates the importance of economic considerations in partner selection strategy. According to Korean academic Min Gyo Koo, economic explanations can be based on three theoretical perspectives: (1) countries with capital-labor comparative advantages that aim to foster inter-industry trade; (2) countries with similar factor endowments (product specialization) that aim to foster intra-industry trade; and (3) countries with geographical proximity that aim to reduce transaction costs (2006: 141–42). This means that, from an economic point of view, a country would consider negotiating an FTA with another country in different regions if there are opportunities for expanding intra- or inter- industry trade and with a country in the same region if costs to trade can be substantially reduced.

Thus, it is unsurprising to encounter feasibility studies conducted prior to the determination of FTA negotiations. Such studies are attempts at quantifying the

Table 10.2 Projected GDP and export changes based on FTA between Japan and Asian Countries (Source: Adapted from Kawasaki 2003)

	China	S. Korea	Indonesia	Malaysia	Philippines	Thailand
Real GDP	0.45 (3.06)	0.12 (2.45)	0.06 (3.01)	0.08 (5.07)	0.03 (3.03)	0.24 (20.09)
Export	2.52 (9.88)	0.70 (4.18)	0.41 (4.68)	0.29 (5.31)	0.19 (5.16)	0.83 (25.79)

Note: Figures in percentage; Figures in ( ) are expected changes for Asian countries

projected macroeconomic gains of trade pacts in order to justify the need for such agreements. The study by the ASEAN-China Expert Group prior to the establishment of China-ASEAN FTA (CAFTA) negotiations noted that exports between ASEAN and China will more or less double with ASEAN's real GDP to increase by USD5.4 billion (0.9%) and China's by USD2.2 billion (0.3%) (ASEAN Secretariat 2001).

As for ASEAN-Korea FTA, their Expert Group in 2004 reported that ASEAN's GDP would rise at an average of 0.13%[3] and Korea's by 0.05% with all countries benefiting economically although Thailand and Indonesia are likely to reap the most from their exports exceeding a billion dollar (South Korea FTA 2004). In the case of ASEAN-Japan FTA, the Joint Expert Group reported in 2002 that ASEAN's exports would increase by 44.2% and Japan's by 27.5%, with a 1.99% increase for ASEAN real GDP and 0.07% for Japan (METI 2002).

Other studies on bilateral FTAs based on the use of the computable general equilibrium (CGE) model have also shown equally positive figures. Japan's FTA with external regional countries such as Chile and Australia are anticipated to impact positively on domestic economic growth. With Australia, Japan will increase its real GDP by 0.03 ~ 0.13% (2.3 trillion yen) while Australia will gain 0.66 ~ 1.79 percentage point (3.3 trillion yen) (MOFA 2006a). With Chile, real GDP and exports will jump 0.49 and 15% (USD380 million) respectively for Chile and 0.002 and 42% (USD290 million) respectively for Japan (MOFA 2005). A study by Kawasaki (Table 10.2) shows that bilateral FTAs between Japan and a number of East Asian countries are expected to reel positive effects for all sides, although the rate of changes would appear greater for the Asian side due to their economic size in comparison to the Japanese economy.

From the above table, it is clear that bilateral FTAs can expand trade and achieve higher economies of scale due to the static effects of trade creation. However, countries that are excluded are estimated to incur losses due to the trade diversion effect. Table 10.3 shows how the economies of excluded countries are negatively impacted by the various FTA combinations in the region. It also shows that the larger the FTA becomes, i.e. more countries join, the higher the economic gains will be for the members. This indicates that there are explicit commercial incentives for countries to prefer regional over bilateral agreements.

---

[3] This figure is based on the average of six ASEAN countries – Indonesia, Malaysia, Philippines, Singapore, Thailand, and Vietnam.

Table 10.3 Projected GDP changes among various FTA partnerships in East Asia (Source: Adapted from Kawasaki 2003 and Tsutsumi 2004)

	JPN-CHN	JPN-SIN-KR	JPN-ASEAN	CHN-ASEAN	JPN-KR-ASEAN	JPN-CHN-ASEAN	JPN-CHN-KR-ASEAN
Japan	0.450	0.009	0.380	−0.070	0.038	0.790	0.061
S. Korea	n/a	0.207	n/a	n/a	0.274	n/a	0.366
China	3.060	−0.004	−0.270	0.970	−0.019	3.680	0.497
Singapore	−0.340	−0.180	4.530	5.640	0.985	5.660	1.176
Indonesia	−0.260	−0.008	3.660	1.920	1.294	4.080	1.319
Malaysia	−0.420	−0.009	9.270	6.780	1.731	10.790	1.813
Philippines	−0.270	−0.007	3.960	2.790	1.119	4.670	1.152
Thailand	−1.060	−0.039	25.750	10.130	3.409	27.160	3.576
Vietnam	−0.590	−0.013	13.710	11.880	2.215	19.650	2.403
US	n/a	−0.001	n/a	n/a	0.003	n/a	0.001
World	0.090	0.005	0.220	0.100	0.070	0.340	0.096

Note: Figures in percentage

Despite the favorable figures in support of (region-wide) FTA expansion and consolidation, states continue to take the short term measure of escalating their collection of bilateral agreements. Though this does not bode well for the region, a number of reasons explain such a move. Firstly, negotiating for a region-wide FTA requires strong political will from member economies, which is lacking due partly to the overzealous consensus culture and is, hence, time consuming. The ASEAN way and the various political systems inevitably make it difficult. Secondly, states find bilateralism within their control and therefore easier to incorporate into their respective trade policies. Thirdly, bilateralism reduces states' chances of falling behind their competitors in a rapid changing global economy.

Thus, trade figures alone are incapable of explaining the trend of bilateral FTAs being preferred over regional ones among countries in East Asia. There is a need to take into consideration the political/strategic factors that states inject into their selection process in search for the right FTA counterparts. As FTAs are used to deepen political relationships, their impacts go well beyond trade interest.

10.2.2 Political/Strategic Factors

A feasibility study report filled with numerical analyses on the economic effects of a FTA may be helpful in justifying to the masses a country's choice of partnership but hardly explains the political calculations and strategic intent that influences that choice. It is a latent factor since it involves security concerns related to a country's foreign policy strategy (see Tanaka 2001). In this section, six factors have been identified to elucidate the important role that politics play in the selection of FTA partners. They are the energy resources concern, the gateway consideration, negotiation experience, the domino effect, political (re)positioning and international status and, lastly the concerns of domestic actor.

10.2.2.1 The Energy Resources Concern

For countries experiencing a scarcity of energy resources such as Japan or which are hungry for more energy supply like China, FTAs can serve as a means to securing long-term access to those needed resources. Japan, for example, which has been very careful with choosing its partners, for example made a rather quick decision to engage the Gulf Cooperation Council (GCC) without requesting for a feasibility study.

Then Foreign Affairs Minister, Taro Aso (2006) explained that "(u)ntil now, we have been entering into negotiations with partner countries only after completing a study with private sector academics and the like. However, in the case of negotiations with the Gulf Cooperation Council, (…) we will intentionally pass over that preliminary step. I think it should go without saying that the six Persian Gulf states of the Arabian peninsula which comprise the GCC make that Council an extremely valuable partner for Japan in the area of energy security policy, insofar as Japan depends on its member nations for 75% of her petroleum needs and over 23% of her natural gas needs". As of March 2010, the two parties have yet to conclude and put their FTA into effect. While the reason for the delay is unclear, Japan has been reported to have requested preferential treatment in securing oil from the GCC including emergency situations and during war (Masaki 2006). Japan made a similar request to Indonesia, and their FTA that took effect on 1 July 2008 has a provision ensuring stable supply of oil and liquefied gas to Japan.

In such cases, FTAs can become a useful tool for securing crucial resources that are being sought by a growing list of countries for economic development. Japan's need to act fast reflects its competition with China which has been aggressively combing the earth from Africa to Eastern Europe for oil supply.

10.2.2.2 The Gateway Consideration

With enterprises regionally organized, an FTA with a country in a different region can serve as an entry point to take advantage of the economies of scale that the region provides. This is the reason why Mahathir was strongly against the Singapore–New Zealand FTA because he saw it as a back-door into ASEAN. However, AFTA's rules of origin requiring at least 40% of local content would theoretically make such advancement ineffective. Nonetheless, New Zealand has been able to capitalize on its FTA with Singapore by approaching other members of ASEAN to sign similar deals.

The gateway factor also played an important role in Mexico's decision to consider Japan for an FTA. It saw an opportunity to diversify its trade networks and engage East Asia. As American University academic Mireya Solis (2005) aptly pointed out, the FTA for Mexico was "about trade diversification, extending the FTA network for the first time into Asia, and preventing disinvestment".

What about the Japan-Switzerland FTA that came into effect on 1 September 2009? Pure economic reasoning is incapable of explaining Japan's move to approach Switzerland for a partnership. Trade between the two sides only amounted to about USD11.6 billion annually, a tiny fraction of the more than USD216 billion in annual trade between Japan and China in 2009. Most goods have already been subjected to low or no tariffs and yet the report by a joint governmental study group in January 2007 called for the launching of negotiations. The main reason that makes Switzerland an ideal partner for Japan is that it "can offer a key gateway to Japanese exports and investments destined for the greater European market" since it is strategically located at the center of Europe (Ajima 2009). This is important primarily because Japan does not have an FTA with the EU,[4] unlike South Korea which has an FTA with EFTA (effective 2006) and is in negotiations with the EU. Japanese businesses will be able to overcome competition by utilizing Switzerland's FTA with the EU to gain access into the vast European market (ibid.).

10.2.2.3 The Negotiation Experience

Negotiating FTAs require acquired skills that can only be sharpened and improved with on-the-job training. As such, countries looking for their first partner may not have the skills and know-how to successfully conclude negotiations and would therefore choose partners that offer the least problems. Certain countries are eager to go beyond WTO requirements to include other features such as labor, healthcare and environment, which then make negotiations a complicated process.

When Japan decided to change direction and adopt a more favorable attitude towards FTAs, it chose Singapore for its first experience. Negotiations took only a year and were relatively easy since most of Singapore's products were already low in tariffs and there was no notable agricultural sector that could derail the whole process. As a result, Japan was able to gain the necessary bargaining and operational skills before embarking on more strenuous negotiations with countries such as Mexico and South Korea.

South Korea, on the other hand, chose Chile over Singapore as its first FTA partner. The reason for selecting Chile and not neighboring countries like Singapore remains uncertain but scholars have noted the role of learning in negotiating with a more experience Chile and agricultural issues provided the Korean negotiators with the needed hands-on experience (Cheong 2002; Min 2006).

Eventually, countries gain confidence and are able to take on more difficult partners as well as know-how to overcome difficult issues. This was reflected in a speech by Japan's Taro Aso (2006) who stated that "because we have a stock of experience in various negotiations until now, we have become able to show partner countries

---

[4] It would be a formidable challenge for Japan and the EU to conclude an FTA in the short term period because of the agricultural sector that is highly subsidized by both economies.

right at the beginning an example of what the end product will ultimately look like, and we can then start to formulate the new EPA with that as a model. We have taken this approach in working with Vietnam, Brunei, and India, for example".

10.2.2.4 The Domino Effect

Since FTAs have the capability to divert and create imbalances in trade, decisions taken by neighboring countries can create a domino effect that leads others to make similar changes, even if there is reluctance to do so. The best example to illustrate this point is Malaysia. Malaysia has been strongly supporting the AFTA process and saw bilateralism as a destabilizing factor to regionalism. It was not pleased when Singapore signed its first FTA with New Zealand and then with Japan. As Singapore expanded its FTA list and observed similar moves made by Thailand and the Philippines, it realized that it could no longer defend AFTA or stay disinterested. It could no longer abstain and continue to incur economic costs, realizing that getting ASEAN as a group to negotiate with other countries would be simply time consuming (Okamoto 2006: 241–42). Fearing exclusion, Malaysia had no choice but to join the FTA bandwagon, selecting Japan as its first FTA partner in early 2004 before taking on the US, Pakistan, Australia and so forth.

Singapore's actions have brought about a domino effect on neighboring countries like Thailand, the Philippines and Malaysia, and their decisions to go beyond AFTA further influenced Indonesia and Brunei to join the trend as well. Having completed an FTA with Japan, Indonesia is also considering separate agreements with the US, Pakistan, Australia, New Zealand and India. These countries tend to select similar partners to avoid market undercuts and minimize economic disadvantages. In Northeast and other parts of Asia, China's FTA with ASEAN has caused a chain reaction with Japan, South Korea, India, Australia and New Zealand taking similar steps.

10.2.2.5 The Political (Re)positioning and International Status

Strategic calculations that take into consideration political positioning and international status are as important as trade figures, if not more. China's proposal for an FTA with ASEAN best illustrates this factor. The proposal came at a time when many of the Southeast Asian countries were recovering from the Asian financial crisis and feared that such recovery would be dampened by China's rapid economic rise and its ability to absorb huge amounts of FDI. China took that opportunity to allay fears by offering an economic partnership and the proposed Early Harvest Program has proven to be decisive.[5] Apart from appeasing ASEAN, it was an approach to build political stability and enhance China's regional influence (Sheng 2003; Kwei 2006: 129).

---

[5] While political considerations marked China's initial FTA proposal to ASEAN, the commitment to negotiation and the unfolding cooperation have helped both sides to see the economic benefits.

By reducing the negative perception that China's neighbors have on China through FTAs, it has greatly enhanced its credibility. FTAs became the bridge that strengthened China's relationship with Southeast Asian countries and repositioned China as a reliable supporter of regional cooperation. In addition, China has managed to gain international recognition as a market economy because it had made clear to all its prospective partners that such recognition is pivotal to any FTAs. Though China has already been recognized as an economic powerhouse, it was seeking international political recognition. To a large extent, China has succeeded to do so as observed by its ability to deny Taiwan an FTA.

Economically, Taiwan has a strong trade history with many East Asian countries and it would be ironic that those countries would not be interested in engaging Taiwan. Yet, Taiwan has been unsuccessful in getting support for its FTA proposals. The reluctance of countries such as Japan, Singapore, Malaysia and Thailand to accept Taiwan's offer is mainly to avoid angering China. In 2002, China's then foreign trade minister, Shi Guangsheng, gave a strong warning that "if such countries sign free trade agreement with the Taiwan authorities, they are bound to bring political trouble to themselves" (People's Daily Online 2002). To avoid confrontation, Japan's Ministry of Foreign Affairs issued a statement in 2002 that read: "Taiwan is a separate customs territory under the WTO Agreement, and while the possibility of concluding an FTA with a WTO member is theoretically and technically a potential subject for consideration, Taiwan's tariff rates are already low, so tariff reductions achieved through an FTA would not produce major benefits for both sides" (MOFA 2002). This reasoning fails to hold up when Japan's FTA with Singapore is observed, which has equally low/zero tariffs. Furthermore, it does not sit well with the fact that Japan's exports to Taiwan in early 2000s was nearly twice as large as Singapore and that Taiwan was listed as the ninth ideal partner compared to Singapore at 18th in terms of real GDP impact (Kawasaki 2003: 25; Ravenhill 2006: 30).

For smaller nations, however, FTAs may mark a shift in a state's political position on issues such as trade and investment liberalization. Despite the difficulties in negotiating with major powers such as the US, the readiness of small nations like Malaysia, Singapore and Thailand to take on the US reflects their tenacity to further integrate their economies into the global market. As John Ravenhill explained that "(i)t may be in the strategic interests of the smaller economy to make more concessions on trade liberalization than its stronger partner if its participation in the agreement is intended, for instance, to be a means of signaling its commitment to liberalization, and thereby an attempt to increase its attractiveness to potential investors" (2006: 29). It becomes a strategic move when states use FTAs to reposition themselves to achieve particular aims.

10.2.2.6 The Domestic Actor Concern

The role of domestic actors can influence the selection process of FTA partners. The degree of influence broadly depends on who the actors are and what the states' political systems would be. Highly democratic states with dynamic societies will take the views of domestic actors more seriously than autocratic and dictatorial ones. In other words, there is a higher level of awareness and participation in democratic societies. Domestic actors refer to interest groups such as business organizations, non-governmental organizations (NGOs) and even bureaucratic groups in various ministries. Business associations with certain vested interests may lobby their governments to pay attention to certain countries by highlighting particular issues that deserve government intervention. In the case of the Japan–Mexico FTA, the Nippon Keidanren (1999) played a critical role in lobbying its government to address the imbalances of Japanese businesses paying higher tariffs in Mexico compared to their counterparts from the US and the EU. The Federation of Korean Industries did the same thing when it urged Seoul to sign a deal with the EU as a way to reduce the high tariffs that the EU has maintained on Korean products (The Chosun Ilbo 2006).

Different interests among bureaucrats and inadequate policy coordination among ministries can affect the preference of partners. In developed economies, negotiating with a developing country purely for trade can be unattractive since the real GDP growth is extremely small. To increase the benefits, big nations prefer to negotiate for a comprehensive agreement that goes beyond the WTO framework to include labor, environment, government procurement, technical cooperation and etc. This means involving more ministries than otherwise required.[6] It is not only coordination which becomes complicated, differences in opinion also arise.

In Japan, there had been coordination problems between the Ministry of Foreign Affairs (MOFA) and the Ministry of Economy, Trade and Industry (METI). When Japan decided to pursue FTAs, it launched an FTA headquarter and established an FTA division in the Economic Affairs Bureau under MOFA. The division is tasked to plan, draft, unify and coordinate responses. However, this has brought about disagreements between MOFA and METI on how Japan should approach its FTA strategy. For example, METI had favored a multilateral approach with ASEAN as it was concerned that a China-ASEAN FTA would lead to the investment of Chinese firms impacting on Japan's carefully built business and production networks in Southeast Asia. MOFA, on the other hand, preferred a bilateral approach thinking that separate FTAs would be more feasible considering ASEAN countries' different stages of development and would allow Japan to negotiate more comprehensively (Terada 2004; Soesastro 2005).[7] The outcome was a dual approach strategy that focused on establishing bilateral FTAs with the older ASEAN members before concluding a plurilateral one with ASEAN.[8] This has undeniably affected the selection process of partners and the level of comprehensiveness of the negotiated agreements.

---

[6] Malaysia's FTA with the US actually involved 19 negotiation teams representing various ministries and agencies (Bernama 2007).

[7] There are also reasons to believe that such differences stemmed from the approach that these two ministries take towards FTA. MOFA sees FTA as a broad comprehensive agreement that should best be approached bilaterally while METI is more concerned with trade issues and thus defined it in narrower terms.

[8] Though ASEAN has publicly expressed dissatisfaction with such an approach citing solidarity concern, member countries privately support it as it allows them to negotiate and demand for more benefits from Japan in competing with other members (personal discussion with a MOFA official, July 2006).

10.3 The Impact of FTA Proliferation on Human Security

The discussions above show that economic and strategic interests concerning states are clearly embedded into their foreign trade policies and thus affect how states select their FTA partners. This section probes further by asking whether states are aware of or have given ample consideration to the impact of FTAs on human security. By revisiting some of the bilateral FTAs that are in the process of negotiation or have been concluded, this section discusses the various human concerns and challenges that the states have not properly addressed in their pursuit of FTAs.

The lack of consideration for human security in FTA policy is reflected in the high-speed pace of states entering and signing trade pacts. Calling FTA development in East Asia the "do-it-quick" and "do-it-soon" agreements, the late Malaysian academic Noordin Sopiee stated that "(n)o more the hesitant, patient, step-by-step, go-slow, take-it-easy, calculate-all-the-costs, examine-all-the-possible-negatives, be-cautious approach. It is remarkable how many are now prepared to jump straight into the most serious commitments, quite obviously before doing all their sums, so obviously without adequate national study, still less, preparation" (2004: 29).

In many cases, states' apparatuses are stretched thin due to multiple negotiations at a given time and the relatively short period allocated for negotiation. States are able to negotiate swiftly partly because of the absence of active participation from the general public. Negotiators are either not sensitive enough to solicit feedback or the state may see problems arising from structural transformation as domestic matters and thus takes the approach of concluding now and addressing the ramifications later. As the Thai authorities noted on their website, "(w)ith freer trade, Thai local companies will also encounter an increasing level of competition, which could result in the crowding out of less competitive firms and industries. And the political, social, and cultural repercussions of a more open environment could also be high. Nonetheless, it is clear these negative ramifications can be effectively dealt with through proper preparations, adjustments, reforms, and through joint efforts and intensify cooperation from all sides" (Thai FTA, n.d.).

However, no amount of preparations, adjustments and reforms can fully shield a country from the negative impacts of FTAs. The experience of NAFTA has shown that there are winners but there are also losers (Engardio et al. 2008; Costantini 2009).[9] The recent global economic crisis further brought home the point that states, especially developing nations, do not have the capability to protect their societies from the outside forces of change. More so in this globalized age where states have less control over their borders. Although governments can provide stimulus packages to slowdown the effects, ordinary citizens do lose jobs and their life long savings. Thailand's political upheaval that started with a *coup d'état* back in September 2006 further exhibits the limitation if not the ineptitude

---

[9] Even after 15 years, NAFTA has not been able to provide a permanent solution to the problem of illegal Mexican immigrants entering the US in search of economic security.

of states to safeguard the human interest of their people. This means that the chances of human security being compromised are high. It is high when civil societies are prevented from playing their roles in providing valuable inputs or inputs that are not taken into serious consideration such as in the selection and negotiation process of FTAs.

The problem lies in how states and societies perceive the value of FTAs. While states focus on the big picture (macro-economy) and worry less about the human impact, individuals are cautious and concerned with how trade pacts can affect their personal wellbeing. Labor mobility and influx of foreign skilled labor threaten existing social safety nets causing unemployment to those who are incapable of change, primarily those who live in the peripheries of society. The following subsections provide an assessment of the discrepancies of perception between the people and the states.

10.3.1 Human Concerns in Bilateral FTAs with Japan

Asian reactions to FTAs with Japan have been rather mixed. Most Asians see Japan favorably. Japan's relatively moderate foreign policy, its widespread production networks and the technical assistance under the Official Development Assistance (ODA) program have helped to contribute to smoother negotiations. Its less demanding attitude on environment and human rights issues in comparison with the US also help to reduce contentious problems. In East Asia, Japan has FTAs with ASEAN, Brunei, Indonesia, Malaysia, the Philippines, Singapore, Thailand and Vietnam. It is negotiating with Australia, India and trying to restart a stalled negotiation with South Korea. The following discussion focuses on two concluded agreements, namely the Japan-Thailand Economic Partnership Agreement (JTEPA) and the Japan-Philippines Economic Partnership Agreement (JPEPA).

These two agreements have been more problematic compared to others such as the Japan-Singapore EPA (JSEPA) or the Japan-Malaysia EPA (JMEPA) which have hardly received any resistance despite little public consultations. There were scarcely any protests as if either large segments of the societies trusted their governments in negotiating with Japan or many were oblivious to the existence of such negotiations. Then Malaysia's Trade Minister Rafidah Aziz's call on the private sector to provide input showed a general lack of interest from the public (Bernama 2005). Furthermore, the absence of labor mobility in the JMEPA removed contentious issues that the JTEPA and JPEPA had to face.

Under the JTEPA, 7,000 product items or 97% of total trade are covered with both sides agreeing to eliminate tariffs on industrial (except automobiles) and most agricultural products within 10 years. Rice, wheat and barley were among the list of items excluded from the pact. On the movement of natural persons, Japan is to ease entry restrictions for Thai cooks and cultural instructors while the acceptance of care workers and spa therapists have been left opened to further negotiations.

Objections to the JTEPA have been manifold. Various groups from NGOs and the academia to local media and business groups in Thailand were taking a much more cautious line than the government, worried at how the FTA will impact people's livelihoods. Issues that have cropped up during negotiations include the origin of raw materials in textile and garment ('yarn forward' versus 'fabric forward' principle) and the issues of steel and auto.[10] Local manufacturers and business associations were against the idea of opening up the steel and auto markets fearing stiff competition from Japan. Together with foreign auto makers, they were also worried that the idea of a 'Detroit in Asia' would be undermined by a bilateral FTA with Japan.

Even after the negotiation process has concluded, Thai NGOs continue to work to uncover and highlight parts of the agreement that they deemed inappropriate. The postponement of the signing ceremony due to Thailand's general election and later the collapse of the Thaksin government have allowed the NGOs ample time to obtain the documents, study the impact and thrash out the contentious issues. Two issues raised were toxic-waste and micro-organism patenting, fearing that there could be a hidden agenda. On the former, the fear was that tariff abolishment could increase trade in disposed waste exposing Thai people to environmental and health hazards. While Thailand may have laws in place, the argument was that it does not have effective mechanisms to enforce the laws and control the elimination of banned waste products, thus creating opportunities for abuse (Bangkok Post 2007). On the latter, the fear was that allowing Japan to patent microbes would cost Thailand several hundred billion baht a year as the rights to the country's micro-organism assets would go to Japan (The Nation 2007). These issues and the way the NGOs and other concerned groups had to work around the lack of transparency in the negotiation process illustrated the lack of sensitivity of the state towards the peoples' concerns with the 'fine prints'.

In the JPEPA, toxic waste became an issue as well. It was uncovered in the finalized document which was concluded in July and signed in September 2006. The Basel Action Network (BAN) with offices in Seattle and Quezon City is an NGO that opposes global toxic trade. In January 2007, they produced a report calling the JPEPA "a step in Japan's greater plan to liberalize hazardous waste trade in Asia" and argued that:

> ...the inclusion of tariff reductions for hazardous wastes is not simply a technicality, nor an insignificant byproduct of the poker game of trade negotiations. It is a legally significant move and is in fact part of a deliberate strategy now in play by Japan in a global chess game. The game plan is to overturn the Basel Convention's obligations to minimize transboundary movements of hazardous waste and strictly control its trade, to replace this norm with one that finds waste but another commodity to be freely traded (Basel Action Network 2007).

---

[10] 'Yarn forward' means that 100% of the yarn must come from either Thailand or Japan to qualify for lower tariffs while 'fabric forward' requires fabric to be made in either country irrespective of the yarn origin.

The report noted the statement released by the Japanese embassy that "the Government of Japan…does not allow the export of toxic and hazardous waste… unless the government of such a country approves such export." In reply, it stated that "it does not say Japan will refrain from export of hazardous wastes…Rather it notes that a country must approve such import. With the JPEPA in place, legally Japan will be well placed to *insist* that the Philippines *'must approve'* such export." Whether or not Japan will export toxic waste to Asian countries[11] remains to be seen but incorporating it into its bilateral FTAs has not only made it legal but overrides the Basel Convention.

Another issue in the JPEPA is the movement of natural persons pertaining to nurses and care workers. The Philippines had initially demanded that Japan accept Filipinos based on demand and qualification and not on quota or volume limit (Manila Bulletin 2005). However, Japan offered to allow a year-on-year quota of about 200 nurses and care workers. This offer was strongly rejected by the Filipino side as it was seen as too small a number (Asia Times 2005). The failure to agree on the figure was one of the reasons that had led to a year of delay in finalizing the agreement compared to the JMEPA.[12] While the Philippines failed to get Japan to lift the quota requirement, it has been agreed that Japan will accept up to 400 nurses and 600 caregivers between the fiscal year 2007 and 2008.

Japan's willingness to accept more than originally discussed could be partly due to the change of tide of Japanese establishments accepting foreign workers. Nevertheless, there are preconditions. Specificities have been inserted into the JPEPA that could make it harder for qualified Filipino nurses to apply and create restrictions for those who fulfill the conditions. The document on labor movement notes that a qualified nurse with work experience of 3 years and a certified caregiver (with a bachelor degree) under Philippine laws can apply for a stay in Japan for 1 year of which the first 6 months will be for Japanese language training and followed by practical training under Japanese supervision, before preparing to take the designated national examination (MOFA 2006b).[13] Not only do such prerequisite set a tall order for Filipinos, two of their biggest challenges would be to master the Japanese language and pass the national exam.

A Level 1 or 2 of the Japanese Language Proficiency Test would be needed to have an adequate command of the language. Unless a substantial amount of language preparation is done in the home country, it is near impossible to master it in 6 months. In addition, there are medical jargons that need to be learned in preparing for the board exam and the JPEPA clearly stipulates that only three chances are given for the newcomers. This unfortunately is just the tip of the iceberg. Elderly people in rural areas are also known to be heavy users of colloquial

---

[11] Similar clauses are found in JMEPA and JSEPA although they have received less public attention than in Thailand and the Philippines.

[12] Part of the reason for the delay was due to the clash of interests between Japan's MOFA, METI and the Ministry of Justice (MOJ).

[13] Nurses can extend their stay for 2 more years and caregivers 3 more years.

dialects and some have reservations toward foreigners. The challenges presented to Filipino workers are enormous and are not balanced up by the incentives offered to them.

The conditions laid down in the JPEPA demonstrates that while the Filipino government has negotiated to provide legal pathways for its citizens to seek better lives, which is the main driving force for Filipinos to venture abroad, it has not ensured that those pathways are sufficiently secured. The fact that Filipino health workers could be sent back with zero achievements should they fail to fulfill the stringent requirements means that they are taking a great risk with no guarantee of job security. The JPEPA could end up creating losers and contributing to the number of illegal immigrants.

For those who succeed, they are faced with the possibility of discrimination and abuse. Already, Japanese nurses have been worried about their job security, calling for better working conditions instead of accepting "cheap labor" (The Japan Times 2006). Certainly, there are issues that can strain the relationship between Japanese and Filipino nurses who are fundamentally dependent on their Japanese counterparts for guidance. Abuse could come from unfair employment conditions such as extra workloads, longer shift hours and lower income. This warrants attention since problems with low and unpaid wages of foreign trainees in the machinery and agricultural industries have been well documented.[14]

10.3.2 Human Concerns in Bilateral FTAs with the US

In East Asia, the US has an FTA with Singapore (USSFTA) that came into effect in 2004, has signed one with South Korea (USKFTA) in 2007 but has since asked for renegotiation, and has put its negotiations with Thailand (USTFTA) and Malaysia (USMFTA) on hold. Inspired by the USSFTA, the US's first FTA with an Asian country, it announced a new Enterprise for ASEAN Initiative (EAI) in October 2002 to serve as a framework towards the creation of a network of bilateral FTAs with ASEAN countries. The EAI were encouraged by the show of interest from the other ASEAN members, primarily Thailand, and by geopolitical concerns with the proactive stance of China and Japan towards FTA. US's stance under President Bush was to use FTAs to expedite trade liberalization in Northeast and Southeast Asia and help APEC achieve its Bogor goals (White House 2002). For the Southeast Asian countries, FTAs with the US would bring in much needed FDI and boost trade in competing with China and India.

---

[14] See Advocacy Network for Foreign Trainees (2006) and Kawakami (2008). Some steps have been taken such as the drafting of a guideline on the transparency in job placement by the Ministry of Health, Labor and Welfare, and the support networks that Filipinos residing in Japan are providing to the new arrivals but their efficacy remains unclear.

Absent agriculture and high tariff conditions, issues with the USSFTA have mainly centered on financial liberalization and were miniscule when compared to the USKFTA, USTFTA and USMFTA. The latter three saw a high level of participation from NGOs, associations and the general public, highly apprehensive of their governments seeding too much to the US. Being aware of the US's global reach and dominance in economy and security, and the resentment following the US's hawkish foreign policies, there was also a general fear that the US might muscle its way into forcing Asian countries to open up. Alternative media and internet access have also created a higher sense of awareness on the negative effects of NAFTA and the lack of public engagement in the monitoring of past FTA negotiations.

However, the two major problems with engaging the US have been the inclusivity of US's FTA strategy and the limited negotiation timeframe. On the former, FTAs can be a good instrument to advance US's political interests and that means emphasizing WTO-plus issues such as intellectual property rights, labor rights, procurement, and environmental and investment protection. With such issues, the US could affect political and economic changes in partner countries that are aligned with its overall strategies. After all, bilateral FTAs with small individual countries would have little economic gains for the US (Feinberg 2006). On the latter, Asian countries were rushing to negotiate with the US to meet the July 2007 deadline, when President Bush lost his Trade Promotion Authority (TPA) and the power to broker deals reverted back to Congress from the executive branch.[15] Eager to meet the deadline, Philippines's President Arroyo said that:

> ...instead of having exploratory talks and going through that whole range, we will write a draft and give it to them for them to consider or amend. That's for the business community now to prepare because it's the business community... that have been urging me to go into a free trade agreement... His authority is until June or July... I don't want to start with exploratory talks because it would take years... Now, I'm challenging the business sector. I told Doris Ho... I got President Bush to say yes to the FTA so you write the draft so that we don't have to go through the years and years of negotiations (Tubeza 2006).

Despite reports that the Filipino government would learn from their mistakes with the JPEPA by involving all parties (ISSA News 2007), this is clearly a case that has shown otherwise. The idea of relegating the drafting of a trade deal to a group of business leaders without proper consultations and feedback from various parties simply because of a deadline demonstrated the lack of responsibility of the state to its people by creating an enormous risk that may end up benefiting few but harming the livelihood of many. The US–Philippines FTA has since remained in the proposal stage.

With Malaysia, the USMFTA negotiations started in June 2006 but soon received objections and pressure from local NGOs and consumer groups. FTA Malaysia, a portal site run by three NGOs – Third World Network (TWN), Consumers' Association of Penang (CAP) and Sahabat Alam Malaysia (SAM) – have been

---

[15] Also known as fast-track, it allowed the White House to sign deals that will then be sent to Congress for approval or rejection without amendment.

against the deal from the beginning. Joined by other people-oriented groups like TERAS (Malay Empowerment Group) and JERIT (Network of Exploited Communities) and business entities like the Malay Businessmen and Entrepreneurs Association of Malaysia (Perdasama), they have been voicing their disapprovals from calling for the exclusion of government procurement and taking a more cautious line to disclosing details of the negotiation and stopping it altogether. Negotiations came to a standstill in February 2007 when 58 outstanding issues could not be resolved in time to enjoy the terms of the TPA. However, the Malaysian government had maintained that the USMFTA would not be bound by any timeframe. As other countries lost interest to negotiate with the US after the TPA deadline, Malaysia resumed negotiations in 2008 but only for a brief period and has since been put on hold due to a change in the new administration under Barack Obama, who has yet to finalize reviewing US trade strategies.

With Thailand, the USTFTA has witnessed droves of protesters in large numbers, 10,000 or more at times, demonstrating and calling for "No FTA" with the US. The Thai government started negotiations in 2004 and was nearing completion when the Thaksin government was overthrown in a coup in 2006, which has since led to continuous unsettled political crisis in that country. Thai's NGOs like FTA Watch and sectors of the general public have taken up a wide selection of issues with the Thai government including intellectual property rights (IPR), farming, privatization, labor laws, finance and environment. On IPR, the people were worried that drug patents would make medicine expensive and unreachable to those in need including poor HIV sufferers by preventing the use of locally produced generic drugs. However, Thai's Health Ministry's unprecedented decision to issue licenses for generic versions of heart and HIV/AIDS drugs in early 2007 provides a ray of hope on the issue of health security (Reuters 2007). In other areas such as farming, the people's concerns were captured by Biothai's Witoon Lienjamroon remarks to the chief negotiator, Nitya Pibulsonggram, that, "You, honest bureaucrats, should answer to the public if the liberalization of farm products has benefited only a handful of animal-feed investors who get cheaper soybean and corn while millions of farmers were to go bankrupt. How can we protect our food security?" (Bangkok Post 2005). There were also other issues that revolved around the giving of concessions for public utilities to foreign operators, the inability of local operators to compete in financial liberalization and the acceleration of deforestation to grow profitable single-crop plantations.

Concerned with human rights violations, the National Human Rights Commission of Thailand drafted a report in January 2007 highlighting the possibility of violations should the deal go through and pointing out the ill-preparedness of the government in facing an FTA tsunami (South–North Development Monitor 2007). Concerned, the Commission recommended that all sectors of the society should be involved in the negotiation process and an independent committee be established for appraisal purposes with public hearings scheduled. Not much development has been made since then as all attention has shifted to the domestic political turmoil.

With South Korea, negotiations for the USKFTA started around the same time as Malaysia and have seen a fury of protests and strikes culminated in violent clashes with riot police. Representing some 282 trade unions, farmer's groups and civic societies, the Korean Alliance against the Korea-US FTA (KoA) was at the center of those opposing the USKFTA, including the Korea Federation of Trade Unions, religious groups and the Korean Democratic Labor Party. They saw the deal as highly lopsided and were fearful of how the accord would destroy the farming, automobile and pharmaceutical industries. They were also wary of the loss of jobs and income; issues that are extremely sensitive in Korean society. In 2007, the KoA had estimated that agricultural production nationwide will decrease by 45% with nearly half of the farmers losing their livelihood and citrus-producing farmers on the Jeju island will see the price of their tangerines drop by 59% or USD200 million in annual losses (KoA 2007a).

Apart from highlighting key areas of concern ranging from beef and rice to film quota and anti-dumping regulations, the Executive Director of the Korea Policy Institute, Thomas Kim, wrote in his policy brief on the proposed USKFTA that "concern in South Korea about the FTA is driven by worries about the undemocratic nature of the negotiations and by the possibility of negative policy consequences to various sectors… Readers of independent internet news are more likely to learn that the proposed FTA will further concentrate the power of multinational corporations and erode the rights of governments to determine national policies to protect the rights of workers, farmers, the environment, and cultural institutions" (Kim 2007: 3–4; emphasis added).

The same thoughts were echoed by The American Federation of Labor and Congress of Industrial Organizations or better known as the AFL-CIO and a number of other US civic groups when they declared that, "…the current model agreement, which so far has provided enormous benefits for a disproportionate few, will not likely generate widely shared economic prosperity for the majority of persons in the U.S. and South Korea. Indeed, some of the provisions under negotiation could jeopardize important public interest gains or narrow the policy space of governments to respond to the needs or wants of their citizens" (KoA 2007b). Protests especially from the farming community in Korea have continued to mount even after the conclusion of negotiations with the Chairman of the Korean Advanced Farmers Federation warning that a ratification of the agreement "would result in an agrarian uprising" (The Straits Times 2008).

10.4 Conclusion – Making FTAs People Friendly

While it is still too early to ascertain the kind of implications that FTAs will inflict on East Asian societies, the experiences of NAFTA and the way FTAs have been negotiated by countries in East Asia provide an indication of the kind of negative ramifications that may befall societies in the region. Individuals that are quick to adapt to changes and are technologically savvy will reap the benefits. Those that are less able to do so such as peasants, farmers, small time traders, physically challenged groups and senior citizens will most likely face isolation. They are genuinely concerned with how FTAs will encroach on their livelihoods and obstruct their ability to secure their wellbeing and those of their future generations.

These concerns stem from the general lack of trust on the states' capability to meticulously negotiate on behalf of the people. Because of the impatience of states to quickly conclude negotiations, the possible lack of negotiation skills of officials from smaller nations and the lack of transparency and public engagement in the negotiation process, people are suspicious and worried that their governments will sell them out and endanger social cohesions for the benefit of a small but powerful minority. Moreover, the selection of FTA partners as discussed has been largely based on factors concerning state rather than society. If FTAs are what states want and what governments assume what their societies would want, there will be serious implications on human security and on the state's legitimacy in representing and defending the rights of its people.

States need to reevaluate their priorities to make FTA-related policies a people-centered activity instead of a state-centric one. As representatives of their people, governments need to indoctrinate human security into their trade policies. The notion of whether FTAs are good for states should be aptly replaced with whether they are good for human development.[16] This means that FTAs should not be a state-induced policy but people-sensitive policy and the decision to engage others in FTAs, the choices of FTA partners and the process of negotiation ought to be done collectively. Time and external forces should never be allowed to hold a state and its people hostage or be used as excuses to proliferate FTAs.

Human security is after all about the empowering of the people to take charge of matters that concern them. The people need to play a proactive role by exercising their rights. This means the right to voice their angst, to be informed of developments, and to participate actively through the right channels. Civil societies have an ultimate role to play in ensuring that FTAs signed are just, people-oriented and sustainable. It would be a fallacy to assume that trade liberalization is all that is needed to generate prosperity for all. FTAs should be about lowering poverty, creating equal distribution and driving sustainable development.

References

Advocacy Network for Foreign Trainees. (2006). *Gaikokujin Kenshuusei: Jikyuu 300-en no Roudousha (Foreign Trainees: 300 yen an hour laborers)*. Tokyo: Akashi Shoten.
Ajima, S. (2009, October 15). Japan-Swiss FTA may offset lack of EU accord, *The Japan Times*.

---

[16] Here, it is interesting to note that Bolivia's President, Evo Morales (n.d.) has developed an alternative to the FTA in 2006, calling it People's Trade Agreement (PTA). The PTA aims to safeguard the interests of small nations by calling for a more equitable agreement that promotes development, defends national production and involves active participation from the general public.

Asia Times (2005, July 1). Labor issues to delay Japan-Philippines FTA.
ASEAN Secretariat (2001). *Forging closer Asean-China economic relations in the twenty-first century* (Report by ASEAN-China Expert Group on Economic Cooperation), http://www.aseansec.org/asean_chi.pdf. Accessed 14 Jan 2007.
Aso, T. (2006). Speech at the Japan National Club, http://www.mofa.go.jp/announce/fm/aso/speech0603.html. Accessed 15 Jan 2007.
Bangkok Post. (2005, April 6). 1,200 march to urge dropping of intellectual property from US deal.
Bangkok Post. (2007, January 10). FTA sparks toxic waste dump fears.
Basel Action Network. (2007). JPEPA as a step in Japan's greater plan to liberalize hazardous waste trade in Asia, http://www.ban.org/library/JPEPA_report.pdf. Accessed 19 Jan 2007.
Bernama. (2005, January 27). Malaysia: Private sector told to engage in FTA process.
Bernama. (2007, March 5). Cabinet to state its stand on M'sia-US FTA issue, Kuala Lumpur, http://www.bernama.com.my/bernama/v3/news_lite.php?id=249782. Accessed 8 Feb 2010.
Bhagwati, J. (1991). *The world trading system at risk*. Princeton: Princeton University Press.
Cheong, I. (2002). *Korea's FTA policy: Focusing on bilateral FTAs with Chile and Japan* (KIEP Discussion Paper 02–02).
Costantini, P. (2009, December 15). Winners and losers: The human costs of 'free' trade, *The Huffington Post*.
Engardio, P., Smith, G., & Sasseen, J. (2008, March 19). What you don't know about Nafta, *Businessweek*.
Feinberg, R. (2006). US trade arrangements in the Asia-Pacific. In V. K. Aggarwal & S. Urata (Eds.), *Bilateral trade agreements in the Asia-Pacific: Origins, evolution, and implications* (pp. 95–116). London: Routledge.
ISSA News. (2007, February 28). Philippines pursue U.S. free-trade accord.
Kawai, M., & Wignaraja, G. (2007). *ASEAN + 3 or ASEAN + 6: Which way forward?* (ADBI Discussion Paper 77), Tokyo: Asian Development Bank Institute.
Kawakami, S. (2008). Transformation of the foreign trainee program, *Voices From Japan*, No. 20, Asia-Japan Women's Resource Center, http://www.ajwrc.org/english/sub/voice/20-1-2.pdf. Accessed 10 Feb 2010.
Kawasaki, K. (2003). *The impact of free trade agreements in Asia* (RIETI Discussion Paper Series 03-E-018), http://www.rieti.go.jp/jp/publications/dp/03e018.pdf. Accessed 12 Jan 2007.
Keidanren. (1999). Report on the possible effects of a Japan-Mexico free trade agreement on Japanese industry, http://www.keidanren.or.jp/english/policy/pol099.html. Accessed 20 Jan 2007.
Kim, T. (2007, February 7). Policy brief on the proposed U.S-Republic of Korea free trade agreement, Korea Policy Institute, pp. 1–23.
KoA. (Korean Alliance against the Korea-U.S. FTA) (2007a, February 16). Seventh FTA negotiations end but struggle continues daily, *No FTA Newsletter*, http://nofta.jinbo.net/en/entry/KoA-No-FTA-Newsletter-02162007. Accessed 28 Jan 2007.
KoA. (Korean Alliance against the Korea-U.S. FTA). (2007b, March 12). Five-thousand rally against free trade amidst strong police violence, *No FTA Newsletter*, http://nofta.jinbo.net/en/entry/No-FTA-Newsletter-031207. Accessed 1 Feb 2007.
Kwei, E. (2006). Chinese trade bilateralism: Politics still in command. In V. K. Aggarwal & S. Urata (Eds.), *Bilateral trade agreements in the Asia-Pacific: Origins, evolution, and implications* (pp. 117–139). London: Routledge.
Manila Bulletin. (2005, June 27). No quota under proposed JPEPA, http://www.mb.com.ph/node/128580. Accessed 11 Mar 2007.
Masaki, H. (2006, December 18). Japan's FTA drive, East Asian regional leadership, and the China challenge, *The Asia-Pacific Journal: Japan Focus*.
METI (Ministry of Economy, Trade and Industry of Japan). (2002). *Report on the joint study on the ASEAN-Japan closer economic partnership* (ASEAN-Japan Closer Economic Partnership Expert Group (ACEPEG)), http://www.meti.go.jp/policy/trade_policy/asean/data/ajcepeg_jr_e.pdf. Accessed 12 Jan 2007.

Min, G. K. (2006). From multilateralism to bilateralism? A shift in South Korea's trade strategy. In V. K. Aggarwal & S. Urata (Eds.), *Bilateral trade agreements in the Asia-Pacific: Origins, evolution, and implications* (pp. 140–159). London: Routledge.

MOFA (Ministry of Foreign Affairs of Japan). (2002). Japan's FTA Strategy, http://www.mofa.go.jp/policy/economy/fta/strategy0210.html. Accessed 26 Dec 2006.

MOFA (Ministry of Foreign Affairs of Japan). (2005). *Report of the joint study group on Japan-Chile economic partnership agreement/free trade agreement*, http://www.mofa.go.jp/region/latin/chile/report0511.pdf. Accessed 5 Jan 2007.

MOFA (Ministry of Foreign Affairs of Japan). (2006a). Joint study for enhancing economic relations between Japan and Australia, including the feasibility or Pros and Cons of a free trade agreement, http://www.mofa.go.jp/region/asia-paci/australia/joint0612.pdf. Accessed 5 Jan 2007.

MOFA (Ministry of Foreign Affairs of Japan). (2006b). Agreement between Japan and the Republic of the Philippines for an economic partnership, http://www.mofa.go.jp/region/asia-paci/philippine/epa0609/index.html. Accessed 5 Jan 2007.

Morales, E. (n.d.). A People's Trade Agreement (PTA), alliance for responsible trade, http://www.art-us.org/PTA_html. Accessed 11 Feb 2007.

Munakata, N. (2002). Talking regional, acting bilateral – Reality of 'FTA Race' in East Asia, Tokyo: Research Institute of Economy, Trade and Industry (REITI), http://www.rieti.go.jp/en/papers/contribution/munakata/01.html. Accessed 12 Feb 2010.

Okamoto, Y. (2006). The reluctant bilateralist: Malaysia's new trade strategy. In V. K. Aggarwal & S. Urata (Eds.), *Bilateral trade agreements in the Asia-Pacific: Origins, evolution, and implications* (pp. 232–252). London: Routledge.

People's Daily Online. (2002, June 21). FTA with Taiwan means political trouble: Official, http://english.peopledaily.com.cn/200206/21/eng20020621_98285.shtml. Accessed 23 Jan 2007.

Ramesh, S. (2004). Singapore's FTAs set pace for other ASEAN countries: Lee Kuan Yew, *Channel NewsAsia*.

Ravenhill, J. (2006). The political economy of the new Asia-Pacific bilateralism: Benign, banal, or simply bad? In V. K. Aggarwal & S. Urata (Eds.), *Bilateral trade agreements in the Asia-Pacific: Origins, evolution, and implications* (pp. 27–49). London: Routledge.

Reuters. (2007, February 12). Thailand threatens to produce more copycat drugs, http://www.reuters.com/article/idUSBKK5005820070212. Accessed 13 Feb 2010.

Sheng, L. (2003). *China-ASEAN free trade area: Origins, developments and strategic motivations* (ISEAS Working Paper), Singapore: Institute of Southeast Asian Studies (ISEAS).

Soesastro, H. (2005). *The evolution of ASEAN + X free trade agreements: Implications for Canada* (CSIS Working Paper Series WPE 089), http://www.csis.or.id/working_paper_file/50/wpe089.pdf. Accessed 17 Jan 2007.

Solis, M. (2005). The political economy of the Japan-Mexico EPA: How does a cross-regional initiative affect the future of Japan's regional integration efforts?, *Transcript*, http://www.rieti.go.jp/en/events/bbl/05070401.html. Accessed 16 Dec 2006.

Sopiee, N. (2004). Three views of East Asian integration: The new paradigm of East Asian cooperation. *Japan Echo, 31*(2), 29–31.

South Korea FTA. (2004). http://www.fta.go.kr/storage/str1_view.php?page=3&board_id=273&country_id=. Accessed 6 Jan 2007.

South-North Development Monitor. (2007, January 25). Thai Human Rights Commission attacks FTA with US, Issue# 6176.

Tanaka, H. (2001). Can Japan find a breakthrough? Free trade agreements as foreign policy tools. *Japan Echo, 28*(1), 8–14.

Terada, T. (2004). Thorny progress in the institutionalization of ASEAN + 3: Deficient China–Japan leadership and the ASEAN divide for regional governance, The 21st century center of excellence program, policy innovation initiative: Human security research in Japan and Asia, Tokyo: Keio University.

Thai FTA. (n.d.). http://www.thaifta.com/english/main_fta_eng1.html. Accessed 2 Feb 2007.

The Chosun Ilbo. (2006, August 2). Business lobby group urges FTA with EU, http://english.chosun.com/site/data/html_dir/2006/08/02/2006080261022.html. Accessed 23 Jan 2007.

The Japan Times. (2006, September 13). Philippine FTA to reshape health care.

The Nation. (2007, February 17). NGOs fear there's a hidden agenda in Japan FTA.

The Straits Times. (2008, November 25). Farmers against FTA.

Tsutsumi, M. (2004). Economic impacts of Japan-China-Korea FTA: A CGE model simulation, *Japan Center for Economic Research*.

Tubeza, P. (2006, November 20). Arroyo eyes free trade pact with US by July 2007, *Inquirer.*

White House. (2002). Press release, http://www.whitehouse.gov/news/releases/2002/10/20021026-7.html. Accessed 10 Feb 2007.

WTO Online. (n.d.). http://www.wto.org/english/tratop_e/region_e/regfac_e.htm. Accessed 28 Mar 2010.

Chapter 11
Human Security, Capital Punishment, and East Asian Democracies

Sangmin Bae

11.1 Introduction

Dangerous and destructive political experiences in the twentieth century taught us that it is impossible to protect human freedom and welfare exclusively through the traditional notion of state security-premised upon military defense of territorial integrity. Those who support a new, broader formulation of security believe that if our security apparatuses address more how to eliminate the economic, social, and environmental conditions that generate threats to human well-being, instead of relying merely on the traditional understanding of military threats such as war, terrorism, or the spread of weapons of mass destruction, the world would be a more secure place. The primary goal of a new security policy model is, therefore, not only dealing with issues related to how to prevent and stop war but focusing also on how to eliminate the economic, social, environmental, and political conditions that generate threats to the security of people. Characterized by a shift from the state to the individual as the primary referent of security, this revised paradigm is constructed as an ethical alternative to realist notions of national security (Axworthy 2001; Baldwin 1997; Evans 2004; Gasper 2005; Kay 1997; Newman 2001). National security and international security cannot be achieved without respect for individual security which is the core value of respect for human rights and fundamental freedoms protected and promoted in any society. The interconnectedness of human rights and human security in today's global context are increasingly becoming relevant.

The focus of this chapter is the death penalty, one of major issues on the international human rights agenda. Punishing people with death has a history as old as society itself, and was not considered a human rights violation until the last decades of the twentieth century. Policy regarding the death penalty has been commonly

S. Bae (✉)
Northeastern Illinois University, Chicago, USA
e-mail: sbae@neiu.edu

understood to be the prerogative of national governments and, especially when a heinous crime is involved, people assumed that the state should demonstrate a fair and determined authority by imposing the ultimate punishment. With the increasing interest in human rights safeguards during the postwar period, however, the recognition of the "right to life" as a normative objective gained momentum. Over the past few decades, international bodies have increasingly made statements and adopted policies favoring the abolition of capital punishment on human rights grounds. The Universal Declaration of Human Rights, which was unanimously adopted by the United Nations General Assembly in 1948, declared that "everyone has the right to life, liberty and security of the person" (Article 3), and "no one shall be subjected to torture or to cruel, inhuman or degrading treatment or punishment" (Article 5). Thirty years after the introduction of the Universal Declaration, the United Nations General Assembly adopted a resolution to "progressively [restrict] the number of offenses for which the death penalty may be imposed with a view to the desirability of abolishing capital punishment." The International Covenant on Civil and Political Rights (ICCPR), adopted by the United Nations General Assembly in 1966 states, "Every human being has the inherent right to life." The covenant goes on to describe the path a state must follow if it wishes to continue using capital punishment with the aim of eventual abolition. The United Nations proclaimed its commitment to the abolition of capital punishment even more explicitly in the Second Optional Protocol to the International Covenant Aiming at the Abolition of the Death Penalty, which the UN General Assembly adopted in 1989. The protocol declared that "no one within the jurisdiction of a State Party to the present Protocol shall be executed" (Article 1.1) and that "each State Party shall take all necessary measures to abolish the death penalty within its jurisdiction" (Article 1.2). The only reservations permitted under the protocol are those that would provide "for the application of the death penalty in time of war pursuant to a conviction for a most serious crime of a military nature committed during wartime" (Article 2.1).

Perhaps most importantly, in December 2007, the United Nations General Assembly endorsed the call for all states that still maintain the death penalty to establish a moratorium on executions with a view to abolish the death penalty. The resolution was passed by a 104 to 54 vote, with 29 abstentions. Although UN General Assembly resolutions are not legally binding, a vote calling for a suspension of the death penalty, backed by a majority of countries, would be a significant statement of changing international opinion. At present, around 140 countries are fully abolitionist either in law or practice. The progress in recent years is quite remarkable given that in 1970 only 21 countries were considered abolitionist and in 1980 this number had risen to just 37. The norm that prohibits this "cruel, inhuman, and degrading" punishment has today become a dominant feature among the issues of international human rights as a legitimate focus of global attention.

At the regional level, Europe has always been most active in promoting the norm against the death penalty. As the first international legal instrument to embrace the abolition of the death penalty as a policy objective, Protocol No. 6 to the European Convention on Human Rights was open for ratification in 1983. Since then, states that wish to apply for membership to the Council of Europe have been expected to ratify it prior to admission. Both the European Union and the Council of Europe have explicitly demanded abolition of the death penalty as a formal, non-negotiable condition of membership. While Protocol No. 6 outlaws death sentences generally but it allows countries to retain capital punishment in time of war or imminent threat of war, Protocol No.13 adopted by the Council of Europe in 2002 requires the *total* abolition of the death penalty in all circumstances, permitting no exceptions. Over time, at least in Europe, the trend to abolish capital punishment is a vital component of human rights and human security norms and it has become stronger, more specific, and more subject to pressure from across national boundaries.

Other parts of the globe, including Africa and America, also see the growing movement to abolish the death penalty. In 1990, the Organization of American States (OAS) accepted the Protocol to the American Convention of Human Rights to Abolish the Death Penalty. While Article 4 of the American Convention had already placed severe restrictions to impose the death penalty – only applicable for the most serious crimes; no reinstatement once abolished; not to be used for political offenses or common crimes; not to be used against those aged under 18 or over 70, or against pregnant women – signing this protocol formalizes a state's commitment to refrain from using capital punishment in any peacetime circumstance. The continent of Africa is more ambiguous than its European and American counterparts in the view of the death penalty. Unlike the American Convention of Human Right and the European Convention on Human Rights, the African Charter of Human and People's Rights does not mention anything about the death penalty. Notwithstanding, the African Commission on Human and Peoples' Rights (African Commission) passed a resolution in 1999 and again in 2008 that African States should "observe a moratorium on the execution of death sentences with a view to abolishing the death penalty" (African Commission on Human and Peoples' Rights 2008).

East Asia, however, remains an area in which retention rather than abolition is the norm (Bae 2008a, b, 2009). China plays a leading role, as this country alone regularly accounts for more executions than the rest of the world combined, and applies it to as many as 70 crimes. In 2008, China carried out at least 1,718 executions, 72% of the total world executions (Amnesty International 2009). Japan, on the other hand, remains one of only two advanced democracies in the world (together with the United States) that still practice the death penalty. In Singapore, mandatory death sentences are given for murder, treason, and drug trafficking, giving the small city-state by far the highest per capita rate of executions in the world. In 2008, the majority of executions worldwide were carried out in 12 Asian countries including the aforementioned countries – China, Japan, and Singapore – and Indonesia, North Korea, Malaysia, Mongolia, and Vietnam. Such a predominant concentration of the death penalty makes Asia the most important region of the world when it comes to capital punishment. In fact, over 90% of all executions in the world take place in East Asia (Johnson and Zimring 2006: 89–95).

This chapter compares two major democracies in East Asia – Japan and South Korea – in their use of the death penalty. I address why different democratic countries are at fairly different stages in their movements toward abolition. Japan is one of only two advanced democracies in the world (the other is the United States) that still practice the death penalty. In contrast, South Korea marked 10 year moratorium on death penalty and became abolitionist in practice. Korea's state officials are forthcoming on a wide variety of abolitionist campaigns. The noticeable change in this country is particularly important because there is no external institution or authority enforcing the norm against capital punishment (Bae 2008b, 2009). Focusing on the interaction between the international norm and domestic factors that affect policy change, my analysis seeks to assess whether certain domestic factors help or hinder the impact of a norm concerning human rights and human security.

11.2 East Asia, a Death Penalty-Friendly Region

The notion of human security is both old and new. It is as old as Woodrow Wilson's famous 1918 speech laying out the "Fourteen Points" intended to guide the reconstruction of the world in the wake of World War I, in which he implicitly acknowledged that all nations should advance the living standards and human circumstances of their people. Franklin D. Roosevelt, in his State of the Union speech in 1941, referred to "freedom from fear" and "freedom from want" —terms often found in the UN documents and widely used in definitions of human security. Similar language was also embodied in the Covenant of the League of Nations and, most importantly, in the Charter of the United Nations. The UN Charter committed its member states to providing "higher standards of living, full employment, and conditions of economic and social progress and development, . . . [as well as] solutions of international economic, social, health, and related problems" as preconditions to continuing global "stability and well-being" (Charter of the United Nations, Article 55). A theoretical inspiration for human security came in part from Johan Galtung's peace studies in the 1970s, which emphasized the role of "structural violence," that is, violence built into the social system and expressed in the unequal distribution of power and, as a result, unequal opportunities (Galtung 1971, 1975). But the conceptual development of the idea of human security is new, because it was only after the end of the Cold War that the principles of human security became the focus of much attention in both academic and policy circles. Human security as an international policy agenda was first suggested in April 1991 in the Stockholm Initiative on Global Security and Governance. The Stockholm Initiative championed an alternative security discourse that shifted its focus from "political rivalry and armament" to "a wider concept of security, which deals also with threats that stem from failure in development, environmental degradation, excessive population growth and movement, and lack of progress towards democracy" (1991, 17–18). A timely and influential response to the Stockholm Initiative was the UN Development Programme's 1994 publication of the *Human Development Report*, which further articulated the notion of human security. In that report, the UN's description of the concept of human security closely resembles that of the Stockholm Initiative, moving "from an exclusive stress on territorial security to a much greater stress on people's security" and "from security through armaments to security through sustainable human development" (United Nations Development Programme 1994, 24).

The multilateral and normative nature of human security is even newer to East Asia (Acharya 2003; Tang 2003). The security environment in East Asia has changed since the end of the Cold War especially in terms of its strategic significance as a "hot spot" located at the intersection of the communist powers and free-market democracies. The demise of the Cold War, at the same time, did not have the same impact on East Asia as it had on Europe. Northeast Asia, in particular, is "still distinguished by continuing, if somewhat anachronistic, Cold War alliance systems linking the two Koreas, Japan, China, and the United States in a bilateralized regional security complex" (Kim 2004: 6). Despite dramatic political and social transformations the region experienced in the last few decades, much of the region's key security concerns are state-focused.

Regarding the death penalty, why do Asian countries so frequently impose capital punishment? Under the belief that only heinous criminals are executed, and that executions take place according to authorized and legal procedures, people support the death penalty as the state's legitimate sanction that makes society safer. Most countries that have abolished the death penalty have done so against this general public belief. For them, public opinion was not a principal factor in the abolitionist cause, partly because the choice between abolition and retention was a legal decision requiring judicial review in the courts, and partly because of constitutional protection for the rights of minorities and others who cannot protect their rights adequately through the democratic process. Abolition has, therefore, been a hot-button issue that puts the "good intentions" of the government—that is, its desire to establish international standards domestically—in sharp conflict with the public desire to maintain the status quo (Bae 2007). In addition, East Asian countries are subject to no binding multilateral checks on their domestic policies. With no outside pressure and surrounded by those who equally support capital punishment, Asian countries have little incentive to abolish the death penalty, which may explain why Asia leads the world in its use. In the Asian context, it is easy for those who favor the death penalty to argue that the norm against capital punishment is an imported idea that does not accord with their domestic norms.

In Japan, the death penalty is used sparingly, but its imposition has increased in recent years: one in 2005, four in 2006, nine in 2007, fifteen in 2008, and seven in 2009. By hanging two death row inmates in July 2010, Japan continued executions even after the new center-left government under the Democratic Party of Japan assumed power. The pattern of executions is also very distinct in Japan. All executions take place in extreme secrecy and silence. Neither prisoners nor their families are given advance warning of executions. The Justice Ministry announces hangings only after they have taken place and does so for inconsistent reasons. The names of those executed were made public for the first time only in December 2007. As David Johnson notes, "The Ministry of Justice … does not want prison officials to talk about the death penalty. Those who do talk get punished. In this sense, silence is professional common sense" (Johnson 2006: 253). Over the years, prosecutors in the Ministry of Justice have tended to assign execution dates strategically during the parliamentary recess and holiday periods, apparently in order to minimize publicity and avoid a parliamentary reaction. In 2007, for instance, four inmates, including two men in their seventies, were hanged on Christmas day, just days after Japan's

Diet closed for the year. Such bureaucratic secrecy has served to make the death penalty less salient in the public consciousness and to suppress public debate. Violent crime is relatively rare in Japan, and it has one of the lowest crime rates among industrial nations. Yet Japan, along with the United States, is one of the few advanced industrial democracies that still use the death penalty.

Public opinion surely matters to elected officials in any democracy. A broad problem facing abolition of the death penalty in East Asian countries or anywhere else is the public's common perception that social order would decay and that the country would become more dangerous because of rising crime rates. A public perception that the streets are not safe is not a very fertile ground for abolition of the death penalty. In Japan, since extensive polling started in 1953, support for the death penalty has never fallen below 50%. Despite ups and downs over time, pro–death penalty opinion managed to rise above 70%, reaching 80% at times (79.3% in 1999 and 81% in 2005, for instance) (*Japan Times*, 20 February 2005). The crime wave of the 1990s in Japan has led to a public clamor for tougher measures in Japan.

The government hardly expresses its position on the issue. Death sentences and executions are not commented on. State officials practice a "better not to talk about it" strategy (Johnson 2006: 256). According to Minister of Justice Hideo Usui, the death penalty is "simply not a social issue in Japan" (Struck 2001). However, recently appointed ministers felt the need to make public statements. After carrying out four executions on December 25, 2006, Justice Minister Jinen Nagase said: "I am aware of various opinions on the issue, but nearly 80% of the people in this country have no objection to the existence of the death penalty .... I don't have any plan to change the current justice system." Justice Minister Kunio Hatoyama, a staunch supporter of capital punishment, appointed in 2007, using the simile of "a conveyor belt," declared that executions should be carried out systematically (*Agence France-Presse*, 26 December 2006). The recent action of Justice Minister Keiko Chiba, a former member of the Japan parliamentary league against the death penalty, shows that politicians can act contrary to what they say or believe in. In July 2010, she signed the execution orders of two inmates, witnessed the executions, and said afterwards that she wanted to establish "a study group on the death penalty to determine whether the system should be maintained" (*Yomiuri Shimbun*, 29 July 2010).

Whenever possible, political leaders emphasize that the retention of the death penalty is the will of the Japanese public. Before the UN General Assembly in November 1982, the Japanese representative stated, "The majority of the Japanese people support the retention of the death penalty for criminals who have committed especially abominable crimes, and approve of it as an effective deterrent against such criminals" (Schmidt 2001: 61). This line of argument has been repeated over the years. In an interview for the *Washington Post* in January 2005, Hideo Takasaki, a senior official of the Ministry of Justice's criminal affairs bureau said, "We believe that the decision whether to keep or abolish the death penalty should be the decision of each individual country, and should be based on the public sentiment of each country, and the crime situation in each country" (Lane 2005). When the UN General Assembly adopted the Second Optional Protocol to the International Covenant on Civil and Political Rights Aiming at the Abolition of the Death Penalty, only two industrialized countries voted against it: the United States and Japan.

Prisoners can apply for pardons based on the Amnesty Law, which empowers the cabinet to commute death sentences. However, the prime minister has used this right only three times in the past four decades—in 1969, 1970, and 1975. This is in stark contrast to South Korea's case, where a single president (Kim Dae-jung) commuted 13 death sentences to life imprisonment during his 5 year tenure. Even politicians who oppose capital punishment rarely speak about their view on capital punishment to their constituents. Of the 762 members of the Diet, 122 had joined "the Diet Members League for the Abolition of Capital Punishment (*shikei haishi o sokushin suru giin renmeikai*) in 2003. But this number shrank to 72 in 2008 (Makino 2008). Only two or three of these Diet members officially acknowledge their views to the electorate, and the rest, fearing punishment at the ballot box, remain silent (Johnson 2006: 256).

Since the United Nations' Development Report suggested a holistic approach to security in 1994, some countries took the initiative in promoting this new concept. Japan, in particular, has been one of the most seminal advocates and the largest donor to this UN-led innovative human security campaign. Japan adopted the principle of human security as a pillar of foreign policy and its language is widely used in official policy documents (Akiyama 2004). Japanese prime ministers, foreign ministers, and other top representatives have made numerous speeches specifically on Japan and human security. Japan established a Trust Fund for Human Security within the United Nations in 1999, its contributions amounted to $300 million by 2007, making it the largest trust fund established through the UN (Ministry of Foreign Affairs of Japan).

Assessments of Japan's active role in human security vary, however: "Japan is no longer branded as an aspiring military power by its domestic and international critics" (Lam 2006: 141–159), "Compared to the success of Canada, Japan's human security policy presents many limits and failures" (Ho 2008: 101–112), and "Japan's involvement in human security serves its neorealist interest in 'normalization'" (von Feigenblatt 2007). Any study of human security, if it is to be sincere, cannot avoid engaging in highly controversial debates regarding the role of the government and its political motives. No matter what intentions the Japanese government might have, the country's generous contribution to the global project on human security has been highly appreciated by the United Nations and other international organizations. It is, therefore, a puzzle why Japan is unwilling to embrace the widely-accepted norm against the death penalty while this country greatly contributes to the UN-led human security project. The abolition of the death penalty and the advancement of human security, in principle, come from the same spirit: the protection and promotion of the basic rights of human beings.

In contrast, South Korea has maintained a moratorium on executions since the election of President Kim Dae-jung in December 1997, and no executions occurred under the Roh Moo-hyun government. In legislation, bills on the abolition of the death penalty have been presented to the National Assembly three times, in 1999, 2001, and 2005. In 2003, the Constitutional Court declared unconstitutional several death penalty provisions in special criminal acts on the ground of disproportionality (Korean Constitutional Court 2003). The Supreme Court handed down a decision in February 2002 on a murder case in which the Military Court had twice ruled in favor of the death sentence. The Court ruled as follows: "The death penalty was too severe as the crime was committed on impulse, and the defendant has had no trouble with the law in the past and had been faithful to his military duties before committing the criminal act … he has ample potential to correct himself" (*Hankyoreh*, 23 February 2002). It was unprecedented for the Supreme Court to overturn the lower court's judgment on the ground that the defendant had the potential to reform. Similar rulings have been made in the criminal courts. In February 2004, a person who committed a heinous murder was sentenced to life imprisonment instead of receiving the death penalty. In the concurring opinion, the court stated, "If this crime had happened 10 years ago, the death penalty might have been applied. Yet considering the growing social concerns about the death penalty and its relations with human rights, we sentence him to life imprisonment. Human rights are entitled to everyone including those who have committed the worst crimes" (*Donga Ilbo*, 5 February 2004). In May 2005, the criminal court also sentenced a person who had committed multiple homicides to life imprisonment. The court stated, "It seems inevitable to impose the ultimate punishment on the most heinous crime such as this one. But the death penalty is a truly exceptional punishment that a civilized country's judicial system can impose. It is allowed only in special and objective situations that can be justified by the responsibility for the crime and aim of the punishment" (*Hankyoreh*, 13 May 2005). A series of recent court decisions, in marked contrast to Japan's Supreme Court decisions in favor of the death penalty, and the suspension of executions for the past 9 years suggest that Korea distinguishes itself from its neighbors, gradually moving toward a death-penalty-free society.

Korea's National Human Rights Commission (NHRC) cited the right to life as the primary grounds for its recommendation of abolition. The NHRC contends that capital punishment violates not only the right to life but also provisions against disproportionate punishment and cruel and unusual punishment (The National Human Rights Commission of Korea). Several legislative initiatives are noteworthy. The first of its kind in Korea, the Special Bill for the Abolition of the Death Penalty was submitted in 1999 to the National Assembly with the assent of 91 of the 299 members. The major premise of the Bill is to remove the provision of the death penalty from the Criminal Code and the Special Act, and to make life imprisonment the maximum punishment. Two years later, in 2001, the bill commuting the death penalty to life imprisonment was again presented to the National Assembly. This time it carried stronger political weight, since it was submitted with the signatures of 155 lawmakers from both the ruling and opposition parties. This number exceeded the 137 needed to pass a bill in the 273-seat unicameral National Assembly. For a bill to be enacted, however, it must first be approved by a majority of the 15-member Legislative and Judiciary Committee before being sent to a floor vote in the Assembly. These two attempts, however, went nowhere: the bills could not even pass the Legislative and Judiciary Committee of the National Assembly. In 2005, the debate over the death penalty was revived in the National Assembly for the third time in 6 years, when a group of 175 lawmakers again submitted the abolition bill. As the same bill has been repeatedly presented, more and more lawmakers have joined the cause and put their names to it. They share the view that it is a contradiction to take the life of a criminal in the name of justice, that doing so is at odds with the idea of human dignity and the right to life guaranteed by the Constitution. According to Representative Yoo Ihn-tae, who took the lead in drafting the 2005 bill, "it is contrary to the spirit of the Constitution that the government wields the power to take the life of a human being." Echoing his senior lawmaker Chyung Dai-chul, a major proponent of the 2001 bill to abolish the death penalty, Yoo called the abolition an "irreversible global trend" as more and more countries are joining the movement to abolish the death penalty worldwide (*Hankook Times*, 4 March 2008). To end capital punishment, according to them, is to join an international human rights project.

The abolitionist movement in South Korea seems to stimulate public debate on the death penalty, which until recently had been almost entirely absent. As the debate has continued, public support for the death penalty has lessened. According to a 2001 poll conducted, 36% of 838 respondents over the age of 20 opposed the death penalty, compared with 34% in 1999 and 20% in 1994 (*Korea Herald*, 4 December 2001). Other polls have yielded similar findings. The Korea Survey Research Organization poll in 2002 found that 54% favored the death penalty and 45% were against it. When the same questions were asked in 1992, 67% were in favor of the death penalty, while only 20% opposed it (Chyung 2002: 11). Gallup Korea's survey confirmed that opponents of capital punishment have significantly increased over the years: 20% opposed it in 1994, 31% in 2001, and 40% in 2003. In 1994, 70% of Koreans reportedly supported the death penalty; this had dropped to 55% by 2001, and to 52% by 2003 (Gallup Korea 2003). Certainly a majority of South Koreans still support capital punishment, yet a growing number favor its abolition (Bae 2009).

While hopes for abolishing the death penalty were growing among human rights advocates, the Constitutional Court upheld the retention of the death penalty in South Korea. The Constitutional Court ruled in February 2010 that the death penalty does not violate the constitution saying that: "The death penalty is a kind of punishment that the current constitution expects, and cannot be seen as a measure that profoundly infringes upon the dignity of human life." Lee Kang-kook, president of the Court said executing serious criminals helped "protect innocent ordinary citizens and significant public interests" adding that "society needs to change more before it is scrapped" (*Yonhap News*, 25 February 2010). It was the second time after 1996 that the Constitutional Court of South Korea has ruled in favor of the death penalty.

One might argue that the Court's 5–4 decision in 2010 proves that support for the death penalty has decreased in the Constitutional Court compared to a 7–2 verdict in 1996. But most human rights advocates expressed regret over the decision arguing that it might be influenced by the position of the government. In fact the Lee Myong-bak government, the ruling Grand National Party, and the Ministry of Justice have repeatedly stated that the death penalty is a legitimate form of punishment and the government may consider renewing executions. During the open hearing held in June 2009, the representative from the ministry insisted that "Capital punishment has been proven to have a greater effect than a life sentence in preventing violent crimes …. There is little chance of the system being abused or misused" (*Korea Herald*, 26 February 2010). Kim Kyung-han, the Minister of Justice said: "[I] seriously consider resuming executions." The position of the Ministry of Justice under the Lee administration is in contrast with the ministry's stance on the death penalty in 2006 when it was conducting "a fundamental research on the necessity of the death penalty in order to answer a social and political request to abolish the death penalty" (*Korea Herald*, 24 February 2006). The ruling of the Constitutional Court in 2010 and the changed position of the Ministry of Justice in recent years demonstrate how easily issues related to the death penalty are influenced by the executive in South Korea. Would the verdict of the Constitutional Court have been the same if Korea had a President who opposes the death penalty? Wouldn't the Ministry of Justice have continued to review the possibility to end the death penalty if the President was supporting abolition? In light of the history of Korean politics where the judiciary is often criticized for its lack of independent power, it seems very unlikely that the death penalty will be abolished by the courts independently in South Korea without active support and coordination from the government.

Previous research suggests a weak correlation between political turnover and a state's death-penalty policy. The European experience showed that once the death penalty was abolished, it is very likely to remain so even if a different government takes over (Bohm 2003; Zimring and Hawkins 1986). Asia, however, provides counter-examples, such as Bangladesh, Indonesia, Japan, Malaysia and Thailand, whereby the death penalty was reinstated after several years of disuse (Johnson and Zimring 2006: 93). David Johnson and Franklin Zimring stated that, "If formal abolition happens there [in South Korea] and is followed by an orderly transition to a government of the right, … then it will become an important test of how quickly abolition gets institutionalized in East Asia" (2008: 110). In this sense, the resilience of South Korea's moratorium on executions will be tested under the administration of Lee Myong-bak. If South Korea joins its Asian neighbors and returns to practicing the death penalty, it will strengthen the argument of the impenetrability of international human rights norms in East Asia. If, however, South Korea continues on its path towards formal abolition, it will demonstrate that the international norm against the death penalty is capable of establishing roots even in death-penalty-friendly Asia.

11.3 Conclusion: "If It Ain't Broke, Don't Fix It!"

When the public favors an international norm, it is obviously easier for the government to formally embrace it. Even if political leadership does not favor a particular norm, a state may adopt it. One example is the norm of democratization, which can be forced by internal or external power against the will of an authoritarian leadership. When an international norm is in conflict with values and practices established in the domestic sphere, political actors are likely to find that appeals to the international norm are ineffective in garnering support for a particular policy. Thus, when a norm does not resonate with public opinion, political leadership is essential for its adoption. In the case of the death penalty, the general public in most countries supports to keep it, suggesting that the abolition is likely to require strong political leadership.

Undoubtedly the role of political leadership in South Korea under the administrations of Kim Dae-jung and Roh Moo-hyun was crucial in the government's adoption of an international norm, mostly because the norm was unpopular among the majority of the population. In achieving de facto abolition of capital punishment, South Korea's case indicates that the state can nonetheless endorse an international human rights norm even when it does not resonate with domestic preference. Political leadership may be as significant as widespread domestic opinion and beliefs—and often more important—in bringing international norms of human rights and human security into the domestic arena and bringing about policy change.

Another interesting point about the abolition of the death penalty is that it was abolished more quickly in countries that experienced radical regime change. Much of the empirical research has been conducted to suggest a positive correlation between the occurrence of important historical events (such as wars, revolutions or major crises) and the likelihood of policy change. Many of these key events are hypothesized to trigger elite learning (Jones 1994; Keeler 1993; Levy 1994). Drastic political transformation or political crises often create a sociopolitical context for governance uniquely conducive to the passage of reforms. The political transition captures and broadens the imagination of policymakers, leading them to question commitments to existing norms and practices. They "open the window for reform," and decision-makers are more willing to listen to new ideas espoused by transnational actors or regional governments (Keeler 1993: 434). As Bryan Jones points out, it is very likely that the sudden flurry of interest caused by "discontinuous and non-incremental" transformation leads to and influences changes in a nation's political agenda (Jones 1994: 87). At the international level, some type of discrete events or political shocks, such as "world wars, acts of terrorism, or horrific human rights abuses" can provide the impetus for international legal change to occur (Diehl, Ku and Zamora 2003: 57–58). When a regime changes drastically from authoritarianism to democracy, the new government usually adopts different kinds of human rights discourse in order to distinguish itself from the former authoritarian rule that marginalized human rights norms and actors.

The history of the European Convention on Human Rights is a good example. After the catastrophe of two world wars, followed by the vulnerability of their postwar democracies, western European countries created the Convention in order to combat both communist subversion and the resurgence of fascism. A common human rights framework and standard, enforced by a supranational court, was accepted by sovereign states in the hope to stabilize and neutralize any unrest in the new democratic regimes in Germany, Italy, and France. In the case of the death penalty, Germany after Nazism, Italy after fascism, and Portugal, Peru, Nicaragua, Brazil, Argentina, the Philippines, Spain, and most recently East Timor and Rwanda all abolished capital punishment after emerging from periods of severe repression, suggesting a certain relationship between the degree of human misery and constitutional progress.

This insight explains in part why Japan continues to practice the death penalty. Since the end of World War II, Japan enjoyed distinctive democratic regimes, which are stable, continuous, and legitimate. Though Japan was certainly a losing power, it was not treated as such. Defeated in war, occupied, and considered to be of central importance in Asia's regional order during the Cold War, Japan became a key client of the United States first, and then a close ally. Mainly due to its strategic significance and partly due to what it suffered from the bombings of Hiroshima and Nagasaki, Japan was hardly asked to apologize by Western powers or forced to have the feeling of remorse or guilt. When the United States has enhanced its self-perceptions about "a triumphal history" (Kahn 2005: 199), Japan stood by without lessening its own desire for greatness. In Japan, political leaders enjoy extreme stability and political continuity, having little incentives to comply with an unwanted norm and enact bold reforms. The stability of the domestic democratic system is an important force for the explanation of noncompliance. The extreme stability in their democratic system hinders political actors from adopting new norms and changing their existing local norms and beliefs. Democratic stability and legitimacy have constructed an unwavering identity through time. Therefore, any political and legal attempt to improve their democratic system that already works is pointless and may even be detrimental ("If it ain't broke, don't fix it").

References

Acharya, A. (2003). Guns and butter: Why do human security and traditional security co-exist in Asia? *Global Economic Review, 32*(3), 1–21.
African Commission on Human and Peoples' Rights. (2008). ACHPR/Res.136 (XXXXIIII).08: Resolution calling on state parties to observe the moratorium on the death penalty. http://www.achpr.org/english/resolutions/resolution136_en.htm.Accessed 5 May 2010 .
Agence France-Presse. (2006, December 26). Japanese minister vows more executions.
Akiyama, N. (2004). Human security at the crossroad: Human security in the Japanese foreign policy context, IPSHU English Research Report Series 19, Hiroshima: Institute for Peace Science of Hiroshima University.
Amnesty International. (2009). Death sentences and executions in 2008. http://www.amnesty.org/en/library/info/ACT50/008/2009/en. Accessed 5 May 2010.
Axworthy, L. (2001). Human security and global governance: Putting people first. *Global Governance, 7*, 19–23.
Bae, S. (2007). *When the state no longer kills: International human rights norms and the abolition of capital punishment*. Albany: SUNY Press.
Bae, S. (2008a). Is the death penalty an Asian value? *Asian Affairs, 39*(1), 47–56.
Bae, S. (2008b). The abolitionist movement in death penalty-friendly Asia. In J. Yorke (Ed.), *Against the death penalty: International initiatives* (pp. 220–246). London: Ashgate.
Bae, S. (2009). South Korea's de facto abolition of the death penalty. *Pacific Affairs, 82*(3), 407–425.
Baldwin, D. (1997). The concept of security. *Review of International Studies, 23*(1), 5–26.
Bohm, R. M. (2003). The economic costs of capital punishment: Past, present, and future. In J. A. Acker, R. M. Bohm, & C. S. Lanier (Eds.), *America's experiment with capital punishment: Reflections on the past, present, and future of the ultimate penal sanction* (pp. 572–594). Durham: Carolina Academic Press.
Chyung, D.C. (2002). Capital punishment abolition campaign in Korea and its prospect. Paper presented at a seminar on justice and human rights in council of Europe observer states: The abolition of the death penalty. Tokyo, Japan, 4–5 May.
Diehl, P., Ku, C., & Zamora, D. (2003). The dynamics of international law: The interaction of normative and operating systems. *International Organization, 57*(1), 43–75.
Donga Ilbo (2004, February 5) Life imprisonment for murderers.

Evans, P. (2004). Human security and East Asia: In the beginning. *Journal of East Asian Studies, 4*(2), 263–284.
Gallup Korea. (2003, September 27). Gallup poll: Should the death penalty be abolished?.
Galtung, J. (1971). A structural theory of imperialism. *Journal of Peace Research, 8*(2), 81–117.
Gasper, D. (2005). Securing humanity: Situating 'human security' as concept and discourse. *Journal of Human Development, 6*(2), 221–245.
Hankook Times (2008, March 4). Human rights movement – Korea's campaign to abolish the death penalty.
Hankyoreh (2002, February 23). Supreme court made a decision on a murder case.
Ho, S. (2008). Japan's human security policy: A critical review of its limits and failures. *Japanese Studies, 28*(1), 101–112.
Johnson, D. T. (2006). Where the state kills in secret: Capital punishment in Japan. *Punishment & Society, 8*(3), 251–285.
Johnson, D. T., & Zimring, F. E. (2006). Taking capital punishment seriously. *Asian Journal of Criminology, 1*, 89–95.
Johnson, D. T., & Zimring, F. E. (2008). Law, society, and capital punishment in Asia. *Punishment & Society, 10*(2), 103–115.
Jones, B. D. (1994). *Reconceiving decision-making in democratic politics*. Chicago: University of Chicago Press.
Kahn, P. W. (2005). American exceptionalism, popular sovereignty, and the rule of law. In M. Ignatieff (Ed.), *American exceptionalism and human rights* (pp. 198–222). Princeton: Princeton University Press.
Kay, C. (1997). *Globalisation, competitiveness and human security*. London: Routledge.
Keeler, J. T. S. (1993). Opening the window for reform: Mandates, crises, and extraordinary policy-making. *Comparative Political Studies, 25*(4), 433–486.
Kim, S. S. (2004). *The international relations of Northeast Asia*. Oxford: Rowman & Littlefield.
Korea Herald (2001, December 4). Anti-death penalty: a prayer for the dying.
Korea Herald (2006, February 24). Debate on death penalty.
Korea Herald (2010, February 26). Court rules death penalty constitutional.
Korean Constitutional Court. (2003). Han Ba 24 (Decision of 27 November).
Lam, Peng Er. (2006). Japan's human security role in Southeast Asia. *Contemporary Southeast Asia: A Journal of International and Strategic Affairs, 28*(1), 141–159.
Lane, C. (2005). Why Japan still has the death penalty. *The Washington Post*, 16 January. http://www.washingtonpost.com/wp-dyn/articles/A11306-2005Jan15.html. Accessed 5 May 2010.
Levy, J. S. (1994). Learning and foreign policy: Sweeping a conceptual minefield. *International Organization, 48*(2), 279–312.
Makino, C. (2008). Death penalty – Japan: No "conveyor belt" executions – Abolitionists, *Inter Press Service News Agency*, 12 March. http://ipsnews.net/news.asp?idnews=41561. Accessed 5 May 2010.
Newman, E. (2001). Human security and constructivism. *International Studies Perspectives, 2*(3), 239–251.
Schmidt, P. (2001). *Capital punishment in Japan*. Leiden, the Netherlands: Brill.
Stockholm Initiative on Global Security and Governance. (1991, April 22). *Common responsibility in the 1990s: The Stockholm initiative on global security and governance*. Stockholm, Sweden Prime Minister's Office.
Struck, D. (2001). On Japan's death row: Uncertainty by design. *The Washington Post*, 3 May.
Tang, J. T. H. (2003). A regional approach to human security in East Asia: Gglobal debate, regional insecurity and the role of civil society. Paper read at international conference on human security in East Asia, Seoul, South Korea.
The Cabinet Office of Japan. (n.d.). Public opinion survey on the death penalty. http://www8.cao.go.jp/survey/h16/h16-houseido/index.html. Accessed 5 May 2010.
The National Human Rights Commission of Korea. (n.d.). Sahyŏngjedoe daehan kugminuisikjŏsa [Public opinion survey on the death penalty]. http://library.humanrights.go.kr/global/docs/s_detail.html?mastid=20242. Accessed 5 May 2010.

United Nations Development Program (UNDP). (1994). New dimensions of human security. *Human Development Report*. New York: Oxford University Press.

von Feigenblatt, O. (2007). Japan and human security: 21st Century ODA Policy apologetics and discursive Co-optation, Ph.D. Dissertation. Bangkok: Chulalongkorn University.

Yomiuri Shimbun, T. (2010, July 29). Chiba: It was my duty to watch – Justice minister says death penalty discussions should start a new. http://www.yomiuri.co.jp/dy/national/20100729TDY02T09.htm. Accessed 1 Aug 2010.

Yonhap News (2010, February 25). Constitutional court rules in favor of death penalty.

Zimring, F. E., & Hawkins, G. (1986). *Capital punishment and the American agenda*. New York: Cambridge University Press.

Chapter 12
An Emerging Human Security Threat on Pacific Island States: Analyzing Legal and Political Implications of Territorial Inundation*

Chih-Chieh Chou

12.1 Introduction

The Inconvenient Truth, Al Gore's documentary film rewarded by an Oscar in 2007, elicits conflictual discussions and diverse views on the effects of climate change in the United States and other industrialized states. The climate crisis has particularly jeopardized small island states even more than developed ones, and the threats there are already present. As Paul Telukluk, the Minister for Lands, Energy and Environment of Vanuatu, said: "The impacts of climate change are cross cutting and affect all sectors. Most of Vanuatu's economic sectors are climate sensitive and are often affected by climate extremes" (Willie 2001). Actually, the tsunami disaster in December 2004 inundated half of Mahe, the Capital of Maldives, a small island state (SIS) in the Indian Ocean. The Maldives Tourist Office even ran an ironic advertisement urging tourists to come and visit Maldives before it is too late (*Space Daily* 2005). A storm hitting the South Pacific in November 2003 caused many islands to be completely submerged, including 95% of the territory of Kiribati and nine uninhabited islands in Tuvalu, another two small island states.

The international community appears to be gradually acknowledging the phenomenon of sea level change produced by global warming, a major effect accompanied with the deterioration of the global ecological system. Global tides rose by an average of between 10 and 20 cm over the twentieth century, a trend to which global warming "has contributed significantly" (BBC News 2001a). Over the next 100 years, the global average for sea-level rise is expected to be 5 mm a year (IPCC 2001).

---

*This work is mainly supported by the Landmark Project of National Cheng Kung University titled "Nexus between Sea Level Change and Nationhood: Strategy on Political and Legal Consequences of Territorial Inundation" (A0110), and is part of a research project titled "Practice and Development on Human Security in Regional Governmental Organizations" (NSC 99-2410-H-006-062). The author wishes to express his gratitude to the anonymous reviewers for their insightful comments.

C.-C. Chou (✉)
National Cheng Kung University, Tainan, Taiwan
e-mail: ccchou@mail.ncku.edu.tw

A new report suggests sea-levels in the Asia-Pacific region could rise by up to 16 cm by 2030 and up to 50 cm by 2070. A half-meter rise would affect more than 100,000 km of coastline (Friends of the Earth Australia 2007: 3; Panichi 2001). As early as November 2001, Tuvalu announced that its entire people would migrate to New Zealand as a result of its slowly diminishing geographic territory (Kirby 1999, 2004). In 2002, Koloa Talake, the Prime Minister of Tuvalu, had further threatened litigation in the International Court of Justice against Australia, claiming industrial pollution was contributing to the inundation of his country: this threat was withdrawn after the election (*Space Daily* 2002a; BBC News 2002). Speaking at a Commonwealth meeting in February 2002, Talake said: "Flooding is already coming right into the middle of the islands, destroying food crops and trees which were there when I was born 60 years ago. These things are gone, somebody has taken them and global warming is the culprit" (*Space Daily* 2002b).

Attempting to boost the visibility of their plight, Tuvalu, Kiribati, and other small island states have raised the issue of sea level change at various international fora, including the United Nations, the South Pacific Forum, and the South Asian Association for Regional Cooperation (SAARC) (Allen 2004: 755). With support from the UN, they have also worked in response to this situation through the Alliance of Small Island States (AOSIS) – which includes 43 island states and territories as members – established at UN level in 1993. The scenario raises various questions of marine ecological conservation, sustainable development, challenge of sovereignty, and people's relocation and immigration, and contained several emotional appeals: a humanitarian concern for displaced people, sensitivity to Third World poverty, and moral questions about who was responsible versus who was suffering (Lockhart et al. 1993; Chou 2005: 8).

As a North–south issue, sea level change had resonance, for it seemed particularly cruel that small and poor island states like Tuvalu and Kiribati were to be the first major victims of global climate change (Hay 2001; Kirby 1999). Pacific island states have received the most attention on this issue due to their particularly fragile ecosystems and persisting stereotypes as peaceful tropical island paradises. Despite this, these incidents do not receive very much attention internationally. The major polluting nations remain slow to cut their production of greenhouse gases. Even in the SAARC regional forum, global warming and sea level change was but one issue among many.

It was also a controversial issue. The connection between industrial pollution in the North and sea surges in island states is difficult to prove. While the science was arcane, the argument caught the attention of some journalists and environmental activists. The issue has been studied widely. The UN's Intergovernmental Panel on Climate Change (IPCC) has estimated a global average change of 5–25 cm by 2030 and up to 20–70 cm by 2070 (Watson et al. 1998; UNEP 2007). These estimates have been subject to criticism as both over-and under-estimating the phenomena. However, whatever impacts do occur, they will not be uniform over the entire globe. Certain countries are far more vulnerable to the effects than others (Gillespie and Burns 2000: 17; Paterson 1996: 12). Rising seas pose many challenges, the worst being the displacement of local inhabitants, victims of environmental changes over which they have little control.

Sea level change potentially impacts all coastal states. The danger to small states is simply more extreme: loss of scarce arable land or even inundation: vanishing completely beneath the waves. While not a major international issue, even in the field of environmental politics, sea level change is significant for numerous reasons that range from ecology to humanitarianism. Even small amounts of land loss in tiny Tuvalu, only 10 square miles of land lying only 15 ft above sea level, has the makings of a major humanitarian disaster.

The loss or disappearance of state territory also raises issues of law and sovereignty. Land loss changes the boundaries of territorial waters and Exclusive Economic Zones (EEZ), important for their economic value. Complete inundation raises the question of residual rights of a state that has "vanished" in an unprecedented way. What happens if a state loses a large portion of its territory to a "natural" process that is attributed to the industrial activities of, or based in, other states? Sea level change is a sovereignty question for both sinking states and for those alleged to be responsible (Henkin 1990; Hurrell 2000; Philpott 2001). Small island states may face the loss of territorial statehood but polluting states could face international accountability (or at least challenges) for their domestic economic activities.

The scenarios discussed here are predicted (not with any certainty) to occur over the next 50–100 years, a very long time in the world of policy making. However, the issue raises interesting questions for international relations theory. What is the abstraction called "the sovereign state" and how is it related to, or distinguished from, the physical reality of territory? The issue of sea level change is challenging because of the traditional connection drawn between territory and state sovereignty. The Westphalian nation-state is defined according to its territory and its boundaries with other territories. Does the erosion of physical territory produce an erosion of sovereignty? Does this have any significance for the future of the sovereign state as presently conceived? Can sovereignty exist separately from territory? This chapter attempts to explore these questions, based on existing understandings of international law and the principle of sovereignty.

12.2 Sunken Territory and Sovereignty

12.2.1 Identifying the 'Sea Level Change' Problem

Among the loss of biodiversity, desertification, deforestation, global warming, ozone depletion, and various forms of pollution, Sea level change is also one of major issues of the broader phenomena of global climate change. The rise in average temperatures around the world, known as global warming and the greenhouse effect, is an outgrowth of industrial society. Global warming is the predicted outcome of an increase in atmospheric carbon dioxide that increases the amount of solar radiation retained by the Earth's atmosphere. Atmospheric carbon dioxide has increased dramatically in the past century, due to the use of fossil fuels and the burning of forests. One predicted effect of this increased global temperature is the melting of the vast reservoirs of ice in glaciers and in polar ice packs. The amount of ice at the poles is tremendous. For example, if the West Antarctic icecap were added to the world's oceans, it would raise global sea level by 5–7 m (Kellogg 1989: 54).

However, the science of global warming remains controversial. It is difficult to separate events caused by natural variations or changes and those attributable to human activity. Natural fluctuations may have multiple causes; some sea level changes observed in recent years may be due to the *El Nino* phenomena. Other studies claim that Pacific islands are not sinking and that the Antarctic is getting cooler rather than warmer (Weart 2006; Sports 2002). The consensus position developed over the past two decades is that the mean global temperature has risen by between 0.3°C and 0.6°C in the past century (*Space Daily* 2001; Paterson 1996: 9). Evidence of the effects of this increase is seen in the shrinking of glaciers and the "poleward and altitudinal shifts of plants and animal ranges" as tropical species migrant northward, southward and to higher elevations (Tiempo 2001). The consensus view is that this trend will continue in the next century. Sea level change is one of numerous effects predicted by global warming models.

If the consensus view is correct and global warming and sea level change are occurring, the impact will not be equally distributed around the world. Coastal states are of course the most vulnerable, especially those with large coastal populations. States with dependence on oceanic resources (fishing, oil, trade, tourism) will suffer more should sea levels change. However, as Paterson (1996: 78) noted, not all coastal states are equal in responsive capacity. Both Bangladesh and the Netherlands are sensitive to changes in sea to level and both have large populations in vulnerable areas. They are, however, certainly not equal in their access to technology and financial resources to combat sea level change.

States that are most vulnerable to sea level change are the small island states scattered around the globe, some in chains or clusters and others solitary. These island states cannot easily be typified. They range from fairly large, heavily populated places, like Cuba (11 million people) to tiny atolls with populations in their thousands, like Kiribati and Maldives in the Indian Ocean. The smaller SISs are the most vulnerable, as many lie only a few feet above sea level and have no imaginable hinterland. Their populations are therefore more susceptible to displacement, should land be lost to the sea.

12.2.2 Legal Fundamental of Sovereignty

International politics is defined by sovereignty to a degree far greater than any other concept (Strange 1996; Katzenstein 1996; Jackson 1999). Even the notion of power is premised on the assumption that actors are sovereign and wield power in the name of and for the protection/promotion of, state sovereignty. Authority is dispersed internationally and no one locus of authority legitimately predominates (Hurrell 2000; Henkin 1990). International organizations may serve as moral authorities or as expressions of collective will, but they do not hold sovereignty. That remains the exclusive privilege of the state.

Sovereignty itself is a term with many subtle facets. Several scholars of international relations have attempted to unravel the concept of sovereignty and drawn different conclusions. Steven Krasner's 1999 book *Sovereignty* breaks the concept down into functional elements. There are four basic meanings of sovereignty according to Krasner, three of which emphasize authority and control. The first, domestic sovereignty, refers to "the organization of public authority within a state and to the level of effective control" (1999: 9). The second meaning is interdependence, control over cross-border activities. Westphalian sovereignty refers to "the exclusion of external actors" from domestic authority. These three senses all relate to the issue of controlling the destiny of an entity. The fourth meaning Krasner cites does not stress control but rather is a membership trait: mutual recognition and international legal sovereignty.

The concept of sovereignty is strongly connected to territory and territorial jurisdiction (Charney 1999: 863–865; Jackson 1990). The basic understanding of international law and diplomatic practice is that a state needs to have territory to qualify as a state. Members of the UN are all territorially constituted states with recognized and regulated, though not always uncontested, borders. However, what Krasner defines as "Westphalian sovereignty" is not an essential feature of UN membership. The UN and the US accepted the membership of the Ukrainian and Belorussian republics of the USSR as UN members, when clearly neither was yet sovereign in any sense. India became a founding member of the UN when still a British colony. One could also question how much Westphalian sovereignty UN members Micronesia, Palau, and the Marshall Islands actual have when the US handles their defense. These anomalies aside, no non-territorial entity is a member of the UN.

Despite the emphasis on territory, there are exceptions. Certain entities, such as the Palestinian Authority or governments in exile have been accorded diplomatic recognition despite their lack of *de facto* control over territory. However the exceptions themselves speak to the importance of land: governments in exile and liberation movements both claim to represent a legal or moral claim to land. Sovereignty remains tied to territory. Even when claims of legitimacy are based on a "people's" aspirations, those aspirations are territorial based. Therefore, "people" and "nation" are given a "territorial connotation," not an ethnic or cultural one (Gottlieb 1993: xiii; Douglas 2006). The emphasis on land is more parsimonious: territory is concrete, measurable and more easily set by boundaries. Identity, loyalty, and affinity are more amorphous and subjective.

However, sovereignty is still based in part on population. An authority without subjects is not a state. Territory must be inhabited, at least partially, for it to be regarded as a state. Inhabited, arable lands, and regions that can sustain human habitation are all part of a state's territory (Ruggie 1993; Wendt 1992). However, the population is still assumed to be present in a coherent, distinguishable parcel of land. Territory and population must coincide for sovereignty to be possible (Schachter 1997). A dispersed population without a homeland may be recognized as a nation (think of the Jews before the setting up of the state of Israel), but would not be recognized as sovereign.

The final qualifications for sovereignty are diplomatic in nature. An entity must be able to engage in international relations with other states, and enjoy the recognition by other states as a member of the international community. Such recognition would accord the state the potential to join international bodies, sign treaties, enjoy privileges of diplomatic immunity, and international legal equality. However, non-state actors may play a role in diplomacy. Rosenau argues that international relations is less about sovereignty and more about relational principles of authority and bargaining (1990: 40–42). Such bargaining is not the sole purview of states, since international NGOs (like Greenpeace) play a vital role. Nonetheless, states remain the primary actors in international law and diplomacy; NGOs pay a role but mainly in efforts to shape state action.

Despite the importance of the sovereign state to diplomacy, the state itself is not defined clearly under international law. The clearest definitions of international law are located in treaties, the most basic being the Vienna Conventions that govern diplomatic relations and treaty law.[1] The Conventions are highly specific on certain points, but not regarding the characteristics of a state, the *Vienna Convention on the Law of Treaties* (1969, I, Article 2) goes to great lengths to define the terms "treaty," "full powers," "reservations," and other key concepts but does not define the term "state." States are defined only in regards to their acceptance of the Convention. What exactly constitutes a "state" is left undefined.

This silence is due to several factors. First, there may be a sense that the issue is self-evident. Only states are members of the UN, only states operate embassies with diplomatic immunity, and only states, or organizations of states, sign treaties. As only a state can be party to a treaty, all those that are parties to a treaty are states. Beyond this circular reasoning lies the political issue of statehood. To clearly define what constitutes a "state" would be to create a clear standard that various aspirants to statehood could appeal to. This could encourage challenges from entities or movements claiming the status of "states."

Within the field of international relations theory, the concept of the state has also been central (Waltz 1979; Wendt 1992; Watts 2000). The accepted characteristics of state are more clearly defined, as discussed above. An entity with territory, people, and a government therefore merely requires the assent of other states to be regarded as a state. Nonetheless, the smallest of the world's states have long been a challenge to conventional notions of sovereignty and the idea of the territorial states. The smallest of the SISs pose the toughest questions. Many discussions of the power of the state as the primary actor in IR have fumbled on what small states like Kiribati really signify internationally (Jackson 1990; Hurrell and Kingsbury 1992; Schachter 1997). With few resources, small populations, and little landmass,

---

[1] The Vienna Conventions in chronological order relate to: diplomatic relations, 1961 (cited here as, Vienna I), consular relations, 1963 (Vienna II), treaty law, 1969 (Vienna III), successor states and treaties, 1978 (Vienna IV) treaties between involving international organizations, 1986 (Vienna V).

many SISs are often regarded as oceanic versions of Liechtenstein, states only in a technical sense. Economically and political dependent on larger states (usually former colonial powers), the smallest of the SISs appear as a theoretical afterthought.

12.2.3 Sovereignty of Sea "Territory"

Whether the sovereign state is clearly defined in international law or theory faces many challenges. All nation-states, as conventionally conceived, are under pressure from many directions. A distinction should be made between challengers seeking to rend a state into fragments and those threatening to bypass the state as a social form. For example, a Quebecois nationalist may seek to break up the existing Canadian state but only to create a new independent state of Quebec. Such secessionist movements do not threaten the *idea* of the state. In fact, such efforts embrace the idea of the state, complete with flags, anthems, territory and currency. This type of challenge to the state is significant primarily as a general historical trend away from empires and multi-national states. The primary importance of secessionist movements to the issue of sovereignty is scale: how small can a political unit be before it ceases to exercise real sovereignty over its destiny? However, secessionist movements do not question the notion of sovereignty itself.

More significant to the question of sovereignty are challenges to the authority of the state from non-territorially based actors (Chou 2009: 144–146). State authority is based primarily on the right to use force and the ability to command the loyalty (or at least submission) of its population. Alternative sources of authority pose a threat to certain states as great as secessionist movements. Transnational movements based on various identities, ethnic, linguistic, cultural or religious are one source of individual loyalty that can transcend the state. Such movements appeal not to state loyalty but to identity. Control of territory is less important than the identity, the ideology, or the cause.

The consolidation of economic and financial power in transnational corporations (TNCs) is a second challenge to sovereignty. Globalization also includes non-commercial transactions: information and ideology. Discursive networks (political, environmental) operate independent of, and sometimes in opposition to, states. The best example of these are anti-globalization demonstrations that have occurred around the world, not led by any organized movement but rather a loose correspondence of beliefs held together by the global communications system. Globalization, discursive networks, and transnational identities may represent coordinated political action that is not based on state affiliation.

The power of TNCs to threaten sovereign states has been exaggerated and rejected by most scholars of international relations, including the author of *Sovereignty at Bay* (Vernon 1981). However, states are still vulnerable to challenges to their authority over people and their effective control of territory. As states are not equal in capabilities, certain states are far more vulnerable. The USA faces less danger from the power of TNCs, or sea level change, than Micronesia.[2] The key understanding is that the state is unlike any other institution in that is enjoys the power of jurisdiction and loyalty. While other actors, like TNC may enjoy authority over people, property, and functions, they are not in a position to replace the state as the prime actors in international relations (Strange 1996: 46). While TNCs and in different ways NGOs have assumed authority and functions internationally, they lack other key resources, such as the command of civic loyalty and the legitimate use of force that states enjoy.

12.2.4 Identified Consequences of Sea Level Change

The nation-state persists despite the challenges of TNCs, NGOs, secessionists, and other groups. Sovereignty remains an exclusive legal privilege of states. States also enjoy the physical sources of sovereignty: population, geographic size, natural resources, knowledge resources (technology and education), and legitimacy (Waltz 1979; Chou 2009: 121–122). These resources are not held equally by all states and many states may lack one or more. States continue to maintain their special place in world politics.

However, the issue of sea level change poses a new riddle. Accepting the consensus scientific position as a point of departure, what are the political implications of this phenomenon? The physical effects can be enumerated fairly easily, indeed some of the effects have been observed. The impacts on human life and society range from the subtle to the catastrophic, with the poignant cinematographic images of *Waterworld* to support the latter. The actual impacts of global warming are less cosmic in scale (Tiempo 1999). However, rising average temperatures of even a few degrees would have major effects on climate belts, agriculture, distribution of flora and fauna, and put added pressures on vulnerable local environments. The economic damage of these various changes is more difficult to estimate, although the UN Environmental Program put the figure at US$150 billion per year (UNEP 2007: 82).

One important impact of climate change is disruption or destruction of agricultural productivity. Changing patterns of rainfall, slightly changed growing seasons, and the introduction of tropical pests into temperate regions are three probable impacts of changed global temperature. Changing patterns of rainfall could also contribute to the existing phenomena of desertification. However, it is more honest to say that patterns of agriculture will be altered under global warming scenarios. Far northern altitudes (such as northern Canada and Russia) may actually see an increase in agricultural production due to longer growing seasons (Young 1999; IPCC 2001).

Sea level change itself has numerous potential impacts. One obvious impact is damage or loss of coastal lands. Rising sea levels would erode beach areas, destroy

---

[2] As the US is responsible for Micronesia's security, one might even question whether Micronesia, as with Palau and the Marshall Islands, is fully sovereign, despite their UN seats and embassies.

barrier islands, and possibly displace inhabitants (Edgarton 1991: 25–27). The loss of these coastal features would make those regions more vulnerable to storm damage and flooding (Paterson 1996: 85). The coastal areas of many countries, including China, Bangladesh, the USA, and Egypt, are densely populated and vulnerable to such coastal erosion. Land areas do not need to be entirely flooded for there to be economic or other consequences. Higher sea levels also pose a threat to fresh water supplies if salt water contaminates coastal aquifers (Peterson 1996: 85). Salt-water contamination has implications for drinking water, industry, and agriculture. Disposal of wastewater is also a potential difficulty, especially in population concentrations (Gourbesville 2006). Sea level change also threatens destruction of local ecosystems, including natural habitats for wildlife. This is an environmental issue, as well as an economic one. The loss of aesthetic features like beaches or reefs could negatively impact valuable tourist industries.

Partial or total disappearance of land areas would affect states' claims to territorial waters and Exclusive Economic Zones (EEZs). Claims to oceanic resources are based on a state's territorial expanse. An EEZ is an extension of its (sovereign) territorial sea, itself derived from a state's coastline.[3] Both the territorial sea and the EEZ are drawn from the same coastal baseline as the territorial sea. Loss of coastline or islands would contract the claimable zones. Certain claims may even be based on sovereignty over uninhabitable islands or rocks, if the area has sustained economic activities like fishing or drilling.

The living resources of the EEZs and territorial waters are often important for domestic consumption as well as for export. EEZs, which may be up to 320 km distant from shore, allow states to claim exclusive rights to economic resources located therein (UN *Law of the Sea Treaty*, Article 56). The mineral, oil and fishing resources of those waters may be claimed, though the waters themselves remain free for navigation (Buck 1998: 94). Some EEZs comprise far more ocean area than the territory of their claimants. For instance, Tuvalu with only 26 km^2 of land, claims 900,000 km^2 in EEZ ocean space (Watson et al. 1998: 338). Loss of small islands would have the biggest impact, potentially contracting EEZs by hundreds of square kilometers.

The loss or degradation of territory has implications for loss of living space. The issue is not simply space, for arable land and inhabitable terrain are always less than the total area of an island. Small islands states are vulnerable to even small changes. While most SISs do not generally contain large populations, most have fairly high population densities, and many inhabitants live close to shore, especially on atolls. Internal migration of populations, if even possible, would increase already existing population pressures. Even small changes in coastline can force populations to move, internally or internationally. Recently in one of the islands off 'mainland' Papua New Guinea, 1,500 people were reportedly being resettled as their island was sinking (*Space Daily* 2004). For very small states like Tuvalu, sea level changes of 20–70 cm would be simply catastrophic.

---

[3]Convention on the Territorial Sea and the Contiguous Sea, 29 April 1958, Part I, Art. 1; UN Law of the Sea, Part V, Art. 57.

The movement of people poses a final set of implications of climate change: cultural and social implications. Lands partially or totally lost to the sea would threaten small, heavily localized, and already vulnerable, indigenous cultures. The dislocation and dispersion of populations would have devastating consequences for local and national cultures. This would include the loss of ancestral and culturally significant lands and sites as well as the disruption of cultural ties between members of scattered communities. Indigenous languages would also suffer if already small populations were to be dispersed around the world into larger, more hegemonic cultures. Traditions and cultural identities could disappear.

12.2.5 Consequences of Inundation

The worst-case scenario of sea level change is the complete inundation of an island state. While not a certainty, it is this possibility that has alarmed the governments of Tuvalu, Kiribati and Maldives. Sea level change will likely occur slowly enough that populations can be relocated and governments will continue in some form even if the territory of the state vanishes. The human suffering and cultural damage of these changes is not to be ignored. Another issue, one that poses a challenge to conventional ideas of sovereignty, is what happens politically and legally if the territory of a state vanishes completely?

The central issue in a "post-territorial" scenario would be the rights, if any, of the surviving populations and their representatives. The worst-case scenario of total inundation lacks any precedent in international politics. There has never been an instance of a sovereign entity physically disappearing. National borders have frequently been changed and states may vanish as autonomous units, but never as geographic realities. Inundation raises the possibility that a nation state would cease as a territorial entity. The population, however, would continue to exist, most likely as refugees, nomads or immigrants.

The political and legal problems that would arise in such a scenario are numerous and speculative. However, there are several issues that can be identified, based on current practice and theory:

1. Population displacement and continued collective identity, if any. If the population of Tuvalu were forced to leave sinking islands, would they retain any collective identity? This has various cultural and ethical implications as discussed. It is also a legal issue. Will displaced populations be recognized as having any collective rights?
2. Diplomatic Issues. All states discussed here have signed treaties, both bilateral and multilateral. They therefore have both treaty rights and obligations. To what extent will those rights and obligations be recognized and supported? To what extent would inundated states be permitted to participate in international bodies, forums and other diplomatic activities as recognized actors?

3. Immunity. The issue of diplomacy also raises the issue of the diplomatic immunity of individuals acting on behalf of inundated states. Will the governments of such inundated states and their representatives be, or continue to be, recognized as diplomatic agents with the immunities traditional conferred to such agents?
4. Property and assets abroad, and international debt. The status of embassies would be another legal issue, along with the control of property and assets in other countries. If a population is dispersed, who controls and enjoys the benefits of property and assets abroad? In the same vein, what is the status of international debts?
5. Claims to former territorial waters, EEZs and the resources therein. Would an inundated state have claims to its former territorial waters or EEZ? Such waters could still have enormous economic value. Would small features (islands, rocks, reefs) not capable of habitation but capable of economic activity serve as a residual territorial basis for sovereignty?

12.2.6 Compensation for Victim States

In either the best or worst case scenarios, what are the alternatives available to SISs? Part of the challenge in this issue is the lack of a precedent. Minor loss of territory due to natural processes does occur, for the Earth is a dynamic system. What makes the changes discussed here different is the alleged human induced cause of global warming. The effects of the change therefore cannot be left to impersonal fate or nature as natural erosion but may be laid at the feet of responsible (and culpable) human agencies. If some states shoulder a greater share of the blame for sea level change, does this make them legally liable? It has been well established in international law that a state that harms another state is liable. To date, such cases have been primarily focused on the laws of war and commercial relations. The principle of state liability also exists for inadvertent harms, such as damage done by off course or reentering space objects. These cases however are based on established customs or treaties; liability or environmental harm is not established automatically.

The responsibility of individual states for global warming is not clearly stated in treaties. The UN Framework Convention on Climate Change (UNFCCC) has struggled with the issue of responsibility (Ellison 2003; Paterson 1996: 75). Clearly, the developed countries have produced the bulk of greenhouse gases in the past, but are not alone in producing them today. In addition, developing countries wish to expand their own industrial activities and modernize the consumption patterns of their populations. Notions of equity may demand the right of the South to develop, despite environmental costs, as the North has done. At the same time, developed countries are unlikely to accept sole responsibility for the problem and the solution. The compromise, apparent in the UNFCCC Preamble, assigns the developed countries a greater role in reacting to the problem but not blame or liability. Indeed, this greater role given to developed countries is premised as much on their greater capacity to act than to their greater share in creating the problem (UNFCCC 1992). The Article 3[1] of the UNFCCC identifies "common but differentiated responsibilities and respective capabilities." In international negotiations leading to the Rio and Kyoto agreements, developed countries resisted any specific statement of responsibility (UNFCCC 1992). Responsibility for global warming was placed at the door of all states, though not equally. This could be the basis for liability.

However, any legal recourse poses two major problems for affected states. Establishing that certain states have produced atmospheric carbon dioxide is relatively easy. It is clear which states have historically engaged in industrial activity. Establishing a connection between specific states' pollution, the global warming phenomena, and specific instances of sea-level change is a far more daunting task. To what extent is global warming a human-produced phenomenon? How much, if any, sea-level change can be attributed to global warming or other human activity? Is sea level change in Tuvalu largely due to industrial pollution in the developed countries, to pollution originating in nearby Australia, or to economic activity, agriculture, and other human pressures occurring in Tuvalu itself? These are scientific questions on the surface, but determining the source of responsibility will not be a solely scientific decision. Political considerations will play a bigger part in assigning responsibility.

Scientific research cannot with any certainty establish what portion of global warming is directly caused by human activity, how much is a natural process, and what local effects are driven by human or natural factors. In addition, the scientific community itself is divided and a vocal minority rejects the consensus view. The judgment therefore cannot be based on clear overwhelming scientific evidence.

The second problem facing litigants is the ability of states to opt out of international legal proceedings. The US has in the past withdrawn itself from the International Court of Justice's jurisdiction on short notice. Australia, however, has accepted the jurisdiction of the Court without reservations and therefore would be vulnerable to suits brought by island states (BBC News 2003).

Should impacted states receive compensation for damages caused by sea level change, it could take one of three forms. The same means could be employed without legal suits, should developed countries decide to act on this issue. One possible method of compensation would be financial. Polluting states could pay monetary damages to compensate for loss of tourism or fishing revenue, or pay for relocation costs. Should populations be dispersed, monetary payments could be made to individuals. This could be similar in concept to compensation paid by the German and Japanese governments' victims of atrocities during the Second World War.

A second form of compensation would be technology transfer to affected states. Technology does exist to protect and reverse the affects of coastal erosion. States responsible for greenhouse gas emissions could pay for the restoration or protection of endangered areas (such as barriers against beach erosion or flooding), when those solutions were technologically feasible. Desalination technology could be employed when local water sources are contaminated.

A third form of compensation could be expanded or special migratory rights. Tuvalu has asked both Australia and New Zealand to accept greater numbers of Tuvaluan migrants. While Australia has refused to consider this proposal, New Zealand has agreed to accept more Tuvaluan immigrants over a 30 year period (Kirby 2004; Panichi 2001). This approach would be useful in scenarios were sea level change is minor; it would prove essential in an inundation scenario.

Nevertheless, migratory rights are problematic. Even though Tuvalu and other SISs generally have small populations, developed countries have resisted the influx of refugees and other migrants. Developed countries are increasingly inhospitable to refugees, and immigrants, regardless of their status (legal, illegal, refugee and otherwise) are lightning rods for political conflict in many countries of destination. Moreover, how do governments deal with a population of 11,000 claiming *environmental* asylum (Paterson 1996: 11)? The question does not end with SISs. Can opportunities granted to South Pacific refugees get extended to other, much more populous states? Bangladesh comprises a large, densely concentrated population that is very vulnerable to changes in sea level. Therefore, migratory rights would not be an easy option for the developed countries to propose.

12.3 Sovereignty Without Territory? Possible Solutions in International Law

Stemming from the above analysis, then, how does the loss of territory necessarily mean the loss of statehood? The simplest legal outcome would be to regard territory loss as a natural process that changes nothing about international law or practice. The states that have vanished simply cease to be subjects of international law. Without territory above water, with a dispersed population, diplomatic recognition is withdrawn. Embassies would lose their status and the world moves on. This is one scenario in the case of territory loss.

The problem with this scenario is that a legal person does not cease to exist without leaving a legacy, any more than a natural person. The law of successor states is well established, partly in the 1978 *Vienna Convention on the Succession of States in Respect to Treaties.* This treaty sets out in broad terms that successor states are bound by treaties signed by predecessor states (Art. 34). Even though the Soviet Union disintegrated, Russia was recognized as its legal successor state. The other former Soviet republics were bound to some degree to treaties signed by the USSR before December 1991. The problem lies once again in the connection of the state to territory. The Soviet Union disappeared, the territory did not; it was merely divided up into 15 new states. A possible answer lies in those entities that do not fully share the attributes of statehood discussed previously. There are three alternative models of sovereignty that are not new to international law or relations and could be used as basis for post-territorial sovereignty.

12.3.1 Sovereignty with a Territorial Veneer

Notwithstanding the discussion so far, there are entities in international politics for which the claim of territorial sovereignty is weak. The best known case in the contemporary international system is probably that of the anomalous status of Vatican City/The Holy See, recognized by many governments as a sovereign state. The Vatican

City State holds sovereignty over 108.7 acres of land within the territory of Italy. While not a member of the United Nations, it does enjoy permanent observer status as a non-member state. Vatican City, with a small territorial fig leaf, exists as a territorial sovereign. However the same entity is also the Holy See, the administrative centre of the Roman Catholic Church that does not claims sovereignty based on territory (Damrosch 2001: 291; Henkin 1990). Exactly where does sovereignty lie in the case of the Vatican/Holy See? The Permanent Mission to the UN is in the name of the Holy See. Some states recognize the Vatican, others the Holy See. In a sense, the Holy See represents a non-territorial sovereign that claims sovereignty even if it did not control the 108.7 acres and its small population of permanent residents. The Vatican/Holy See therefore represents a possible model of sovereignty which is not solely or primarily based on territory.

12.3.2 Stateless but Sovereign

The state is not the only actor in which sovereignty could conceivably rest. Medieval authority was dispersed and overlapping and not based solely on territorial jurisdiction. A second possible model of post-territorial sovereignty deconstructs sovereignty and removes it from the state. Sovereignty has been considered an attribute of the state since the end of the Middle Ages in Europe. The Treaty of Westphalia is a widely accepted, if arbitrary, benchmark that established the territorial state as free of the authority or influence of any other actor. That Treaty, as Krasner notes, marks a new emphasis: "territoriality and the exclusion of external actors from domestic authority structures" (Krasner 1999: 14). Multiple or intersecting sovereignties operating on the same patch of land were soon to fade as a working concept (even though they have reappeared in today's world). The fiction of equality between sovereignties also became an important factor. Sovereignty as we understand it today is not the first or final word on the concept.

Therefore, sovereignty could be placed in a different entity, such as a population. In a sense it is a major revision of the concept of sovereignty: placing it in human beings rather than a territory. Specific ethnic groups have been given special recognition based on culture, language, or religion. The sovereignty of Native American nations over their internal affairs is one such example. These communities lack all the attributes of sovereignty, but are recognized based on characteristics beyond land. Therefore, this could form a model of legal authority (of some degree) being placed in something other than a recognized state. However, it is crucial to maintain a legitimately selected leadership that can only be achieved if the concept of sovereignty is applied to a group of people defined by culture and linguistic. Following the definitions used by Krasner, such a people (or nation) would have Westphalian and international legal sovereignty but would not necessarily exercise control over a territorial unit or wield domestic sovereignty (that is, have the ability to fully regulate its "citizens") therein. Applied to inundate states, sovereignty based on people would allow displaced people collective rights, even if they reside in the territory of other states.

Gottleib made such a case in *Nations Against State,* in which he proposed a "states plus nations" model to resolve conflicts. Gottlieb's model would supplement existing state sovereignty with non-territorial national sovereignty. Disputed territories would have dual identity, sundering nationality from citizenship. This would allow an individual to claim cultural identity-based nationality in a group and citizenship protection from an established state (1994: 3, 24). Gottlieb also envisions how extensive functional cooperation between states would establish cross-border institutions (1994: 5).

There are no examples in the contemporary international system where sovereignty and diplomatic recognition is granted to a population without territory. There are transnational national groups, without states, but nonetheless maintain a collective identity, the best know example being the Roma (also called Gypsies, though that term is rejected by most Roma). International NGOs claiming to represent the Roma operate to promote Romani culture, language, legal protections, and identity. However, like organizations claiming to recognize other cultural-ethnic groups, the Roma are not regarded as sovereign or recognized as a nation, but as the citizens of their respective states.

12.3.3   Government in Exile

The third model, better established in international law, is the government in exile. Here a recognized government continues to operate with its sovereign rights, despite not being in effective control of its territory. Governments in exile operate under the assumption that they have legitimacy, and would exercise sovereignty over territory and authority over a population.

During the Second World War, several governments in exile were recognized by the Allied powers as the *de jure* governments of occupied states. They participated in international conferences and signed treaties (Damrosch 2001: 313). The government of Kuwait continued to be recognized by all except Iraq as the legitimate government of the territory of Kuwait throughout the Iraqi occupation. The concept is not limited to wartime situations. US recognition of the three Baltic States continued after the Second World War and until those states won *de facto* independence from the USSR in 1991. National liberation movements (like the Palestine Liberation Organization) are in a sense a variation on the government in exile model, although such movements usually claim to represent *a provisional* government yet to be established.

The difficultly of applying the government in exile concept to inundated states is that the concept is based on an assumption that the condition is temporary. If Tuvalu slips beneath the Pacific, its government would most likely never regain its territory. The "states" claiming government in exile status would exist in a shadowy condition: recognized by some states and continuing to press their claims upon the rest of the world. As only states can bring suits before the International Court of Justice, this would likely be the primary benefit of post-territorial recognition. However, it would not be certain that all states would recognize the government of an inundated state as a government in exile. If such recognition would be used to press for migratory rights or monetary compensation, many governments would be loath to offer, or even withdraw, recognition.

Ultimately, diplomatic recognition is a political act, and states may in a sense do what they wish (Krasner 1999: 15). If anarchy is what states make of it; the same argument could be applied to sovereignty. States could recognize a new form of sovereignty that allows the perpetuation of some collective legal rights of displaced populations. Beyond providing legal models for inundated states, these models also offer alternative ways to conceive of sovereignty. By challenging the link between sovereignty and territory, it is possible to see beyond world politics as merely a collection of similar actors, or following Rosenau, a duopoly of sovereignty-bound and sovereignty-free actors. With small island states leading the way, it is possible to look beyond both sovereignty and the state to a more complex and richer conceptualization of world politics where there are many networks, loci, and types of status shaping individuals, group, and global affairs.

12.4 Concluding Remarks

In a final twist of irony, although Tuvalu's request in June 2001 to Australia to allow increased immigration was rejected, Australia asked Tuvalu to accept Middle Eastern refugees it had turned away from its shores (BBC News 2001b). This incident is emblematic of how SISs suffer from the disregard of more powerful states. SISs have little to bargain with except moral principles. Their small size, lack of resources, and limited voice on the world stage erodes their influence. They have no strong economic or resource-based clout to use against anyone. As sea level change is an arcane subject with irregular political resonance, many other issues more closely tied to security and prosperity will crowd it off the agenda.

The cost of sea level change may very well be narrowly borne by SISs, at least at first. The broader significance of sea-level change will not be fully understood until the model of major climate change becomes part of a scientific and political consensus. Until then, this issue must compete for attention with many other, potentially more important issues. The recognition of this issue as a problem deserving of concerted action may depend on when a major archipelagic state in the Asia Pacific impacted by climate change, like Japan or Taiwan, decides to make this issue the core of its international diplomatic efforts.

References

Allen, B. J. (2004). The Pacific Islands: Background to the region. In Europa regional survey of the world: the far east and Australasia. (pp. 750–757). New York: Routledge.
BBC News. (2001a, August 17). Islanders press bush on global warming.

BBC News. (2001b, November 13). Sinking islands urged to accept migrants.
BBC News. (2002, March 4). Tiny pacific nation takes on Australia.
BBC News. (2003, November 16). UN attacks Australia's Asylum Policy.
Buck, S. (1998). *The global commons*. Washington: Island Press.
Charney, J. (1999). Rocks that cannot sustain human habitation. *American Journal of International Law, 93*(4), 863–878.
Chou, C. C. (2005, February 22). We Cannot Ignore Island Nations. *Taipei Times*, p.8.
Chou, C. C. (2009). State authority vs. international norm: Impacts of legitimacy on practice of international human rights law. *Chengchi Law Review, 109*, 113–176.
Damrosch, L. F. (2001). *International law: Cases and materials* (4th ed.). St. Paul: West Group.
Douglas, L. N. (2006). *Global governance and the quest for justice*. Oxford: Hart Publication.
Edgarton, L. T. (1991). *The rising tide: Global warming and world sea levels*. Washington, DC: Island Press.
Ellison, J. (2003). How South Pacific mangroves may respond to predicted climate change and sea-level rise. In A. Gillespie & B. William (Eds.), *Climate change in the South Pacific: Impacts and responses in Australia, New Zealand and small island states* (pp. 289–300). Netherlands: Springer.
Friends of the Earth Australia. (2007). *A citizen's guide to climate refugees*. http://www.foe.org.au/resources/publications/climate-justice/CitizensGuide.pdf. Accessed 20 Apr 2010.
Gillespie, A., & Bums, W. (2000). *Climate change in the South Pacific: Impacts and responses in Australia, New Zealand, and small island states*. Dordrecht: Kluwer Academic Publishers.
Gottlieb, G. (1993). *Nations against state*. New York: Council on Foreign Relations.
Gourbesville, P. (2006). Sustainable coastal wastewater management promotion and hydroinformatics. Working paper (U.M.R. 5661 of C.N.R.S.), France: University of Nice.
Hay, J. (2001). Small islands and the JPCC. *Tiempos* 40/41 (September), http://www.cru.uea.ac.uk/tiempo/floorO/recent/issue4041/t4041a4.htm. Accessed 20 Apr 2010.
Henkin, L. (1990). Law and politics in international relations: State and human values. *Journal of International Affairs, 44*, 183–208.
Hurrell, A. (2000). International law and the changing constitution of international society. In M. Byers (Ed.), *The role of law in international politics: Essays in international relations and international law* (pp. 327–347). Oxford: Oxford University Press.
Hurrell, A., & Kingsbury, B. (1992). *The international politics of the environment. Actors, interests, and institutions*. New York: Oxford University Press.
IPCC. (2001). *Climate change 2001: Summary for policy makers*. New York: UNIPCC.
Jackson, R. H. (1990). *Quasi-states: Sovereignty, international relations and the third world*. Cambridge: Cambridge University Press.
Jackson, R. H. (1999). Sovereignty in world politics: A glance at the conceptual and historical landscape. *Political Studies, 47*, 431–456.
Katzenstein, P. J. (1996). Introduction. In P. J. Katzenstein (Ed.), *The culture of national security: Norms and identities in world politics*. New York: Columbia University Press.
Kellogg, W. (1989). Carbon dioxide and climate changes. In S. Fred Singer (Ed.), *Global climate change: Human and natural influences* (pp. 37–66). New York: Paragon House.
Kirby, A. (1999, June 14). Islands disappear under rising seas, *BBC News Online*.
Kirby, A. (2004, October 9). Pacific islanders flee rising seas, *BBC News Online*.
Krasner, S. (1999). *Sovereignty: Organized hypocrisy*. New Jersey: Princeton University Press.
Lockhart, D. G., Drakakis-Smith, D., & Schembri, J. (1993). *The development process in small island states*. New York: Routledge.
Panichi, J. (2001). That sinking feeling. Pacific Islands Report. http://www.pireport.org. Accessed 12 Oct 2001.
Paterson, M. (1996). *Global warming and global politics*. London: Routledge.
Philpott, D. (2001). Usurping the sovereignty of sovereignty. *World Politics, 53*(January), 297–324.
Ruggie, J. G. (1993). Territoriality and beyond: Problematizing modernity in international relations. *International Organization, 47*(4), 140–174.

Schachter, O. (1997). The decline of the nation-state and its implications for international law. *Columbia Journal of International Law, 36*(1–2), 7–23.
Space Daily. (2001, August 25). Pacific Atolls Can't Find Out Whether They Will Sink.
Space Daily. (2002a, March 28). Global warming not sinking Tuvalu- but maybe its people are.
Space Daily. (2002b, March 27). No evidence Pacific rising to engulf Tuvalu, scientists say.
Space Daily. (2004, December 13). Now another island group sinking into the Pacific.
Space Daily. (2005, March 14). Pacific nations air their fears before the UN.
Sports, P. (2002, January 18). Guess what? Antarctica's getting colder, not warmer. *Christian Science Monitor.*
Strange, S. (1996). *The retreat of the state.* Cambridge: Cambridge University Press.
Tiempo. (1999). JPCC third assessment: Impact, 40/41 (September), http://www.tiempocyberclimate.org/portal/archive/issue4041/t4041a5.htm. Accessed 8 May 2010.
Tiempo (2001). Global temperature 2001., 43 (December) http://www.tiempocyberclimate.org/portal/archive/issue43/t43a6.htm. Accessed 8 May 2010.
UN Environmental Program. (2007). *UNEP annual report.* UK: UNER Publications.
Vernon, R. (1981). Sovereignty at bay ten years later. *International Organization, 35*(3), 517–29.
Vienna Convention on Diplomatic Relations. (1961). 18 April. http://untreaty.un.org/ilc/texts/instruments/english/conventions/9_1_1961.pdf. Accessed 11 Oct 2009.
Vienna Convention on the Law of Treaties. (1969). 23 May. http://untreaty.un.org/ilc/texts/instruments/english/conventions/1_1_1969.pdf. Accessed 11 Oct 2009.
Vienna Convention on the Law of Treaties between States and International Organizations or Between International Organizations. (1986). 21 March. http://untreaty.un.org/ilc/texts/instruments/english/conventions/1_2_1986.pdf. Accessed 11 Oct 2009.
Waltz, K. N. (1979). *Theory of international politics.* New York: McGraw Hill.
Watson, R., Zinyowera, M., & Moss, R. (1998). *Regional impacts of climate change: An assessment of vulnerability.* Cambridge: Cambridge University Press.
Watts, A. (2000). The importance of international law. In M. Byers (Ed.), *The role of law in international politics: Essays in international relations and international law* (pp. 5–16). Oxford: Oxford University Press.
Weart, S. (2006). *The discovery of global warming.* Boston: Harvard University Press.
Wendt, A. (1992). Anarchy is what states make of it: The social construction of power politics. *International Organization, 46*(2), 391–425.
Willie, R. (2001). Vanuatu minister urges plan for climate change. *Pacific islands report* (February 4). http://webcache.googleusercontent.com/search?q=cache:bQIwmpEotPcJ:pidp.eastwestcenter.org/pireport/special/cofa_special.htm+Pacific+Islands+Report+February+2001&cd=1&hl=zh-TW&ct=clnk&gl=tw. Accessed 20 Apr 2010.
Young, O. R. (1999). *The effectiveness of international environmental regimes: Causal connections and behavioral mechanisms.* Boston: MIT Press.

Index

A
Abad, M.C. Jr, 6, 149
Abolition of the death penalty, 218, 219, 222–224, 227
ADB. *See* Asian Development Bank (ADB)
AFC. *See* Asian Financial Crisis (AFC)
African Charter of Human and People's Rights, 219
African Union (AU), 149
Agriculture, 69, 81, 121, 123, 125, 174, 179, 209, 238, 239, 242
Akaha, T., 5
Alles, D., 157
Alliance of Small Island States (AOSIS), 232
American Convention of Human Rights, 219
Annan, K., 7, 8, 60
APT. *See* ASEAN plus three (APT)
ARF. *See* ASEAN Regional Forum (ARF)
Aristotle, 34
ASEAN. *See* Association of South East Asian Nations (ASEAN)
ASEAN Charter, 10, 137, 146, 170
ASEAN plus three (APT), 139–141
ASEAN Regional Forum (ARF), 10, 145, 149, 188
ASEAN way, 135, 137, 146, 152, 185, 198
Asian Development Bank (ADB), 119, 120, 137, 169,
Asian Financial Crisis (AFC), 2, 24, 139, 145, 201
Asian food crisis, 186
Association of South East Asian Nations (ASEAN), 10, 64, 119, 120, 135–152, 157–160, 163–165, 167–170, 181, 183–186, 188, 193–199, 201, 203, 205, 208

Australia, 10, 32, 101, 118, 123, 140, 141, 148, 150, 159, 162, 174, 179, 193, 194, 196, 197, 201, 205, 232, 242, 243, 246
Axworthy, L., 1, 6, 217

B
Bae, S., 217
Baker, S., 82, 83, 85, 87–89
Bilateral, 22, 101, 102, 118, 142, 164, 186, 193–198, 201, 203–209, 221, 240
Bilateral social security agreement, 102
Bin, Y., 20
Birth control, 63, 66, 89
Birth rates, 61, 89,
Border areas, 27, 124, 125,
Borderlands. *See* Border areas
Borders, 1, 21, 27, 61, 62, 66, 77, 81, 82, 84, 119, 124, 125, 127, 176, 180, 235, 245
Brunei, 99, 101, 136, 139, 186, 201, 205
Burma, 82, 85, 86, 88, 159, 166, 167, 178
Burmese, 77, 82, 84, 85, 88, 91, 149

C
Cambodia, 11, 32, 61, 69, 79, 81–83, 85, 86, 115, 116, 118–122, 126–129, 131, 136, 148, 151, 178, 179, 186, 187, 194
Campbell, J.R., 173
Capital punishment, 12, 217–228
Catholic Church, 95, 105, 106, 109, 244
Chen, L., 45, 52–54
Chenoy, A.M., 60
Child labor, 86, 87

Child migrants, 77, 86, 87
Child prostitution, 85, 89
Child Protection and Development Center (CPDC), 80, 86
China, 1, 11, 17, 20–22, 24, 25, 27–29, 31, 39–56, 59, 61–63, 68, 69, 101, 102, 117, 118, 120, 123, 124, 139–143, 145, 150, 151, 175, 176, 181–182, 184, 187, 194, 195, 197–203, 208, 219, 221, 239
Chosun, I., 20, 203
Chou, C-C., 231
Civic rights, 99, 102
Civil society, 54, 55, 61, 64, 65, 107, 117, 119, 120, 122, 128, 129, 138, 146, 149, 150, 183, 185, 187
Civil society actors. *See* Civil society
Civil society organizations. *See* Civil society
Clark, W.C., 32
Climate change, 3, 11, 31, 68, 117, 135–152, 174, 177, 179, 180, 188, 231–233, 238, 240, 241, 246
Cold War, 3–6, 60, 61, 65, 115, 119, 120, 135, 139, 147, 152, 220, 221
Commission on Human Security (CHS), 7, 19, 23
Compensation form, 241, 242, 246
Comprehensive Economic Partnership in East Asia (CEPEA), 194
Constructivism, 146
Cooperation, 2–4, 9, 10, 12, 24, 26–29, 54, 115, 118–120, 122, 128, 135, 137–139, 141–147, 150–152, 157, 159, 162–165, 169, 174, 177, 179, 182, 184–188, 196, 199, 201–204, 232, 245
Copenhagen School, 136, 138, 146
Crime, 1, 2, 8, 10, 50, 71, 95, 100, 104, 135, 139, 145, 146, 149, 176, 218, 219, 222, 224, 225
Critical security, 24, 32, 116, 117
Croll, E., 49
Cuba, 234
Culture, 11, 35, 61, 69, 104, 123, 157, 198, 244, 245
Cyclone Nargis, 5, 12, 23, 24, 135, 137, 145, 150, 159, 161, 165, 169, 177, 180–182
Cyclones, 137, 174, 176

D

Dae-jung, K., 223, 227
Death penalty, 12, 217–227
Decentralization, 64, 65, 119

Deforestation, 68, 116, 119, 121–123, 127, 139, 141, 143–145, 152, 174, 180, 210, 233
Democracy, 22, 23, 136, 148, 149, 166, 220, 222, 227
Demographics, 59, 121
Depoliticization, 145–151
Deregulation, 99, 100
Diem, D., 62, 63
Dikötter, F., 47
Disaster diplomacy, 159, 161
Disastermanagement, 163
Displacement, 69, 119–124, 232, 234, 240
Distinction (between natural disasters and other components of human security), 158, 159
Doi Moi, 64–65, 68, 70
Domestic actors, 199, 202–203
Domino effect, 199, 201
Dosch, J., 145
Dupont, A., 24

E

East Asia
  future of, 1–12
  international relations of, 1
  peoples of, 1, 10, 12
  states and societies in, 9, 10
East Asia (region), 1–12, 115, 116, 118–120, 123, 127, 131, 193–195, 198, 199, 204, 205, 208, 211, 219–226
East Asia Free Trade Area (EAFTA), 194, 195
East Asian
  community, 9
  region, 3, 4, 62, 121, 127, 141
  regionalism, 9
Economics, 41, 65, 122, 184, 195, 196
Edström, B., 10
El Nino phenomena, 234
Emmerson, D.K., 135, 146, 149, 150
Employment, 30, 42, 54, 61, 65, 66, 71, 83, 85, 86, 89, 98, 99, 103, 104, 127, 160, 205, 208, 220
Energy resources, 5, 137, 143, 152, 198, 199
Energy security, 137, 141–145, 150–152
Environment, 60, 61, 67–71
  degradation, 30, 115–127, 130, 131, 135, 178, 180, 220
  insecurity, 115–131
  security, 6, 12, 115–117, 125–127, 131, 138, 148
  threats, 12, 177
Equal distribution, 212

Ethnic minorities, 61, 62, 68–70, 124, 125, 129, 176
EU. *See* European Union (EU)
European Convention on Human Rights, 218, 219, 227
European Union (EU), 21, 141, 150, 151, 168, 181, 194, 219

F
Filipino family, 105, 109
Filipino migration, 95, 96, 105, 106, 108
  economic benefits, 98
  infrastructures, 99
  social stakes, 109
Fires in Indonesia, 144, 183
First World, 63, 141, 152
Food, 3, 5–7, 10–12, 19–21, 23, 39, 59, 60, 67–70, 86, 105, 123–125, 137, 147, 158, 160, 167, 174, 178, 179, 184, 186, 188, 210, 232
Food insecurity, 3, 137, 178
Food safety, 179
Foreign direct investment. *See* Investment
Foreign Investment, 70, 71, 118, 122, 124, 128
Free Trade Agreement, 12, 194, 202, 209
French Colonialism, 61, 62
Fresnoza-Flot, A., 95
Fukushima, A., 4, 7

G
Gender, 11, 41–43, 48–50, 52–56, 67, 75, 77, 79, 82–85, 88, 89, 91, 105, 111.
  See also Women
Gender roles, 41
Geneva Accords, 62
Gerstl, A., 135
Global climate change, 177, 179, 188, 232, 233
Globalization, 2, 6, 9, 60, 61, 69, 76, 101, 120, 182, 185, 237
Global warming, 138, 141, 174, 231–234, 238, 241, 242
GMS. *See* Greater Mekong Subregion (GMS)
Gorbachev, M., 4
Gottlieb's model, 245
Government in exile, 245–246
Government procurement, 203, 210
Grassroots groups, 129, 130
Grayson, K., 32–34
Greater Mekong Subregion (GMS), 2, 119–121, 151

Greenhouse gas emissions, 137, 141, 143, 151, 242
Gulf Cooperation Council (GCC), 199

H
Hampson, F.O., 95
Hayes, A.M., 39
Haze, 137, 138, 141–145, 152
Health, 5–7, 11, 12, 19, 21, 23, 24, 39–48, 53–55, 60, 66–68, 70, 71, 75, 78, 80, 81, 84, 89–92, 95–99, 102, 124, 144, 147, 148, 158, 160, 173–189, 200, 206, 208, 210, 220
Health insecurity and roots of conflict, 187–188
Helmke, B., 135
Hinsley, F.H., 33
HIV/AIDS, 11, 30, 39–56, 75, 85, 88–92, 100, 173, 176, 184, 187, 210
  blood and plasma selling, 39
  commercial sex workers, 45, 46, 54
  condom, 44–49, 51, 63, 76, 88, 89
  general population, 40–47, 50–52, 54, 66, 70
  growth period, 40
  injecting drug users, 39
  intravenous drug use, 41, 187
  mother-to-child-transmission, 40
  self-perceived risk, 44, 47–48
  sexual transmission, 40, 53
  stigma and discrimination, 47, 53
Hmong, 125
Hobbes, T., 33
Hocké, J.P., 26
Housing, 60, 65, 67, 68, 71, 96, 187
Hubert, D., 22, 60
Hughes, C.W., 2, 5, 21, 51, 123, 129
Human development, 2, 4–7, 9, 19, 25, 33, 116, 137, 147, 212, 220
Human health challenges and regional security, 175–178
Human health threats, 173–189
Humanitarian concern, 23, 24, 232
Humanitarian disaster, 5, 165, 166, 233
Humanitarian intervention, 7, 33, 34, 148, 166, 181, 185
Human rights, 2, 6, 8, 12, 18, 19, 21–23, 25–28, 30, 33, 34, 60, 77, 78, 82, 84–86, 92, 97, 107, 109, 136, 141, 143, 147–150, 159, 205, 210, 217–220, 224–227
  abuse, 6, 49, 77, 78, 84, 86–88, 95, 97, 98, 103, 108, 206, 208, 225, 227
  universal, 2, 8, 25, 26, 39, 67, 91, 158, 218

Human security, 17, 39, 59, 75, 95, 115, 135, 157, 173, 193, 217
  challenges, 1, 3, 8, 39, 59, 62, 68, 71, 80, 81, 84, 91, 115–117, 125–131, 145, 147, 148, 173–180, 182, 184, 185, 187, 188, 204, 207, 208, 232, 233, 236–238
  concept, 3–7, 11, 209, 242,81, 96, 136, 145–147, 220
  definition, 9, 25, 39, 96, 157, 158, 173, 220
  development of, 3, 8
  in East Asia, 1, 3–10, 12
  framework for, 4
  multidimensionality, 97
  portfolio diversification approach to, 95
Human trafficking, 1, 11, 50, 75–81, 88, 90, 97, 104, 187
Hunger, 4, 6, 19, 21, 30, 60, 97, 173, 179, 184
Hydropower, 116, 119, 121, 122

I
Illegality, 28, 52
Il-Sung, K., 198
India, 10, 48, 96, 140, 141, 150, 159, 164, 169,176, 193, 194,201, 205, 211, 231, 234, 235
Indonesia, 1, 2, 12, 65, 101, 136–139, 141–145, 148, 149, 152, 159–165, 168, 174–176, 179, 182–183, 187, 194–199, 201, 209, 215, 226
Industrialization, 67
Infant mortality, 21, 178
Insurance, 99, 101, 102, 158, 169–170
Interference (political), 148, 158, 170
International accountability, 233
International community, 8, 12, 18, 24, 29, 31, 32, 34, 143, 148, 160, 180, 181, 231, 236
International Covenant on Civil and Political Rights (ICCPR), 218, 222
International human rights, 12, 217, 218, 225–227
International human rights norm. *See* International norm
International intervention, 7, 28, 168
International Labor Organization (ILO), 79, 80, 82, 85, 92, 104
International NGOs, 167, 236, 245
International norm, 220, 226, 227
International relations, 1, 19, 24, 29, 33, 34, 97, 117, 175, 176, 233, 235–238
International security, 217

Intra-regional, 119, 120, 193
Investment, 3, 64, 70, 71, 109, 118–124, 128, 142, 143, 151, 179, 187, 195, 196, 199, 200, 202, 203, 209
Irregular migration, 75–92, 97

J
Japan, 1–5, 7, 10, 12, 22, 23, 99, 104, 118, 120, 139, 140, 145, 150, 151, 193–203, 205–208, 219, 221–223, 226–228, 246
Jeffreys, E., 51

K
Kant, I., 34
Kawakami, S., 208
Keidanren, 203
Kennan, G., 33
Khagram, S., 32
Khmu, 125
Kim, C.S., 18
Kiribati, 231, 232, 234, 236, 240
Koh, D.W., 20
Koh, J., 17
Korean constitutional court, 223
Krasner, S., 235, 244, 246
Kyoto Protocol, 139–142

L
Labor, 11, 19, 21, 22, 61, 62, 65, 67, 75–81, 84–89, 91, 92, 95–109, 121, 122, 125, 184, 196, 200, 203, 205, 207–211
Land, 63, 66–69, 75, 77, 85, 86, 105, 116, 121–123, 125, 143, 165,179, 183, 233, 235, 238–240, 244
Land relations, 116, 121, 123
Lao PDR, 115, 116, 118, 119, 121–123, 125–127, 131
Lao People's Democratic Republic. *See* Lao PDR
Laos, 11, 61, 85, 86, 136, 151, 176, 178, 179,186, 194. *See also* Lao PDR
Legal Support for Children and Women (LSCW), xi, 79, 81–85
Legitimacy, 28, 43, 119, 126, 128, 129, 136, 138, 146, 148, 152, 212, 228, 235, 238, 245
  political legitimacy, 43, 119, 126
Liotta, P.H., 30, 31
Loescher, G., 18, 26, 27

Index

M
Machiavelli, N., 33
Malaysia, 1, 2, 63, 65, 99, 118, 120, 136, 142–144, 159, 177, 180, 183, 193, 194, 196–198, 201, 202, 204, 205, 208–211, 219, 226
Maldives, 159, 231, 234, 240
McDuie-Ra, D., 115
McGeown, K., 83
McRae, R., 242
Media, 47, 54, 95, 105, 108–109, 135, 141, 161, 166, 167, 206, 209
Mekong Commission, 120
Mekong region, 11, 115, 117, 126
Mekong river. *See* Mekong region
Mekong River Commission (MRC), xi, 119–122, 186
Migrant domestic workers, 103, 104
Migrant Filipinas, 103, 108, 109
Migration, 6, 11, 18, 28, 33, 51, 59, 61–63, 65–66, 69, 71, 75–92, 95–110, 121–123, 125, 136, 137, 140
Migratory rights, 242, 243, 246
Military, 4, 5, 9, 18, 22, 23, 27, 32, 59–63, 82, 136, 147–150, 157, 160, 162, 164, 166, 167, 169, 173, 175–177, 180, 217, 218, 223, 224
Millennium Development Goals, 116, 184
Mining, 116, 121, 123–124
Minorities, 61, 62, 68–70, 124, 125, 129, 176, 221
Mobility, 22, 66, 97, 205
Mongolia, 219
Moo-hyun, R., 223, 227
Morgenthau, H.J., 33
Movement, 17, 26, 28, 34, 62, 65–68, 70, 96, 98, 99, 117–119, 129, 160–162, 166, 205–207, 219, 220, 225, 235–237, 240, 245
MRC. *See* Mekong River Commission (MRC)
Multilateral, multi-sectoral cooperation, 143, 188
Myanmar, 5, 23, 24, 32, 120, 136, 137, 143, 148–150, 159, 161, 164–169, 173, 176, 177, 179–182, 187, 194
Myong-bak, L., 225, 226

N
National honor, 95–110
National security, 6, 30–33, 59–71, 135, 145–148, 150, 164, 176, 187, 188, 203. *See also* State security
Natural disasters, 7, 12, 20, 24, 30, 116, 135, 157–170, 173, 174, 176–178, 180, 183, 188

Natural resources, 31, 118–121, 123, 124, 139, 140, 174, 238
  extraction, 118, 119
  management, 119, 121, 128
Negotiation process, 205, 206, 210, 212
Neorealism, 146
NGOs. *See* Non-Governmental Organizations (NGOs)
Noncompliance, 145, 228
Non-Governmental Organizations (NGOs), 2, 5, 10, 41, 55, 61, 76, 78, 79, 95, 96, 105, 107–108, 117, 119, 128, 129, 141, 162, 166, 167, 169, 180–182, 203, 206, 209, 210, 236, 238, 245
  networks, 107, 108
Non-interference, 7, 12, 34, 135, 146, 149, 157, 159, 164, 165, 168–170, 176, 183, 185
Non-intervention, 148, 158, 168, 181
Non-state actors, 2, 12, 59, 60, 95–97, 105–110, 115, 116, 128, 130, 131, 138, 236
Non-traditional security, 24, 30, 138, 146
Normative, 24, 32, 116, 147, 218, 221
Norms, 19, 26, 33, 55, 81–84, 88, 115, 128, 131, 164, 219, 221, 226–228
  normative, 221
North Korea, 6, 17–21, 25, 28, 29, 31, 32, 219

O
Obama, B., 150, 151, 210
Ogata, S., 7, 209
Overseas Filipino workers, 99

P
Partner selection, 196–203
Paterson, M., 232, 234, 239, 241, 243
Pattaya, 77, 80, 83, 85–87
Peace building, 117
Peacekeeping, 148, 149
Peace process (Aceh), 161
People's Republic of China
  All China Women's Federation, 42
  civil society, 54, 55
  condom, 44–49, 51
  cultural revolution, 43
  female suicide rates, 49
  floating population, 51
  Four Frees and One Care, 54
  human trafficking, 50
  One Child Policy
    domestic violence, 49, 50
    sex selective abortion, 50
    son preference, 49, 50

People's Republic of China (*cont.*)
  premarital sex, 44–46
  reform and opening, 43, 44
  Regional Women's Commission, 42
  rural health system, 53
  SARS, 54, 55
  sex education, 44, 45
    contraceptives, 45
  sex workers, 45–47, 50–52, 54
  traffic of women, 50, 51
  women, 39–43
Pearson, E., 79–82, 85, 92
Philippines, 1 , 11 , 65, 95–110, 135, 136, ,
    149, 174, 179, 186, 194, 196–198,
    201, 205, 207, 209, 227
Philippine state, 96, 98–105
Police, 21, 50, 81, 84, 86, 87, 90, 162, 173, 211
Political neutrality (of natural disasters), 157–170
Political patronage, 129, 130
Politicization, 130
Politicized, 32, 128–131
Pollution, 116, 124, 140, 144, 174, 177,
    182–183, 232, 233, 242
Population and Community Development
    Association (PDA), 89, 92
Post-conflict societies, 59
Post-territorial state, 240, 243–245
Poverty, 4 , 10 , 30, 31, 60, 64, 66, 68, 70, 75,
    77, 80, 82–85, 89–91, 116, 119,
    124, 126, 135, 137–139, 147, 160,
    177–179, 184, 186, 212, 232
Privatization, 53, 64, 65, 126, 210
Proliferation of, 162, 193–212
Public opinion, 12, 221, 222, 226

Q
Quebecois nationalist, 237

R
Raad, D.F., 32
Regime change, 227
Regime security. *See* State security
Regional, 1–12, 27, 28, 31, 44, 59–61, 80, 88,
    115–131, 136–147, 149–152, 157,
    158, 162–165, 167, 168, 173–189,
    193–198, 201, 202, 218, 221, 227,
    228, 232
Regional cooperation, 9, 141–147, 150, 152,
    157, 182–186, 202
Regionalism. *See* East Asian
Regional trade agreement, 193
Relief, 150, 157, 159–162, 164, 166–169, 174,
    180–182, 188

Reproductive rights, 11, 59, 71
Resettlement, 62, 63, 65, 69, 122, 124, 125
Responsibility to Protect (R2P), 8, 148, 150,
    166–168, 181, 185
Rosenau, 236, 246
Rouge, K., 32
Rules of origin, 194, 199
Russia, legal successor state, 243

S
Sandler, S., 198
Sea level change, 12, 231–234, 238–242, 246
Secessionist movements, 237
Second Indochina War, 59, 63, 69
Severe acute respiratory syndrome (SARS),
    5, 24, 54, 55, 145, 174, 175, 183–185
Shifting/swidden cultivation, 123
Sichuan earthquake, 181–182
Singapore, 99, 104, 118, 136–138, 140–144,
    149, 151, 162, 177, 183, 186, 193,
    194, 197–202, 205, 208, 219
Small island state (SIS), 231–234, 239, 246
Smith, P.J., 138
Social protection, 101
Social rights, 101
Social security, 23, 97, 99–102
South Asian Association for Regional
    Cooperation (SAARC), 232
South Korea, 12, 17, 18, 20, 21, 31, 99, 102,
    118, 120, 139, 140, 194, 196, 197,
    200, 201, 205, 208, 211, 219, 223,
    225–227
Sovacool, B.K., 143
Sovereignty, 1, 7–9, 12, 19, 242–25, 27, 34,
    126, 135, 144–146, 148–150,
    157–170, 175, 181, 184, 185,
    232–241, 243–246
  sovereign state, 233, 236, 237, 243
  sovereignty with a territorial veneer,
    243–244
  sovereignty without territory, 243–246
  Westphalian sovereignty state, 235
St Augustine, 34
State authority, 237
State-centric, 137, 146, 149, 152, 212
Stateless but Sovereign, 244–245
State liability, 241
State security, 1–4, 6, 7, 9, 23, 27, 28, 30, 97,
    136, 147–150, 217
States plus nations, 245
Strategic interest, 202, 204
Strategic interests, 202, 204
Street children, abstract, 11, 21, 76, 85–88,
    90, 91

Index

St Thomas Aquinas, 34
Supranational, 158, 169, 227
Sustainability, 3, 123, 140
Sustainable development, 7, 9, 116, 121, 139, 140, 143, 186, 212, 232
Sustainable security, 11, 29–33

T
Tadjbakhsh, S., 60
TAGP. *See* Trans-ASEAN Gas Pipeline Infrastructure Project (TAGP)
Teh, B.C.G., 1, 193
Territory, 11, 183, 202, 231–246
Terrorism, 4, 6, 34, 135, 138, 139, 142, 145, 146, 217, 227
Thailand, 1, 2, 6, 11, 65, 75–92, 118–122, 124, 125, 135, 136, 143, 144, 150, 158, 159, 164, 174, 176, 179, 186, 187, 193, 194, 196–198, 201, 202, 204–208, 210, 226
The Inconvenient truth, 231
The Ministry of Justice. *See* The Ministry of Justice in Japan
The Ministry of Justice in Japan, 207, 221, 222, 225, 226
The Vatican City State, 243, 244
The Vienna Convention on the Law of Treaties, 236
Timber. *See* Deforestation
Tobin, K.A., 59
Todtan bunkhan, 83
Toxic waste, 206–207
Trade liberalization, 2, 196, 202, 208, 212
Trade Promotion Authority, 209
Traditional security, 1, 3, 9, 11, 12, 19, 24, 30, 157, 162, 163, 169
Trafficking in Persons (TIP), 75, 77, 78, 80
Trafficking Victim's Protection Act (TVPA), 78
Trans-ASEAN Gas Pipeline Infrastructure Project (TAGP), 137, 142, 143
Transnational, 2, 9, 12, 33, 60, 64, 105, 115, 117–120, 127, 128, 136, 144, 145, 150, 151, 157, 159, 169, 170, 176, 188, 227, 237, 245
Transnational cooperation, 144, 151
Transnational Corporations (TNCs), 237, 238
Transnational investment. *See* Investment
Transnational threats, 2
Truoung, T.D., 67
Trust Fund for Human Security, 223
Tsunami, 5, 24, 135, 137, 145, 157–165, 168, 169, 176, 187, 188, 210, 231
Tuvalu, 231–233, 239, 240, 242, 243, 245, 246

U
UN Framework Convention on Climate Change (UNFCCC), 140, 141, 241, 242
UNDP. *See* United Nations Development Program (UNDP)
UN General Assembly, 164, 218, 222
United Nations, 2, 4–6, 23, 34, 39, 55, 60, 63, 66, 70, 71, 75, 128, 139, 140, 147, 149, 150, 158, 159, 165–168, 173, 178, 180, 181, 218, 220, 223
United Nations Development Program (UNDP), 5–7, 9, 12, 39, 60, 67, 68, 96, 97, 115–117, 136, 147, 158, 173, 184, 185
United Nations Security Council, 166
United States, 5, 10, 18, 62, 63, 99, 101, 148, 150, 160, 166, 174, 181, 193, 219, 221, 222, 228, 231
Universal Declaration of Human Rights, 25, 218
Urbanization, 31, 62, 66, 67, 70, 122, 140
Use of force, 78, 142, 238

V
Vietnam, 2, 11, 34, 59–71, 85, 115–122, 125–129, 131, 135, 136, 143, 151, 174, 179, 186, 194, 197, 198, 201, 205, 219
Vietnam War, 5, 34, 60–63

W
Walzer, M., 34
Water, 116, 122, 124, 125, 128
Water wars, 177
Westphalian nation-state, 233
Westphalian sovereignty. *See* Sovereignty
Wetzler, J., 75
Women, 1, 7, 11, 21, 39–55, 63, 65–67, 70, 78–85, 88, 95, 96, 98, 103–109, 117, 124, 125, 130, 160, 219
World Trade Organization (WTO), 64, 193, 195, 196, 200, 202, 203, 209

X
Xia, G., 45

Y
Yop, H.J., 21